USS BLUEGILL SS-242
NUI KA PILIKIA O KA MOANA

U.S.S. TINOSA
S.S. 283

U.S.S. BECUNA
SS-319

USS CATFISH
SS 339

USS DIODON

SS 404
U.S.S. SPIKEFISH

SS 419
TIGRONE

TORO
SS 422

USS PICKEREL
SS 524

USS DOLPHIN
555

USS LAFAYETTE
SSBN 616

USS JAMES MADISON SSBN-627

BENJAMIN FRANKLIN
SSBN 640

IMUA
SSBN 642
KAMEHAMEHA

SSBN 658
Mariano G. Vallejo

USS NAUTILUS

USS HALIBUT
SSGN 587

590
VIDETE PRIUS
USS SCULPIN

SSN 594
USS PERMIT

VENATOR-NECATOR
TULLIBEE
SSN 597

USS LANCE

DE PROFUNDIS
254
662
GURNARD

USS DRUM
WEST PAC 74-5
677
STEELY-EYED KILLER OF THE DEEP

SSN 678
USS ARCHERFISH

USS PARCHE
NI PAR EXCELLENCE IV
SSN 683

SSN 711
SAN FRANCISCO
ORO EN PAZ FIERRO EN GUERRA

USS NORFOLK
VI PER CONCORDIAM
SSN 714

MAKA ALA MAU
HONOLULU
SSN 718

USS PITTSBURGH
SSN 720

USS HELENA
SSN 725

SUBMARINE GROUP
EIGHT

SUBRON 14

SUBMARINE SQUADRON SEVENTEEN
PAX PER POTENTIAM

SUBMARINE SQUADRON EIGHTEEN

UNITED STATES
SUBMARINES

UNITED STATES
SUBMARINES

David Randall Hinkle, Editor-in-Chief

Harry H. Caldwell, Editor

Arne C. Johnson, Editor

To: Jean, Joe, Amanda & James
This book is a good summary of all
that we did in the Cold War.
with love
Dad/Grandpa

NAVAL SUBMARINE LEAGUE
SONALYSTS, INC.
HUGH LAUTER LEVIN ASSOCIATES, INC.

Naval Submarine League

The Naval Submarine League is a professional organization for submariners, the submarine industry, and proponents of submarines. The primary mission of the Naval Submarine League is to stimulate and promote awareness of the need for a strong U.S. Submarine Force.

The League strives to identify submarine issues affecting the common defense and national security of the United States. It also seeks to act as liaison and promote better communications among the military and academic and business communities. In addition, the Naval Submarine League provides a forum wherein views and perceptions can be focused and examined.

Finally, the League is dedicated to the support of the heritage, loyalty, patriotism, and memory of the many loyal submarine officers and men who have served and gone before us.

Naval Submarine League
Post Office Box 1146
Annandale, Virginia 22003

Sonalysts, Inc.
215 Parkway North
Waterford, Connecticut 06385

Published by Hugh Lauter Levin Associates, Inc.
Published with the cooperation and assistance of the Naval Submarine League.

© 2002 Sonalysts, Inc. All rights reserved.
Sonalysts Representative: A. Lisa Mackie

Design: Lori S. Malkin
Project Editor: James O. Muschett
Sonalysts Project Leader: Don C. LaForce
ISBN 0-88363-103-2
Printed in Hong Kong
Distributed by Publishers Group West
http://www.HLLA.com

All photography and illustrations courtesy U.S. Navy unless otherwise credited.

Contents

A Word to the Reader

This book exists to celebrate the U.S. Navy's Submarine Force, by setting forth in prose and pictures the story of its development through the first 100 years.

Although the selected time frame excludes some of the earlier key events in the history of U.S. submarines, we have made exceptions for Bushnell's *Turtle* and the Confederate submarine, *Hunley*. This is because *Turtle*, designed and built for the Revolutionary War, recognized and addressed all the problems of using a submersible to attack an armed warship. *Hunley* took submarine development a step farther by actually sinking an enemy vessel. By 1900 technology had caught up with this concept. John P. Holland—after several tries—produced *Holland VI*, the first viable submarine, which he sold to the U.S. Navy.

Today's submarines are fully capable of supporting an aircraft carrier battle group or operating completely independently. Our Navy's multimission Submarine Force operates around the clock and around the world. Armed with sophisticated torpedoes and long-range cruise missiles and equipped with complex sonar, navigation, and combat systems, attack submarines provide national commanders with a formidable asset to support United States strategy. The nuclear attack submarine USS Jefferson City (SSN 759) is shown operating with elements of the USS Enterprise (CVN 65) Task Group during 1996 operations in the Persian Gulf.

We chose to use this landmark as the starting point for our story. To close out 100 years of U.S. submarine development, we offer glimpses into the future by some highly qualified prognosticators.

The authors and editors have really enjoyed the work involved in assembling this book. All of us are familiar with the submarine story and are delighted at the opportunity to share it with a wide audience. In doing so we have tried to be accurate, educational, and entertaining. Some old tales have been repackaged—some material is brand new.

Regarding statistics such as numbers of men lost, ships sunk, total tonnage, etc. in World War II, there are no absolute numbers agreed upon. However, the approximations used by various authors are close to the real losses suffered in that great war.

We view the book as analogous to a small museum. Flipping through and looking at the pictures should be enjoyable. If your interest is piqued, read the captions and become better informed. If you're hooked, read the text and you will become much better informed. Above all, we hope you enjoy the book.

David Randall Hinkle
Editor-in-Chief

Arne C. Johnson
Editor

Harry H. Caldwell
Editor

"We, who survived World War II and were privileged to return to our loved ones at home, salute the gallant officers and men of our submarines who have lost their lives in that long struggle. We shall never forget that it was our submarines that held the lines against the enemy while our fleets replaced losses and repaired wounds."

—FLEET ADMIRAL
CHESTER W. NIMITZ

World War II submarine veterans arrayed in their distinctive and colorful vests and hats frequently take part in ceremonies honoring their former shipmates and counterparts who lost their lives during the war. This particular ceremony took place on 6 December 1991 at the Pearl Harbor Submarine Base as part of an observance of the fiftieth anniversary of the Japanese attack on Pearl Harbor.

A Century of Silent Service

A Century of Silent Service: Chronology

Captain Arne C. Johnson, USN (Ret)

Pages 8–9: *A line of submarines alongside USS* Holland *(AS 3) represent the range of boats used by the submarine force at the start of World War II. The boats are (from left) USS* Nautilus, Narwhal, Shark, Dolphin, Porpoise, Pike, *and* Tarpon.

Above: *USS* Georgia *(SSBN 729) cruising the Hood Canal at dawn, near the Trident Refit Facility in Bangor, Washington.*

Since *Holland VI* was accepted in 1900, our submarines have evolved from small submersibles with limited capability to proven warfighters to today's nuclear-powered, multimission warships. A century of technological innovation, undersea exploration, and adaptation to changing strategic and defense needs have made today's Submarine Force ready to respond across the spectrum of conflict.

Noteworthy is the immense contribution during World War II in which U.S. submarines sank over 4,800,000 tons of Japanese merchant ships and 214 naval vessels. Fifty-two of the 288 U.S. submarines and 3,505 men who manned them were lost.

In the Korean War, U.S. submarines consistently patrolled hostile waters on covert missions.

With the advent of nuclear power under Admiral Rickover, our attack submarines became the premier antisubmarine warfare (ASW) force and accomplished extremely sensitive missions of great importance to our national security. Strategic submarines made over 3,000 deterrent patrols during the Cold War while safely and reliably controlling the nuclear weapons under their responsibility.

Today, the Submarine Force enters its second century of service conducting complex operations demanding a stealthy, mobile, high-endurance platform with great firepower. This dominant undersea force is manned by extraordinary people with superb support forces and backed by the finest families.

—ADMIRAL HENRY G. CHILES, JR., USN (RET)
Chairman of the Submarine Centennial Committee

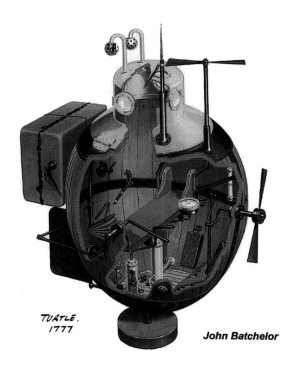

TURTLE,
1777

John Batchelor

1776

7 Sep—**Turtle**, a one-man submarine built by 34-year-old Yale graduate David Bushnell of Saybrook, Connecticut, unsuccessfully tries to attach a keg of gunpowder to the hull of **HMS *Eagle***, Admiral Howe's flagship, anchored in New York harbor. However, the powder keg exploded in the harbor prompting the American General Putnam to exclaim, "God 'scurse 'em, that'll do it for 'em."

1801

3 Jun—Robert Fulton's submarine **Nautilus** dives to a depth of 25 feet and remains there for more than an hour.

1864

17 Feb—The Confederate submarine **H. L. Hunley** is the first to sink an enemy ship in combat when it rams its spar torpedo into the hull of the Union screw sloop **USS Housatonic** off Charleston, South Carolina. **Hunley** sinks and is lost during escape transit.

1888-1895

—Bureau of Construction and Repair design competition brings inventor John P. Holland a Navy contract to build the unsuccessful steam-powered **Plunger**.

1900

■ **Birthday of U.S. Submarine Force**
11 Apr—John P. Holland sells his internal combustion, gasoline-powered submarine, **Holland VI**, to the Navy for $160,000, after demonstration trials off Mount Vernon, Virginia. This marks the official birth date of the U.S. Navy's Submarine Force.

HOLLAND (Hull length: 53 feet, 8 inches)

E-CLASS (Hull length: 135 feet, 3 inches)

12 Oct—**USS Holland** is commissioned, Lieutenant H. H. Caldwell commanding.

1909

—The Electric Boat company begins building the F class (SS 20 through 23) and the E class (SS 24 and 25). These are the first submarines to be powered by diesel engines.

1912

5 Mar—The Secretary of the Navy establishes the Atlantic Submarine Flotilla, commanded by Lieutenant Chester W. Nimitz.

1915

21 Mar—**USS F-4** (SS 23), the first U.S. submarine to be lost at sea with no survivors, founders off Honolulu.

1916

19 Jun—Submarine Force, U.S. Atlantic Fleet, is established.
29 Aug—Congress authorizes construction of sixty-eight new submarines.
—**E-1** (ex **Skipjack**) (SS 24) is the first U.S. submarine to cross the Atlantic under her own power.

—The Bureau of Construction and Repair and the Bureau of Steam Engineering initiate design of the faster 15-knot, 800-ton *S*-class.

1917

■ **United States enters World War I.**
Jan—Submarine School is established at Submarine Base, New London, Connecticut.
4 Mar—The Appropriations Act of 1917 adds eighteen more boats to the submarine construction program. The Navy uses resources from the Naval Emergency Fund for twenty more.

14 Apr—**USS L-4** (SS 43) goes on an antisubmarine patrol the day Congress declares war. This marks the first war patrol of a U.S. submarine.
28 Jun—Submarine Force, U.S. Pacific Fleet, is established.
Oct—Four K boats deploy to the Azores.

1918

22 May—**USS L-1** (SS 40) conducts a torpedo attack on a German submarine near the Scilly Islands, UK. The Germans take *L-1* under fire. This is the first U.S. submarine to be attacked by an enemy vessel.

1920

1 Sep—**USS S-5** (SS 110) sinks off the Delaware Capes with the bow on the bottom and the stern out of the water. The crew escapes through a hole cut in the tiller room, some two days after sinking.

1925

25 Sep—**USS S-51** (SS 162) is rammed and sinks off Block Island, Rhode Island. Captain E. J. King, commanding officer Submarine Base New London, supervises salvage operations.

1927

17 Dec—**USS S-4** (SS 109) is rammed and sinks off Provincetown, Massachusetts. The inability to rescue trapped survivors leads to the development of the McCann rescue chamber.

1929

10 May—"Momsen Lung" is tested by Lieutenant Charles Momsen and Chief Gunner C. L. Tibbals from a depth of over 200 feet.

1930

15 Aug—The first submarine escape training tank is placed in operation at the Submarine Base, New London.

1933

—The Washington Navy Yard makes twenty sets of quartz and steel echo-ranging equipment, a major development in sonar (SOund NAvigation and Ranging) technology.
27 Oct—**USS Porpoise** (SS 172) is the first U.S. new construction submarine to have electric drive and high-speed diesel engines.

1935

—The importance of submarine operations in the Pacific, Caribbean, and the South Atlantic leads the

S-40 (Hull length: 219 feet, 3 inches)

Navy Department to install the first submarine air-conditioning system on board **USS *Cuttlefish*** (SS 171), in spite of space constraints.

1936

15 April—The keel is laid for **USS *Salmon*** (SS 182), lead ship in a new class designed to accompany the fleet. The *Salmon*-class boats, instead of having riveted hull joints, were of all welded construction.

1939

23 May—**USS *Squalus*** (SS 192) sinks during a practice dive off the coast of Portsmouth, New Hampshire. By using the McCann rescue chamber, thirty-three men are saved.

1940

—The Navy initiates construction of the long-range fleet submarine (*Gato* class to be followed by the *Balao* and *Tench* classes). These boats become the "workhorses" of World War II.

1941

■ **United States enters World War II.**
—The first radar for submarines becomes operational.

7 Dec—**The Japanese attack Pearl Harbor,** bringing the United States into World War II. U.S. submarines are overlooked during the attack. The Submarine Force becomes indispensable while the rest of the fleet recovers.
10 Dec—**USS *Seadragon*** (SS 194) and **USS *Sealion*** (SS 195) in Cavite, Philippines, are attacked by Japanese aircraft. Ensign Samuel H. Hunter in *Seadragon* is instantly killed, the first submarine casualty of World War II. Four men in *Sealion* are killed, and *Sealion* is so badly damaged that it is scuttled on Christmas Day—the first U.S. submarine destroyed in World War II.

15 Dec—**USS *Swordfish*** (SS 193) torpedoes a large freighter for the first confirmed sinking of a Japanese ship by a U.S. submarine.
31 Dec—Admiral Chester W. Nimitz, a veteran submariner, takes command of the U.S. Pacific Fleet, on board **USS *Grayling*** (SS 209).

1942

27 Jan—**USS *Gudgeon*** (SS 211) sinks the Japanese *I-173,* the first confirmed sinking of an enemy warship by a U.S. submarine in history.

JAPANESE WWII MARITIME LOSSES[*]

	TO SUBMARINES		TO ALL CAUSES	
	SHIPS	TONNAGE	SHIPS	TONNAGE
1942	139	593,165		
1943	308	1,366,962		
1944	548	2,451,914		
1945	152	449,276		
Total	1,152	4,861,317	2,535	8,897,393

As published by the Joint Army Navy Assessment Committee

1945

■ **World War II ends.**
14 Aug—**Japanese agree to surrender terms; hostilities are terminated.**

GATO (Hull length: 311 feet, 7 inches)

—By V-J Day, U.S. submarines have sunk 5 million tons of Japanese naval and merchant shipping at a loss of fifty-two U.S. submarines and more than 3,500 valiant men.

—Fleet consists of 6,768 active units; 232 are submarines. The defense budget is $83 billion, representing 89.5 percent of federal spending. Fleet Admiral Ernest J. King is the Chief of Naval Operations (CNO); James V. Forrestal is Secretary of the Navy.

—U.S. Navy begins study of German U-boat technology and future ASW problems. Work begins on new sonar, weapons, and propulsion systems.

15 Dec—Fleet Admiral Chester W. Nimitz becomes CNO.

1946

■ **Cold War develops.**

—Captain Hyman G. Rickover arrives at Oak Ridge to begin study of atomic energy.

—Greater Underwater Propulsion Power (GUPPY) program for World War II fleet boat modernization begins.

1947

—First two GUPPY submarines, **USS *Odax*** (SS 484) and **USS *Pomodon*** (SS 486), complete conversion.

12 Feb—**USS *Cusk*** (SS 348) fires the first **Loon** guided missile from a submarine.

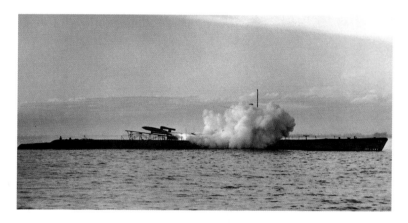

—**Regulus** missile program begins.

—**USS *Irex*** (SS 482), the first fleet snorkel submarine, completes conversion.

1948

—Bureau of Ships forms Nuclear Power Branch, with Captain Rickover assigned as head.

—Westinghouse signs contract with the Atomic Energy Commission to build the Bettis Atomic Power Laboratory, beginning the Submarine Thermal Reactor (STR) design using pressurized water.

—Submarine Squadron SIX in the Canal Zone conducts tests with **USS *Tusk*** (SS 426), concluding that submarines are the best ASW platforms against snorkeling submarines.

20 Jan—***Cusk*** (redesignated SSG 348) is the Navy's first guided-missile submarine.

1949

18 Apr—Construction of newly designed fast attack submarines (6) commences with the keel laying of **USS *Tang*** (SS 563).

9 May—Submarine Development Group TWO is established to conduct ASW research and development. Captain Roy S. Benson is first COMSUBDEVGRU TWO.

26 Aug—**USS *Cochino*** (SS 345) suffers a catastrophic electrical fire and is lost at sea. ***Tusk*** rescues crew but six ***Tusk*** crewmen and one man from ***Cochino*** are lost during high sea rescue operations.

1950

■ **President Harry S. Truman authorizes the construction of the first nuclear-powered submarine.**

—Bureau of Ships begins design work on swimmer delivery vehicles (SDVs).

1951

—Bureau of Ships signs contract with Westinghouse and Electric Boat for **USS *Nautilus*** (SSN 571), the first nuclear-powered submarine.

1952

14 Jun—Keel laid for ***Nautilus*** at the Electric Boat Company in Groton, Connecticut.

1953

—Fleet consists of 1,122 active units, including 110 submarines (all diesel). The defense budget is $52.8 billion, representing 69.3 percent of federal spending.

—First submarine thermal reactor prototype reaches initial criticality.

—Atomic Energy Commission approves the Submarine Fleet Reactor (SFR) project. This leads to the S3W and S4W reactor designs.

—Keel is laid for **USS *Seawolf*** (SSN 575), the second nuclear-powered submarine, at Electric Boat. This submarine is designed with the submarine intermediate reactor (SIR) using liquid sodium coolant.

8 May—**USS *Tunny*** (SSG 282) prototype SSG conversion is recommissioned. She is the first U.S. submarine equipped to fire surface-to-surface **Regulus** missiles.

5 Dec—**USS *Albacore*** (AGSS 569) is commissioned. Designed to test new submarine technology, her most important innovation is her teardrop-shaped hull form.

NAUTILUS (Hull length: 323 feet, 10 inches)

1954

30 Sept—**Nautilus**, the world's first nuclear-powered ship, is commissioned, Commander E. P. Wilkinson commanding.

1955

17 Jan—**Nautilus** sends the historic message, **"Underway on nuclear power,"** signaling a new era in both submarine warfare and maritime propulsion.

7 Oct—The **X-1**, the U.S. Navy's first midget submarine, powered by hydrogen peroxide, is placed in service.

1956

18 May—Construction of newly designed fast attack submarines (3) commences with keel laying of **USS Barbel** (SS 580). It has an **Albacore** hull form and a single propeller for improved submerged performance.

3 Dec—The Navy terminates participation in the U.S. Army's **Jupiter** missile program and begins pursuing the development of the **Polaris** missile submarine.

1957

23 Dec—**USS Skate** (SSN 578), the first submarine to be powered by the submarine fleet reactor, is commissioned.

—**Regulus II** missile program is terminated to free funds for the Polaris project. SSGNs on order are recast as SSN-593-class attack submarines. Existing **Regulus I** submarines continue operations.

1958

3 Aug—**Nautilus is the first ship to pass beneath the North Pole,** on a four-day, 1,830-mile voyage from the Pacific to the Atlantic.

6 Oct—**Seawolf** completes a sixty day, completely submerged 13,000 mile cruise. This demonstrates the submerged endurance of a nuclear-powered submarine for a normal war patrol.

1959

15 Apr—USS **Skipjack** (SSN 585) is commissioned, the first submarine combining nuclear propulsion with the **Albacore** hull form and the first submarine powered by the S5W reactor.

10 Nov—USS **Triton** (SSRN 586) is commissioned. She is the first and only dual reactor submarine in the U.S. Navy.

30 Dec—USS **George Washington** (SSBN 598), the first of the "41 for Freedom" fleet ballistic missile (FBM) submarines, is commissioned, Commander J. B. Osborn commanding.

1960

4 Jan—USS **Halibut** (SSGN 587), the first and only nuclear-powered, **Regulus** guided missile submarine, is commissioned.

10 May—**Triton completes the first submerged circumnavigation of the Earth,** following Ferdinand Magellan's route and covering more than 41,000 miles in eighty-four days.

20 July—While submerged off the coast of Cape Canaveral, Florida, **George Washington successfully fires two Polaris A-1 missiles** with a range of 1,200 miles.

SKIPJACK (Hull length: 251 feet, 10 inches)

25 Aug— **USS *Seadragon*** (SSN 584) charts the Northwest Passage and surfaces at the North Pole, where the crew plays baseball.

15 Nov—**George Washington** departs Charleston, South Carolina, on the first operational deterrent patrol with the **Polaris** missile system.

1961

3 Aug—**USS *Thresher*** (SSN 593) is commissioned at Portsmouth Naval Shipyard, the first unit of what will be a class of fourteen submarines.

1962

2 Aug—**Skate** and **Seadragon** rendezvous under the ice and surface at the North Pole.

8 Nov—**USS *Ethan Allen*** (SSBN 608) fires six **Polaris** A-2 missiles (1,500-mile range) on the Atlantic missile range.

1963

—**USS *Sam Houston*** (SSBN 609) is the first **Polaris** submarine assigned to a Mediterranean patrol.

10 Apr—**Thresher** is lost during a test dive 220 miles east of Boston. SUBSAFE, a wide-sweeping redesign and upgrade of submarine systems and procedures, is initiated as a result of this accident.

23 Apr—**USS *Lafayette*** (SSBN 616), lead ship of the third class of SSBNs, is commissioned.

— **Polaris** A-3 missile with a 2,500-mile range becomes operational.

1964

—**Halibut** makes the last **Regulus** patrol.

21 Aug— **USS *Daniel Boone*** (SSBN 629) is the first fleet ballistic missile submarine permanently assigned to the Pacific.

1965

18 Jan—President Lyndon B. Johnson announces plans to develop **Poseidon** C-3, a more powerful missile than the **Polaris** A-3.

1966

6 Dec—**USS *Queenfish*** (SSN 651) is the first ***Sturgeon***-class attack submarine to be commissioned.

1967

1 Apr—**USS *Will Rogers*** (SSBN 659) is commissioned. This completes the building of the "41 for Freedom" FBM submarines, two years ahead of schedule.

12 Aug—Submarine Development Group ONE is established to prosecute deep submergence development. Captain A. G. Butler is first COMSUBDEVGRU ONE.

1968

—At the height of the Vietnam War, the fleet consists of 932 active units, including 156 submarines (diesel and nuclear).

5 Jun—**USS *Scorpion*** (SSN 589) is lost during her transit from the Mediterranean Sea to Norfolk.

17 Aug—**USS *Dolphin*** (AGSS 555), a small, deep-diving, diesel-powered research and development submarine, is commissioned.

GEORGE WASHINGTON (Hull length: 381 feet, 7 inches)

1969

27 Oct—NR-1, the Navy's only nuclear-powered deep diving research submarine, is placed in service.

1970

—The first deep submergence rescue vehicle (DSRV), designed for quick deployment in the event of a submarine accident, is launched.

— **Poseidon** missile conversions begin on SSBN-616-class submarines.

1972

—Design work begins on the **Tomahawk** cruise missile. This is the U.S. Navy's first cruise missile since **Regulus**. Design work begins on a submerged-launch version of the **Harpoon** anti-ship missile.

1973

16 Feb—The Secretary of the Navy announces Bangor, Washington, as the initial base for **Trident** submarine operations. **Trident** is the third generation strategic missile system (following **Polaris** and **Poseidon**).

1975

27 Jun—USS *Tigrone* (AGSS 419), the last surviving World War II fleet submarine in the U.S. Navy, is decommissioned.

1976

13 Nov—USS *Los Angeles* (SSN 688) is commissioned at Newport News, Virginia, as the first of a new class of attack submarines. She is outfitted with the S6G reactor plant.

1977

—The U.S. Navy consists of 523 active ships, including 118 submarines (3 diesel, 115 nuclear). The defense budget is $95.1 billion, representing 23.4 percent of federal spending.

1978

—Submarine Base Kings Bay, Georgia, is established for Atlantic fleet **Trident** submarine operations.

1979

—Ten SSBN 616-class submarines begin upgrades for **Trident** C-4 missile systems.

1980

30 Mar—Nautilus is decommissioned at Mare Island Naval Shipyard.

1981

—President Ronald Reagan plans a 600-ship navy with 100 attack submarines.

11 Nov—USS *Ohio* (SSBN 726), the first *Trident*-class submarine, is commissioned. She is outfitted with the S8G reactor plant and twenty-four missile launch tubes.

1982

1 Feb—**Admiral Hyman G. Rickover is relieved by Admiral Kinnaird R. McKee** as the director of nuclear propulsion.

1983

—**Tomahawk** cruise missile becomes operational.

—USS *Sam Houston* (SSN 609) and USS *John Marshall* (SSN 611) (ex SSBNs) begin conversion as swimmer delivery platforms.

—Design work begins on the *Seawolf* (SSN 21) class to succeed the SSN 688, *Los Angeles* class.

—The dry deck shelter, a modular housing capable of being fitted onto the deck of a submarine for swimmers and swimmer delivery vehicles (SDV) lockouts, is introduced.

1987

—U.S. Navy consists of 594 active units, including 139 submarines (3 diesel, 136 nuclear). The defense budget is $274 billion, representing 27.3 percent of federal spending.

1988

6 Aug—USS *San Juan* (SSN 751), the first improved 688-class submarine (688I), is commissioned. Improvements include a strengthening of the sail and the relocation of the fairwater planes to the bow.

17 Dec—USS *Tennessee* (SSBN 734), the first **Trident** submarine employing the D-5 missile system, is commissioned.

1989

—USS *Memphis* (SSN 691) becomes a research platform to test advanced submarine technology.

21 Mar—The first submerged test launch of the eight-warhead **Trident** D-5 missile is made by *Tennessee* off Cape Canaveral, Florida.

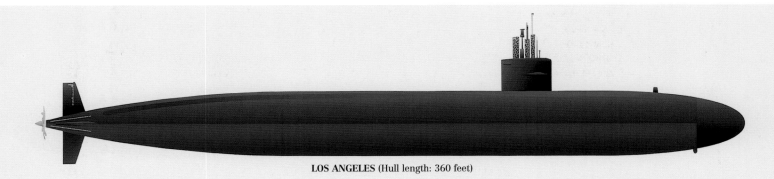

LOS ANGELES (Hull length: 360 feet)

1990

—**USS *Scamp*** (SSN 588) becomes the first nuclear-powered submarine to be dismantled as part of the U.S. Navy's Submarine Recycling Program at Puget Sound Naval Shipyard. This program leads to a safe and effective process for disposing of decommissioned nuclear-powered submarines.

1 Oct—**USS *Blueback*** (SS 581), the last diesel-powered attack submarine in the U.S. Navy inventory, is decommissioned.

1991

—The U.S. Navy consists of 529 active units, including 121 nuclear-powered submarines.

—**USS *Louisville*** (SSN 724) and **USS *Pittsburgh*** (SSN 720) fire the first **Tomahawk** cruise missiles from a submarine in combat during the Persian Gulf War.

1992

—The SSN-21 construction program is terminated with three boats authorized.

1994

9 Mar—**USS *Mariano G. Vallejo*** (SSBN 658), one of the original "41 for Freedom," is the last to be deactivated.

1996

13 Sep—**USS *Cheyenne*** (SSN 773), the 62nd and last unit of the SSN-688-class submarines, is commissioned.

1997

—U.S. Navy consists of 365 active ships, including 91 nuclear-powered submarines. Defense budget is $258.3 billion, representing 16.1 percent of federal spending.

19 Jul—**USS *Seawolf*** (SSN 21) is commissioned in Groton, Connecticut. She is outfitted with the S6W reactor plant.

6 Sep—**USS *Louisiana*** (SSBN 743), the 18th and last ***Trident*-**class submarine, is commissioned.

1998

11 Dec—**USS *Connecticut*** (SSN 22) is commissioned.

—**Tomahawk** cruise missile strikes from submarines against targets inside Iraq emphasize a shift from "blue water" operations to the littorals.

—General Dynamics and Newport News announce a cooperative effort to build the SSN 774-class submarine. Each shipyard will build specific subassemblies for each boat.

1999

2 Sep—**USS *Virginia*** (SSN 774) keel laying ceremony is held at Quonset Point, Rhode Island. With construction started at Electric Boat in Groton, Connecticut, and Newport News, Virginia, *Virginia* is the lead ship of a new class of attack submarines. She is expected to be completed in 2004.

2000

■ **Submarine Centennial—U.S. Submarine Force commemorates 100 years of "Silent Service."**

VIRGINIA (Hull length: 377 feet)

OHIO (Hull length: 560 feet)

THE Early Years

The First Skipper

Captain Harry H. Caldwell, USN (Ret)

My father, Lieutenant Harry H. Caldwell, USN, had the privilege
of commanding our Navy's first submarine. Born in St. Louis,
Missouri, in 1873, he grew up in Quincy, Illinois, on the Western frontier. He was bright and industrious. At age 14, after
one year of high school, he won an appointment to the U.S. Naval Academy, from which he was graduated in 1891.

By the time he put *Holland* in commission on 12 October 1900,
Lieutenant Caldwell had worked with the boat for three months and
sensed that this radical new weapon might have a major impact on the
future practice of naval warfare. In a letter to his mother dated the same
day, he wrote, "I hope to do great things in the way of developing this new
means of warfare, which I think will revolutionize naval methods." Later
in the same letter he said, "At any rate it is some distinction to be the first
naval officer who has ever manipulated a submarine boat."

Lieutenant Caldwell was then 27 years of age, tall, slender, well-
mannered, and rather elegant in appearance. A veteran of sea duty in the
Atlantic, Pacific, Far East, and Great Lakes, he was completing a most
interesting tour as Flag Secretary to Admiral George Dewey, a tour that
included the Battle of Manila Bay. His assignment to command *Holland*
was in part the result of Admiral Dewey's interest in the submarine.

In March of 1900, Admiral Dewey had attended a demonstration
run on the Potomac by *Holland* that he (and members of the Congressional
Naval Affairs Committees) had watched from the deck of a yacht. John
Holland had invited the admiral to embark in the submarine for a submerged operational demonstration. He declined politely, but authorized
Lieutenant Caldwell to embark in his place. Having made at least two trips
in the submarine before its purchase by the Navy, he was slightly better
informed about its operation than any other line officer at the time the Navy
crew was selected. By coincidence—or perhaps not—Lieutenant Caldwell

USS Holland *underway with launch in tow.
Note* Holland*'s towing pendant rigged to
the bow.*

Pages 20–21: USS Holland *at the Naval
Academy was the ship used to introduce
naval cadets from the class of 1902 into the
mysteries of submarines. Lieutenant Caldwell
observes as naval cadet H. G. S. Wallace
negotiates the hatch. Other naval cadets are:
J. H. Blackburn (at mast); J. W. Woodruff
(behind the hatch); and W. J. Moses (beneath
the flag).*

Opposite: USS Holland *as she might have
appeared in 1901. When fully rigged for
surface with all ballast tanks dry,* Holland
*rode comfortably when in protected waters.
The deck topside was a pleasant place to ride
in good weather—quiet enough to hold a conversation, which was an impossibility below
decks when the engine was running. However,
the wake from a passing ship could fill one's
shoes. ("* Holland *Underway," Jim Christley)*

USS Holland's crew pose on board in the summer of 1901 at Newport, Rhode Island. Lieutenant H. H. Caldwell, the commanding officer, is in the turret. Chief Gunner's Mate W. H. Reader, the chief of the boat, and Chief Machinist's Mate Barnett Bowie, the senior engineering rating, are (left to right) in the foreground. Adjacent to the turret (L to R) are Gunner's Mate Second Class Augustus Gumpert and Gunner's Mate Second Class Arthur Callahan. Standing to the rear (L to R) are Gunner's Mate First Class Harry Wahab, Gunner's Mate First Class O. Swanson, Warrant Gunner Owen Hill, and Electrician's Mate Second Class W. Hall. Gunner Hill succeeded to command Holland in 1903 and later put USS Grayling in commission as commanding officer. Wahab fired the first U.S. Navy submarine torpedo.

was assigned for temporary duty at the torpedo station in Newport, Rhode Island, ostensibly to learn about torpedoes and electricity. Soon after his arrival he was asked by Commander N. E. Mason, commanding officer of the torpedo station, to pick a crew for *Holland*, which had been delivered there in June of 1900. Picking the crew included serving as officer-in-charge and overseeing operational training of the Navy crew by the four-man civilian crew that had earlier delivered the boat to Newport.

The longer he worked with *Holland* the more interested Lieutenant Caldwell became in the boat, its capabilities, and its military potential. In August of 1900, *Holland* practiced sneaking up at night on an alerted target. In September, during a fleet exercise that pitted a defensive force of surface torpedo boats (and *Holland*) against a blockading squadron, *Holland* appeared during the night close aboard the battleship *Kearsarge*, seven miles south of Newport; Caldwell shouted through a megaphone, "Ahoy, *Kearsarge*, you are blown to atoms! This is *Holland*!" Lieutenant Caldwell made the front page of the New York newspapers and was heard by a national audience.

By the time *Holland* was placed in commission a new and more urgent mission had emerged. *Holland* would be used to train crews for the

next six boats, "improved *Holland*s" or *Adder* class, ordered in August of 1900. The broad pattern of operations for *Holland* evolved into spending the summers at the Newport Torpedo Station and the winters in Annapolis, where the converted yacht *Gloucester* was made available as a tender to provide messing and berthing for *Holland*'s crew. *Holland*'s young skipper explained his choice of Annapolis for wintering in his 12 October letter: "My object in going to Annapolis is not for the benefit of the cadets, but because that is a place with a good machine shop, etc., where it will be warm enough to run the boat most of the winter and train officers and men for the new boats." It is possible that its proximity to Washington, D.C., played a role in the choice of Annapolis for winter operations.

Despite finding favor with Congress and the press, *Holland* did not lack for detractors within the Navy. Seeing money spent on such a "toy" as an unwarranted drain of funds from the Navy appropriation, several short-sighted battleship admirals took every opportunity to point out *Holland*'s deficiencies.

One of *Holland*'s perceived failings was its apparent need to be towed wherever it went. In order to confirm or disprove this flaw, *Holland* was ordered to proceed to the Norfolk Navy Yard under its own power—escorted, but not under tow. A trip on Chesapeake Bay in January can be bracing. On 20 January 1901, while in Norfolk, Lieutenant Caldwell's comments were expressed in a letter home to his mother:

> *My trip down here was a decidedly hard one for me but was to my mind a success, which made up for any hardship. We left Annapolis at one o'clock in the afternoon and ran all that night, so I got no sleep for thirty-six hours, and was wet through most of that time. The following night we anchored and arrived here on Thursday. Fortunately, I suffered no ill effects from my repeated drenching with spray, although it was very cold.*

Holland VI *underway in open water with the hatch shut. In this condition, the visibility of the conning officer is limited to squinting through 1 by 3-inch glass ports set in the wall of the access trunk, so it can be expected that he will open the hatch for a better look around as soon as he can. (Jim Christley)*

Ensign H. H. Caldwell as he appeared about 1895. This portrait was made in Vallejo, California, probably to satisfy requests from family members back home in the Midwest.

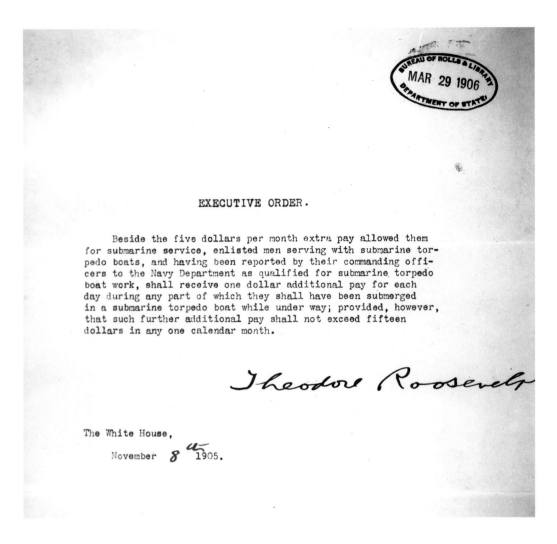

MAR 29 1906

EXECUTIVE ORDER.

Beside the five dollars per month extra pay allowed them for submarine service, enlisted men serving with submarine torpedo boats, and having been reported by their commanding officers to the Navy Department as qualified for submarine torpedo boat work, shall receive one dollar additional pay for each day during any part of which they shall have been submerged in a submarine torpedo boat while under way; provided, however, that such further additional pay shall not exceed fifteen dollars in any one calendar month.

Theodore Roosevelt

The White House,
November 8th 1905.

Holland VI *is shown moored, probably at Perth Amboy, New Jersey, early in 1898. The man just forward of the turret is standing on the pressure hull with his torso protruding through a deck hatch in the superstructure. Note the ladder being used as a brow.*

The question of *Holland*'s mobility apparently was answered and did not come up again.

Early in their association, Lieutenant Caldwell developed a deep respect for the competence of *Holland*'s crew. To reward their fine performance he proposed that submarine crew members be authorized to draw extra money in addition to their regular pay. Finally in December 1900 he was able to report: "The Navy Department has at last agreed to my recommendation to give the men extra pay, though I had to keep at them a long time in order to get it. Of course, it does not apply to the officers." The extra pay, $5 per month, seems small today but was substantial in 1900. More than the dollars, the prestige of qualifying for extra money based on professional competence probably served as an incentive to volunteer for submarine duty.

Holland spent the next two summers, 1901 and 1902, in Newport and the winters in Annapolis training the crews for the A-boats, demonstrating *Holland*'s unique capabilities to foreign naval attachés and other important guests and, while in Annapolis, indoctrinating small groups of naval cadets. In 1902 President Theodore Roosevelt came to Annapolis to present diplomas to the graduating class of naval cadets. In the afternoon he observed (from the surface) while *Holland* was put through her paces by Lieutenant Caldwell and his crew. Three years later Roosevelt became the first president to make a dive in a submarine when USS *Plunger*, an *Adder*-class boat, took him out for a couple of hours in Oyster Bay, Long Island, near Roosevelt's summer home. One serendipitous outcome of this trip was an order to pay submarine crewmembers $1 a day for each day they made a dive, not to exceed $15 per month.

USS Holland *is seen overtaking a coastal schooner in New York Harbor. Technology pushes forward into the twentieth century. (Photo: Leo Shea and Paterson Museum)*

A major factor in crew training was to recognize the inherent hazards of submarine operations, to emphasize discipline, and to stress safety. Hazards characteristic to submarines included: catastrophic loss of depth control; fire or explosion of gasoline, the boat's fuel; carbon monoxide poisoning resulting from leaks in the engine exhaust system; fire or explosion of hydrogen given off by the main storage battery incident to battery charging; and chlorine gas generated by the inadvertent contamination of battery electrolyte with salt water. Learning to anticipate and avoid such hazards was vital to the survival of *Holland* and its crew, and indeed to the whole submarine program. A major calamity to *Holland* would have fueled the detractors' opposition to submarines and could have set the submarine program back significantly.

Holland VI *on 20 April 1898 is shown preparing for a trial dive in the choppy waters of Raritan Bay in New York's outer harbor. The picture is taken from one of the two tugs carrying the inspection party. The trial—whose purpose was to confirm for the Navy inspectors that the boat could dive—was a success, as* Holland VI *stayed down for an hour and ran circles around the inspectors' tug boat.*

Through a combination of skill, caution, and luck, Lieutenant Caldwell and his crew avoided sinking the boat or killing any crew member, although two serious accidents did occur. In one case, while underway at night and preparing to dive in Narragansett Bay, the wake of a bay steamer washed over *Holland*'s hatch before it was completely secured. Enough water sloshed in before the hatch could be secured to overcome the 100 pounds of positive buoyancy *Holland* normally carried when submerged, and the submarine dropped to the bottom in 95 feet of water. This was in excess of the boat's designed maximum operating depth, 75 feet; but the boat's hull held. *Holland*'s crew was able to restore its proper trim, blow ballast tanks, and return to the surface.

The other casualty occurred in August 1902. *Holland* was moored for the night at the Brooklyn Navy Yard and had charged her battery from shore power. By the end of the charge the battery was gassing heavily. When charging was secured, the boat was shut up for the night. The following morning the crew came down to the submarine and opened the hatch. When Hall, the duty electrician, went aboard to start the ventilation blower, the high concentration of hydrogen in the boat's atmosphere was ignited by a spark in the ventilation blower motor controller. While relatively little material damage occurred, Hall was severely burned and spent several weeks in the hospital. This was one of the first of the many submarine battery explosions that would occur through the next 100 years.

It is a tribute to the care and attention exercised by *Holland*'s crew in training future submarine crews that despite occasional accidents and individual personnel casualties, no U.S. submarine was lost during the first fifteen years of operation.

After two years of pioneering with *Holland*, Lieutenant Caldwell was detached late in 1902 to join a new battleship being built at Philadelphia. This was not completely his preference; however, Admiral Dewey thought it was time he returned to the mainstream of his profession, the surface Navy.

By the time Lieutenant Caldwell was relieved as commanding officer, he had successfully completed crew training for the A-boats and had displayed *Holland*'s military potential for harbor defense. Building on *Holland*'s performance, the U.S. Navy would steadily exploit new technology and rely on exceptional personnel to design, construct, and operate submarines of increasing capability in the future.

USS Holland *shares a graving dock with the Russian battleship* Retvizan *at the Brooklyn Navy Yard in 1901. With each centered over its respective keel blocks, they wait for the dock to be pumped dry. The disparity in size suggests a large child and his rubber duck.*

T H E
Legacy of Holland VI

Captain Harry H. Caldwell, USN (Ret)

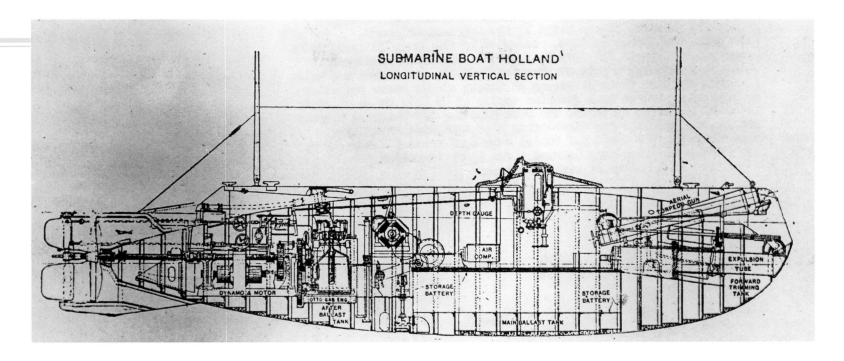

SUBMARINE BOAT HOLLAND
LONGITUDINAL VERTICAL SECTION

When the U.S. Navy bought *Holland VI* on 11 April 1900 from the Holland Torpedo Boat Company, it acquired the world's first viable submersible warship. Designed by John P. Holland, the brilliant Irish-born inventor, *Holland VI* outclassed the competition, foreign and domestic, principally because it provided separate power sources for propulsion while on the surface and submerged.

The following excerpt from a descriptive specification written by Engineer Charles A. Morris in 1899 sets forth some of the principal features of the boat:

> *She is 53.3 feet overall, largest diameter is 10.3 feet; draft in cruising position, 8.5 feet; draft in a diving position, 11.5 feet; 63 tons light displacement and 75 tons submerged. Her speed varies from 6 to 10 knots according to power used. The radius of action with gasoline alone is 1,300 knots; with gasoline and electricity, 1330 knots, allowing 30 knots for electricity* (sic). *The air reservoirs contain 30 cubic feet of air at 2,000 pounds per square inch. (for "knots" read "nautical miles"—Editors)*

> *The hull is parabolic, spindle-shaped. It is constructed of steel plating; the frames are of angle iron which are all perfect circles, the largest being 10.25 feet placed a little forward of amidships, tapering to both ends and all set up from a center line through the ship. This construction will resist a pressure of 35 pounds per square inch, which is sufficient to allow her to dive to a depth of 75 feet.*

> *The boat has a 45 horsepower Otto gas engine connected so as to drive the propeller or dynamotor for charging the batteries. The dynamotor can also be connected to drive the propeller. These connections are made by friction clutches. The dynamotor is connected to run at any speed or power from 10 horsepower to 150 horsepower.*

This sectional view of Holland VI *shows the boat in its final (1899) configuration with the steering and diving planes located aft of the propeller, the aft-pointing Zalinsky dynamite gun removed, and a very modest fairwater installed fore and aft of the turret. Note that the "expulsion tube" is an 18-inch-diameter torpedo tube, and that the item marked "aerial torpedo gun" is the 8-inch barrel of the remaining Zalinsky dynamite gun and has nothing to do with torpedoes.*

Holland VI *comes off the marine railway in 1898 after completing work in the shipyard at Elizabethport, New Jersey. Note the oversized colors the boat is wearing.*

Opposite: Holland VI *in Little Peconic Bay, Long Island, New York, in 1899. The man behind the hatch is believed to be Frank T. Cable, the boat's captain.*

Top: *Freshly painted* Holland *on the blocks on marine railway, probably at Raritan, New Jersey.*

Above: *Bow view of USS* Holland *moored at Newport in June 1901. Prominent on the boat's bow is the cap for the muzzle of the dynamite gun. Note the widened portable decking for use in port.*

Opposite, bottom: *USS* Frank Cable *(AS 40), a submarine tender, was named for the submarine pioneer in recognition of his major contributions to early submarine development.*

In addition to these features *Holland VI* was well armed. A single 18-inch-diameter torpedo tube in the bow carried a Whitehead torpedo with space and weight reserved for two spares. Further, *Holland VI* mounted a Zalinsky pneumatic dynamite gun with an 8-inch bore on the centerline forward, elevated approximately 15 degrees. This weapon, in whose patents John Holland held a financial interest, could lob a 200-pound projectile carrying up to eighty pounds of guncotton a distance of half a mile. The gun was trained by maneuvering the boat, and range was adjusted by using the trimming tanks. It could be fired with the submarine submerged and the tip of the bow at or just below the surface.

This system did not work too well, was seldom used, and so was omitted from future submarines. The Zalinsky gun, a direct descendant of the catapult, remains of interest because it is also the first submarine ballistic missile system to feature an underwater launch.

Holland VI was designed by John Holland to prove and demonstrate his concept of a submarine boat. It was financed by money he raised privately, so the design was not compromised by extraneous and unrealistic operational requirements. An earlier submarine building experience, the design and construction of *Plunger* under Navy contract, had left John Holland frustrated. In 1893 he had won a competition sponsored by the U.S. Navy to design a submarine boat; however, after construction began,

THE DOG STORY— *Captain Harry H. Caldwell, USN (Ret)*

USTB Holland *was not immune to casualties. In fact, most operational accidents that would threaten submarines for the next 100 years previewed on* Holland*. As* Holland *was the Navy's first operational submarine, this is no great surprise.*

On a night in 1901 Holland *was underway on the surface near Rose Island in Narragansett Bay getting ready to submerge. A Long Island Sound steamer passed nearby, kicking up a wake that washed over the little 53-foot submarine, sending her to the bottom in about 95 feet of water. Ballast tanks were blown and* Holland *returned to the surface, wet inside and out.*

Chief Gunner's Mate W. H. Reader, the chief of the boat, wrote:

> This accident caused us to wonder how we could escape should we be unable to rise to the surface. Later, at Annapolis, we tried an experiment. A dog had attached itself to our crew; and one day, with Captain Caldwell's approval, we put the dog in the torpedo tube, closed the inner door, opened the outer, and applied fifty pounds of air into the tube. On deck we expected to see the dog shot to the surface, but only bubbles appeared. We imagined that the dog had become jammed in the outer door, but closing the door slowly we found no obstruction. The tube was blown out, and there was the dog, perfectly dry and unharmed. The tube being inclined and admitting air too quickly, prevented the tube from filling up completely, the dog remaining between the inner door and the air inlet.

There remain unanswered questions: Did the heroic anonymous dog stay attached to the crew? Did he volunteer to participate in any more personal escape experiments? History is silent in this regard.

Navy bureaucrats loaded it with unrealistic operational requirements that could not be met with current technology.

John Holland's new submarine, *Holland VI*, was a warship. Like a fish, it was built to travel underwater. Its shape was optimized for running submerged, with only a few obstructions to the flow of water over the hull. There was very little flat deck topside, which introduced obvious hazards to safe surface operations—particularly when underway at sea.

Mr. Holland's submarine was a little hydrodynamic jewel. A self-taught student of marine engineering, he had learned much from designing, building, and operating his five previous submarines. He showed his genius as an inventor by adapting new technologies to his purpose as they evolved. Although *Holland VI* was well ahead of most competitors, it was not without flaws.

Holland VI commenced builders' trials early in 1898, and for the next two years John Holland practiced running the boat, conducted trials for the Navy, and made demonstration runs for foreign naval attachés, newspaper reporters, and practically anyone who showed interest. This activity resulted in some minor changes and one major one. In response to a Navy inspection board's criticism of the boat's sluggish steering performance, the stern of *Holland VI* was rebuilt in 1898 to move the propeller forward of the rudder and stern planes. With this arrangement, the propeller wash impinged on the control surfaces, ensuring better steering and diving performance.

By 1899, even before he sold *Holland VI* to the Navy, John Holland designed her successor, *Holland VII*. After acquisition by the Navy, submarines built to the *Holland VII* specifications became the *Adder* class. This Mr. Holland referred to as an "improved" *Holland* when discussing it with members of the Congressional Naval Affairs Committee.

Frank T. Cable was an electrician working for the Electro-Dynamic Company of Philadelphia when, in 1897, he was sent to Elizabethport, New Jersey, to repair the main motor in Holland VI. *He repaired the motor and soon thereafter joined the Electric Boat Company, where he became captain of the trials crew for* Holland VI *and a trusted friend and advisor to John P. Holland. As the company's trials crew skipper, he conducted the sea trials for each boat built by the Electric Boat Company and trained the first Navy crew on* Holland VI.

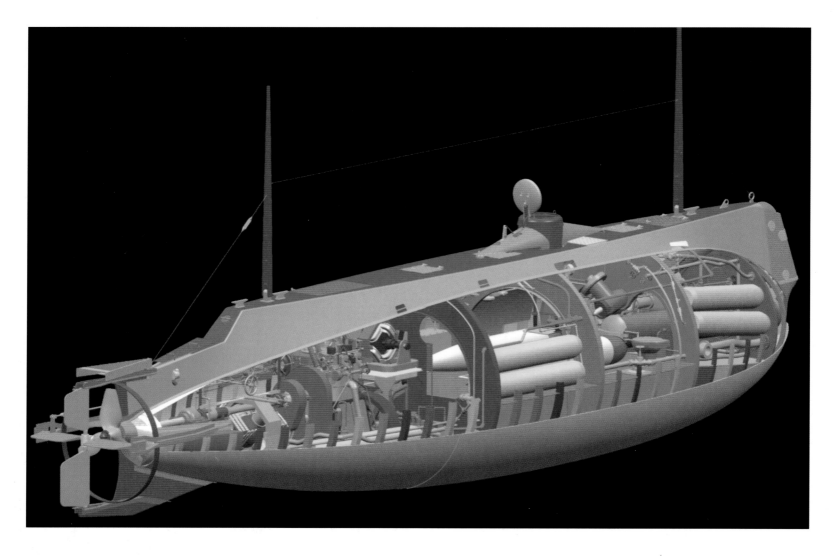

This cutaway view of Holland VI is a computer model created by Gary McCue using the CATIA® system. The same system is being used to design the Virginia-class submarines today. The Holland model was created to demonstrate the system. (CATIA® is a registered trademark of Dassault Systemes, France)

Fulton (pictured here) was the prototype for the Adder class. She was built by the Electric Boat Company in 1903 and underwent tests off Newport, Rhode Island, in 1904. This shot was taken at the completion of a submerged full speed endurance run in Narragansett Bay. Note the differences from Holland: forward superstructure is cut down (made possible by omitting the dynamite gun); the conning tower fairwater is larger; and a fixed periscope (with trials flag attached) is mounted just forward of the hatch. Fulton never joined the U.S. Navy, but was sold to Russia in 1904.

A review of the improvements built into *Holland VII* reveals some of the principal flaws found in *Holland VI*. The main points of comparison between *Holland VI* and *Holland VII* were:

SIZE—*Holland VII* was 10 feet longer and a foot and a half beamier than her predecessor, with the displacement nearly doubled. The new class was roomier and more comfortable, particularly with the dynamite gun omitted.

POWER—*Holland VII* had a 180 horsepower (hp) gasoline engine compared to *Holland VI*'s 45 hp. Electrical horsepower was increased from 50 hp in *Holland VI* to 70 hp in the new class.

ARMAMENT—*Holland VII* lost the Zalinsky pneumatic dynamite gun and its ammunition, but it carried two additional spare torpedoes instead.

SUPERSTRUCTURE—After *Holland VI* joined the Navy, she was fitted out with removable topside decking to extend the width of the superstructure while the boat was in port. *Holland VII* added a crude frame bridge structure to raise the commanding officer's height of eye and keep him a little drier when underway on the surface.

PERISCOPES—When built, neither *Holland VI* nor *Holland VII* were outfitted with periscopes. It is difficult to see how operations were possible without this critical item. Once the submarine's hatch was shut, the only way to see out was through one-half-inch-thick bars of glass set in the walls of the turret. Periscopes were soon installed in *Adder*-class boats, but not backfitted into *Holland VI*.

From this list of evolutionary improvements, it appears that *Holland VI* was small and cramped, underpowered, and wet during surfaced operations. It allotted valuable space to an ineffective weapon and was practically blind when the hatch was shut. With these shortcomings corrected, the follow-on *Adder* class served through World War I, most notably providing coast defense in Manila Bay, showing the flag throughout the Philippine Islands, and training newly recruited men and officers for duty in future submarines.

Holland VI—after joining the U.S. Navy and becoming USS *Holland*—lasted a scant five years on active duty. Her initial training mission complete, *Holland* now was rendered obsolete by newer and larger submarines. She languished in Annapolis until 1905, when she was placed in reserve at Norfolk, Virginia.

In her brief career *Holland* demonstrated the potential of the submarine to level the field between great and lesser naval powers. The opaqueness of the sea permitted the submarine to choose its own battles and to use the element of surprise to great advantage. All that remained was for technology and imagination to bring improvements to the platform and weaponry. This evolution has been going on for the past 100 years, with every prospect that it will continue.

Holland underway, fully rigged for surface. Rectangular holes in the superstructure permit the flow of water to and from the free-flooding space above the pressure hull during diving and surfacing.

Protector, *Simon Lake's first warship, was completed in 1902. Since the U.S. Navy was slow to accept* Protector, *it was sold to Russia in 1904.*

Pioneer Ship Builders

*J*ohn Holland has been referred to as the "father of the submarine." An Irish schoolteacher who emigrated to the United States in 1873, he designed and built submarines, initially to assist the Fenians in their avowed effort to destroy the all-powerful British navy. Holland was a self-taught engineer whose special talent was to recognize the synergy of modern developments and to incorporate them into a submarine design where they could best be used. For example, he recognized that the internal combustion engine offered great promise as a prime mover on the surface. At the same time he saw the potential of using improved electric storage batteries (another new development) with an electric motor to turn the propeller when submerged. Noting that the gasoline engine could further be used to charge the storage batteries when depleted, Holland was able to put together the tidy and effective propulsion package that powered Holland VI. At the same time John Holland applied his genius to hull design. Shaping his submarine in conscious imitation of the porpoise, he strove for optimum submerged performance. Thus was conceived the tear-drop hull, with a near optimum ratio of length to diameter.

The problem with this approach was that Holland VI *was a submersible—not a submarine—whose submerged activities were severely restricted by the capacity of the storage battery.* Holland VI *conducted surface operations most of the time, with submerged operations generally limited to practice attacks and other specific training evolutions. The low freeboard and lack of topside protection from wind and waves inhibited operations in rough weather.* Holland VI *proved John Holland's submarine theories and design, but it was left to Mr. Lawrence Y. Spear, Holland's successor as senior engineer and designer at the Electric Boat Company, to modify the submarine hull and superstructure configuration to improve surface operating characteristics. Fifty years*

later nuclear power replaced the storage battery and the internal combustion engine as the driving force for propulsion surfaced and submerged. This breakthrough provided a nearly unlimited power supply that permitted the submarine to operate submerged at all times except when entering and leaving port. It became timely and appropriate for submarine design to revert to John Holland's concepts, emulating the clean lines of nature's sea creatures.

John Holland was not the only talented American submarine inventor. A young competitor named Simon Lake appeared at the office of the Secretary of the Navy in 1893 with an armful of drawings he had prepared in response to a request to design and build a submarine for the Navy. Like Holland, Simon Lake was an engineer from New Jersey who had been fascinated by submarines since boyhood as a result of reading Twenty Thousand Leagues Under the Sea *by Jules Verne. While Lake did not win the 1893 competition (the more experienced Holland won), his design did attract some capital and he found himself constructing* Argonaut *at the Columbian Iron Works and Dry Dock Company on building ways adjacent to those being used to erect* Plunger *under John Holland's supervision.*

Above: The Irish-born inventor, John P. Holland (1841–1914), came to the United States when he was 32 years old, and he brought notes and drawings on submarines with him. In 1878, John Holland finished construction of *Holland I* and demonstrated it for the Fenians, who had funded it. Over the next eighteen years, he designed and built four more boats before *Holland VI* was constructed. He learned from each iteration and applied the lessons to the design of *Holland VI*.

The two boats were very different, reflecting the different motivations of their inventors. All Holland's submarines were warships—built for combat, well armed and highly maneuverable. Lake's Argonaut was designed with commercial applications in mind. It dove and surfaced with a level keel, was fitted with wheels to run over the sea bottom, and included a diver's lock and hatch rigged so that crewmembers could exit from the submarine to the seabed. Lake expected to use Argonaut commercially to explore the bottom, harvest shellfish, or visit shipwrecks. He espoused the tactic of submerging his boat with a level keel. To facilitate this procedure he installed diving planes at both ends of the boat.

Simon Lake moved into the design and construction of warships with his submarine Protector, built at his yard in Bridgeport, Connecticut; Protector was sold to Russia in 1904. In later years he designed and built submarines for the U.S. Navy, including O-boats, R-boats, and S-boats, but competition from the Electric Boat Company and the Portsmouth, New Hampshire, Navy Yard forced the Lake Torpedo Boat Company out of business in the building vacuum caused by the cessation of World War I hostilities.

Above: USS *Holland* drydocked at New York Navy Yard in 1901. The clean lines of the underwater hull, unmarred by even a bilge keel, are clearly evident.

Left: A brilliant and imaginative engineer schooled at the Franklin Institute, Simon Lake (1866–1945) provided the only real competition for John Holland. Lake's first boats, *Argonaut* and *Argonaut Jr.*, were designed for commercial rather than military use. In 1902 he built his first warship, the submarine *Protector*, which he soon sold to Russia. Lake is credited with conducting the first open-ocean submarine operations with *Argonaut* in 1897. Although the Lake Torpedo Boat Company of Bridgeport, Connecticut, built several submarines of his design and of Portsmouth Navy Yard design through World War I, the excess of existing U.S. Navy submarines at war's end and the lack of commercial interest put Simon Lake's submarine company out of business.

THE
Early Days

Admiral William J. Crowe, Jr., USN (Ret)

Above: *Rigged for surface exercises, with her pipe stanchion and canvas con (conning station), a D-class submarine heads out past a coastal schooner loaded with pilings for new submarine piers at Submarine Base, Groton, Connecticut, c. 1916. On the left is the large naval coaling facility that dominated the Thames River shoreline at this period. (Victor Mays)*

Opposite, top: *The Confederate submarine H. L. Hunley is shown in a pen and ink drawing with wash dated 1902. (R. C. Skerrett)*

As I prepared my remarks for a June 2000 Naval Submarine League banquet, it kept coming back to me that we are celebrating 100 years of history. Yet most of the material I found was devoted to the last sixty years of the century. I would like to focus on the early days of our service—the forty years before Pearl Harbor. It is not a well-known story, but it is an amazing one.

For centuries men had dreamed of probing the undersea world and some had in mind military weapons. The most well-known in our country was the attack of CSS *Hunley* on USS *Housatonic* anchored off Charleston Harbor. In the process, the first rule of submarining was violated. Both ships were sunk.

During the late 1800s several European nations experimented with weaponizing a submersible with some success. The U.S. Navy, while mildly interested, was "stand-offish"—money was tight and emphasis was given to building capital ships.

In the United States two brilliant inventors, following different paths, designed military submarines—J. P. Holland and Simon Lake. The Navy, in its wisdom, insisted on a series of competitions primarily devised to put off making a serious decision. Holland ultimately prevailed, and in April 1900 delivered to the U.S. Government its first ready-made submarine. It was given the imaginative name of USS *Holland* and not surprisingly an accompanying number of SS 1.

She was 53 feet in length, 10 feet in diameter, displaced 63 tons. Her operating depth was 75 feet. On the surface she was powered by a 45-horsepower gasoline engine.

This article is adapted from the banquet address by Admiral William J. Crowe, Jr., USN (Ret) to the Naval Submarine League Symposium on 16 June 2000.

CONFEDERATE SUBMARINE

During the War between the States, the Confederates made several submarines out of iron cylinders. Each was powered by husky men turning a long crankshaft attached to an outboard propeller. The weapon system consisted of a pole extending out over the forward end of the submarine, with an explosive charge attached to the end of the pole. This was rigged to explode upon contact with the side of an enemy ship. After many trials and some loss of life, CSS Hunley *was ready for action. On 17 February 1864 she set out from Charleston, South Carolina, to attack the Union frigate* Housatonic. *Her approach was successful, and* Hunley *exploded her weapon against the ship's side, sinking the frigate.* Hunley *drew off about four miles where she fired a blue signal which told those on shore the action was complete and the Union ship was on the bottom.* Hunley *was not heard from again until 1995, when she was discovered about four miles off Sullivans Island. In 2000* Hunley *was raised to the surface and barged to a conservation laboratory where she will undergo preservation for at least seven years. After meticulous refurbishment it is planned to display CSS* Hunley *at the Charleston, South Carolina, museum.* Hunley's *proud place in history is ensured— she is the first submarine to sink an enemy warship.*

—*CAPTAIN HARRY JACKSON, USN (RET)*

A machine shop, drawing room, docking facilities, and basin at New Suffolk, New York, was leased by the Holland Torpedo Boat Company (later to become the Electric Boat Company) in 1899. This small harbor was the nation's first operational submarine base. In the foreground is an A-boat proceeding to moor outboard of two other A-boats.

Lieutenant Chester W. Nimitz, center, commanding officer of a "Mother Ship" for six or seven U.S. submarines is shown here with four other officers and Mr. W. Crowell, an architect, on 1 October 1911 at Newport, Rhode Island. The writing identifying two of the officers is Fleet Admiral Nimitz's.

Perhaps more importantly, a word should be said about the general climate. *The New York Times* reported "*Holland* may or may not play an important part in the navies of the world in the years to come." *The New York Times* was no better then at predicting than it is today. Within the Navy the bulk of the officer corps took little notice. They considered the whole concept as a nuisance, or at best a novelty.

Fortunately, a small group did believe that the submersible had promise. One of these individuals was of high rank and rather well

USS Plunger, *an Adder-class submarine, shown here, was numbered SS 2 in 1920 even though USS* Adder *was commissioned first. The tall ventilator pipe shown on the aft deck of the boat is an air intake for the gasoline engine. The three small glassed ports are clearly shown in the hatch cover.* Fulton *and USS* Porpoise *are moored across the basin.* Fulton *was the company's prototype for the class. She was sold to Russia in 1904.*

Opposite, bottom: *The entire B class is shown in a snow-covered drydock in the New York Navy Yard. The other ship in the dock is the converted yacht USS* Hist, *a veteran of Cuban operations during the Spanish American War, and subsequently one of our first submarine tenders.*

known, Admiral George Dewey, who was also head of the General Board. He threw his weight behind the initial *Holland* purchase. Incidentally, the first commanding officer of *Holland* was Lieutenant H. H. Caldwell, who had been an aide of Dewey. I often wondered if he was a volunteer.

When you think about it, the U.S. Navy in 1900 had just finished fifty years of unprecedented change: wood to armor, sail to steam, etc., and had just prevailed in a major war at sea—the Spanish American War. Now came two groups of upstarts (whippersnappers) demanding recognition. They had even more radical proposals—seaborne aircraft and submersibles. It was tough medicine for a service that was deeply rooted in Mahan and traditional surface-to-surface actions.

It's interesting to note that *Holland* preceded the first naval airplane by eleven years. But the romanticism of aviation exploits and the lack of commercial usage for submarines stifled comparative progress.

Nevertheless, the civilian inventors and later the associated builders were aggressive crusaders. They saw submersibles as a niche market and a viable maritime weapon. They carried their case to both the Administration and Congress. For its part, the Navy played a subsidiary role both in the design and in generating the necessary support. I have often thought the obvious difference in the amount of visual imagery between air and undersea combat capabilities also had an effect on general recognition of submarine potential.

We should give great credit to those civilians who were the prime drivers moving the Navy in this new direction—not only Holland and Lake, but also Mr. Frank Cable, Holland's confidant and economic advisor. I would especially include Mr. L. Y. Spear. He had spent ten years as a naval constructor and left the Navy as a lieutenant to join J. P. Holland's submarine building company, which later became Electric Boat. He spent the next forty years overseeing Electric Boat construction. He died in 1950.

WWI TACTICS

At the start of World War I, one of the tactics was for a submarine to lie quiet on the bottom near the entrance to a port. The submarine could hear and sometimes identify the noise radiated from an approaching submarine. This caused the Navy Department to authorize a committee to investigate the possibility of detecting submarines by the sounds radiated from their operation. The War Committee, which included Dr. Reginald A. Fessenden, made the USS L-9 submarine available for the target. The Committee also had a motor launch outfitted with instrumentation to listen and record the sounds from the submarine. The captain of L-9 complained that the sound boat was always on his tail. This was the beginning of today's fabulous sonar systems.

—CAPTAIN HARRY JACKSON, USN (RET)

L-class submarines are photographed alongside their tender in Ireland during World War I. Impressed by the successes of British submarines against the German U-boats, the U.S. sent twelve submarines to the European war zone. They were based in the Azores and southwest Ireland. Although the L-boats in Ireland made a number of contacts with enemy submarines, they never sank one.

Above: *The crew of USS B-3 (SS 12) lined up topside in Cavite, Philippines. The crew consists of one officer, three CPOs, and nine enlisted men including one fairly large fellow third from left. The submarine had only limited headroom and this gent may have had a rough time of it below deck. These boats operated in the warm waters of Manila Bay with gasoline engines, open-topped batteries, poor ventilation, and no air conditioning or refrigeration. Their supplementary compensation was $5 a month, plus $1 a dive to a maximum of $15 per month.*

Given the lack of submarine expertise at the higher levels and the absence of any central authority for developing a mission or support structure, it is rather astonishing how many boats were built in the first few years. They were not ships but boats, since they could be carried on ships. Ultimately, the slang term was expanded to "pig boats." I guess that was progress of sorts.

After *Holland*, the next seven submarines were characterized as A-boats. From 1903 to the early 1930s, the classes were designated alphabetically as A, B, C, D, E, etc. The letters were followed by numbers for administrative purposes. Each class, of course, was designed to increase modestly in size, speed, depth, crews, and equipment carried.

The fundamental challenge was to expand and refine the Navy's knowledge of submerged operations and to steadily improve the pig boats and associated equipment to prove they could be a viable weapon system. The technical problems were formidable: unsafe structures, unreliable

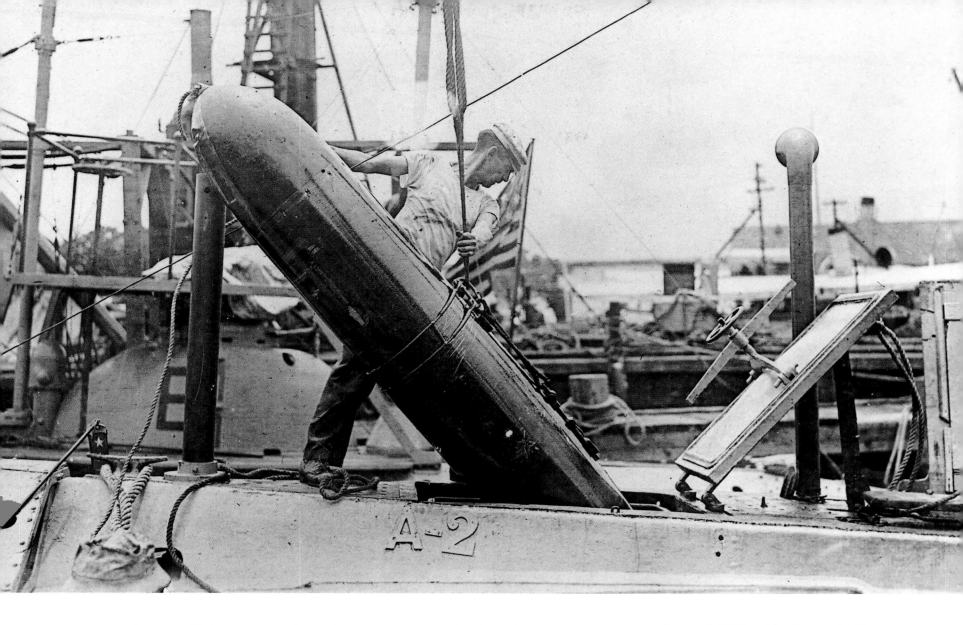

engines, inefficient storage batteries, poor communications, inadequate optics, primitive metallurgy, poor construction techniques, and on and on.

The early boats were fickle mistresses. Breakdowns and accidents were a way of life. Major casualties were always in the back of everyone's mind. Improvements didn't spring full-grown onto the scene. Most solutions came after hundreds of hours of trial and error—and there were lots of errors.

Added to this were trying living conditions. Space was severely cramped. Gasoline and later oil fumes were constant. Berthing compartments were unventilated and normally wet. Privacy was almost nonexistent and the one commode was a full-view model indelicately dubbed the throne. Admiral Charles A. Lockwood commented that "sanitation arrangements at best were meager and defied description"—a kind way of putting it. The boats were best known for their constant odors and smells.

There was a great story about a skunk. It seems that after one liberty-port evening, a sailor returned to the boat leading a skunk on a leash. The duty officer told him he could not bring the skunk aboard the submarine and the sailor asked "Why not, if other ships have mascots?" "It's the

Above: A-2 *(SS 3), originally named* Adder, *takes on a torpedo at the Navy Yard in Cavite, Philippine Islands. This photo, taken about 1912, shows the torpedo being loaded tail first. The conning tower, shown to the left of the sailor and below the torpedo's warhead, belongs to another A-class boat on the far side of A-2.*

Bottom: M-1, *shown here, and the T-class submarines were designs that proved to be the direct forerunners to the Gato-, Balao-, and Tench-class fleet submarines. It was hoped, in the years around World War I, that a submarine could be devised to operate as a unit of a battle fleet. It would travel at fleet speeds, submerging to engage enemy ships as the two fleets closed. The problem that was to prove intractable was speed. The standard fleet speed was higher than that obtainable by the diesel-engine-powered submarines of the time. As propulsion and ship designs improved, the strategy changed and submarines, instead of being tied to fleets as escorting units, turned into offensive weapons that operated in a far-ranging and independent mode.*

Opposite, bottom left: A-2 *(SS 3) is shown with her entire crew topside in Manila Bay prior to World War I. The two men to the right, on the stern, are leaning on the signaling bell. The two tall masts are fixed periscopes.*

Opposite, bottom right: *Work on the early boats did not take the heavy drydocking and cranes that are required today. This photo of A-2 (SS 3), taken in Cavite in 1913, shows the boat pulled ashore on a small marine railway and her bottom and stern being worked on.*

Right: *Looking forward in the torpedo room of a D-class submarine, the four handwheels, two on the left and two on the right, are the breech door operators for the four tubes. Instead of muzzle doors as later tubes had, this Electric Boat-designed submarine had a rotatable bow cap with two openings. Along with the obvious simplicity of these early boats was a notable lack of safety features and interlocks.*

Opposite, top left: *Looking aft through the engine room of a D-class submarine, the two engines seen, one on each side, were direct-drive gasoline engines with most of their moving parts out in the open. The use of gasoline was fraught with dangers as most of the fittings were prone to working loose and leaking, thus causing toxic and flammable vapors to build up. On at least one early boat, these gas fumes caught fire and killed the entire crew. In addition, the engines required constant attention and adjustment. Diesel engines in later submarines were safer and became more reliable.*

Right: *A diving stand of a D-class submarine is shown. As with the helm, normal operation of the planes was by electric motor. Hand operation was with the handwheel seen here. There is only one hand wheel because this class of submarine had no bow planes. The ladder on the left led to the conning tower and topside.*

Right: *The internal helm stand of a D-class submarine. The watertight door to the torpedo room is seen to the right of the helm wheel. The helm wheel motor is attached via gearing to the transmission shaft, which ran aft to the rudder linkage. Directly above the helm wheel is a mirror into which the helmsman looked to obtain a view of the magnetic compass repeater above. Normal steering was by an electric switch that operated the motor.*

smell," was the officer's explanation. The sailor replied, "Oh, he'll get used to it same as I did." Then there was the canned food and Navy gasoline, coffee—black, hot as hell, and strong as a cannon.

Complicating the picture—funds were always short. There were no senior officers with direct submarine experience and no overarching organization to coordinate, prioritize, and fight for the needs of the boats.

Still, the real story was the people. It took time to build a corps of people who were knowledgeable and dedicated advocates. It's exciting to trace how that eventually came to pass.

Fortunately, the pig boats with all their faults, from the outset attracted a stream of young officers and enlisted men with adventurous spirits. They were fascinated by the newness of the concept, by the technical challenges, by the ever-present dangers, by the camaraderie of small ships, and the opportunities for early responsibility. They didn't fully understand the potential of their boats, but they were enthusiastic believers. In essence they were a special breed, just as they are today.

If you peruse the list of commanding officers and wardrooms you can see that some healthy seeds were being planted. Ensign Nimitz took command of the *C-5* in 1910. This was the first of his five submarine commands. Charles Lockwood's name appears often—he ultimately

Top, left: *Vice Admiral Charles Lockwood started his submarine career on A-boats in Manila Bay. He described early submarine life in* Hell at 50 Fathoms. *During World War II he served as Commander Submarine Force Pacific Fleet (COMSUBPAC) and directed the highly successful operations of the Pearl Harbor-based submarines.*

Top, right: *USS* H-3 *(SS 30) on the surface in 1914.* H-3 *ran aground on the California coast while operating with USS* Milwaukee *(CL 21) and USS* Cheyenne *(BM 10) in December 1916. The crew was rescued by the U.S. Coast Guard using a breeches buoy from the sandy beach. A salvage attempt was made with* Milwaukee *putting over cables to tow the little submarine off the beach. In the attempt,* Milwaukee *herself got broadside to the surf and was forced ashore at Samoa Beach. The cruiser and the submarine both became the subject of an intense salvage effort. The submarine was hauled across the sand on log rollers to Humboldt Bay and relaunched. The cruiser was heavily pounded by the surf, and a storm the following year broke her back. She was scrapped in place.*

commanded some eight different boats, including a captured German U-boat. These were only two from a large number that reached flag rank; some were later prominent in the submarine hierarchy: Nelson, Bingham, Whiting, McWhorter, Gygax, Munroe, Daubin, Frazer, English, Withers, Quigley, David Taylor, Lewis, Denfeld, Whiley, Wilkes, Styer, Murray, Will, Crawford, and Low.

Occasionally, an individual or an unexpected event would intervene and assist in one way or another. In 1905, President T. Roosevelt rode an A-boat in Long Island Sound for a few hours, against the advice of his Secret Service. Shortly thereafter he recommended and succeeded in getting an expanded submarine pay bill. It called for $1 for each dive to a limit of $15/month. It applied only to enlisted men and spawned the phrase "a dollar a dive and six months pay if you don't come up."

The most important event of the early years was World War I. It provided the kind of cold water shock the force and the Navy needed. There was little direct participation. Twenty boats were sent to Ireland and the Azores to assist the Royal Navy in harbor defense—hardly

A brood of submarines—"mother ship" USS Holland *(AS 3) with ten S-boats and the giant V-2 in San Diego harbor.*

Above: *The* H-2 *(SS 29) submerges in the Hudson River during a recruiting drive in 1919. The H-class boats were built both for the U.S. Navy and for export. During the early days of World War I, several boats were built covertly for the Royal Navy and for the Russian navy. The boats built for Russia were eventually taken into the U.S. Navy as USS* H-4 *through* H-9.

Middle: *USS* N-2 *(SS 54) being loaded with weapons in the early 1920s in New London, Connecticut. These boats were used for harbor defense during World War I and conducted antisubmarine warfare (ASW) patrols during 1917 and 1918 out of New London and Block Island. Here,* N-2 *is taking a torpedo warhead on board. The davit was normally erected for recovery of practice torpedoes from the water. The ten men shown topside comprise nearly half the boat's crew.*

Left: *USS* Alert *is an example of the various types of ships that served as submarine tenders prior to World War I. Built as an iron gunboat in 1874, she became the mother ship for the first four submarines assigned to the Territory of Hawaii in 1914. She is similar to another gunboat turned tender, USS* Castine, *who had to beach herself to avoid sinking when* C-4, *one of her brood, rammed her with a periscope.* C-4 *was approaching the anchored tender while running submerged. The commanding officer turned the periscope over to a gunner's mate with the order "split the* Castine *in two." Before the commanding officer took the scope again, the periscope struck the* Castine *amidships. While the gunner did not split* Castine *in two, he did make a sizable penetration.*

prestigious. But Germany's U-boat exploits combined with some amazing British feats were a tonic for the whole community.

Money began to flow into the business. The O- and R-class boats were expedited and this fiscal spurt ultimately led to the S class, which became the mainstay of the force until the middle 1930s. In 1917 the Secretary of

Above: *USS* Bushnell *is shown with USS L-1 (SS 40) and L-3 (SS 42) in Bantry Bay, Ireland, during World War I. These boats made ASW patrols in operating areas in the Western Approaches for most of 1918. The boats ran submerged all day and surfaced at night patrolling back and forth along convoy tracks looking for German U-boats. Living conditions on board limited the time the boat could spend underway to a week to ten days. They were small boats with scant provision for habitability, but they were the best available in 1917. The newer O-class boats were on the way when the war ended in November 1918.*

Right: *USS K-6 (SS 37) is shown in 1916. Although the use of hull numbers and the two-letter ship type designator was not made official until July 1920, this boat wears its hull number in white on a black background.*

the Navy (after the sinking of the *F-4*) acknowledged the need for more sophisticated training and authorized the establishment of a submarine school in New London, Connecticut—thus on-the-job training became the follow-on practical phase rather than the sole method of indoctrination.

This Lake designed N-class submarine, USS N-7 (SS 59), is shown on builder's trials. These boats operated out of New London, Provincetown, and Block Island on ASW patrols during 1917 and 1918.

USS L-3 (SS 42), an Electric Boat design, is shown off Provincetown, Massachusetts, in September of 1915 prior to its commissioning the following April. After commissioning, the boat spent a year in training and working up while operating out of New London. In 1917 she deployed to the Azores and Queenstown, where she patrolled in the war zone until November 1918.

U.S. officers eagerly read everything published on the German and British operations. More significantly, after the Armistice, Great Britain gave us six of the surrendered U-boats for study.

Above all, the war highlighted the need for central direction or a total submarine approach. Captain Thomas Hart (later Commander in Chief of the U.S. Asiatic Fleet in World War II) had been placed in command of those units sent to Europe.

In 1918 he was given responsibility for overseeing a total submarine program. This was a watershed step. The force was coming out of the doldrums. Soon a broader and more meaningful vision of the future

The crew of USS L-11 (SS 51) gets a breath of fresh air (and a cigarette) most likely in the port of Haulbowline, Ireland, where the L-boats went for repairs during their overseas deployment in 1918. The L-11 overhauled here in June and July of that year. She bears the number AL-11 to differentiate her from the British L-class boats also operating in the same area. USS L-11 made thirteen patrols out of Punta Delgada and Queenstown during the last part of 1917 and most of 1918.

Lake designed USS L-6 (SS 45), and the Navy split the design and construction of L, N, O, R, and S classes between Electric Boat and Lake. The Lake L-boats had superstructures that could be closed off and made watertight for more surface buoyancy. The ports that could be opened to make the superstructure freeflooding are visible along the sides of the boat. The Lake boats generally had three periscopes. Simon Lake built submarines for the U.S. Navy with varying degrees of success, and his designs were notably different from those of John Holland and the Holland Torpedo Boat Company (later Electric Boat Company) under Issac Rice and Frank Cable. These submarine designers and builders carried on a war of patents and marketing until after World War I.

Top: *Modern submarine surface communication is shown World War I style. A crewman uses signal flags on the forward deck of USS L-1 in Queenstown in 1918. The three football-shaped objects on pedestals in the foreground are sonar hydrophones.*

Above: *Submarine School was established in the brick building pictured here and located on the Submarine Base in Groton, Connecticut, in 1917. Shown is Building 3, which is still in use as the headquarters for Commander, Submarine Development Squadron TWELVE, and Commander, Submarine Squadron FOUR.*

Right: *USS K-2 (SS 33) is shown in striped dazzle camouflage in 1916. There are three known photos of K-class boats (most likely all the K-2) with this type of striped paint scheme. One has wider stripes and one has very narrow stripes. It is believed that the schemes were painted as a trial that proved unsuccessful, and no submarines actually used the dazzle paint scheme. This type coloration and design was used to disguise the shape of a ship and confuse an observer trying to determine what direction it was heading.*

began to emerge within the community led by Hart. As he advanced in rank he remained interested, involved, and influential in future submarine programs.

By the 1920s operating submarine officers were becoming more and more involved in specifying ship requirements and in every aspect of construction. For example, one of the most pressing challenges was to develop reliable diesel engines to meet the demands of long patrols without mother ship support. The force began training its own diesel experts, even sending officers overseas to become knowledgeable on foreign developments.

During World War I, government yards commenced designing and building boats. Predictably, they were more responsive to the views of the operators than the civilian yards. This, in turn, precipitated a genuine schism between Electric Boat and the Navy, which lasted for many

Submarine Tender USS Argonne *(AS 10) with the V-1 and V-6 alongside dressed for Navy Day, October 1930.*

An R-class submarine and the captured German U-111 pass during the 1919 Victory Bond Tour. The U-111 was one of a group of U-boats brought to the United States as war reparations and for studies by the Navy to learn about German submarine technology. The U-111, after study, was sunk off the East Coast as a gunnery target in July 1921.

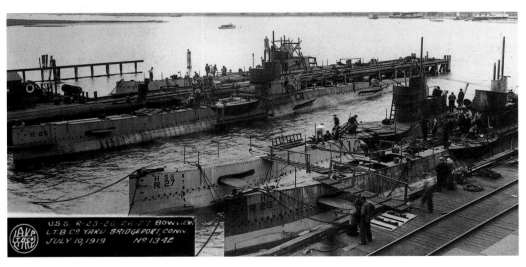

Three R-class submarines lie alongside the fitting-out docks at the Lake Torpedo Boat Company in Bridgeport, Connecticut, in July 1919. Like N, O, and S classes, the R class is divided into the Electric Boat variant and the Lake variant. These three boats are representative of the Lake variant (R-25 through R-27). The H number visible above the R designator on the bow of the two near boats is the Lake company hull number.

years. In that period the long-running problem of the diesel engine was worked out with General Motors and Fairbanks Morse. The dream of a fast, long-range boat at last became practical.

Another fortunate intervention occurred in 1925 when Captain E. J. King was ordered to command the Submarine Base at New London.

Above: *USS* Beaver *(AS 5) at Olongapo, Philippine Islands, March 1929, with six S-boats alongside. All the S-boats pictured made war patrols in World War II, first primarily in the Philippines, later in the Aleutians. Three of them sank Japanese freighters, earning the combat pin for successful war patrols.*

Right: *The crew of* S-44 *is preparing to recover a practice torpedo. In the center of the photo, a man is sitting on the bow plane with a boat hook in hand as the remainder of the topside personnel get ready to rig lines to the torpedo loading davit. The torpedo will be returned to the submarine's torpedo room and readied for another exercise shot.*

Below: *USS* Savannah *(AS 8) is photographed with three S-boats making a port call in Portland, Oregon. Berthing and messing facilities were so primitive in early submarines that tenders usually accompanied the boats for extended excursions.*

He gained considerable publicity in subsequent salvage operations. In the process he became a staunch supporter of the undersea community. This support lasted all his life. In 1923 he recommended a special device be designed to be worn by qualified submariners. Hence the dolphins we wear so proudly. One can readily see whence the strong support for the boats by leadership in World War II came.

One other aspect of early submarine life deserves special mention. Submarines were not a top agenda item in the press or the public mind,

except when a sinking focused all eyes on the undersea community. There were a disturbing number of these tragedies. Such crises highlighted the risks of working below the surface and more importantly, the character and resourcefulness of the men engaged.

Before 1915 there had been accidents, even deaths, but no sinkings. The age of innocence ended that year. *F-4* was lost off Hawaii with all hands. By 1927 the U.S. Navy held second place in the submarine funeral cortege of navies with 146 casualties and 13 major accidents. The list of sinkings is chilling.

- *F-1* rammed by *F-3* off the coast of California in 1917. Five men survived.

- *H-3* stranded off the California coast in 1916. No loss of life occurred.

- *S-5* sank off the Delaware Capes in about 170 feet of water on 1 September 1920. Thirty-eight crewmen escaped.

- *S-48* on builder's trials off Bridgeport, Connecticut, in 1921 sank in 70 feet of water. The after half of the boat flooded; the crew escaped through a forward torpedo tube.

- *S-51* was struck by the SS *City of Rome* on 25 September 1925, and sank off Block Island in 132 feet of water. Only three survived.

A diver descending to the sunken F-4 *is photographed ninety feet below the surface. The successful recovery of* F-4 *was a major event in the history of Navy diving and salvage. Navy diver Frank W. Crilley was awarded the Medal of Honor for a heroic act while taking part in the extremely deep diving activities.*

- *S-4* was struck by USCG *Paulding* in 1927 off Provincetown, Cape Cod, in about 110 feet of water. All forty hands were lost, although some remained alive for almost seventy-two hours.

- USS *Squalus* off Portsmouth, New Hampshire on 23 May 1939 sank in 240 feet of water. Twenty-six men were lost; thirty-three were saved.

Every one of these incidents exudes high drama. I found the *S-5* rescue a miraculous story of great determination and resourcefulness by the crew. She sank when the forward torpedo room was accidentally flooded preventing a successful surfacing. In a desperate move all the main ballast tanks were blown to bring the stern out of the water. The result was a 70-degree down angle with the nose stuck in the mud; 17 feet of the stern extended out of the water. The crew was literally walking on the bulkheads; the decks had become bulkheads. There were thirty-four men on board, crowded into the after compartments. All kinds of problems were overcome, but they were still trapped with no electricity other than flashlights. The commanding officer, Lieutenant Commander "Savvy" Cooke, crawled into the tiller room with two chiefs. After eight hours of exhausting effort, using a breast hand drill, they drilled a 3/4-inch hole through the pressure hull (3/4-inch). Several more holes were drilled and connected with handsaws and chisels. The effort produced a hole of 1 1/2 inches by 4 inches. It was large enough to push a stick with the captain's shirt on it out of the hole. By then the main problem was putrid air and a lack of fresh water. After a painful wait, SS *Alanthus*'s Captain Johnson was attracted by the odd sight. The ship's captain approached this small Tower of Pisa in a rowboat. Using the small opening the following conversation took place:

Left: *The SS* Alanthus *with the SS* George W. Goethals *aided in rescuing the crew of the USS* S-5, *which sank with a flooded torpedo room on 1 September 1920 off the Delaware Capes.*

Above: *USS* S-5 *is shown on the surface just after commissioning. In September 1920, off the Delaware Capes, a 5-inch pipe burst in the forward torpedo room sinking the S-5. After blowing tanks to raise her stern out of the water, the crew, using hand tools, laboriously cut a 4-inch hole in the pressure hull above the water. The skipper waved a shirt on a pole through the hole to attract a passing ship; that ship enlarged the hole in the hull, permitting the crew to escape. When the official salvage team arrived and attempted to lift and tow the submarine to shallower water, the cables snapped and she was lost forever.*

Left: *This plate was cut from the stern of USS* S-5 *to provide egress for the crew from the damaged submarine. The plate reads "Removed from the United States Submarine S-5 to allow the crew of that vessel to escape after being imprisoned 37 hours. The S-5 while engaged in diving exercises flooded a forward compartment and sank at 2:00 p.m. Sept. 1, 1920 in 165-feet of water. After repeated efforts, the crew managed to bring the stern of the vessel to the surface. The vessel was lying at an angle of 60 degrees with the bow resting on the bottom. The crew managed to cut a small hole in the hull and by an improvised signal attracted the attention of a passing steamer* Alanthus. *Later the Pan-American steamer* George W. Goethals *arrived on the scene. The chief engineer of that vessel, Mr. W. G. Grace, assisted by the chief engineer of* Alanthus, *Mr. C. Jacobson, working with a ratchet drill and chisel, removed this plate and at 3:00 a.m. Sept. 3, 1920 the crew of S-5 numbering 38 men were rescued."*

Johnson: What ship is this?"
Cooke: *S-5* U.S. Navy."
Johnson: "Who is speaking?"
Cooke: "Lieutenant Commander Charles Cooke, commanding."
Johnson: "Where is your destination?"
Cooke with disgust: "Hell by compass!"
Whereupon both laughed.

Alanthus, using hoses, managed to get pure air and fresh water into the boat and to remove some of the foul air. As other units arrived on the scene, the small hole was gradually enlarged. The entire crew escaped through that small window after a fifty-one-hour ordeal.

It's hard to overestimate the impact of these events on our history. First, each incident was an intense learning experience. A host of mechanical improvements followed every crisis. Most obvious were the advances in submarine rescue and salvage operations. In 1915 there were no preplanned procedures or equipment to deal with a boat on the bottom.

By 1939 when *Squalus* went down, specialized submarine rescue vessels were part of the Force. Admiral Momsen's famous lung was stan-

Opposite, top: *This view shows R-26 being fitted out in the Lake Torpedo Boatyard at Bridgeport, Connecticut. The bow planes rig into slots in the superstructure in the Lake variant as opposed to the Electric Boat scheme of folding flat alongside the bow.*

Opposite, bottom: *All personnel of the basic submarine classes received a qualification course in the training tank on the use of submarine escape devices. Facilities permitted escapes from a bell at any depth up to 100 feet and from locks at 18, 50, and 100 feet. Periodic refresher training was given to submarine personnel serving afloat.*

dard equipment on 211 boats. Crews were trained in escape techniques. Escape training towers had been erected at New London and Pearl Harbor. Extensive efforts were made to develop a rescue chamber. This effort was ramrodded by Captain A. R. McCann aided by A. I. McKee, an engineering duty officer, who was later associated with the Electric Boat Company for years.

Incidentally, it is not well known, but over the interwar period seven enlisted divers were awarded Congressional Medals of Honor for their work on rescue and salvage operations. In fact, a host of records for individual divers were set (depth, etc.). By 1940 the U.S. Navy led the world in deep-water search and exploration. We have never relinquished that position. Similarly, these events drew attention to the need for special bases and logistic tenders to support the operating boats.

Admiral Lockwood in his book *Hell at 50 Fathoms* discusses these disasters at length. One of his general comments is priceless:

> *Submarining, like other engineering progress, is a matter of trial and error, of learning by mistakes, mechanical as well as human. If we had waited for ultimate perfection to come from the drawing boards the fleet submarine that helped win WWII and the ballistic missile super sub that may prevent WWIII would never had dipped keel into water.*

Another note should be included. The last commanding officer of *S-4* was Lieutenant Commander Roy Jones. Mrs. Jones, who had stood by remarkably calm throughout the ordeal, told the press that when her six-year-old son grew up she hoped he too would choose the Navy. Roy K. Jones, Jr., did—both the Naval Academy and submarines.

Just as significant, these tragedies were media events and, in a bizarre way, inspired the admiration of the public for those who man submarines, as well as considerable criticism of the Navy for neglecting these problems. It also brought home the risks and the fact that special people are required to do this dangerous work. Congress reacted similarly and became more receptive to handling submarine appropriation requests, although such sympathy was short lived—just as it often is today.

Taking a step backward and looking at the period of 1900 to 1940 as a whole, it's people who stand out. It was not the golden age of

submarining—that was to come later. But although demanding, it was a necessary era. Those engaged directly didn't always have a clear vision of the submarine possibilities, and by 1940 many significant challenges still remained, including untrustworthy torpedoes and a well-thought-out strategy.

Nevertheless, the flaws of those pioneers were strongly outweighed by the virtues. From the outset capable people stepped up—men of unbelievable determination and perseverance. In retrospect, it's incredible how many stayed the course—we were the beneficiaries. These pioneers were willing to take the high risks associated with this pioneering effort and, no matter what the obstacles, to build a viable structure for the force. They were willing to devote their souls and talents to realizing their dreams, no matter how blurred.

By 1940 there was a special command structure, an extensive logistics infrastructure, an all-embracing training program, and a number of knowledgeable submariners ready to ascend to high positions. By 1940 the fleet boats, the best submarines in the world at the time, were coming out of the yards.

These men gave us the one consistent thread that runs throughout the history of the community. The most priceless legacy those men left was a set of values for those who probe the depths that is still with us today. We should always pay homage to those men: Spear, Hart, Nimitz, King, Lockwood, Fife, Momsen, McKee, McCann, Styer, Yarnell, and many besides naval officers. It can truly be said that our subsequent achievements rested on the shoulders of giants.

Put simply, over the last century, America's submariners have risked, served, fought, and on occasion died so that Americans might have a safer and freer life. In the process, they have given a full measure to the Navy, the nation, and the free world. I can think of no higher praise.

USS Narwhal (SS 167) presents a handsome figure running at high speed on builder's trials off Provincetown, Massachusetts, in July 1930. Note the raised deck amidships and her two 6"/53 deck guns.

Attaching cables from towing locomotives and warping into position to enter upper Gatun Lock, four C-class submarines and the submarine berthing ship, USS Severn, transit the Panama Canal in April 1914. The Navy made extensive use of the Panama Canal, constantly shifting naval forces between the Atlantic and Pacific depending on the current threat to U.S. interests around the world.

Submarine Roots

Captain Donald H. Kern, USN (Ret)

Is it a fact, rumor, or myth that Alexander the Great, in 332 B.C. seized an opportunity to explore the world beneath the waves in a glass sphere? The story goes on to refer to chains or rings used to secure an access door; that skins of goats were used for seating comfort; that two people joined Alexander on the adventure; and that food and drink were provided indicating more than a few moments of submergence was planned. But—how did they provide adequate air habitability? No mention is made of a hose to the surface for air replenishment. Alexander's submersible sphere generates a plethora of design and technological questions when trying to sort out whether the story is fact, rumor, or myth.

Irrespective of the story's validity, its durability no doubt has tweaked many inventive minds over the centuries to attempt the design and construction of submersible craft. In 1775, David Bushnell, a Connecticut Yankee, was convinced that he could construct a submersible that would be capable of causing the destruction of British warships blockading American harbors. With minimal support from the Connecticut government, and encouragement sans dollars from General Washington and Benjamin Franklin, Bushnell managed to build a creditable wood planked "pressure hull" with caulked seams aptly named Turtle, to be used for an attack against a British warship.

The name Turtle evolved from the shape of his craft. Two sea turtle shells placed together edge to edge with the head or forward end of the shells toward the sea surface provide a rough visual picture of the shape of the hull. The volume and height of the interior was just large enough for one man standing in an upright position. The source of power for propulsion was human. Three shafts were installed to turn two-bladed, windmill type propellers. One was located in the bow for forward and aft motion; one topside, for vertical up and down motion; and, in addition to a small rudder, a third propeller was located on the side of the hull to provide horizontal rotation. Bushnell understood

that these propellers would help the operator control the craft once it was submerged. However, to submerge, and then maintain a neutrally buoyant condition, he must somehow find a way to adjust the total weight of Turtle. This problem was solved by simply opening a foot-operated sea cock that allowed water to flood into the bilge until a crude depth gauge—a mercury barometer connected through the hull to measure sea pressure—indicated Turtle was submerged. To bring his craft back to the surface or to control overflooding and leakage from hull seams or from the seals used around shaft penetrations, a foot-operated pump forced water out of the hull against sea pressure. An emergency flooding situation could be countered by dropping a lead weight attached to the keel.

Air habitability of sorts was provided via two brass tubes extending a short distance above the hull and fitted at the top with float valves (the first snorkel?). A magnetic compass provided a general sense of direction, but navigation was primarily visual, using glass ports in a small cylindrical extension of the pressure hull fitted on top of the hull. With Turtle's hull submerged and the cylinder just above the sea surface, the operator's head could be positioned inside the cylinder; this would allow a limited view, via the glass ports, for steering. A serious problem was lack of illumination to enable an operator to see valves and

Top: Cutaway drawing of Turtle underway. The right-hand turns the screw, the left-hand steers, and feet operate the flood valve and bilge pump. (Courtesy of Connecticut River Museum)

Opposite, top: Sergeant Ezra Lee rises out of Turtle in an attempt to affix a bomb to the rudder of a British ship in New York Harbor in 1776. (Courtesy of Connecticut River Museum)

Right: In 1776 Sergeant Ezra Lee is the first American submariner—a volunteer, as are those who follow in his footsteps.

other control mechanisms and to read the depth gauge and compass. Bushnell soon found that candle illumination rapidly exhausted the oxygen available in the very small internal hull volume. His solution was foxfire, a luminescent fungus that grows on decaying wood. A small cork of foxfire floated on top of the depth gauge mercury column, and a small piece attached to the compass needle made their positions visible in the total darkness of the submerged hull. Operation of controls, pumps, and valves was dependent upon operator memory and sense of feel.

Turtle's primary mission was to sink a British warship at anchor in an American harbor by delivery and attachment of an explosive charge to the hull of the enemy ship. For this mission stealth was an essential characteristic and consisted of two elements: first, the cover of darkness and second, a submerged weapon delivery vehicle. Bushnell's weapon of choice was a keg of gunpowder carried on the exterior of the hull. The delivery scheme was simple: while partially submerged, drift with the tide to the immediate vicinity of the British target using the limited propulsion and directional controls available; submerge when alongside the target to place Turtle under the target's hull. With Turtle properly positioned the operator must then put the critical element of the submersible's weapon system into play—turn the crank driving a vertically oriented external auger bit until the auger bites securely into the target's wooden hull. Then release the auger bit by allowing it to pull out of the auger's grasp leaving it planted in the British ship's hull. A line attached to the bit led to the keg of gunpowder and Turtle's operation order

then directed it to pull, or more realistically, paddle away from the target. The departure of Turtle would cause the line attached to the bit to pull the powder keg away from its mounting on Turtle and at the same time it would pull the lanyard on the igniter timer. The operator listening to

the external noises and knowing what was about to occur did not, we can be sure, have to be instructed to crank furiously away from the target. This was Bushnell's planned modus operandi; however, Bushnell, the designer, elected not to be the operator of Turtle to carry out the intended mission. He was fortunate to find a volunteer to serve as operator—Army Sergeant Ezra Lee. It would not be difficult to believe that any modern day professional engineer, involved in submarine design, would pay a tidy sum to have been afforded the opportunity to play "fly on the wall" when Bushnell first described to Sergeant Lee, the operation of Turtle.

Sergeant Ezra Lee trained well and made two valiant attempts to sink a British ship in New York harbor—both attempts failed primarily due to the inability to successfully drive the auger into the hull of the target ships. Although Bushnell failed to produce a submarine system that could be credited with delivering the first sinking of an enemy ship, he did identify the key and vital elements that must be incorporated and integrated to produce a successful military submarine design.

The noted British naval historian, Commander Richard Compton-Hall, MBE, RN, believes the Turtle saga is mostly an American myth. Be that as it may, it is *our* myth—and we like it!
—THE EDITORS

Trouble Below
Submarine Sinkings, Rescues, and Salvage

James Christley, EMCS (SS) USN (Ret)

USS F-4 (SS 23), a 330 ton "F" class submarine was built at Seattle, Washington, and transferred to Hawaii in 1914. On 25 March 1915, during a routine dive a few miles off Honolulu, F-4 sank in 51 fathoms of water with the loss of her twenty-one crewmembers.

Officers examining the hull of USS F-4 that sank after a catastrophic hull failure due to leaking battery electrolyte. The loss was the first U.S. Navy submarine to sink with all hands at sea. In this view taken from off the port bow, F-4 is rolled 120 degrees to starboard and shows the port bowplane in the center. Note the enormous hole in the hull created by the implosion when F-4 sank below crush depth.

The ocean is a hazardous place, and submarines are as susceptible to the hazards as other ships. Unlike a ship designed to ride only on the surface of the ocean whose compartments will collapse as the ship sinks, a submarine may carry all or a portion of its crew to the bottom alive if it sinks in shallow enough water. Should this happen, efforts turn to effecting an escape from inside the submarine or a rescue from outside. Apart from lifting the entire submarine to the surface, which could be done in the early days when submarines were smaller and lighter, there are two main ways to rescue the crew. The crew can equalize the pressure inside the boat with sea pressure outside, open a hatch, and swim out individually. The pressure inside must be raised quickly and the escaping crew must swim out quickly or suffer effects of the bends and carbon dioxide poisoning. Once outside, each man must remember *not* to hold his breath as he rises to the surface. As he ascends, the air in his lungs expands with the decrease in pressure and if he does not breathe out continuously, he will rupture his lungs. Once on the surface, the escape survivor is exposed to weather conditions at the surface while he waits to be picked up. The preferred method of rescue is to bring a rescue chamber to the submarine's hatch and to unload the crew into the chamber. The rescued men are then transported in the chamber to a place of safety. This method requires that the rescue vessel transit to the site of the sinking and that takes time. Because the air available to the submarine's crew is limited, and most likely contaminated with high levels of carbon dioxide, time is a critical item in short supply for the crew on the bottom.

In the early days the only method of rescue available was to hoist the entire submarine to the surface. This could be accomplished by using heavy lift salvage cranes or floodable pontoons. One hoped that these would be available and could be brought to the scene and used quickly enough. This method alone proved inadequate in the first several submarine sinkings in Britain, France, and Russia.

Top: *USS S-4 (SS 109) is shown on the surface just after commissioning in 1919. In December 1927, while surfacing off Cape Cod, she was struck by the U.S. Coast Guard cutter* Paulding, *and sank in 102 feet of water. Several men trapped in the torpedo room communicated with rescuers for a time by tapping on the hull but all eventually perished.*

Above: *The submarine rescue ship* Falcon *(right) and fleet tug* Wandank *over the sunken USS* Squalus *during rescue operations, May 1939.*

Page 61, top: *USS* Falcon *(ASR 2), commissioned in 1918 as a minesweeper, was reclassified as a submarine rescue ship in 1929. She conducted salvage operations in 1921 on USS S-5 (SS 110). In September 1925, she successfully salvaged S-51 (SS 162) after it was rammed and sunk off Block Island. She served as the operating platform for the successful rescue of the surviving crewmen of USS* Squalus *(SS 192) in 1939.*

Page 61, center: *The USS S-51 sank after being struck by SS* City of Rome *in 1925. The submarine was refloated eight months later (shown here) by a salvage crew and divers operating from USS* Falcon.

59

BRAVE SHIPMATE— ROBERT HAMILTON

On 28 October 1923, USS O-5 (SS 66) was crossing Limon Bay toward the entrance to the Panama Canal. SS Abangarez struck O-5, opening a large hole and causing massive flooding. The submarine started sinking rapidly stern first. Some of the crew who were topside were thrown into the water, and a few others made their way topside and were saved. In all, sixteen of the crew were rescued. Five were missing. These included Chief Electrician's Mate Lawrence T. Brown and Torpedoman's Mate Second Class Henry Breault. Breault had been working in the torpedo room when the collision occurred. He headed up to the main deck, but realized that Chief Brown was below—asleep. Instead of going over the side, Breault headed back below to get Brown. He shut the deck hatch over his head just as the bow went under and water started to pour in. The submarine settled to the bottom in 42 feet of water. Breault found Chief Brown and together they fought their way through the rising water in the battery compartment to the torpedo room. Having shut the watertight door, they waited in the darkness for rescue, which they hoped would come before their air ran out.

The water was only 42 feet deep that close to the port of Cristobal, but the only way to rescue the men was to lift O-5 out of the mud using pontoons or cranes. However, the nearest pontoons were more than 2,000 miles away, and the only two cranes capable of the job were on the canal, trapped inland by a mudslide that had closed the waterway for the first time in seven years.

As diver Sheppard Shreaves, a civilian employee of the Panama Canal Company, worked to prepare O-5, other crews cleared the landslide from the canal. Almost eight hours passed before one of the cranes could make it past the obstruction, and it would take hours more to make it to the accident site. Shreaves worked with a firehose to cut a trench in the mud of the harbor floor so he could pass cables under O-5. As he worked, Shreaves tapped on the hull to let the crewmen know work was still underway. Breault and Brown knocked back, but as the hours passed and the air grew stale, the knocks grew weaker.

The morning after the accident the crane was in place and the cables were ready. The teams took up the slack; however, the weight of the boat and the suction of trying to pull it clear was too much, and the 4-inch cable snapped. They slung another harness, but it snapped as well. Finally, on the third try, thirty-one hours after Breault had sealed himself in with Chief Brown, O-5 pulled free and lifted toward the surface.

Breault, who had served four years in the British navy before joining the U.S. Navy in 1920, received the Medal of Honor from President Calvin A. Coolidge for his selfless act. Shreaves was honored with the Congressional Lifesaving Medal and a gold watch from the Coco Solo Submarine Base, where O-5 was homeported. Breault remained in the Navy after the accident and even sought a waiver to remain in the service when he was diagnosed with a serious heart condition. He died at the age of 41 a few days before the United States entered World War II.

The bow of USS *O-5* (SS 66) is hoisted to the surface by barge-mounted heavy lift cranes near the entrance to the Panama Canal. A collision with SS *Abangarez* sank the submarine. Henry Breault shut the hatch, which is seen just above the water's edge, to save a shipmate as the bow went under. Thirty-one hours later the bow was raised freeing Henry Breault and Lawrence Brown from a slow death.

In 1908, an intrepid young ensign, Kenneth Whiting of USS *Porpoise* (SS 7), used the 18-inch torpedo tube as a trial escape chamber. He had himself closed in the tube and when it was flooded, had the outer door opened and swam out. The effort suggested the basic design elements of the escape trunks used in later submarines.

The first U.S. submarine to sink while operating at sea was USS *F-4* (SS 23). On 25 March 1915, she suffered a catastrophic hull failure while diving just off Honolulu harbor. Ships arriving on the scene found bubbles of air and oil coming to the surface, which indicated to many that the crew might be alive and attempting to pump or blow their ballast tanks. Divers prepared to descend to render assistance and to prepare the submarine for lifting if the crew couldn't get the boat back up. It lay in over 300 feet of water, a depth well below any previously attempted by a diver. Chief Gunners Mate Jack Agraz and Chief Gunners Mate George B. Evans, at great personal risk, each dove to depths of more than 200 feet three times that day in a vain effort to reach the bottom and to find *F-4*. The search was resumed by dragging, and as hope for a successful rescue faded, the rescue turned into a salvage effort. The hull of *F-4* later was raised and studied to determine what had gone wrong. Investigators found that leaking battery electrolyte, primarily sulfuric acid, had corroded the plating and structural members under the battery well, which was also the top of the forward ballast tanks. When the boat dove, the increased pressure on the plating caused it to fail catastrophically, sinking the boat and killing the crew.

MEDAL OF HONOR CITATION FOR TORPEDOMAN'S MATE SECOND CLASS HENRY BREAULT

For heroism and devotion to duty while serving on board the U.S. submarine O-5 at the time of the sinking of that vessel. On the morning of 28 October 1923, the O-5 collided with the steamship Abangarez *and sank in less than a minute. When the collision occurred, Breault was in the torpedo room. Upon reaching the hatch, he saw that the boat was rapidly sinking. Instead of jumping overboard to save his own life, he returned to the torpedo room to the rescue of a shipmate whom he knew was trapped in the boat, closing the torpedo room hatch on himself. Breault and Brown remained trapped in this compartment until rescued by the salvage party thirty-one hours later.*

Torpedoman's Mate Henry Breault receives the Medal of Honor from President Calvin Coolidge.

USS S-4 (SS 109) is shown being settled on blocks in a Boston Navy Yard drydock. She was raised in March 1928 after having been sunk in a collision the previous December. The large cylindrical objects are pontoons that were used to raise the submarine. The pontoon is flooded with water and sinks to the bottom near the submarine. It is then attached to the submarine with chains, which are threaded from one pontoon through tunnels under the submarine and attached to another pontoon on the other side. After several pairs of pontoons are so attached, air is blown into the pontoons, expelling the water. The buoyancy provided lifts the flooded submarine toward the surface.

In the preceding chapter "The Early Days," Admiral Crowe lists early submarine sinkings and describes the miraculous rescue of the crew of USS *S-5* (SS 110).

On 17 December 1927, an accident occurred that accelerated the improvements in submarine escape and rescue equipment and procedures. USS *S-4* was surfacing off the tip of Cape Cod when she was rammed by the USCG cutter *Paulding*. The *S-4* settled to the bottom in water merely 102 feet deep. The battery compartment was flooded, six men had gone forward into the torpedo room and were trapped there. The other men in the crew had closed themselves in the control room and the engine room. When the ventilation line in the battery compartment collapsed and debris clogged the bulkhead isolation valve, the control room began to flood and the crewmembers in the control room retreated to the engine room and motor room.

By 11 a.m. USS *Falcon* had arrived from New London. She commenced dragging operations to try to locate the downed boat and when she did, she put divers over into the cold and increasingly rough

The hull of USS S-4 is being towed into the Boston Navy Yard on 16 March 1928. S-4 was sunk off Provincetown, Massachusetts, on 17 December 1927. Although most crewmen perished soon after the sinking, six men survived for several days in the torpedo room as rescuers desperately tried to assemble enough equipment to raise the bow of the boat. The death of these men provided strong motivation to devise methods for allowing the crew to escape safely and for rescuers to extract the crew from a sunken submarine.

water to get to the stricken submarine. By the time the divers reached the deck, the men in the engine room and motor room had succumbed to the buildup of chlorine and carbon dioxide. The six men in the torpedo room were alive and were trying to communicate by tapping on the hull. The boat had been down for twenty-four hours and the time for rescue was growing short. The bow of the boat had to be lifted to the surface to effect a rescue. At that time, no other way of freeing the crewmembers was available even in that relatively shallow water. Although the salvage of S-51 in 1925 had demonstrated that cranes alone were useless, pontoons and cranes were the only hope of rescuing

St. Mary of the Harbor Church in Provincetown, Massachusetts, on the tip of Cape Cod, contains a simple wooden memorial cross, dedicated to the men who perished in the USS S-4. The church holds an annual memorial service on 17 December in honor of the crew. S-4 was accidentally rammed by a Coast Guard cutter off Provincetown on that day in 1927 and sank in 102 feet of water. The painful inability to rescue the crew, after the central compartments flooded, intensified efforts to develop safer submarines, including escape and rescue devices to save those trapped below. Quick-operating doors, heavy compartment bulkheads, the Momsen lung, and the McCann rescue chamber were only a few of the many features devised to save men trapped in a submarine. This simple memorial and annual service is appreciated by those who go down into the sea in service to their country.

The submarine S-4 is shown here alongside USS Falcon (ASR 2) in 1928. She was used for many years to test various submarine rescue concepts. Operating out of Key West in 1929 and 1930, then in New London in 1931, S-4 was sent to Pearl Harbor in 1932, where she was decommissioned in 1933. She was sunk as a target near Pearl Harbor in May 1936.

While still in the hands of the civilian builders, S-48 (SS 159) was on trials in Long Island Sound off Bridgeport, Connecticut, when during a dive, water flooded into the submarine through an unsecured ballast tank access. Settling to the bottom in relatively shallow water, the crew emptied the forward ballast tanks and raised the bow above the surface. They then escaped through a forward torpedo tube.

the crew. As the call went out for heavy lift cranes and pontoons, *Falcon* readied divers to get air hoses down to the boat to replenish the air supply to the men in the torpedo room. Suddenly a severe northeast storm blew up and diving operations had to be suspended. Sixty-two hours after *S-4* sank, the final signal from the six men trapped below was received, P-L-E-A-S-E H-U-R-R-Y. Eventually an air hose was fitted

Left: *USS* R-6 *(SS 83) sank in October 1921 in San Pedro, California, due to a malfunctioning torpedo tube. After being submerged for fifteen days, she was refloated through the efforts of the crews of* R-6, R-10 *(SS 87), and USS* Cardinal *(AM 6).*

Above: *Lieutenant Momsen is shown using a battery-less underwater telephone in a test of the flooded escape chamber he had built on the deck of USS* S-4. *He has removed the mouthpiece of his rebreather "lung" that was later renamed the Momsen lung.*

to the C-tube sonar fitting and air was pumped in. But it was too late; the six men had perished. The death of *S-4*'s crew and the painful inability of the Navy to rescue them inspired efforts to improve submarine escape and salvage techniques.

One sign of the increased importance now accorded to submarine salvage and rescue was the formal redesignation of *Falcon* (AM 28) and USS *Widgeon* (AM 22) from minesweepers to submarine rescue vessels in 1929. Now a full-time unit of the Atlantic Submarine Force, *Falcon* (ASR 2) acted as tender and rescue vessel for the submarines on the East Coast. The ship went with the submarines on fleet exercises as far south as the Canal Zone. When a new submarine or a recently overhauled submarine was scheduled for a deep dive on sea trials, *Falcon* would attend.

Lieutenant Charles Momsen, USN, developed a rebreather "lung" that could be used by a crewman of a sunken submarine to escape from the boat and ascend to the surface. It could be used in conjunction with a lockout chamber that was designed and backfitted in some S-class and *V*-class boats and was included in the design of new construction submarines. In a parallel effort, Momsen, Commander A. I. McKee, and Commander A. R. McCann designed and built a rescue chamber based on the diving bell principle. This device, a small pressure-tight chamber with a hatch in the top and one in the bottom along with air and communication fittings, could be attached to a cable and pulled down to the deck of a disabled submarine with a downhaul winch mounted in the bell. There it would be clamped to the submarine hatch. Then, the water between the chamber's and submarine's hatches would be blown out, at which time both hatches could be opened and personnel transferred to the chamber. The crewmembers could then be hoisted in the chamber to the rescue ship. The chamber concept was tested and proved successful. By late 1938, the mooring technique had been tested and a new mooring system for *Falcon* was designed. Laying a four-point moor with her large anchors, the rescue vessel could be positioned carefully over the disabled submarine and could lower the bell to the deck with some accuracy. A marker buoy releasable from inside the submarine and tethered to it would indicate the location of the stricken submarine.

Falcon was in New London with the McCann Rescue Chamber when, on 23 May 1939, USS *Squalus* (SS 192) submerged for a test dive

This is a closeup of an early version of the McCann Rescue Chamber. The lower skirt fitted on to a flat circular surface surrounding the forward and after torpedo room hatches on a submarine. The chamber was equipped with ballast chambers, an air-operated winch, and controls for raising and lowering. Once seated, the water between the submarine's hatch and the lower chamber hatch was blown out. Then, both hatches were opened, and the rescued submarine crewmen would climb up into the upper portion of the chamber for the trip to the surface.

The McCann Rescue Chamber is photographed alongside USS Falcon *during the rescue of* Squalus *crewmen.*

USS Squalus *(SS 192) was raised and renamed* USS Sailfish *(SS 192); she served her country well throughout World War II. After the war, the conning tower, bridge, shears, and a portion of the superstructure were removed to become a memorial at the Portsmouth Naval Shipyard in Kittery, Maine. The site has been used for memorial services over the years, including the memorial service for the USS* Thresher *(SSN 593) in 1963.*

only to flood through a jammed main induction valve. *Falcon* immediately started her practiced salvage procedures. The submarine marker buoy had been released by *Squalus* and the word was passed through its telephone to USS *Sculpin* (SS 191) that there were survivors trapped on the bottom. Shortly after, the line parted and contact was lost. The tug *Penacook* started to drag with grapnels to find the lost boat. The next morning *Falcon* arrived at the scene just off Portsmouth, New Hampshire. With the help of *Sculpin*, *Penacook*, and others, they established good contact with the downed submarine. *Falcon*'s anchors were deployed and the rescue started. A wire cable was attached to *Squalus*'s forward torpedo room hatch by divers. The other end of this cable was fed to the downhaul reel in the bell. The bell was also attached to *Falcon*'s large salvage lift boom by another wire cable. The divers inside the bell would adjust the ballast to ensure neither wire was overloaded. During the first and second trips, the bell worked flawlessly. The third trip also went well, then the fourth and final trip to the sunken submarine was made. The last of the surviving crewmen were taken aboard the bell and it started its ascent. Then, the downhaul cable winch jammed. This winch, which pulled the bell down to the submarine's hatch, was also used to control the ascent. Now the bell could not move in either direction, up or down. A diver from *Falcon* hurried down to the stuck bell and tried to free the winch, but he was unable to clear the problem. He found that the cable that attached the bell to *Falcon* had frayed badly and only one strand remained intact. The operators of the bell slowly adjusted buoyancy to settle it on the bottom. Another diver went down to attach another cable but the attempt failed. Finally, as

Above: *Members of the Navy's Deep Submergence Unit slide the submarine rescue chamber (SRC) from an Air Force C-5A Galaxy. The Republic of Singapore navy, the Japanese Maritime Self-Defense Force, the Republic of Korea navy, and the U.S. Navy were conducting a regional submarine rescue exercise in the South China Sea in September 2000.*

the buoyancy of the chamber was carefully adjusted to keep the tension on the frayed cable to a minimum and to keep the bell from rocketing to the surface (perhaps into the bottom of *Falcon*), the crew of *Falcon* slowly pulled by hand the chamber up 200 feet to the surface. As the swells rose and fell lifting the rescue ship, the men raced back and forth on her deck maintaining a gentle pull on the bell. Finally just past mid-

Above: *The U.S. Navy's SRC deploys from MV* Kendrick *to dive to the Republic of Singapore submarine* Conqueror *on 9 October 2000 during joint naval exercises in the South China Sea. The SRC will dive to the ocean floor more than 200 feet below, dock on the "disabled" submarine, and practice evacuating sailors. In a real life rescue, the SRC could safely deliver six sailors per trip to the surface.*

Left: *The surviving crewmembers of USS* Squalus *(SS 192) huddle in the cold damp of the torpedo room while awaiting rescue. Each man moves as little as possible. Each breath inhales precious oxygen and exhales poisonous carbon dioxide. As the carbon dioxide level rises, first comes lethargy and confusion, then slumber, and finally death. John Groth, a Naval artist, painted his conception of this event for a 1966 Navy Memorial Museum display on the sinking of* Squalus *and the rescue of the survivors.*

The McCann Rescue Chamber is shown on the aft deck of USS Chowanoc *(ATF 100) in 1953. The rescue chamber and its attendant apparatus could be transported by submarine rescue vessels (ASRs), salvage vessels (ARSs), and fleet tugs (ATFs). This expanded the range of ships that could respond to a submarine casualty. These ships trained in the use of the apparatus at regular intervals.*

night on 25 May, thirty-nine hours after *Squalus* had sunk, the last of the surviving crewmen reached the open air and the deck of *Falcon*. Thirty-three men were saved from certain death by the heroic crewmen and the ubiquitous *Falcon*. *Falcon* stayed at the site after the rescue and served as the base ship for the divers who worked to salvage the boat.

During the following four years the Submarine Force was again at war. In wartime there is very little chance if any for rescue or escape. Yet in one instance the equipment invented and tested by Commander Momsen was put to use and saved the lives of submariners who would otherwise have been trapped on the bottom.

USS *Tang* (Commander Richard O'Kane) was having good hunting in the area near Turnabout Island at the north end of the Formosa Strait on 24 October 1944. When the last torpedo on board was fired at a freighter during a night surface attack, disaster struck. The rudder of the torpedo jammed hard over after it was launched. The torpedo circled around and detonated against *Tang*'s hull near the maneuvering room. The ship bottomed with its aft compartments flooded. Nine men had been thrown into the water from the bridge; the remainder of the crew were either already dead or were trapped in the forward compartments of the

Left: *From the early 1930s to the mid 1990s, the escape training tank towers at New London and Pearl Harbor (shown) were dominant structures on those bases' waterfronts. The tower houses a 110-foot column of water with entrance or egress chambers at various levels. Trainees entered these chambers and practiced the fundamentals of submarine escape. The towers were first used for Momsen lung training; then after World War II, buoyant ascent was taught. The final individual escape method used in the tank was the Steinke hood. Divers worked and trained in the tank. When submarine crews and submarine school students trained, the tank's water column was populated by divers who instructed and monitored every step of the training and were ever vigilant to ensure safety.*

Bottom, left: *USS* Kittiwake *(ASR 13) is typical of the* Chanticleer-*class submarine rescue vessels built during and just after World War II. She was commissioned in 1946 and operated along the East Coast during workup and training. She was present as the duty ASR at Cape Canaveral, Florida, when USS* George Washington *(SSBN 598) fired the first Polaris missile in July 1960.*

Bottom, right: *USS* Skylark *(ASR 20) spent most of her service life operating out of New London, Connecticut. She was in attendance during USS* Nautilus's *(SSN 571) initial sea trials in 1954. In 1963,* Skylark *was standing by when USS* Thresher *(SSN 593) sank during deep submergence trials off Portsmouth, New Hampshire. Visible amidships are two of the four buoys, called "spuds," which are used to attain a "four point moor" over a specific point in the ocean. The winches on the bow and stern then can control the precise position of the ship. On the stern is the rescue chamber used to retrieve the crew from a sunken submarine. The large tripod aft on the ship is used to handle the rescue chamber, as well as perform other salvage tasks.*

Above: *The crew of a sunken submarine might escape through the on-board escape trunk with an ascent to the surface using the Steinke hood—a combination of an inflatable life vest and a hood that contains a quantity of air, which allows the person to breath normally during the ascent. This photograph shows Commander Walter Mazzone and Lieutenant Harris Steinke using the 110-foot escape training tank to demonstrate the viability of the device.*

Top right, and right: *The Steinke hood, named for its developer, Lieutenant Harris Steinke, is shown during development testing. In the photo with the hoods removed, are Commander Walter Mazzone (right) and Lieutenant Steinke.*

Opposite: *Alongside in Rota, Spain, USS* Billfish *(SSN 676) serves as the support and transport for the deep submergence rescue vessel mounted on her stern.*

submarine 180 feet below. One officer had escaped from the conning tower as the ship was sinking. He and three other crewmen swam all night and were picked up by a Japanese ship the next morning.

As the boat came to rest on the bottom, the survivors took stock of the situation. Those who escaped the carnage aft crowded into the forward end of the boat. They started to destroy classified equipment, records, and logs. During the night they had to endure another depth charge attack. Gathering in the forward torpedo room, the crew started to make an escape using Momsen lungs and the escape trunk. A total of thirteen men left the ship in this manner. Of the men who escaped, only eight were known to have reached the surface. Five of these men survived until morning and were taken prisoner by Japanese vessels in the area, as were four who had escaped from the bridge area as the boat sank. All nine captured crewmembers survived their imprisonment in Japanese prisoner of war camps.

On 10 April 1963, the worst single disaster in our submarine history occurred. USS *Thresher* (SSN 593) sank during its post shakedown availability sea trials. The ocean bottom where she went down was 8,300 feet deep, far below the collapse depth for the pressure hull. There was no

A Sturgeon-class submarine transits on the surface carrying a DSRV on its after deck. The white markings on the sail, sail planes, and around the forward escape trunk are used to provide high visibility waypoints for training the submarine and the DSRV crew.

DSRV-1, Mystic, *is pictured on board USS* Dallas *(SSN 700) in Operation Sorbet Royal 2000, a NATO submarine rescue exercise off the Mediterranean coast of Turkey. This NATO exercise tested the ability of submarine rescue vehicles from various nations to operate with submarines of other nations.*

chance of rescue. One result of the investigation and testing that was done to determine the cause of the disaster was a comprehensive program for increasing the inherent safety of all submarines. This SUBSAFE program undertook a redesign of all seawater piping and all other hull fittings. The quality assurance (QA) on these systems and all hull penetration components would be the same as for the pressure hull. This QA program included a full, traceable documentation track for all construction, installation, and repair; complete radiographs of each weld; and full hydrostatic pressure testing of each system. In addition, the SUBSAFE program changed the design of the main ballast tank blow system to ensure the ballast tanks could be blown free of water quickly under emergency conditions. The number of seawater system penetrations was minimized, then each set of hull valves and backups was set up to be hydraulically operated from a central location. Thus, in an emergency, the entire internal set of hull isolation valves could be closed in seconds. It took time to implement the changes and the delays added to construction of new submarines had to be melded with the backfitting of SUBSAFE items to older operational submarines

One such boat, which had received a partial SUBSAFE modification, was USS *Scorpion* (SSN 589), which was lost when she sank in the mid-Atlantic while on transit back to Norfolk, Virginia, from an overseas deployment in May of 1968. As in the case of *Thresher*, *Scorpion* sank in water far deeper than her collapse depth.

Work continued on submarine safety and rescue technology. Submarine crews could survive in their boats at depths shallower than their collapse depth but greater than those that could be reached by the McCann

rescue chamber or from which the crew could escape using an individual escape device. By 1971 two rescue vessels of a new type were built. Deep submergence rescue vessels (DSRVs) named *Avalon* and *Mystic* were small air-transportable submarines that could be carried on the back of a mother submarine and conveyed to the vicinity of the sunken boat. Once there, they could attach to the escape hatches of the disabled submarine and take rescued crewmen aboard for transport back to the mother submarine. They exercise constantly to perfect their rescue capabilities and procedures. Fortunately they have not been called to action to effect an actual rescue.

More recently, as the DSRVs are approaching the end of their designed service life, new technologies such as remotely operated vehicles (ROVs) and deep diving suits have been considered for submarine rescue. A new immersion and escape suit has been procured to replace

DSRVs like Avalon *shown here, are equipped with a complex maneuvering system that uses pinpoint navigation and underwater control to mate with a crippled submarine. Some of the ducts with internal propellers can be seen on the bow and stern.*

Two converted GUPPY II submarines, USS Cochino (SS 345) (above) and USS Tusk (SS 426) (right), are forever linked. When Cochino suffered a disastrous electrical fire in the Barents Sea in 1949, the smoke, fumes, and flames forced Cochino's crew topside where they huddled in, on, and around the sail. Tusk steamed to assist. Then, in a daring rescue hampered by stormy frigid seas, she rescued Cochino's crew. During the effort Tusk lost six of her own crew, washed overboard and drowned. One man from Cochino also was lost. Cochino sank shortly after. Without Tusk's heroic effort, few if any of Cochino's crew would have survived.

USS Scorpion (SSN 589) was a Skipjack-class nuclear fast attack submarine. She was lost at sea in the mid-Atlantic while making a transit to her homeport of Norfolk, Virginia. The boat went down in water over 12,000 feet deep. Although the wreckage has since been located and studied, the exact cause of her sinking has not been determined. The depth of the ocean in most parts of the world is well beyond the depth at which the submarine's hull will collapse; thus, in most of the submarine's domain, rescue is impossible.

the simpler Steinke hood, which is currently in use. The new escape suit will better protect an individual from exposure during and after escape from a sunken submarine.

During the 100-year history of the U.S. Naval Submarine Force, the United States has lost sixty-five submarines. Of those, one was lost in a collision during World War I, and fifty-two were lost during World War II. Losses were studied, where possible, and the lessons learned were incorporated into submarine operations and training. In most of the peacetime losses (twelve), the hulls were salvaged and studied. The lessons learned from these losses changed submarine design, operations, and crew training. The loss of *Thresher* brought about a profound change in submarine design, construction, and maintenance. This program has been successful in ensuring that proper quality assurance is maintained in submarine construction and maintenance. The Submarine Force has suffered heart-rending tragedies. Our tradition requires that our shipmates who made the ultimate sacrifice did not do so in vain.

The last U.S. diesel-electric submarine lost at sea by accident was USS Stickleback *(SS 415), a Guppy IIA conversion. During antisubmarine warfare training exercises on 27 May 1958 in the operating area about 20 miles south of Pearl Harbor,* Stickleback *lost propulsion power, then depth control while maneuvering at high-speed submerged. This resulted in* Stickleback *inadvertently surfacing directly in front of her ASW antagonist, USS* Silverstein *(DE 534). In the resulting collision* Silverstein's *prow sliced through both the outer and pressure hulls of* Stickleback *just forward of the forward battery-control room bulkhead.*

The destroyer escort's commanding officer held Silverstein's *prow snugly in the cavity it had carved in* Stickleback's *flank. This initially restricted the rate of flooding, enabling the submarine's crewmembers to secure the compartments that were not breached and to make their way topside.*

Prodigious efforts were made to control the flooding while heading under tow for shallow water, but to no avail. Stickleback *sank about six hours after the collision. There were no personnel deaths or injuries.*

75

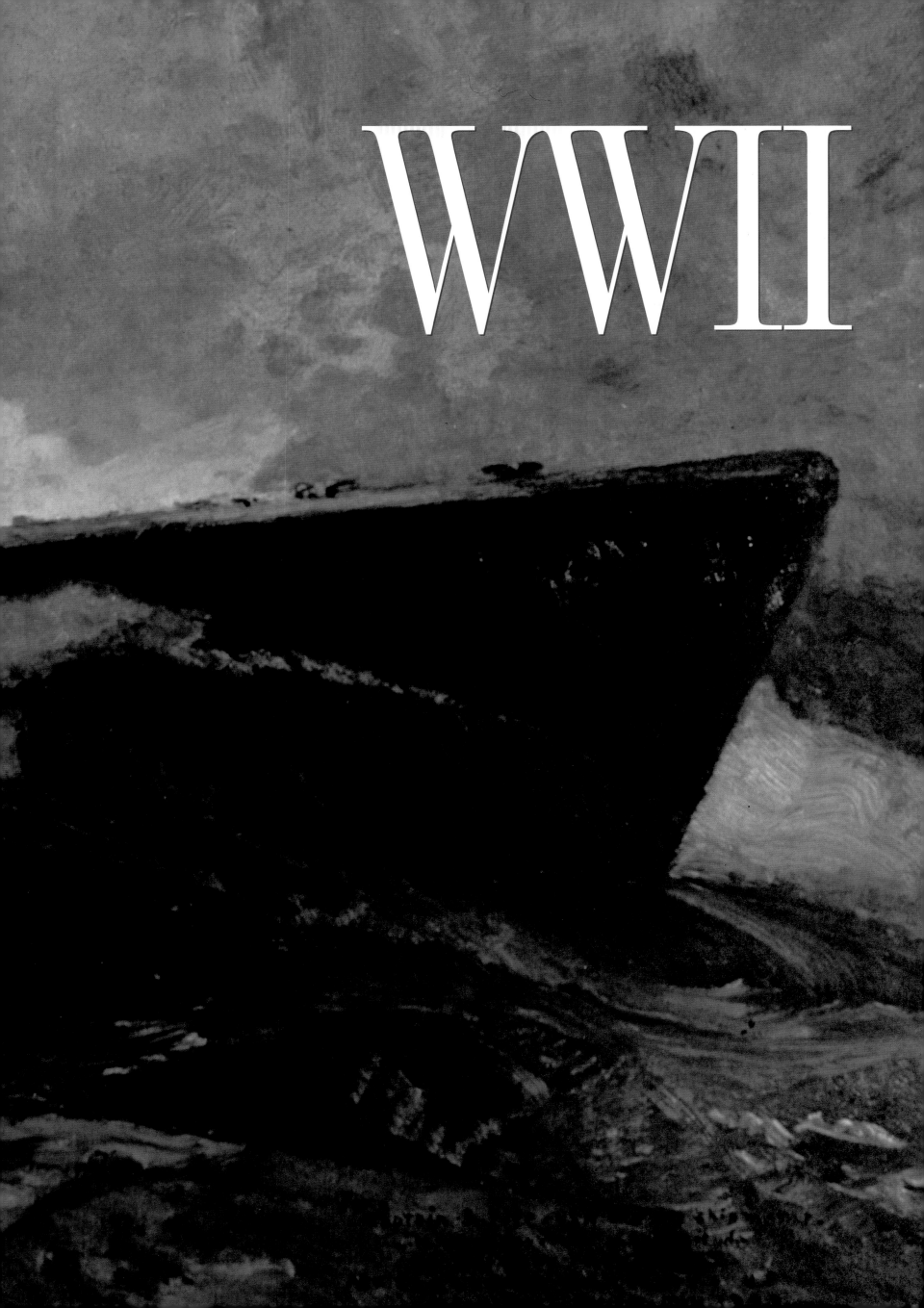

WWII

Submarine Operations in World War II

Rear Admiral Maurice H. Rindskopf, USN (Ret)

Seen through the periscope of USS Drum *(SS 228), the Japanese merchant ship* Taihaku Maru *goes down quickly after a successful torpedo attack.*

"It was to the Submarine Force that I looked to carry the load until our great industrial activity could produce the weapons we sorely needed to carry the war to the enemy. It is to the everlasting honor and glory of our submarine personnel that they never failed us in our days of great peril."

—CHESTER W. NIMITZ
FLEET ADMIRAL, U.S. NAVY

I t is clear from Admiral Nimitz' heartfelt commendation to the Submarine Force that submarine operations in World War II were successful. However, the road was not smooth nor was the trip easy.

Prior to World War II, submarines in the Pacific Ocean were divided between the U.S. Asiatic Fleet, commanded by Admiral Thomas C. Hart, based at Manila, and the U.S. Pacific Fleet, commanded by Admiral H. E. Kimmel, based at Pearl Harbor. At the start of the war the preponderance of submarines—six S-boats and twenty-three fleet boats—were Manila based. The Pearl Harbor contingent totaled twenty-one fleet boats; however, eleven of these were on the West Coast for overhaul, repairs, conversion, or shakedown cruise.

It was fortuitous that the fleet submarine design, which evolved in the 1930s, was ideally suited to the missions and tasks to which the submarines would be assigned. They were capable of sustained operations, unsupported for periods up to sixty or more days, including sufficient fuel capacity to enable them to transit from Pearl Harbor to the Japanese Empire and operate there for thirty days or longer. Their ten torpedo tubes provided ample firepower to ensure success in torpedo attacks, and their twenty-four torpedo capacity was generally matched with their other attributes.

On the other hand, the S-boats were old and difficult to maintain. Their endurance and radius of operations limited them to patrols closer to their bases. Their four torpedo tubes and twelve torpedoes of lesser capability than those in fleet boats, and their more primitive fire control system further constrained them in such attacks.

The author of this chapter, Lieutenant Commander Rindskopf, shown (above) in 1944. Rear Admiral Maurice H. Rindskopf was a 1938 graduate of the U.S. Naval Academy and entered the Submarine Force in July 1940. He commissioned USS Drum (SS 228) just prior to the start of World War II as fourth officer (torpedo and gunnery). He completed eleven war patrols in Drum —the last two as commanding officer. At the age of 26, Rear Admiral Rindskopf was the first of his class and the youngest officer to command a fleet submarine. He was awarded the Navy Cross, Silver Star Medal, and Bronze Star Medal for his service in Drum. —THE EDITORS

Top, left: *Miniature battle flag. Admiral Rindskopf's memento of his eleven war patrols in USS* Drum (SS 228).

Page 76–77: "USS Growler" (SS 215) was painted by McClelland Barclay in 1943 and given to Commodore James Fife. Barclay, the famous artist, was killed in action shortly thereafter when the ship in which he was embarked was torpedoed by an enemy submarine. The Australian kangaroo bow was put on Growler at Brisbane, Australia, after the submarine's original bow was irreparably damaged in ramming a Japanese gunboat north of Rabaul on the ship's fourth war patrol. It was in this action that her first commanding officer was killed. Commander Gilmore, lying on the bridge of his ship, mortally wounded by machine gun fire, ordered his ship submerged with his famous words, "Take her down." Growler was sunk with all hands on her eleventh patrol in the South China Sea in November 1944. The painting was presented to the Submarine School by Rear Admiral Fife in memory of the immortals—McClelland Barclay, Howard Gilmore, and USS Growler. ("USS Growler," McClelland Barclay)

The initial wartime patrols from both Pearl Harbor and the Manila area were, with few exceptions, unaggressive and unproductive. Many commanding officers sought refuge from possible enemy attack at deep submergence—some firing torpedoes on doubtful sonar data. Others used doctrine to set torpedoes at depths designed to run under the target keel to maximize the damage from the installed magnetic

Above: Pearl Harbor, 7 December 1941, battleship row went up in flames. Here the forward superstructure and Number Two 14" triple gun turret of the sunken Arizona *(BB 39) are afire following the explosion of the ship's forward magazines. Burning oil made escape and rescue efforts a nightmare. Admiral Nimitz (inset) breaks his flag in the submarine USS* Grayling *(SS 209) and takes command of the Pacific Fleet, 31 December 1941.*

With battleship row burning in the background, sailors at the Pearl Harbor submarine base do their futile best to disrupt the Japanese onslaught. Note the sentries with rifles in the lower right corner.

HEROIC TENDER

USS Pigeon *(ASR 6), a small submarine rescue vessel, had a brief period of heroic service as a submarine tender during the first days of World War II.* Pigeon *was in the Cavite Navy Yard with her steering gear under repair when Japanese planes attacked on 10 December 1941.* Pigeon *was tied up to the minesweeper* Quail *(AM 15) with steam up, ready to get underway using* Quail's *steering gear. At the time of the attack,* Pigeon *and* Quail *were clear of the docks. Lieutenant Richard "Spittin' Dick" Hawes, commanding officer of* Pigeon, *observed that the submarine USS* Seadragon *(SS 194) was damaged and about to be engulfed by fire in her berth. Lieutenant Hawes maneuvered* Pigeon *and* Quail *back through heavy bombing and strafing to haul* Seadragon *stern first to safety. The heat was so intense that it blistered the ship's paint and melted the brim of Hawes's cap.* Seadragon *was repaired by USS* Canopus *and was back at sea by 16 December 1941.* Pigeon *was awarded the Presidential Unit Citation for this action— the first warship to receive the award in World War II.*

Lieutenant Hawes immediately found and mounted two 3-inch guns and twelve 50-caliber machine guns on Pigeon. *By the end of December,* Pigeon *had received her second Presidential Unit Citation for shooting down several planes and bombarding enemy troops.* Pigeon *was the only surface warship to win two such awards in World War II. This valiant ship and crew remained with* Canopus *in the Philippines until after* Canopus *was scuttled in April 1942. In May, a dive-bomber sank* Pigeon; *most members of its crew were captured and held in the POW camp at Cabanatuan, Philippines.*

USS *Pigeon* (ASR 6) is seen at full "dress ship".

exploder and came up empty when the torpedoes failed to explode. Most of the sinkings that were claimed on return to port were not corroborated in postwar analyses. Many patrols were cut short by materiel problems; not a few resulted in the relief of the commanding officer by his request or otherwise.

An important day for the U.S. Submarine Force was 6 March 1942, for it was then that USS *Drum* (SS 228) arrived at Pearl Harbor from her building yard in Portsmouth, New Hampshire. She was the first new construction submarine to arrive amidst sunken ships and black oil. She would be followed over the next three years by seventy-one more *Gato*-class boats, 100 *Balao*-class, and eleven *Tench*-class boats that made war patrols.

Drum arrived with an officer complement of five, four chief petty officers, and sixty-one crewmembers. As the demand for manning new construction submarines increased, the officer complement grew to eleven, with six chiefs and sixty-eight crewmembers. After each war patrol, every submarine expected to lose trained officers and men with replacements assigned from the "relief crews," who performed routine maintenance on returning submarines while the crew spent two weeks at a rest facility. In Pearl Harbor, that arduous task was carried out at the famous Royal Hawaiian Hotel.

Back in the continental United States submarine building yards were increasing production and the rate of ship completions accelerated. As the number of submarines and support facilities grew, the submarine campaign against the Japanese spread throughout the Pacific region, outlined as follows:

Above: *A chief torpedoman's mate in the torpedo shop of USS* Griffin *(AS 13) adds another casualty to a scoreboard of Japanese shipping sunk by S-boats operating from Australia. The S-boats joined the fleet shortly after World War I, and were seventeen years old when pressed into combat in World War II. At the outbreak of the war, several S-boats were operating as East Coast defense units in the Atlantic. Shortly after Pearl Harbor, they were sent on the 10,000-mile trip to Australia, where they played a big part in stopping the Japanese drive to the south early in 1942. The flags shown indicate the types of ships— plain flag with sun in center, merchant ship; flag showing sun's rays, man-of-war. These flags also indicate ships claimed to have been sunk. Damaged ships are not shown.*

Right: *A submariner meets an "Aussie" at a rest camp near Brisbane, Australia.*

Above: *This pair of periscope photographs records the fate of IJNS* Patrol Boat number 39 *sunk by USS* Seawolf *(SS 197) on 23 April 1943. Patrol Boat number 39 was an obsolescent destroyer of about 1,000 tons.*

Two submarine recruiting posters—the "fighting fish" and "Hit 'Em Where It Hurts! Join the Submarine Service"—from January 1942.

Dates	Operating Base	Operating Areas
1941 (December)	Manila	Luzon, Indochina
1941 to 1945	Pearl Harbor	Japanese Empire, Mid-Pacific Islands, East China Sea
1942 to 1943	Alaska	Alaska, Kuriles
1942 to 1945	Fremantle and Brisbane, Australia	Solomons, Indochina, South China Sea

In Pearl Harbor, support was provided in the main by the submarine base, while in Australia, submarine tenders, with limited assistance from shore facilities, provided all necessary repairs, torpedoes, fuel, and food. In Alaska, the base at Dutch Harbor did its best to succor the men who went to sea under miserable conditions in obsolescent S-boats, which were barely up to the missions assigned. By basing submarines as shown, support loads were distributed and transit times to operating areas were reduced. Some areas could be covered effectively only from the forward bases. As numbers of submarines increased, assigned areas grew smaller, and forces were available for varied special missions. Advanced bases were also established at Midway, Guam, Subic Bay, and other sites to reduce transit time to operating areas.

The U.S. Submarine Force was not a battle-tested organization when the war commenced. Operational training had been stylized with most, if not all, torpedo attacks conducted at periscope depth against targets with known masthead heights (necessary for estimation of range), limited speed, and familiar zig-zag plans. Installed sonar was rudimentary and its ability to track targets with sufficient accuracy to generate an effective torpedo solution was essentially nonexistent. Further, there was little knowledge of sound in the sea, which complicated the use of sonar in both an offensive and defensive role.

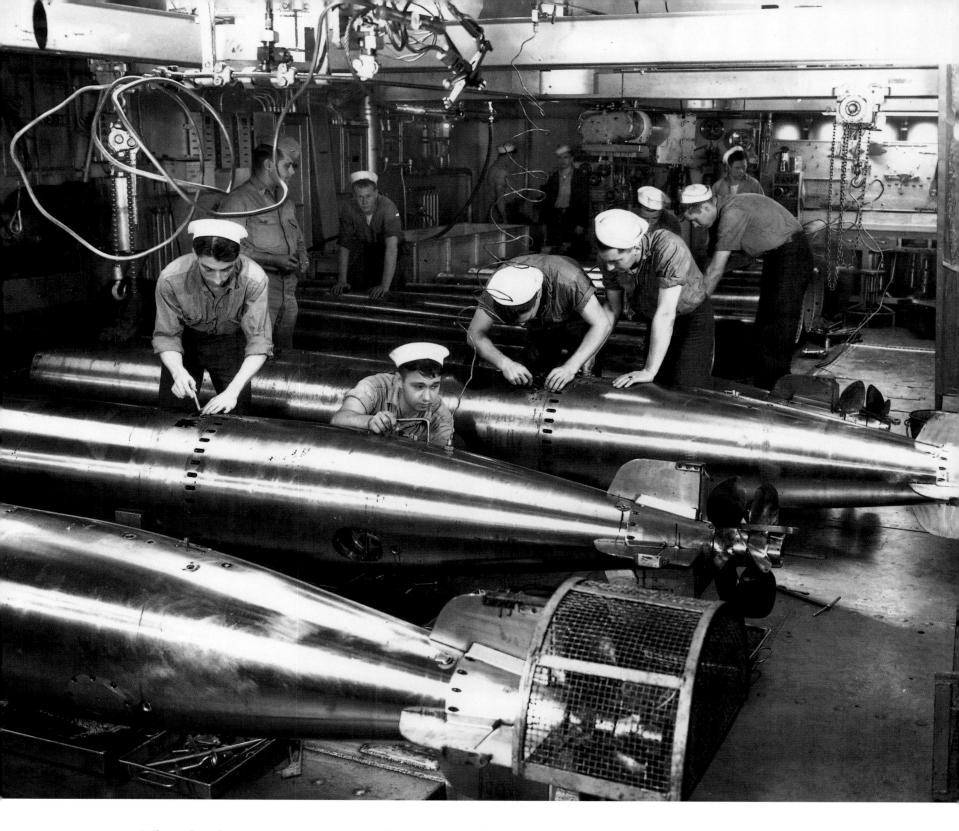

When the shooting war commenced, skippers suddenly were confronted with targets at night—targets that would not be there when a daylight periscope attack was feasible. Thus, the night surface attack was born. These attacks were generally made with meager data on target course and speed and a vague estimate of range. Further, they were normally snap shots, initiated within minutes of sighting. And yet, some were successful! It was not until after the initial war patrols had been completed that radar was introduced to the force. First, an air early warning system, the SD, was installed on a retractable mast aft of the periscopes. It was nondirectional, and of limited range, and the signal was detectable by both Japanese aircraft and ships.

By mid-1942, a surface search radar, the SJ, was installed on the forward face of the periscope shears above the bridge. This equipment, with a range of some eight miles against an average merchant ship, revolutionized night surface attacks. It enabled the submarine to track even unseen targets, to gain optimum firing position by running ahead of the target or convoy, to consummate effective torpedo attacks, and to evade escorts on the surface at night. The initial equipment was unreliable;

The torpedo shop of USS Fulton *(AS 11), in June 1943, is shown here. Known as the "Mother Ship," the submarine tender supplied weapons, fuel, food, and repair parts to her "brood." She also furnished electric power and repair, medical, dental, chaplain, postal, and communication services to submarines alongside.*

Periscope photograph of Mount Fujiyama was taken by USS Trigger *(SS 237) while on patrol off Tokyo Bay in 1943. U.S. submarines took the war into Japanese home waters, sinking ships within sight of the sacred mountain.*

Top, left: *USS* Sand Lance *(SS 381) loads torpedoes from the dock at an advanced base.*

Top, right: *The 5"/25-caliber gun crew of USS Sea Dog (SS 401) is shown in action. The first loader (partly obscured by the gun captain) is shown inserting a round into the breech. During World War II, submarines used their guns to some advantage when they encountered Japanese targets too small to torpedo. Each submarine mounted one or two medium-sized guns (3", 4", 5", or 6"), at least one rapid fire 20mm or 40mm gun, and two or more 50-caliber machine guns. Submarines made unsteady gunnery platforms, rolling and pitching even in the lightest seas. Nonetheless, a conservative 200,000 tons of enemy shipping fell to submarine guns.*

Below: *Vice Admiral Charles A. Lockwood, USN, Commander Submarines, U.S. Pacific Fleet, from February 1943 until the end of the war, was a brilliant and innovative officer with an extensive submarine background. He was much admired by his subordinates, who referred to him as "Uncle Charlie."*

however, radar technicians, added to the crew after intensive schooling, made a difference.

The fleet boats opened the war with a limited supply of the standard torpedo Mark (Mk) 14, a straight running weapon with a range of 4,500 yards at 46 knots, and 9,000 yards at 31.5 knots. Most ships carried twenty-four torpedoes, fired from six bow and four stern tubes. These torpedoes were equipped with the secret Exploder Mk VI with a magnetic influence trigger. It was designed to run under a target, to detect the change in magnetic field caused by the ship's hull, and set off the 600-pound Torpex warhead.

In the 1930s, exploder tests were conducted against the cruiser USS *Indianapolis* (CA 35) and two destroyers but these only investigated

"GOOD MORNING, CHIEF" — BUD GRUNER

USS Skate *(SS 305) had rescued Japanese sailors from two ships previously sunk on different occasions. It was observed that prisoners were thankful to have been saved. They relished the good treatment given them, the ample tasty food, and the friendly relations that developed between them and our crew.*

You must also understand that a wartime submarine crew is small and composed of highly intelligent men who in the wartime environment rapidly became a close-knit family. Further, there was little space on board a submarine for prisoners. As a consequence, steps had to be taken to ensure that a prisoner was placed in an area where he had a bunk, was guarded so that he could do no harm to the ship, and then given a job under close supervision so that he had no time to brood over his capture and make plans for destruction of the ship or its war-making equipment.

It so happened that Skate *rescued a Japanese sailor after sinking a ship in the Sea of Japan. The prisoner was bunked in the after torpedo room and assigned work as a compartment cleaner in the after engine room. His job was to wipe down the two large diesel engines and keep the compartment clean. Two* Skate *motor machinist mates who stood watch in this engine room were both intelligent and imaginative. They decided that it was their duty to educate the prisoner in the ways of submarine life.*

The first lesson was to teach the prisoner that the chief motor machinist mate in charge of the main propulsion plant was the most important man on board ship. That was largely accomplished by means of hand gestures. When the prisoner understood that, they taught him to conduct a ceremony for occasions when the chief would inspect the engine room each morning. The purpose of the ceremony was to show proper recognition for the chief's important status. To accomplish this, they taught the prisoner a few words of English and practiced the ceremony with him until he was able to deliver a letter-perfect formal greeting. The ceremony consisted of the prisoner standing on the deck plates between the two engines with his arms at his sides in Japanese style and making a low bow to the chief. This was accompanied by the proper inhalation hiss and the greeting spoken with proper humility, "Good morning, Chief."

This went over so well with the chief that the engine room crew decided to augment the prisoner's vocabulary. They did so by adding a few words to the greeting without divulging their meaning to the prisoner. A day soon arrived when the prisoner was able to say his lines perfectly, and all was ready one morning when the chief entered the engine room. The prisoner made his customary low bow to the chief accompanied by his customary hiss as he inhaled. Then he announced, with great deference, "Good morning, Chief, you big son of a bitch!"

Lieutenant Commander W. P. Gruner, commanding officer of USS *Skate* (SS 305) flanked by Lieutenant (jg) West and Lieutenant (jg) Kay show off *Skate's* irreverent battle flag. *Skate's* illustrious career covered seven war patrols during which she sank thirteen ships and damaged the battleship *Yamato. Skate* was awarded the Navy Unit Commendation for exceptional performance during four patrols.

the effect of the ships' magnetic field upon the exploder. The Mk VI functioned as designed according to the Bureau of Ordnance. However, the bureau denied the Naval Torpedo Station, Newport's request for a hull to be used in a live firing test of the Mk 14 with the Mk VI. This was a critical error which, in the view of some historians, prolonged the war by many months.

In June 1942, Commander Submarines, U.S. Pacific Fleet (COM-SUBPAC) officials noted in a Patrol Report endorsement that in many of the early torpedo attacks, unexplained misses plagued commanding officers. Then, Rear Admiral Charles Lockwood commenced a series of torpedo tests in Australia against a net in which conclusive evidence was obtained that the torpedo Mk 14 ran about 11 feet deeper than set. Even

Opposite, bottom right: *Some of the Japanese ships sunk by submarines were carrying Allied prisoners-of-war being used as slave labor in various parts of the Japanese empire. Here USS* Sealion *(SS 315) rescues British and Australian survivors left to fend for themselves when the Japanese freighter on which they were being transported was sunk by an American submarine.*

Periscope photograph of a Japanese ship listing heavily to port and sending up thick clouds of smoke after being hit by a torpedo from a U.S. Navy submarine.

Lookouts are shown on the alert. Early in the war submarines spent the daylight hours submerged. Later, as more aggressive skippers learned to "crash dive" and modifications were made to the superstructure enabling faster dives, submarines stayed on the surface during the day to increase the probability of finding targets. From the time a plane was spotted, the six to eight men on the bridge would all disappear down the conning tower hatch, and the submarine would be underwater and going deep in less than forty seconds.

Above: *A Japanese transport heads for Davy Jones's locker after absorbing torpedoes fired by USS* Wahoo *(SS 238).*

Right: *USS* Wahoo *(SS 238) took this periscope shot of the stern of the Japanese cargo ship* Nittsu Maru *in the Yellow Sea off China on 21 March 1943. The short horizontal and vertical lines are stadimeter marks that allow the observer to calculate range to a ship if the masthead height or ship length is known or accurately estimated.*

though orders were issued to all submarines to set torpedoes shallower, some torpedoes exploded prematurely; and others failed even when they actually hit a target. Although the prematures were explained by an anomalous signal, it took months to learn that when the torpedo actually hit a target at the optimum 90-degree angle, the firing pin of the exploder deformed prior to activating the detonator. The ultimate solution was to fire so that the torpedo struck the target at an oblique angle even though the target then presented less than its full length.

Another constraining factor in the early stages of the war was the shortage of torpedoes. Commanding officers had been counseled to be frugal in torpedo expenditure. In some attacks only one torpedo was fired, followed by a second if necessary. In other attacks, a spread of three might have been used, when a full spread of six was called for. Torpedo spreads were designed so that the wing torpedoes would pass ahead and astern of the target if the fire control data were accurate. If, however, the data were faulty, or the target maneuvered to avoid the salvo, the spread increased the probability of obtaining a hit. Finally, in September 1943, the torpedo

Mk 14 was deemed operationally effective, the Exploder Mk VI was inactivated, and the shortage of weapons was alleviated. But we still had circular runs and duds.

Warfighting highlighted another area wherein peacetime training had fallen short—knowledge of sound in the sea and the effective use of sonar. In mid-1943, a small but important piece of equipment came to the force. This was the bathythermograph, which measured the temperature of the sea versus submarine depth. It provided the skipper the depth at which thermoclines changed direction. Below that depth, enemy sonar was ineffective because the sound waves bounced upward rather than penetrating to the hiding submarine. Doctrine quickly dictated that every submarine dive to test depth each morning to chart the thermoclines. Then, if evasion after an attack was required, the safe haven was obvious.

A secret more closely held than the existence of the Exploder Mk VI was the contribution of the Intelligence community to success in the war against Japan. Only long after the war have details of the Navy's codebreaking expertise come to light. From June 1942 to the end of the war, submarines were increasingly provided ULTRA (Communications Intelligence) information on the position, course, and speed of Japanese ships, merchant and combat alike, usually in ample time to permit the addressed submarine to intercept.

As the submarines honed their skills, and sinkings of Japanese shipping and warships increased, Japanese antisubmarine warfare became more effective. Larger depth charges set deeper, dropped by better trained forces, took a continuing toll on U.S. submarines, although Japan never put to sea sufficient ASW forces to stem the relentless tide. One of the earliest and most drastic alternatives to conventional periscope depth attacks was the introduction of night surface attacks. Before the advent of the SJ surface search radar, submarines cruising in areas at night were often confronted with targets at close range. Withdrawal to reconnoiter and trail until daylight was not a feasible alternative to immediate attack based upon "best estimates" of target course, speed, and range.

USS Bluegill *(SS 242) just before it was launched at the Electric Boat Company, Groton, Connecticut, on 8 August 1943.*

USS Scorpion *(SS 278) torpedoes a Japanese patrol vessel on 30 April 1943. This view shows debris and water thrown high in the air by the explosion. Vertical object in foreground is a 20mm gun barrel on* Scorpion. *The Japanese had their revenge a year later when* Scorpion *was sunk with all hands in the Yellow Sea. American submarines were victorious, but paid a high price.*

USS Coucal *(ASR 8) was completed early in 1942 and followed the rest of Submarine Squadron Eight to Australia. She left her rescue bell on the dock in Brisbane and spent the rest of the war supporting other ships of the Southwest Pacific with repair services. At various times* Coucal *served as an advanced base in Darwin, topping off submarines with fuel and stores as they headed north into the Dutch East Indies and the South China Sea. Everyone worked hard during World War II, but none harder or more effectively than the submarine rescue vessels.*

The Face of the Enemy

Ray Welch

The submarine USS Stingray (SS 186) was on patrol somewhere off the Philippines in August 1944 when by chance, we sighted through the periscope a dilapidated life raft containing several persons. We detected no movement and were not sure whether they were alive or dead. However, our skipper, Lieutenant Commander Samuel Loomis, USN, decided to surface and investigate. Going alongside we could see four persons in the raft barely alive, if at all, and probably Japanese. What to do? A submarine has no place for prisoners and our training had made us well aware of enemy treachery and willingness to die rather than be captured.

The captain ordered us to bring the captives on board and strip them. Once the cold and frightened Japanese were below, we had to decide where to keep them. We finally settled them on a few blankets laid on the deck of the forward torpedo room and posted an armed guard to watch over them. Our "doc," Robert L. Wood, pharmacist's mate, first class, and several volunteers then commenced the task of bringing them back to life. Their leader soon revived sufficiently to ask in stumbling English for a drink of water and a pistol—apparently anxious to join his ancestors.

After his drink of water, we discovered that the leader understood English writing but had very little speaking ability. By his response to our written questions we slowly learned he was a recent graduate of the Japanese Naval Academy and was an ensign in their navy. The other three captives were enlisted men, including a torpedoman. The last information gave us some pause, since from his blanket he was within easy reach of our torpedoes and torpedo tubes, but he never ever touched them.

We further learned our enemies had served in the Japanese light cruiser Natori, torpedoed and sunk by USS Hardhead *about ten days before. Ten days adrift in an empty life raft with no shelter and only rain water? All were young—about 19 to 23 years old—small, about 5 feet 4 inches, and slender. In comparison with our own crew, they appeared to be just young kids.

Their first few days on board were miserable ones as they slowly regained the ability to drink, retain food, sleep, and get stronger. Stingray crewmembers found frequent excuses to visit the forward torpedo room. Nearly all the crew were probably meeting an enemy face-to-face for the first time. Some also came to see the effects of their ordeal in the life raft; others came out of simple humanity. At any rate our enemies were quickly adopted by our crew. The crew willingly helped the pharmacist's mate in the care and feeding of the enemies, provided clothing, tried out their few Japanese words, and generally let the Japanese captives know they had little to fear. Our cook made ice cream and special dishes for the enemies even though ice cream was not a frequent item on Stingray's menu.

Suddenly they had names—Uncle Donald, Huey, Dewey, and Louie, after the Disney comic strip. The ensign of course was Uncle Donald and acted the part. There was never any question about who was in charge of the enemy group. He often maintained order with the back of his hand but the enlisted men did not appear to resent his physical style of discipline. Uncle Donald answered all the questions we could think to ask. Also, he was an excellent artist and made many sketches describing events in his short career in the navy. He appeared to accept the fact that his part in the war was over.

In the two weeks that followed, our enemies recovered and were put to work making the galley, crew's washroom, and living quarters gleam as never

before. Uncle Donald supervised, of course, but all chatted together happily, no doubt anticipating the next meal our cook—their Number 1 hero—was preparing. There were never any real problems other than those of language.

Eventually we put into Darwin, Australia, to fuel. An Army truck and a squad of well-armed soldiers came to the dock to pick up our "dangerous" enemies. They were first blindfolded and then led to our topside deck, which, because of an extremely low tide, was about 20 feet below the surface of the dock. Still blindfolded, our enemies were forced to grope their way up a rickety wooden ladder and into the truck assisted by Army rifle butts along the way. Our crew did not appreciate the mistreatment and our captain protested; however, the Army insisted that they knew best how to handle "dangerous" enemy prisoners. We wished our enemies good fortune.

There is a sequel. Twenty years after the war ended, I was asked to participate in a joint Japanese and U.S. one-hour TV program to be broadcast live in Tokyo commemorating the end of the war. TV stations in Tokyo and Washington, D.C., were linked so that Uncle Donald in Tokyo could see and talk with the captain and me in Washington.

For about ten minutes we were able to talk to Uncle Donald, learn that he was a commander in the Japanese navy, that he had visited the U.S. and Washington several times on duty, and each time had tried to trace officers of Stingray. He thanked us for saving his life and for treating our enemies so well. For our part the captain and I agreed that it would be great if all enemies of our country could be like Uncle Donald, Huey, Dewey, and Louie.

Above: A Japanese merchant ship is slowly sinking after being hit by gunfire from USS *Tambor* (SS 198). Survivors are thrown lines and hauled on board by crewmembers of the submarine.

USS Skipjack *(SS 184) ship patch*

Guarded by U.S. Marines, three Japanese prisoners taken from victims of USS Spadefish *(SS 411) are marched ashore in Guam. The battle flag of* Spadefish *flies from number 1 periscope.*

With radar, the submarine gained a significant advantage over its targets, particularly those that were not similarly equipped. Targets could be trailed at safe standoff ranges until the convoy disposition was ascertained, and target data carefully refined. Multiple targets were often successfully attacked, and frequently the submarine was able to withdraw and return to the fray with all tubes again loaded. On other occasions, the submarine chose to attack again in daylight from periscope depth. This maneuver was aptly called the "end-around," which was taken from the familiar football play of the same name.

In May of 1942, Commander James Coe of the USS *Skipjack* (SS 184) literally invented the "down-the-throat" shot when he found himself almost dead ahead of an approaching target. His three-torpedo salvo produced one hit, which sank the ship. Later, in mid-1944 (well after the torpedo Mk 14 problems had been resolved), Commander Sam Dealey of USS *Harder* (SS 257) resorted to the down-the-throat attack with a vengeance. In each of five encounters, Dealey found himself the object of angry destroyers. Rather than going deep to evade, he maintained periscope depth firing two or more torpedoes at ranges of 600 to 1,200 yards sinking all five of his attackers. In these short-range attacks, the target bearing down on the submarine position had little time to maneuver, but if it did, it only increased the target size offered to the torpedo.

A corollary to the down-the-throat shot was the "up-the-kilt" shot. This was normally executed out of desperation in encounters where a premature explosion of a torpedo caused the target to turn directly away from the point of explosion. This gave the submarine a target only as wide as the beam of the ship, but the target course was accurately known, and the speed was immaterial. Rapid sinkings were reported when the stern was literally blown off a ship.

In October 1943, the U.S. Submarine Force embarked upon a new tactical concept adopted from the German U-boats in the Atlantic. This was the "wolf pack," consisting of as few as two submarines and as many as six. The concept was attractive at this point in the prosecution of the war because the number of submarines was steadily growing, and reorientation of Japanese strategy reduced the lucrative hunting areas.

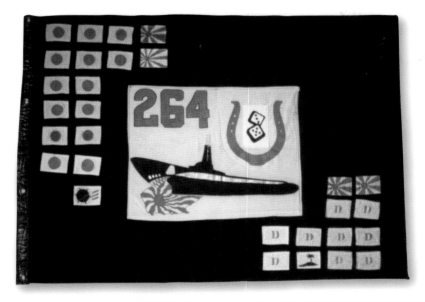

Above, left: *USS* Pargo *(SS 264) battle flag.*

Above: *USS* Haddock *(SS 231) battle flag.*

Left: *USS* Halibut *(SS 232) battle flag.*

Opposite, top left: *This classic photo is the first combat action photograph taken through the periscope of an American submarine in World War II. The destroyer, IJNS Yamakaze, has the Japanese naval insignia visible on the top of the forward gun turret. USS Nautilus (SS 168) took the photo after torpedoing the destroyer on 25 June 1942; however, in many publications it has been incorrectly attributed to USS Wahoo.*

Opposite, top right: *A Japanese merchant ship is torpedoed and sunk by USS Aspro (SS 309).*

The first pack, consisting of USS *Plunger* (SS 179) (Flag), USS *Shad* (SS 235), and USS *Grayback* (SS 208), was under the command of Captain Charles B. Momsen, Commander Submarine Squadron TWO, who was too senior to command a submarine, even at the start of the war. The purpose of the packs was to concentrate fire in key areas, and through coordinated operations supported by short-range radio, bring more torpedoes to the point of attack. At the same time, doctrine had to be developed to ensure the safety of all submarines and to limit radio transmissions so that they did not reveal pack location to Japanese radio direction finding.

Although the early U.S. wolf packs experienced problems with inter-ship communications and found that coordinated attacks were sometimes difficult to consummate, they continued until near the end of the war. However, after Commander Frederick B. Warder, the first wartime commanding officer of USS *Seawolf* (SS 197), took the second pack—USS *Pargo* (SS 264) (Flag), USS *Snook* (SS 279), and USS *Harder* (SS 257)—to sea, he recommended that the senior commanding officer also be put in command of the pack. This procedure, which became the norm, started when Commander Charles Brindupke, commanding USS *Tullibee* (SS 284), patrolled with USS *Halibut* (SS 232) and USS *Haddock* (SS 231). In all, some 116 wolf packs went to sea.

The Submarine Force had been struggling in the opening stages of the war with the Mk 14 torpedo, both with respect to its inadequate

Chow down—the crews' mess was crowded but the food was good.

Combat artist Paul Sample painted this view of the torpedo room of a fleet submarine during World War II. As photography was generally prohibited on submarines, there are very few nonstaged views of the boat's interior from that time.

USS Sea Owl *(SS 405) ship patch*

performance and its inadequate supply. The corrective action on the torpedo and its Exploder Mk VI was previously described. However, alternative paths were being pursued to give commanding officers more freedom of action at the firing point.

The first of these was the modification of the Mk 14 to the Mk 23 under the direction of the Bureau of Ordnance. By eliminating the low-speed, long-range configuration, a higher rate of production was achievable without detriment to offensive power. Experience had revealed that rarely, if ever, had the long-range option been employed with success. With this simple fix, supplies of torpedoes met expenditure rates by mid-1943.

Even before the war, the Bureau of Ordnance had been developing the Mk 2 electric torpedo, a unit with less speed and range than the Mk 14 but wakeless. In 1942, German G7e electric torpedoes had run ashore in the Atlantic and given the Navy an alternative program to the Mk 2. After some organizational problems, Westinghouse Electric Corporation was selected to manufacture copies of the German torpedo, ultimately designated the Mk 18. Although early progress was magnificent, production problems and battery shortcomings delayed the arrival of the torpedo in the force until late in 1943. After some reluctance from commanding officers to shift to the wakeless torpedo because it ran at about 30 knots, and even slower in cold water, the torpedo proved itself and gained wide acceptance. All told, some 10,000 units were delivered, and by mid-1944 the Mk 18 represented about 65 percent of all firings.

At this same time, the first acoustic torpedo emerged from the scientific laboratories. This anti-escort unit was dubbed "Cutie," and later the torpedo Mk 27-0. It contained a nose-mounted sonar, which steered the torpedo toward detected target propeller noise. It was slow, only 12 knots, and had to be fired such that the target passed within its limited acoustic range. Although it had no straight running capability, it could circle or pursue a target for some 5,000 yards. The firing submarine had to remain below 150 feet to ensure that the torpedo did not detect and chase it. Initial operational tests conducted by USS *Sea Owl* (SS 405), under the command of Commander Carter Bennett, an ordnance expert, in late 1944 were successful in sinking two escorts. By war's end some 100 Cuties had been fired resulting in an estimated 31 percent successful attacks. By 1946, this torpedo had been retired and was followed by a more capable Mk 27-4.

Very near end of the war, yet another weapon entered service. This was the Mk 28, which combined some of the attributes of the Mk 14 (straight running to target vicinity), the Mk 18 (battery power), and the Cutie (sonar nose). This torpedo ran at 20 knots to a range of 4,000 yards. Its acoustic capability served to counter inaccurate target data and negated the requirement for spreads. However, its late introduction into the war meant that only fourteen units were fired with four hits reported.

The primary mission of the submarines in the Pacific war was the destruction of the Japanese merchant and combat fleets. However, it was clear to all commands that submarines could operate in areas under the control of the enemy as could no other forces. Thus, early

on, it fell to the Submarine Force to divert its assets and attention to a variety of special missions.

In the first four months of the war, several missions were dispatched to Corregidor to evacuate President Quezon of the Philippines and other senior personnel, deliver much needed ammunition until the surrender of Bataan, and retrieve the few torpedoes that remained in storage.

The success of these missions spawned others, which had not been foreseen when the war started. These included reconnaissance and intelligence collection, especially against the mid-Pacific Islands, which were slated for later invasion. The adaptation of standard photographic equipment for use through the periscope provided vital information about potential landing sites. These same cameras also brought home vivid proof of the sinking of many ships.

Another task performed with daring (because it required operations in very shallow and sometimes uncharted waters) and with skill was the landing, supply, and evacuation of "coast watchers." These were sometimes island natives and frequently Australians, rugged and capable

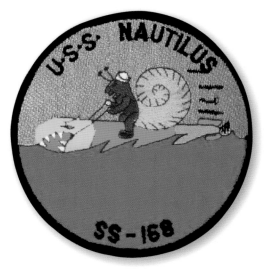

USS Nautilus *(SS 168) ship patch*

Above: *Lieutenant (jg) George Bush is shown being rescued by USS* Finback *(SS 230) off Chichi Jima. In remarks for the Submarine Centennial, President Bush voiced his heart-felt relief on seeing* Finback *coming to his rescue, "I was never so glad to see anything in my life."*

Right: *Trophy flags flying,* Batfish *(SS 310) heads for base at the end of a war patrol.*

USS Trout *(SS 202) crewmen are shown unloading bullion in Pearl Harbor. At the mouth of Manila Bay in January 1942,* Trout *made a run to Corregidor carrying badly needed 3-inch anti-aircraft ammunition to the beleaguered island. On her return trip* Trout *brought with her as ballast two tons of gold bars, eighteen tons of silver pesos, and a large quantity of negotiable securities—in effect most of the solid assets of the Philippine government.*

of living off the land, who maintained radio contact by which they pro-vided data on enemy movements ashore, at sea, and in the air.

Commencing in the fall of 1942, many submarines conducted mine laying missions in the Gulf of Siam, off French Indo-China and the China coast, into the South and East China seas, and in much of the Japanese empire. Some of these early missions were dispatched because of the aforementioned shortage of torpedoes. In one or more such forays, sub-marines reported that the four tubes loaded with mines were the likely reason they failed to sink a Japanese carrier or other target. Further, the effectiveness of minefields was difficult to assess. Rarely did a minelaying submarine see a positive result by witnessing the sinking of a ship.

The first minefields were comprised of Mk X moored, contact mines limited to planting in 250 feet of water, with the case settling at some few feet below the surface. The Mk XII magnetic ground mine was used in later fields. It was triggered by the change in the ambient magnetic field caused by a passing ship and, with its larger charge was effective at depths down to about 100 feet.

Another new mission for submarines was "lifeguarding," the rescue of aviators who were able to bail out after being shot down. This required submarines to monitor the aircraft radio frequencies and to move into position close to target complexes to ensure retrieval of the aviators before the enemy could capture them. Perhaps the most famous rescue occurred

USS Barb *(SS 220) ship's flag displays its many kills from its successful war patrols— including the successful destruction of a Japanese train.*

during the assault on Iwo Jima, the island bastion some 700 miles south of Tokyo on 19 February 1945. There, USS *Finback* (SS 230), Commander Robert R. Williams, rescued Lieutenant (jg) George H. W. Bush, destined to be the forty-first President of the United States.

The story would not be complete without a discussion of the most daring of dangerous missions. As the war proceeded toward its inevitable conclusion, targets became ever scarcer, and commanding officers demonstrated ingenuity of the highest order. In early January 1945, a wolf pack consisting of USS *Queenfish* (SS 393) (Flag), USS *Picuda* (SS 382), and USS *Barb* (SS 220) departed Guam for the East China Sea. After much joint action, which resulted in the sinking of six freighters and several small craft, and damaging others, *Barb* (Commander Eugene B. Fluckey) was left to patrol alone with half her torpedoes remaining. At month's end, she concluded that targets were operating close inshore. Her sweep along the China coast resulted in the radar detection of many ships in Namkwan Harbor. Fluckey's decision to enter the long, ill-charted channel is best described in *Barb*'s eleventh war patrol report.

23 JANUARY 1945:

0000 *Maneuvering through junks which are best indication that area is not mined.*

0112 *First radar indication of possible target concentration at 15 miles.*

0300 *Rounded Incog Island running on 10-fathom curve and confirmed large concentration of ships at anchor with escorts to northeast and southeast.*

0320 *Man battlestations torpedo; well inside 10-fathom curve; single ping depth: 6 fathoms.*

Ship Patches: USS Barb *(SS 220), USS* Picuda *(SS 382), and USS* Queenfish *(SS 393).*

Crewmembers of USS Argonaut (SS 166) read their mail after returning to Pearl Harbor from Makin Island, 26 August 1942. The gun is a 6"/53, the largest deck gun carried on any U.S. submarine.

USS Tirante (SS 420) ship patch.

0352 *Range 6,000 yards, four tubes ready fore and aft; thirty ships at least. Must avoid hitting any target with too many torpedoes—crew tense and ready.*

0402 *Fired four bow tubes at key targets with torpedo run of 3,225 yards. Right full rudder, all ahead standard. Depth now 5 fathoms.*

0404 *Fired four stern tubes, with torpedo run of 3,020 yards.*

0406–0409 *Eight torpedo hits observed on bridge, with explosions, smoke, flames, and sinking ships.*

0413 Barb *headed for open water at 21.8 knots, maneuvering to avoid many junks, but expecting to impale one on bow any moment.*

0633 *Forced down by aircraft in more than 40 fathoms.*

Barb was credited with sinking three merchantmen (19,000 tons) and damaging three others (19,000 tons). Commander Gene Fluckey was awarded the Congressional Medal of Honor.

Equal daring was demonstrated in early April 1945 by Commander George L. Street on USS *Tirante*'s (SS 420) first war patrol, which also commenced in the East China Sea. Subsequently, *Tirante* patrolled off the Japanese empire to detect Japanese forces that could interfere with

This 1943 painting pictures the battle stations torpedo team in the conning tower of a fleet submarine during an approach. ("Up Periscope," George Schreiber)

USS Puffer (SS 268) torpedoes the transport Teiko Maru—later identified as the 15,100 ton French liner D'Artagnan, which had been captured by the Japanese early in the war.

the Okinawa landings, and finally was vectored by an ULTRA intelligence message concerning a large transport at Quelpart Island (Cheju Do) off the southwest coast of Korea. His war patrol report tells the story:

14 APRIL 1945:

0000 *Approaching Quelpart Island from northwestern side.*

0029 *Detected patrol boat with radar, exhibiting suspicion without counteraction.*

0240 *Battle Stations. Single ping soundings every four minutes. Circled small island offshore but cannot make out targets, if any.*

0340 *Approaching harbor from north, with land within a mile. Bridge now can see ships, which are put on torpedo data computer with radar ranges and bearings from target bearing transmitter on bridge.*

0356 *LCDR E. L. Beach, executive officer, on bridge picked primary target. Fired one torpedo as sighting in shot, as captain came to bridge to watch fun. Torpedo missed.*

0359 *Fired two more torpedoes aimed slightly left and were rewarded with a mighty explosion, a thunderous roar, and flames shooting 2,000 feet in air. Additional escorts, identified in light of flames as new Kikura class, were alerted.*

0401 *Captain ordered "Right full rudder, all ahead flank" and immediately countermanded it. Instead, he ordered an attack on the escorts.*

0402 *Fired two torpedoes at one frigate, and another at second.*

0403 *Now, "Right full rudder, all ahead flank."*

0404 *Rewarded with another great explosion. Both frigates disappeared.*

0513 *Original patrol boat now alerted. Too light to evade on surface, so dived for the day.*

Tirante was credited with sinking one ammunition ship and two escorts in the Quelpart Harbor penetration. Commander George L. Street was awarded the Congressional Medal of Honor.

Seaman H. P. Glinski (left) had two toes amputated after being wounded while his submarine was engaging enemy ships. L. J. Lindhe, Pharmacist's Mate First Class, performed the operation on board the submarine with a pair of wire cutters.

Ship patches: USS Cavalla *(SS 244), USS*
Darter *(SS 227), USS* Dace *(SS 247), and USS*
Bowfin *(SS 287) .*

Two epic sea battles in June and October 1944 brought the Japanese naval forces to the brink of extinction. The Battle of the Philippine Sea occurred when U.S. Task Force 58 under Admiral Raymond A. Spruance commenced air attacks against Saipan and Guam as a prelude to the landings on those islands. Admiral Jisaburo Ozawa commanded forces based in the South China Sea, which included nine carriers and the great battleships *Musashi* and *Yamato.* He sortied from Brunei, Mindanao, and Halmahera to "annihilate the U.S. Pacific Fleet with one blow" and to render assistance to the Japanese garrisons on the islands. During his sortie, he was detected by USS *Redfin* (SS 272) Commander M. H. Austin and USS *Seahorse* (SS 304) Commander Slade Cutter, both of whom sent valuable reports to the force commander, stating that the Japanese forces were headed through the Philippine Straits into the Philippine Sea.

On 19 June 1944, the Japanese launched the largest air attack of the war—some 430 planes—from their carriers that could barely reach their targets. In what came to be known as the "Marianas turkey shoot," the Japanese lost 330 aircraft to fighters and to a failure to return to safe decks—all without sinking any U.S. ships. However, USS *Albacore* (SS 218) (Commander James Blanchard) succeeded in putting torpedoes into the new carrier *Taiyo* (much later confirmed as sunk), and USS *Cavalla* (SS 244) (Commander Herman Kossler) sank the first-line carrier *Shokaku.* Finally on 20 June, Admiral Spruance launched a counter air attack, also at extreme range, as Japanese forces were retiring northward to empire waters—216 aircraft sank one carrier and two oilers and further reduced the Japanese air capability to some thirty-five planes. Many aircraft returned safely to their carriers after dark because Vice Admiral Marc Mitscher authorized lighting of decks. Although many pilots were rescued, some eighty U.S. aircraft could not reach the safety of any carrier.

The battle was fought over some 2 million square miles of the Pacific Ocean with no fewer than thirty-nine submarines deployed from Borneo, through the Philippines, east to the Marianas, and north to the Japanese empire. None of these were able to close the retiring Japanese forces for attack.

The Battle of Leyte Gulf developed as a Japanese response to the invasion of the Philippines in the vicinity of Leyte Gulf from the southeast by General Douglas MacArthur and the Seventh Fleet under Admiral Thomas C. Kinkaid. Admiral William F. Halsey and Task Force 38 provided protective support. In brief, after Japanese forces from Singapore rendezvoused at Brunei, Borneo, three task forces were formed. The first consisted of the latest battleships with supporting forces, which proceeded eastward via San Bernardino Strait south of Luzon to attack the landing site from the north. The second force of older, slower battleships proceeded through Surigao Strait south of Leyte, and the third of cruisers and troop carriers was tasked to carry personnel from the Manila area to the west side of Leyte to reinforce the land garrison. These forces were augmented by another from empire waters of cruisers and destroyers under the command of Vice Admiral Shima. A major carrier attack force under Admiral Ozawa sortied from the empire with their remaining 100 flyable aircraft.

Arrayed against these forces, forty-six U.S. submarines were deployed north of Borneo, west of the Philippine Islands, in Luzon Strait and northward to the empire. These submarines provided early warning of the sortie of Japanese forces and inflicted severe damage upon several of the major warships and many supporting merchantmen.

Of particular note is the action of USS *Darter* (SS 227) Commander David McClintock and USS *Dace* (SS 247) Commander Bladen Claggett between 20 and 24 October 1944. Their Fourth and Fifth Patrol Reports respectively relate a magnificent story of tactical excellence, courage, and expert seamanship, as summarized:

20 OCTOBER:

The pack under McClintock's command made the initial detection of the third Japanese task force and chased to no avail. However, their contact reports to force headquarters and other submarines to the north enabled USS Bream *(SS 243), (Commander Wreford "Moon" Chapple), to damage the cruiser* Aoba *with two torpedoes.*

23 OCTOBER:

Shortly after midnight, contact was made with Task Force ONE, heading northeast through Palawan Passage with twelve ships in two columns, with no sonar in operation and little apparent regard for submarine attack. Darter *positioned the two submarines for a dawn submerged attack—*Darter *off the western column;* Dace, *the eastern.*

Depth charge attacks were a boost for church attendance. Crewmembers are crowded into the space between torpedo reloads in the torpedo room for divine services. Submarines did not carry ordained chaplains so services were led by lay crewmembers.

Chief H. A. Stromsoe points with pride to the record of sunken Japanese ships noted on the number 2 torpedo tube inner door. USS S-44 (SS 155) was the most successful of the S-boats in World War II, sinking 17,000 tons (including the heavy cruiser Kako) *during three patrols in the Solomon Islands area from May to August 1942. For these, she won a Navy Unit Commendation. In 1943, S-44 was sunk by a Japanese destroyer in a fury of gunfire during a patrol in the Kurile Islands north of Japan. Fifty-four men (including Chief Stromsoe) were lost—two members of the crew were taken prisoner.*

99

USS Wahoo *(SS 238) moors at Pearl Harbor after a patrol during which she sank a Japanese destroyer and an entire convoy of four ships. She sank the convoy during a fourteen-hour running battle, using both guns and torpedoes. She narrowly escaped destruction by a Japanese destroyer. The commanding officer, Lieutenant Commander Dudley W. Morton, USN, of Miami, Florida, (right) and the executive officer, Lieutenant Richard H. O'Kane, USN, of Durham, New Hampshire, chat on the bridge.*

By 0530, *Darter* had fired a full salvo of ten torpedoes at two cruisers for nine hits. One cruiser was definitely observed to be sinking; the other was at least heavily damaged. Depth charging from four destroyers continued for about an hour as *Darter* evaded.

Dace heard the results of *Darter*'s attacks and began her own approach against a battleship, after permitting two cruisers to pass at very close range. Her six-torpedo salvo at what appeared to be a *Kongo*-class battleship, later identified as the cruiser *Maya*, produced four hits and several monstrous explosions as only magazines could make. Gruesome breaking up noises were accompanied by a lengthy, ever more accurate depth charging from four destroyers. Claggett's description spoke for every submariner in the war: "Four letter-perfect runs were made in which no charges were dropped; tracked them in from forward to aft overhead, with screws audible through the hull. The suspense was worse than the depth charging."

By noon, both submarines had detected one *Atago*-class cruiser dead in the water and generated plans for a joint attack. The target was protected by patrolling destroyers and aircraft. By mid-afternoon the target began movement southeast under tow at slow speed with the submarines seeking favorable attack position. *Darter* ordered both submarines to take position ahead for a submerged night attack.

24 OCTOBER:

At 0007 Darter *ran hard aground on Bombay Shoal. When* Dace *was advised, she broke off tracking the cruiser and closed to within 50 yards of* Darter *to render assistance.* Darter *destroyed sensitive publications and equipment and set demolition charges. Before dawn all personnel were ferried to* Dace *in rubber boats without loss of life. When the demolition charges failed to explode,* Dace *fired four single torpedoes, all of which exploded on the reef in front of* Darter. *Finally, after thirty rounds from* Dace's *deck gun did little damage, she retired with two full crews on board toward Fremantle, Australia. Subsequently, USS* Rock *(SS 274) fired ten more torpedoes with no effect, and later USS* Nautilus *(SS 168) with her 6-inch guns, holed* Darter's *hull.*

In marked contrast to the prior Battle of the Philippine Sea, there was considerable submarine action during the retirement phase of the Battle of Leyte Gulf and in further action in the Luzon Strait against convoys moving south in support of the beleaguered Japanese garrisons. In the days that immediately followed, several wolf packs chased the old battleships *Ise* and *Hyuga*; however, they succeeded only in sinking two tankers and one destroyer.

Concurrently, considerable action was occurring in Luzon Strait west of the fleeing combatants. There, other packs attacked several southbound convoys. In a four-day period, 23 to 27 October, USS *Drum* (SS 228) Lieutenant Commander Maurice (Mike) Rindskopf launched five attacks, fired all twenty-four torpedoes, sank four merchantmen, and damaged two others. USS *Tang* (SS 306) Commander Richard O'Kane continued *Tang*'s marvelously successful career in the Taiwan Strait by sinking no fewer than five southbound freighters. In *Tang*'s final attack against a crippled ship, one of his last two torpedoes circled and struck *Tang*, the ship from which it was originally fired, sinking her instantly.

In the summer and fall of 1943, several submarines had made short forays into the Sea of Japan through La Perouse Strait between the

USS Bullhead (SS 332) comes close aboard a Chinese junk during its first patrol in the spring of 1945. This inspection was done to ensure that a seemingly innocent fishing craft or trading junk was not, in actuality, a picket boat that would radio the position and composition of passing Allied fleet units. In this case, the crew of the submarine provided food to the junk's crew.

A U.S. Pacific submarine sails for Japanese waters. Sunlight silvers the sea. A moving submarine haven protects the submarine from friendly forces. Later near Japanese naval forces, the submarine would transit primarily at night.

★ **Tokyo Bay On Surrender Day** ★
Comsubron-20 ------- 2 Sep 1945 ------- Captain L.S. Parks
U.S.S. Proteus -------------- Captain J.A. Jordan

U.S.S. ARCHERFISH - COMDR. J.F. ENRIGHT	U.S.S. PILOTFISH -- COMDR. A.R. SCHNABLE
U.S.S. CAVALLA -- COMDR. H.J. KOSSLER	U.S.S. RAZORBACK - LT. COMDR. C.D. BROWN
U.S.S. GATO --- COMDR. R. HOLDEN	U.S.S. RUNNER -- COMDR. R.H. BASS
U.S.S. HADDO - ... LT. COMDR. F.C. LYNCH	U.S.S. SEGUNDO -- LT. COMDR. S.L. JOHNSON
U.S.S. HAKE --- COMDR. F.E. HAYLER	U.S.S. SEACAT --- LT. COMDR. R.H. BOWERS
U.S.S. MUSKALLUNGE- COMDR. W.H. LAWRENCE	U.S.S. TIGRONE --- LT. COMDR. V.E. SHUMACHER

USS Proteus (AS 19) with submarines of SUBRON 20 alongside, in Tokyo Bay on Japanese Surrender Day, 2 September 1945.

101

Coming home in May 1945, sailors smile as USS Batfish *(SS 310) comes into San Francisco Harbor, California, after seventeen months' duty in the Pacific. The San Francisco Bay Bridge is in the background.*

Forward submarine bases, such as this one on Guam, shortened turnaround time for repair and reload. Shorter transits saved fuel and extended time on patrol in Japanese waters. Three tenders and two supply ships are pictured (top), *but drydocks were also available. Camp Dealey, the submarine crew rest area* (above) *named for the famous "Destroyer Killer," provided a place for the crews to relax between patrols.*

northern islands of Hokkaido and Karafuto. These excursions were plagued by poor torpedo performance. One such excursion resulted in the loss of one of the stars of the war. USS *Wahoo* (SS 238) (Commander Dudley "Mush" Morton) was sunk by antisubmarine forces as she exited the strait.

As targets became scarcer throughout the Western Pacific in early 1945, Vice Admiral Charles Lockwood, Commander Submarine Force Pacific, and his operations officer, Captain Richard Voge, concluded that the Sea of Japan might offer a wealth of unsuspecting targets. By this time, the high-frequency mine-hunting, frequency-modulated sonar had reached the stage of development where it could be tested against a training minefield, and then against the real thing. Although Admiral Lockwood set himself up as the training officer and accompanied several submarines to sea, he could never convince Admiral Nimitz that he should be allowed to go on war patrol with this equipment.

Thus, in May of 1945, three packs of three submarines each under the overall command of Commander Earl Hydeman penetrated the known minefields in the Tsushima Strait, the southern entrance to the Sea of Japan. In at least two instances, mine cables scraped down the hull of the submerged submarines, but clearing wires around the bow and stern planes staved off disaster. In the short space of ten days, these nine submarines sank twenty-eight ships of over 50,000 tons, suffering only the loss of USS *Bonefish* (SS 223) (Commander Lawrence Edge) in a harbor penetration. The other eight submarines exited through La Perouse Strait at high speed on the surface without incident.

Subsequently, ten or more individual forays into the Sea of Japan achieved modest success. Further, as the power of the mighty U.S. fleet and land-based air forces closed in on the Japanese homeland, many submarines performed lifeguard duties by rescuing pilots shot down in raids on Tokyo and other industrial centers.

Admiral Nimitz and General MacArthur accepted the surrender of the Japanese forces on board USS *Missouri* (BB 63) in Toyko Bay on 2 September 1945. Vice Admiral Lockwood COMSUBPAC was a front-row witness.

Submarine tender USS *Proteus* (AS 19), with submarine rescue vessel *Greenlet* (ASR 10), and twelve submarines— USS *Archerfish*, USS *Cavalla*, USS *Gato*, USS *Haddo*, USS *Hake*, USS *Muskallunge*, USS *Pilotfish*, USS *Razorback*, USS *Runner*, USS *Sea Cat*, USS *Segundo*, and USS *Tigrone*—were moored alongside to recognize their magnificent contribution to the war effort.

To recap U.S. submarine accomplishments in World War II:

> 465 commanding officers made 1,682 war patrols.
> 1,178 Japanese merchantmen totaling 5,053,491 tons were sunk.
> 214 Japanese naval vessels totaling 577,625 tons were sunk.
> 14,748 torpedoes were fired.

During World War II, 52 submarines of a total of 288 were lost from various causes, and 374 officers and 3,131 enlisted personnel were lost of 16,500 who actually made patrols.

CHANGE OF COMMAND — *The Change of Command is a time-honored tradition, which formally restates the continuity of command. In general, the order and content of the ceremony remains as it has been almost since its inception. Custom has established that this ceremony be formal and impressive—designed to strengthen the respect for authority vital to any military organization.*

The uniform for the ceremony is normally "full dress" in keeping with the dignity of the occasion. On board ship the officers and crew are usually formed in ranks so that they may witness the transfer of command. Additionally side boys, honor guard, color guard, and bands may be paraded.

When all preparations are complete and the guests are present, the official party will arrive amid the required ceremonies and salutes. Ranking officers will be piped aboard with boatswain and sideboys. Piping in the days of sail was done by the bos'n to control hoisting of the boatswain's chair in which a visiting officer was brought on board ship from a small boat. Sideboys were assigned to hoist the boatswain's chair and assist the officer on board. The number of sideboys increases with rank. Some say that developed because the more senior the officer, the more stout.

As part of the custom of rendering honors, a gun salute is fired when the senior flag officer arrives. Naval guns in the old days were always kept ready with powder and shot. Once fired, considerable time was required to reload before they could be fired again. Thus, when ships of different nations met or when visiting a foreign state, a gun salute was used to display that a warship was powerless for a time and thus clearly indicated an absence of hostile intent. This custom of gun salutes was later expanded to signify a mark of respect to visiting senior officers and officials. In addition, Navy regulations stipulate that honors for a flag officer being relieved or assuming command shall include a gun salute in conjunction with the hauling down or breaking of the officer's flag.

After the invocation and remarks of the guest speaker and the officer being relieved, both the officer being relieved and his relief read their orders. This formal reading of orders stems from the days when movement of both mail and personnel was a slow process. The reading of orders with all hands present was designed to ensure that only authorized officers held command and that all on board ship were aware of the authenticity of the new commanding officer and the source of his authority.

Upon completion of the reading of his orders and the hauling down of his flag, the departing officer is formally relieved by the officer assuming command. Upon completion of the appropriate honors to the new commander, he will then report to the senior officer present and deliver brief remarks. The ceremony concludes with a benediction and the formal departure of the official party and their families.

The change of command ceremony is nearly unique in the world today; it is the transfer of total responsibility, authority, and accountability from one individual to another. With all its pomp, color, history and tradition, the simplicity of this basic ceremony reflects the great heritage of the U.S. Navy and the honor, courage, and commitment of free men and women proudly serving their nation and the finest Navy in the world.

Commander Lawson P. Ramage, USN, reads his orders to place *Parche* in commission and take command of her on 20 November 1943. *Parche* and Ramage won glory eight months later when they engaged in a nautical dogfight with a large Japanese convoy and its escorts. Remaining on the surface in the middle of the convoy, *Parche* picked off four large merchant ships before departing. For this night's work, "Red" Ramage was awarded a Medal of Honor and *Parche* received a Presidential Unit Citation.

AMERICA'S
Victorious
Submarines
of World War II

Commander John D. Alden, USN (Ret)

The atomic bombs that devastated Hiroshima and Nagasaki brought an abrupt end to an empire already doomed to slow death from economic strangulation. Of the forces that had brought Japan to this condition, most important were the submarines that had inexorably decimated the tankers, cargo ships, and transports that constituted the empire's lifeline to oil and other critical resources from the conquered lands of the so-called Greater East Asia Co-Prosperity Sphere.

When the Japanese attacked Pearl Harbor, the United States had only thirty-eight modern first-line submarines in commission, so the Navy had no choice but to resuscitate obsolete boats from the mothball fleet. Tiny 520-ton O-boats became trainers at the Submarine School in Groton, Connecticut, and slightly larger *R*-class boats actually were sent out against German U-boats in the Atlantic. Overage S-class submarines patrolled in the Caribbean and drew Japanese blood in the southwest

Above: *USS S-44 (SS 155) is shown in 1943. The ball-shaped object on the forward deck is the sonar transducer. The crewmen aft of the hatch are gathered around the muzzle of the 4"/50 deck gun.*

Below: *One S-class and three R-class submarines are nested alongside a pier in New York in 1930. From left, USS R-1 (SS 78), USS R-13 (SS 90), USS R-4 (SS 81), and USS S-22 (SS 127). This photo clearly shows how much larger the S-boats were than the R-boats. The deck gun grew also, from a 3"/50 in the R-boat to a 4"/50 in the S-boat.*

Left: *USS T-3 (SS 61) is shown alongside in the Washington Navy Yard. This view shows the long, clean lines and slender hull form of the T-class. These T-class boats were an early attempt to build a submarine that could operate as an integral part of the battle fleet. They were unsuccessful principally because their engines were unreliable.*

Opposite: *Eight R-class boats are shown alongside USS Camden (AS 6). The Submarine Force began World War II with many old O, R, and S-class submarines, which trained new submariners while conducting submarine operations in the Atlantic and the Pacific.*

One type of submarine design was termed the cruiser submarine. This refers to a large submarine designed to carry heavy deck armament and a large number of torpedoes. The boat was expected to cruise the oceans to search out and sink enemy ships. USS Nautilus (SS 168), formerly V-6, shown here in October 1930, mounted two 6"/53 Mk 17 Mod 1 deck guns—the largest to be carried by U.S. submarines. During World War II Nautilus made fourteen war patrols and is credited with the destruction of six ships for a total of 21,500 tons. USS Argonaut (SS 166) and USS Narwhal (SS 167) were similar in size and also carried 6" deck guns. Narwhal's guns are now on display at the Naval Submarine Base in Groton, Connecticut.

The midships portion of USS Bonita (SS 165), formerly V-3, is shown in her pre-war livery. Alongside is the motor wherry that was carried in the superstructure forward of the deck gun. Considered unnecessary during the war, they were removed from active submarines and were not included in the design of the later Balao and Tench classes of fleet boats.

USS Dolphin (SS 169), a one-of-a-kind boat, was an attempt to build a fleet submarine smaller but with many of the same capabilities as Nautilus and Narwhal. Seen here during sea trials, she was 319 feet long (53 feet shorter than Narwhal). The raised portion of the aft deck was for torpedo stowage.

Pacific and the fog-shrouded Aleutian Islands. Many elderly boats performed unglamorous but essential duties as school boats or practice targets for the crews of antisubmarine vessels, but the brunt of the submarine war in the Pacific was borne by the so-called fleet boats.

The concept of a submarine that could operate with the battle fleet originated before World War I when Congress authorized the Navy's first fleet-type submarines. Such boats would need a surface speed of 21 knots, which required very powerful engines. Because of higher wartime priorities, completion of the T-class was delayed until the 1920s. Unfortunately, U.S. submarine technology had fallen far behind that achieved in Germany, and these boats were failures. The Navy tried again with three V-boats ordered from Portsmouth Navy Yard, but these too were failures.

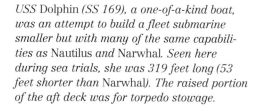

Above: *The Asiatic fleet, primarily based in the Philippines before World War II, moved to Australia in early 1942. S-class submarines like S-39 (SS 144) comprised a small but active part of the early ComSubSoWesPac Fleet and took the war to the enemy. Lacking many comforts of the more modern fleet boats (e.g., air conditioning), these boats patrolled the South China Sea and contiguous waters in an attempt to stem the southward thrust of the Japanese navy.*

Left: *USS* Cuttlefish *(SS 171) is seen here at Portsmouth Navy Yard in 1934. This boat was the test bed for air conditioning, which it was hoped, would help with the condensation and dampness common to submarines.* Cuttlefish *was basically an Americanized U-boat. This design utilized a complete double hull and had an 11,000 nm range at 19 knots.*

The idea of operating submarines directly with the battleship fleet was then abandoned, but the designation "fleet boat" had become accepted for all big, ocean-going U.S. submarines until after World War II.

Six more V-boats followed. USS *Argonaut* was a huge minelayer with a long cruising range but low speed. Two near-sisters, USS *Narwhal* and USS *Nautilus*, were designed as cruiser submarines to act as scouts far ahead of the fleet. Even before they were completed, their planned role vanished as aircraft carriers and seaplanes were viewed as more effective advanced scouts. The concepts of the true fleet submarine, the dedicated minelayer, and the cruiser submarine were all seen as dead ends. Serious engine problems plagued the submariners, who demanded to know why naval designers couldn't just copy the successful German boats of the past war. This called for new thinking, so in 1926 the Chief of Naval Operations (CNO) established the Submarine Officers Conference to "permit general discussion and interchange of ideas leading to improvement of the submarine service." The young submariners finally had a forum from which to make their views heard.

Officers of the USS S-39 (SS 144) posed under the 4"/50 deck gun in Shanghai, China, in 1935. Note Chinese junks in the background. The captain, a lieutenant, is the only dolphin wearer (qualified in submarines). Both the S-39 and the S-36, moored alongside, were lost in 1942 when they grounded on uncharted reefs; the S-36 in January and the S-39 in August. All crewmembers were rescued and lived to fight another day. (Courtesy of Hauber Collection)

A crewman makes adjustments in the engine room of an O- or S-class boat in New London, Connecticut, in 1943. The cylinder heads of the diesel engine are visible in the lower left of the photo.

The next new submarine, USS *Dolphin*, was noticeably smaller than the previous V-boats but had the same number of torpedo tubes. Its general appearance, partial double hull design, and certain interior arrangements foreshadowed the World War II boats, but it still lacked two important features: its engines were relatively reliable but unable to make more than 17 knots, and it suffered from unavoidable leakage through riveted seams. With the final two V-boats, USS *Cachalot* and USS *Cuttlefish*, laid down in 1931, the Navy reduced size even further

and adopted many features of the German U-135 design, including a full double hull. Unfortunately, the pendulum had swung too far; the German-built engines failed and the boats were short-legged and very cramped. However, two major advances were made in their construction: the Electric Boat Company was brought back into the submarine program with *Cuttlefish*, and for the first time welding was used for much of the hull. Welded joints, soon adopted as standard, largely eliminated the problem of oil leaks.

Although the V-boats all survived to serve in World War II, none were first-line patrol submarines. In 1942 *Argonaut* was converted into a transport to carry 120 Marines to raid Makin Island. Shortly thereafter, it was caught by Japanese destroyers and sent to the bottom with 105 men, the greatest number lost on a single submarine during the war. Although big and slow, *Narwhal* and *Nautilus* carried out many valuable special missions. The others were retired after a few patrols and used thereafter as school boats.

Engines still remained the Achilles heel of the Submarine Force, but help was on the way. American diesel manufacturers had finally caught up with German technology and had begun to produce engines for the railroads, which were converting their locomotives from steam to diesel-electric power. The high-speed, light-weight engines would finally enable enough power to be squeezed into a submarine. Even better, with electric drive the engines would no longer have to be coupled directly to the propellers. This would eliminate the problem of shaft vibration and

Top, left: Chief Motor Machinist's Mate Dillow poses between the NELSECO Model 8-EB-15NR diesel engines on board USS S-44 (SS 155). Engines like these were directly connected to a shaft that ran through a clutch, the main motor, another clutch, and to the propeller. This arrangement, called direct drive, was prone to high torsional vibration levels. This, compounded by the speed at which the engines were run, caused bearing damage and shaft failure.

Top, right: USS Tuna (SS 203) is shown off Mare Island just prior to World War II. She made thirteen war patrols from 1941 to 1945 and is credited with sinking 11,075 tons of enemy shipping.

Above: A group of submarines alongside USS Holland (AS 3) show a representative mix of the boats with which the submarine force was equipped at the beginning of World War II. The boats are (from left) Nautilus, Narwhal, Shark, Dolphin, Porpoise, Pike, *and* Tarpon.

Top, left: *USS* Permit *(SS 178) is launched at the Electric Boat Company yard in Groton, Connecticut, in 1936. She made fourteen patrols during World War II sinking over 16,000 tons of Japanese shipping. She ended her days training naval reservists in Philadelphia in 1956.*

Top, right: *USS* Swordfish *(SS 193) is launched at Mare Island Navy Yard in April 1939. At the start of the war this site was the primary submarine repair and overhaul ship-yard on the West Coast and bore the brunt of early wartime ship repairs.*

Above: *The four submarines in Pearl Harbor were not attacked on 7 December. It was a mistake that the Japanese lived to regret. USS* Tautog *(SS 199) moored at pier 2 made thirteen war patrols and sank twenty-three vessels, which ranked her among the top three U.S. submarines in the number of ships sunk. USS* Narwhal *(SS 167), moored at pier 4, made fifteen war patrols, sank eight ships, bombarded airfields and oil tanks with her 6-inch guns, delivered supplies, landed and picked up agents in occupied territories, and evacuated many civilians.*

Right: *This photograph shows the business end of a fleet submarine. USS* Cero *(SS 225) was a Gato-class boat that carried six torpedo tubes forward and four aft. Here in the forward torpedo room, torpedomen stand by for action.*

provide maximum flexibility in locating the machinery and distributing the electricity. By 1933 three engine manufacturers had met the Navy's specifications and Congress authorized the President to use emergency public works funds, appropriated to get the economy out of the Great Depression, to build ships. It was time to make a big leap forward.

Two of the 1933 boats were assigned to Portsmouth Navy Yard with Fairbanks Morse engines and two to Electric Boat with General Motors units. At the same time the yards were given a free hand to design their submarines to meet general performance characteristics set by Washington. Portsmouth built USS *Porpoise* and USS *Pike* as enlargements of *Cachalot*, using the riveted double-hull design. Electric Boat, however, returned to the partial double hull of *Dolphin* and used welding through-out USS *Shark* and USS *Tarpon*, thus uniting for the first time

DEEP DIVE IN LAKE MICHIGAN — COMMANDER JOHN D. ALDEN, USN (RET)

When a submarine has been completed, one of the final tests it must undergo before being accepted by the Navy is to make a dive to its test depth. This is intended to reveal any leaks, which commonly appear at pipe joints, valves, or where masts or electric cables pass through the pressure hull. Such leaks can normally be distinguished from condensation by their

salty flavor. They are usually not serious and can be corrected simply by tightening up the packing around the fitting in question.

A boat built at Manitowoc, Wisconsin, was being inspected by a party of officers from Groton, Connecticut. It was in November and the weather had already turned cold. As we approached test depth, about 400 feet, a few drops of water appeared on a few fittings. The inspection officer, following normal East Coast practice, reached up, put some of the water on his finger, and touched it to his lips. "It's just condensation," he declared, "not a leak." We tightened up the packing anyway. After all, we were in Lake Michigan.

USS *Pompon* (SS 267), a World War II diesel submarine, is photographed on builder's trials in Lake Michigan in April 1943. Landlocked in a fresh water lake 2,000 miles from the sea, *Pompon* eventually reached the Gulf of Mexico and went on to the Pacific where she sank about 9,000 tons of Japanese shipping.

---

the key characteristics that made our wartime submarines so successful—welded hulls and all-electric drive. Although there would still be some backing and filling, these two boats proved to be the models for further development. Their main limitations were too few torpedo tubes (four forward and two aft), a maximum operating depth of only 250 feet, and noisy reduction gears connecting the electric motors to the propeller shafts.

By 1934 Congress had approved long-range plans to rebuild the Submarine Force at the rate of six boats per year. Mare Island Navy Yard (which followed Portsmouth plans) was brought into the program with one of the *Perch* class, to be fitted with a third type of engine made by the Hooven-Owens-Rentschler Company. The navy yards were allowed to use riveted hulls for these boats, which were otherwise duplicates of *Shark*, but shifted to welding thereafter. For the *Salmon* and *Sargo* classes that followed, the Bureau of Engineering adopted a composite arrangement in which two engines were coupled directly to the propeller shafts through

Portsmouth Navy Yard used two drydocks and five building ways to construct submarines in World War II. Here the yard is building three boats at one time in their large drydock. The USS Redfish *(SS 395), USS* Ronquil *(SS 396), and USS* Razorback *(SS 394) are watertight and about to be floated out of dock in January 1944. Steel sections for the next two boats to be built are already stacked in the foreground. Building three at one time proved to be too crowded.*

A 3"/50 deck gun is shown on board USS Silversides *(SS 236) in October 1942. The 3" refers to the gun's bore diameter and the 50 refers to the barrel length measured in bore diameters. In this case, the barrel length is 150 inches. Other deck guns carried by U.S. submarines included the 4"/50 and the shorter 5"/25. The largest guns carried were the 6"/53 guns carried by* Nautilus, Narwhal, *and* Argonaut.

Above: *At the Electric Boat Company, prefabricated hull frame sections await movement from the material yard to the building ways. The use of sub-assemblies and prefabricated parts hastened the building process and allowed submarines to be launched at the rate of nearly three per month from its twenty-one building ways. Other yards built submarines at a frantic pace. Portsmouth Navy Yard's design was built also at Boston and Mare Island Navy Yards. Electric Boat's design was also built at Manitowoc, Wisconsin.*

the reduction gears while the other two drove electric generators. All-electric drive finally became standard with the *Seadragon* class of 1938. In all three classes the number of torpedo tubes was increased to four forward and four aft.

Oddly enough, some influential officers were still pushing for a submarine of about 800 tons, which they believed could be built more rapidly and used on short patrols from advanced bases. The two prototypes, USS *Mackerel* (SS 204) and USS *Marlin* (SS 205), proved to be a step backward and saw no productive combat service in the war.

For the next program the Submarine Officers Conference was asked to establish the characteristics for an ideal general purpose submarine, based on experience gained from the types already in service or under construction. Aside from incremental improvements over the *Seadragon*, the biggest change was the addition of two more bow torpedo tubes and space for two more reloads, an increase that the operators had been seeking for several years. The younger officers also wanted a more powerful deck gun than the standard 3-inch/50-caliber weapon. The older members felt that a bigger gun would encourage the skippers to take unwarranted risks by fighting on the surface, but they agreed to install heavy enough foundations so a 5-inch gun could be substituted later. This feature was quickly taken advantage of when the boats went to war. Six submarines were ordered in 1939—the *Tambor* class—and another six in 1940, which were identical except for having names starting with "G."

The next step was the *Gato* class, which incorporated the machinery and equipment improvements of the previous classes. The only major structural addition was a watertight bulkhead dividing the engine room into two compartments. With some added hull strengthening, it was also possible to increase operating depth to 300 feet. With the war in Europe approaching crisis stage, it was time to freeze a submarine design for mass production, so several peacetime refinements were eliminated. The Navy finally had an ideal prototype, and it was just in time.

Having a good design in hand was one thing, but having the facilities to start mass production was something else again. Hitler's conquests in

Above: *The shipyard in Manitowoc lies on a river that empties into Lake Michigan. This presented special problems in submarine construction that were overcome quickly and in novel ways. Instead of launching stern first from inclined launch ways as in other yards, submarines were launched sideways. They were tipped into the water. The launching splash of USS* Hardhead *(SS 365) as she hits the water is pictured here. The far bank of the river shows clearly. Its narrowness prevented more conventional launch techniques.*

Left: *A hull frame is lowered into place at the Electric Boat Company in 1943. The slot at the bottom fits over the keel. Once set in place, this section is welded to the keel, then hull plates already rolled to shape are welded to the frames. Prefabricating sections like these speeded construction, as individual plates did not have to be cut and fitted on the building ways.*

Opposite, bottom: *A submarine is constructed on inclined ways at most shipyards and launched stern first. Here, the soon-to-be USS* Blenny *(SS 324) is getting started in 1943. The frames are being erected and squared in preparation for the welding of hull plating. In the foreground is the distinctive bullnose, a fairlead through which a towing cable would be fed should the submarine require towing by another vessel.*

Reminders of lost ships and the need to replace them were used to encourage the purchase of war bonds during World War II. This photograph of a huge poster that was used to raise money for the war effort in Connecticut commemorates the USS Dorado (SS 248), built by Electric Boat in Groton, Connecticut, and lost in 1943 with all hands. (Courtesy of Hauber Collection)

Above: The periscope is the eyes of the submarine. Here a new search periscope incorporating the ST radar antenna is about to be installed in a Balao-class boat at an advanced base. Other items visible in the shears are the attack periscope with its slim eyepiece rising high above the SJ surface radar antenna and the air warning SD radar dipole antenna.

Right: The Manitowoc Shipyard took prefabrication to another stage in that entire hull sections were constructed in building sheds then moved to the ways on crawlers. This method of construction is used in modern submarine construction.

Europe finally shook the United States into action. Congress approved a naval expansion program that included a big increase in the submarine force. The first six *Gato*-class boats were followed by twenty-two more. The two navy yards, Portsmouth and Mare Island, were limited in the space available for submarine construction but the Electric Boat Company, the only commercial submarine builder, had room for growth. Along with orders for sixteen boats, the Navy provided funds for a massive expansion of the shipyard. Before this infusion of capital could be absorbed, France collapsed and it looked like Britain might be overrun. The Navy suddenly had to face the possibility of warfare on both coasts, and a shocked Congress reacted by passing the so-called Two-Ocean Navy or 70 Percent Expansion Act in July 1940. This included authorization for forty-three more submarines, and the construction race began.

Each yard had its own specialized facilities and procedures. After its expansion, Electric Boat had the largest number of building ways—twenty-one—which were kept fully occupied by new hulls as two or three were launched each month. Because the yard was more limited in pier space, it kept its boats on the ways for eight or nine months so that they were relatively more complete internally when launched. The shortest building period from keel laying to commissioning was 317 days with USS *Corvina*. All told, Electric Boat completed eighty-two submarines ordered in the wartime programs.

Portsmouth Navy Yard had only five ways but plenty of pier space. It also used its drydocks to lay down two or three hulls at a time and float them out simultaneously. Its method was to prefabricate much of the hull before laying a keel and to launch it as soon as possible. Thus USS *Cisco* spent only 56 days on the ways and USS *Sea Poacher* took only 173 days from keel laying to commissioning. Portsmouth turned out submarines faster than anticipated, so it was given new orders for more higher-numbered boats while Electric Boat was still working on its initial

order. As a government yard, Portsmouth was quick to correct problems encountered during service, whereas the boats delivered from the private yards had to have more last-minute changes made at Pearl Harbor or other advanced bases before going on patrol.

Mare Island had been a new construction yard since 1927, but its facilities were soon fully taxed by overhaul and repair work on all kinds of ships returning from the Pacific combat areas. Even so, it managed to squeeze in seventeen of the new submarines. Its best record was made with USS *Tang*: 273 days from keel to completion, of which 192 were spent on the building ways.

To break the production bottleneck, it was imperative to bring more yards into the submarine construction program, and the Navy turned first to a highly unusual source—the Manitowoc Shipbuilding Company on Lake Michigan. This became a special success story. No Navy submarine had ever been built on the Great Lakes—getting the completed boat to sea took real ingenuity. Canals were widened and bridges raised so the new submarines could be carried down the Mississippi River. The yard was also situated on a river too narrow to allow hulls to be launched in "normal" endwise fashion, so Manitowoc launched them sideways, literally dumping them into the river. The yard followed Electric Boat plans and techniques

The boats that were launched by Manitowoc Shipbuilding Company had to travel from Lake Michigan through a river and barge canal network to the Mississippi River, then to the Gulf of Mexico. Because of the deep draft of the submarine, which would have prevented travel through shallower parts of the system, a floating drydock was used to transport the boat to the Gulf. The periscopes and shears had to be removed to clear low bridges.

USS Fulton *(AS 11) foundry is shown in June 1943. Submarine tender industrial capabilities provided the Navy with the ability to rebuild and repair major equipment on the front lines during World War II. This allowed the submarines to remain on station for the maximum possible percentage of their operating cycles.*

By the end of the war, the stubby 5"/25 weapon had become the main deck gun carried by U.S. submarines. Here, USS Balao *(SS 285), returning from a war patrol, has her 5"/25 gun trained to starboard, showing a Japanese flag and six hashmarks representing small craft destroyed by gunfire. Note the battle flag mounted on the 20mm gun just above the muzzle of the 5"/25.*

Three submarines—USS Bang *(SS 385), USS* Pintado *(SS 387), and USS* Pilotfish *(SS 386)—are alongside USS* Proteus *(AS 19) for supplies and repairs at Midway Island in May 1944.*

but also developed many improvements of its own. Its crews of men and women turned out boats that were unequaled for careful workmanship. Their record was made with *Lamprey*, which was 117 days on the ways and 269 days from keel laying to commissioning.

Later attempts to set up the Cramp Shipbuilding Company of Philadelphia and the Boston Navy Yard as submarine builders proved less successful. Cramp took almost two years to complete its first boat, but ultimately delivered ten by the end of the war. Boston was brought in late in the game—none of its boats saw combat in World War II.

Two new classes of submarines were built during the war. Outwardly both were practically indistinguishable from the *Gato* class, but each had significant improvements. The *Balao* class originated a few months before Pearl Harbor when designers noted that refinements had saved so much weight that extra lead ballast had to be installed as compensation. Why, they thought, couldn't that weight be better used to build a heavier, stronger hull? A few rough calculations showed that the boats could be made capable of diving at least 100 feet deeper without any significant changes to their appearance or interior layout. This would be a tremendous advantage in evading Japanese depth charges. The biggest problem was that no delay in production could be accepted until the *Gato* program was completed. Portsmouth, with a smaller backlog, was able to phase the new design into its building schedule by early 1943. Cramp started out fresh with the heavy-hull design, and the other yards shifted in due course. The change was made so quietly that the Japanese never learned about it; in fact, the diving depth was kept so secret that few nonsubmariners were aware of the change until after the war. While the boats operated routinely at 400 feet, the factor of safety incorporated in their design enabled them to go as deep as 600 feet in emergencies.

The *Tench* class incorporated many detailed improvements over its predecessors. Operationally, the most important was increasing the number of torpedoes carried from twenty-four to twenty-eight. Structurally, it was the elimination of ballast tank vent piping that passed through the torpedo rooms. This seemingly simple change actually required all of the ballast and fuel tanks to be rearranged, so it was undertaken only when there were enough boats under construction to warrant some delay. Portsmouth did the design work and built all but two of the boats that were completed to the original design. (Four were suspended incomplete and redesigned after the war as *Guppy* IIs.) In all, 339 submarines were ordered in the war programs. Of these, 77 *Gato*-class, 119 *Balao*-class, and 25 *Tench*-class boats were completed to their original designs. Most of the rest were canceled when it became obvious that there would be too few Japanese targets left by the time they were completed.

After the boats of the various classes went to war, many changes were made both internally and in outward appearance. Silhouettes were cut down to make the boats harder to detect and extra holes were cut in the superstructure to speed up diving, masts and antennas were added to accommodate new electronic equipment, improved mufflers were installed to reduce engine smoke, and guns were added or moved to different locations. On a few older boats additional torpedo tubes were

installed external to the hull. The torpedoes had to be loaded before leaving port and could neither be reloaded nor reached for servicing while on patrol. This led to some near catastrophes when torpedoes "ran hot" or hung up in the tubes during combat. Major alterations could be made only when a boat was returned to a shipyard for a major overhaul or to repair severe damage. As a result, the outward appearance of the boats varied widely, irrespective of their original design, depending on how much each one had been modified before the war ended.

The best-built submarine in the world, regardless of the type of hull construction or propulsion system, would be of no avail without the ability to sink enemy ships. The main weapon of the submarine was, of course, the torpedo. Deck guns were useful only against weak targets or as a last-ditch means of fending off an enemy. Mines could be laid from torpedo tubes, but submariners detested them because they were dangerous to lay in relatively shallow water and the results could not be observed or verified. The key to success, therefore, was the effectiveness of the torpedoes and their fire control system.

Much has been written about the problems caused by defective and unreliable torpedoes, especially during the first two years of the war. In

A sheet of high-tensile steel is rolled into hull plating at the Electric Boat Company in Groton, Connecticut. The workman holds a template to ensure that the rolled curve is proper. The thickness of this type plate and the frames that reinforce it was increased in the newer Balao-*class submarines. This extended the designed maximum operating depth from 312 feet to 412 feet.*

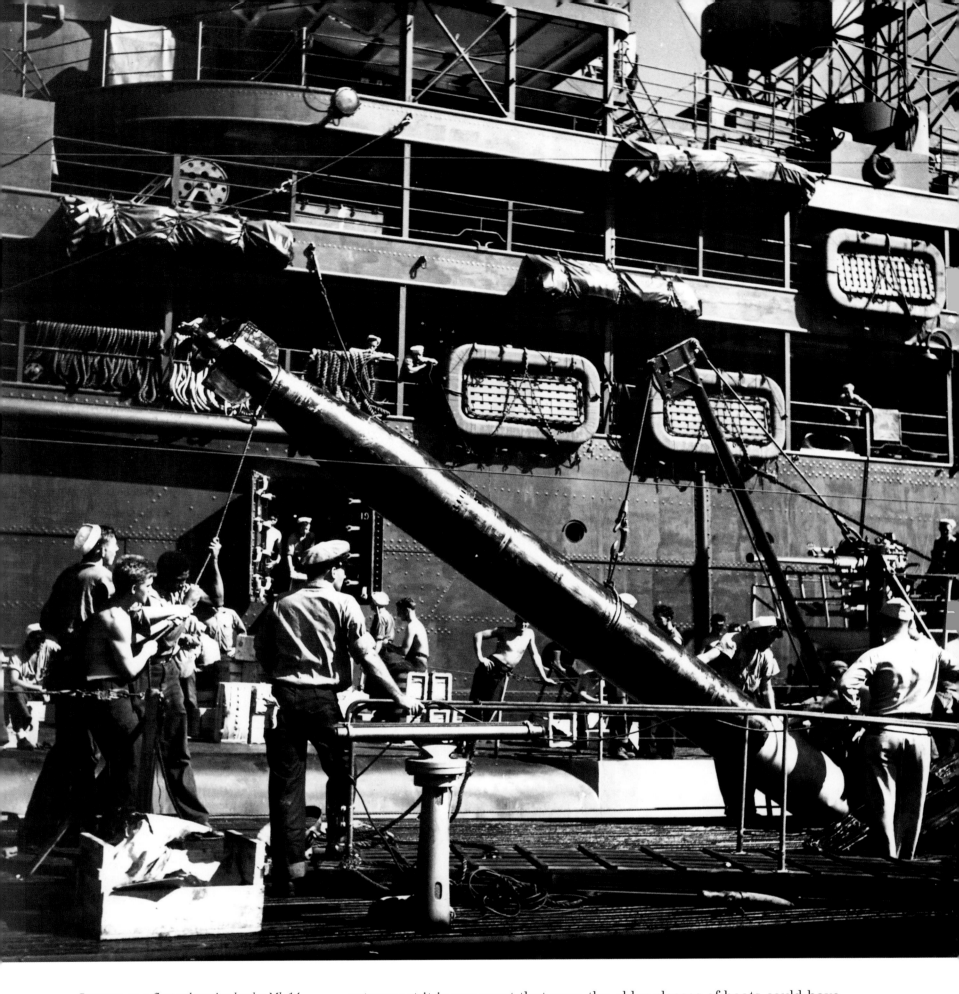

Crewmen on a fleet submarine load a Mk 14 torpedo in 1945. This torpedo, the mainstay weapon of the U.S. submarine fleet, was beset by problems early in the war. When these problems were solved, the weapon became much more reliable and stayed in service with the U.S. Submarine Fleet until 1980.

retrospect it is apparent that even the older classes of boats could have been far more effective than was the actual case, and that even after the most serious defects were believed to have been corrected, our torpedoes continued to malfunction far too often. Our submarines had possessed a reasonably effective fire control system since the mid-1930s. All of the fleet boats had torpedo data computers and remote gyroscope setting systems by which torpedoes could be fired at almost any desired angle. The principal method of aiming them was the periscope, but the boats also had target bearing transmitters on the bridge; further, active (pinging) and passive (listening) sonars could be used to determine the bearing and approximate range of a target. The first submarine radar—the SD

Left: *A Balao-class fleet submarine comes alongside after a long patrol. This boat carries a 20mm gun mount on the forward bridge level with a 40mm gun aft, as well as a 20mm mount on the main deck aft. Note the small flags flying from a line attached to the forward periscope support. These denote Japanese merchantmen claimed as sunk during the patrol.*

Above: *The bridge structure of USS* Trout *(SS 202) is shown as as she comes alongside after her historic trip bringing gold bullion from Corregidor in early 1942. Compare this with the previous photo of the fleet submarine coming alongside after a patrol later in the war. As the war progressed and lessons were learned, the bridge structure was cut down to reduce the silhouette and to give space for larger caliber rapid fire guns.*

aircraft warning set—had been developed by 1940 and the SJ surface search radar began to be installed in August 1942. However, it took many months before all of the earlier boats could be refitted with the new electronic equipment, and submariners could become sufficiently familiar with it to use it to optimum advantage.

Before the war, submarine commanders had been trained to make attacks while submerged. The effectiveness of antisubmarine sonar and depth charges was so overrated that skippers had become overly cautious. War experience soon showed that our submarines were much harder to detect and more resistant to damage than had been feared, and that radar gave them a great advantage in being able to locate and attack targets on the surface. The night surface approach then became the preferred method of attack, because the submarine could use its high speed to get into a firing position and get out again in a hurry, unshaken by depth charges. The submerged periscope attack was still preferred during day-light and became increasingly effective as improved sonars were developed and especially after the ST periscope radar was introduced starting in mid 1944. The bathythermograph enabled submarines to detect temperature layers in the ocean, below which enemy sonars could not easily find them. Other electronic devices such as identification friend or foe (IFF), radar

A submarine departs a forward base in the Pacific. Tenders and floating drydocks made it possible to service frontline boats and get them back on patrol quickly. The relentless pressure decimated Japanese shipping and starved the Japanese war machine. Two weeks of rest and recreation on an atoll were appreciated by submarine crews but still left something to be desired. Time in the rest camp was spent sleeping, eating, drinking beer, writing letters, playing softball, and swimming in the lagoon. After the next patrol the crews could expect to be brought back to a rear base such as Brisbane, Perth, or Honolulu, where there was more to do.

A commander peers through number one periscope in the conning tower of a typical fleet submarine. This view looking aft shows the small space that would be occupied by eight or more people during an attack. Along the port side is the torpedo fire control system and on the other side is the sonar operator's station, radar equipment, and chart table. Behind the photographer are the helm stand and the hatches to the bridge and control room.

detectors and countermeasures, navigation systems (Loran), very high frequency voice radio sets, and frequency-modulated sonar came into service as fast as new equipment could be developed and produced.

Improvements were being made continuously in other areas as well, especially after the Navy began to subject submarine equipment to actual explosive tests. These were started at Portsmouth in the early 1930s to compare the strength of riveted versus welded hulls, then expanded to test other items of equipment. The tests led to better storage batteries, shock resistant mountings, and more reliable fittings ranging from electrical switchboards to shatterproof toilet bowls. A whole series of improvements came about when the newly completed USS *Tambor* was subjected to full-scale explosive tests in late 1940, with the charges gradually moved as close as 100 feet from the hull. Similar changes were made when weaknesses were revealed during actual combat. Diesel engines, pumps, and ventilation fans were steadily improved. Air conditioning became standard starting with USS *Plunger* in 1935, and steady improvements in habitability kept crews healthier and better able to withstand the rigors of sixty to seventy-five day patrols. A major improvement was the introduction of the Kleinschmidt distilling equipment starting with USS *Tunny* in 1942. Submariners finally had a reliable source of fresh water for the duration of a patrol. Submariners were quick to learn the importance of eliminating sources of noise. One of the worst noise generators was the reduction gears, but the submarine could not move without running them. They were finally eliminated when slow-speed electric motors were developed and installed starting with USS *Sea Owl* in 1944. As improvements were built into new boats and backfitted into old ones, the entire submarine fleet became safer and more effective.

The story of our wartime submarines did not end with the surrender of Japan. The boats proved amazingly adaptable to such specialized uses as cargo and transport submarines, radar pickets, tankers for refueling seaplanes, quiet hunter-killers of other submarines, and the first launchers of guided missiles. Fitted with snorkels and streamlined, fleet boats formed the bulk of the Submarine Force for many more years. Their active role in the U.S. Navy finally ended when *Tigrone* was retired on 27 June 1975, but many served even longer in foreign navies. Fortunately, several of the World War II fleet boats have been preserved as memorials where visitors can still see how submariners lived and fought before nuclear power opened a whole new era of undersea operations.

A man's home is his castle, and home is a 6-foot by 2 1/2 -foot bunk. In the foreground is another bunk. A narrow passageway (about 2-feet wide) separates the two bunks, which are top bunks in stacks of three. A ventilation duct (upper center) circulates air when the quiet condition allows the ventilation blower to operate. These upper bunks had more headroom than the bunks below them, thus they were prized.

USS Flasher *(SS 249) comes into port toward the end of World War II. This boat is credited with sinking the most tonnage of any U.S. submarine during the war. She made seven patrols in which she sank 132,383 tons of enemy shipping. Her conning tower shears now form part of the U.S. Submarine Force World War II Memorial in Groton, Connecticut. At this site are inscribed the names of over 3,500 U.S. submariners lost during World War II, as well as stone tablets commemorating the fifty-two U.S. submarines lost during the war.*

Submarine Losses in World War II

Captain John M. Donlon, USN (Ret)

Artist Gerry Levey, a past submarine commanding officer, has captured the drama of USS Darter's *grounding on Bombay Shoal off Palawan Island in the Philippines during a night surface approach on a crippled Japanese cruiser escorted by two destroyers. USS* Dace *can be seen in the background keeping close to* Darter *while the latter's crew is ferried over to* Dace *in two rubber boats.*

Although the Japanese attackers did not include the four submarines present among their "sitting duck" targets at Pearl Harbor, an accurate stick of bombs on the submarine base would have proved worthwhile to the Japanese. The new USS *Tautog* (SS 199) became a thorn in the enemy's side from the beginning, helping to bring down a low-flying intruder in the first few minutes of the raid. *Tautog* then went on to sink twenty-six Japanese ships, first in the number of ships sunk by the Silent Service during the war.

It wasn't long, however, before a submarine was included among U.S. ships sunk. On 10 December, Far Eastern time, just forty-eight hours into the war, USS *Sealion* (SS 195) at Cavite Naval Station in Manila Bay became the first of fifty-two U.S. boats lost during the conflict. *Sealion* was overhauling equipment; therefore, the ship was unable to get underway and proceed to sea. Japanese bombs ruined her propulsion controls. *Sealion*'s own personnel destroyed her hull to make it useless to the enemy.

Submarines patrolled vast regions where they were the only opposition to Japanese predominance on the surface and in the air for many months to come. They learned quickly. Their losses, although severe compared to other U.S. naval forces, were surprisingly small compared to the damage inflicted by our submarines or to the number of enemy submarines destroyed—German losses, 781; Japanese, 130; Italian, 85.

The first loss by direct enemy attack on a specific submarine was USS *Shark* (SS 174), some two months into hostilities in mid-February 1942. Similarly, USS *Perch* (SS 176) succumbed to attacks by Japanese antisubmarine ships two weeks later in what are now Indonesian waters.

Above: *The night of 7 February 1943 saw USS Growler (SS 215) on the surface tracking a target in the vicinity of Guadalcanal. The visibility was poor, but Commander Howard Gilmore and Growler pressed home the attack. As the range closed to less than 2,000 yards, the enemy ship turned and closed at high speed through the mist and fog. Growler tried to turn away, but the two ships met at 17 knots. The bow of Growler was crushed and bent 90 degrees to port as the small Japanese naval auxiliary raked her bridge with machine-gun fire. Ensign W. W. Williams, the junior officer of the deck, and Fireman Third Class W. F. Kelly, a lookout, died at their posts. Other bridge watchstanders, including two lookouts, cleared the bridge. Gilmore, badly wounded and immobilized, ordered the submarine to submerge with the legendary order "Take her down." The Medal of Honor was awarded for his sacrifice. After repairs, Growler fought on but was lost in the South China Sea in November 1944.*

S-boats are moored alongside the tender Canopus *(AS 9). The S-36, moored outboard, made one attack on a Japanese merchantship in December 1941; however, she grounded on a reef in the Makassar Strait, Indonesia, in January 1942 and was destroyed. All hands were rescued.*

123

As with most of her lost sisters, none of *Shark*'s personnel survived the assault. *Perch*, atypically, and later-lost USS *Grenadier* (SS 210) were the only two combat losses whose complements survived the sinkings.

Eleven of our fifty-two losses were caused by other than enemy forces. Three older submarines, USS *R-12* (SS 89), USS *S-26* (SS 131), and USS *S-28* (SS 133), sank in U.S.-controlled waters. Two were estimated to have been accidentally sunk by our own forces—brand new USS *Dorado* (SS 248)

in the Caribbean by aircraft in 1943 and prewar USS *Seawolf* (SS 197) southeast of the Philippines by combined air and surface attacks in 1944.

As if to underscore the problems with U.S. torpedoes, USS *Tang* (SS 306) and USS *Tullibee* (SS 284) were sunk in 1944 by circular runs of their own torpedoes, both during night surface attacks on Japanese convoys. Ironically, *Tang's* torpedo was the last of the full load of twenty-four fired during what proved to be the most fruitful patrol of the war from the viewpoint of the number of enemy ships sunk.

The largest number of losses for which the enemy was known to be not responsible fit the category of "stranding," or running aground. Charts of vast areas of the Pacific war zone were sketchy. Not a few were labeled "from a survey by Capt. James Cook." The four boats driven into the unyielding grasp of reefs, included three S-boats, built to a World War I design and commissioned in the early 1920s. This trio of elder sisters, not equipped with radar or good fathometers, suffered their fates in the first nine months of the war. First to go was USS *S-36* (SS 141) in Makassar Strait in January 1942. A Dutch steamer picked up all personnel after her own crew had destroyed *S-36*. Fog and the Arctic night blinded USS *S-27* (SS 132) five months later in the Aleutians. Unusually strong currents swept her into a rocky basin inside the shoals of Amchitka Island. The crew salvaged materials vital to their survival from the wrecked ship and lived like Robinson Crusoe for a week until Navy flying boats rescued them. Then in August, *S-39* (SS 144) grounded between Australia and the Solomons. Just before the pounding seas ensured complete destruction, her entire crew was rescued by an Australian minesweeper. Loss of USS *Darter* (SS 227) in October 1944 in the southwest Philippines resulted from the commanding officer's calculated risk in an attempt to finish off the third of three Japanese cruisers—all successfully attacked in concert

Above: *USS* R-12 *(SS 89) was lost during a training accident off Key West in June 1943— one of two submarines lost in the Atlantic. R-12 was on a routine training exercise when she suddenly flooded and went down. The other was USS* Dorado *(SS 248), which was never heard from after she departed New London, Connecticut, for Panama. A patrol plane out of Guantanamo, Cuba, received faulty instructions as to the location of the "no attack zone" surrounding* Dorado *and delivered a depth charge attack on an unidentified submarine in the restricted area. A German submarine was also known to be operating in the area and may have picked off* Dorado *during her transit.*

Opposite, bottom: *This closeup periscope photo (far left) shows a sinking Japanese merchantman—a victim of USS* Seawolf *(SS 197).* Seawolf *(left) made fifteen patrols during the war and is credited with sinking twenty-one ships with a combined tonnage of 94,560 tons. A hardworking boat, along with her patrols in which she had fifty-six torpedo battles, she participated in several special operations from the earliest days of the war. It was on such a special mission, transporting U.S. Army personnel and stores to the east coast of Samar, that she was sunk in error by the U.S. destroyer escort,* Richard M. Rowell *(DE 403). The ninety-nine men lost (including the seventeen Army personnel) was the second highest individual casualty total in a single submarine loss in the war.*

USS Argonaut *(SS 166), later classified APS 1 (submarine transport), was the largest of the U.S. submarines to participate in World War II. She was over 380 feet long and had a beam of over 33 feet. Originally built as a minelayer, she had two minelaying chutes and special tubes built into a large stern room. In 1942, she was converted to a cargo carrying and troop transport submarine. The mine laying gear was removed, and the stern room was fitted for troop berthing. She transported Marines for the Makin Island raid. In January 1943 she was on patrol near Rabaul when she was attacked by two Japanese destroyers who were avenging the torpedoing of a third destroyer in a convoy. The two destroyers hammered the water with depth charges;* Argonaut's *bow thrust above the surface and remained there for some time as the destroyers repeatedly hit it with gunfire. Finally, she slid with her crew of 105 men to the depths of the Pacific.*

with teammate USS *Dace* (SS 247). After failed attempts to get *Darter* off the reef, upon which she became stranded in an "end-around" maneuver, the crew destroyed everything useful and all hands were lifted off by *Dace.* Thereby, every member of the ships' companies survived all four catastrophic groundings. *Darter's* crew was transplanted in toto to USS *Menhaden* (SS 377), then under construction at Manitowoc, Wisconsin. *Menhaden's* arrival in the Pacific occurred just as the Japanese surrendered—too late to avenge *Darter's* loss.

The very nature of a submarine's wartime operations makes for uncertainty in determining what went wrong when a boat fails to return from a mission. Independence from day-to-day contact with headquarters (nearly all communications, of necessity, are one-way *to* the ship) means a loss may not be known until long after it occurs. Access to enemy records after hostilities end may shed little light on what happened. The Japanese were wide of the mark in analyzing their antisubmarine actions; they identified 468 "positive" sinkings of U.S. submarines!

Even our own estimates of our losses due to enemy action are clouded by irreconcilable or insufficient data. The complete absence of information prompted assignment of the label "unknown" to five of the forty-one losses

Ship's Company, USS Swordfish (SS 193), is shown at the end of the boat's tenth war patrol. Swordfish's first patrol began the day after the attack on Pearl Harbor. She sank four freighters and damaged a fifth. She later evacuated President Quezon, his family, the vice president, and chief justice from Corregidor. On her tenth patrol the crew, pictured here, sank three freighters. On her thirteenth U.S. war patrol, she was ordered to conduct a photographic reconnaissance of Okinawa. It is now known that many mines were planted around Okinawa as the Japanese prepared for the Allied invasion. Swordfish is one of the eight submarines thought to have been sunk by mines in the Pacific war.

Lieutenant Commander Dudley W. "Mush" Morton is seated at his desk in the small commanding officer's stateroom in the forward battery of USS Wahoo (SS 238). He was lost with her in October 1943. Particularly touching is this reminder that he left a wife and children. The supreme sacrifice made by submariners was most keenly felt by their families who mourn them still.

likely related to enemy efforts. These ships might have succumbed to operational casualties, as could have some of the twelve assessed lost to "possible to probable" enemy causes.

Eight submarines are thought to have been lost to mines. Mines certainly qualify as "enemy action," even though the enemy may not be anywhere in the vicinity when such a weapon takes its toll. Only three of these eight sinkings are classed "probable to certain" losses due to mining. In two cases eyewitnesses survived the war; in the third case, a crewman who did not survive prison camp managed to get a message to insurgents prior to his death. The other five mining casualties were not as routine. All but two of the eight losses occurred in Japanese "home" waters—the Sea of Japan, the Yellow Sea, and the straits leading to them. As targets became scarcer, our submarines pushed into these areas of more extensive minefield coverage. That the United States did not suffer greater losses to mines is a tribute to our improved sonars, our superior commanding officers (and their subordinates), accurate intelligence, and a great deal of good luck.

Our World War II diesel-electric submarines were, of course, basically surface ships capable of submerging. On patrol, they required many surfaced hours each night to charge their batteries in, for the most part, an enemy air preserve. Sharp-eyed lookouts, good radars, and well-drilled crews capable of submerging in seconds provided significant security most of the time. *Grenadier* barely survived a near-miss air attack in the northeast Indian Ocean in April 1943; however, the damage was so great that the ship had to be abandoned the next day. Although the entire crew was picked up by a Japanese merchantman, brutal treatment by their captors resulted in the death of four crewmen. USS *Wahoo* (SS 238), a high scorer, met her end in the Sea of Japan in October 1943 on the enemy's doorstep. In February 1945, USS *Barbel* (SS 316) fell in the southwest Philippines to the last vestiges of Japanese local air supremacy in that region. Air power enthusiasts insisted that control of the air ensured control of the surface beneath. The first and the last of our submarine losses, *Sealion* alongside a pier three days into the war and USS *Bullhead* (SS 332) at sea a few days

USS Runner (SS 275) is pictured as she departs Portsmouth Navy Yard for sea trials in October 1942. She was lost eight months later on her third war patrol, most likely to one of the many mines laid to protect the Hokkaido Coast.

Crewmen clamber through the conning tower upon surfacing. The bridge crew consisted of the officer of the deck, a junior officer of the deck, the quartermaster of the watch, and lookouts, all of whom stood on the open bridge, after bridge deck, and in the periscope shears. This painting was commissioned by Abbott Laboratories and given to the Navy Combat Art collection; it resides in the Navy Art Museum at the Washington Navy Yard. ("Up the Hatch," Thomas Hart Benton, Navy Combat Art Collection)

USS Sealion (SS 195) was damaged by a Japanese bombing attack on Cavite in December 1941 and scuttled because the damage could not be repaired. In 1945, after the islands were recaptured, the hulk was photographed where she sank.

prior to war's end, resulted from enemy air action alone. In all, five losses are attributed to airplanes alone—tragic, indeed, but not bad for a force doing its job with little or no air coverage of its own.

The "traditional" antisubmarine surface ship, the only truly effective World War I weapon against the submarine, accounted for more U.S. losses (sixteen), than any other cause during World War II. Thus, Japanese surface forces, including those working in concert with aircraft, were involved in twenty-two of the total of forty-one losses to enemy forces.

Loss of USS *Herring* (SS 233) on her eighth patrol in June 1944 was most unusual. This veteran of Atlantic patrols had given a good account of herself during the invasion of North Africa and claimed a kill against a German U-boat when operating in the Bay of Biscay. But having disposed of two anchored Japanese merchant ships off Matsuwa in the Kurile Islands during her eighth patrol, she sustained two direct hits from a shore battery. *Herring* went down immediately—the only U.S. submarine to fall to land-based "surface" gunfire.

The previous year, also in the Kuriles, eighteen-year-old USS *S-44* (SS 155) was gunned down by a destroyer, mistaken by *S-44* in poor night visibility for a small merchant vessel. Earlier in the Solomons, she had sunk three ships, including a gunboat and a heavy cruiser, IJNS *Kako*, the first major Japanese warship to go down at the hands of our submarines.

The largest U.S. submarine prior to the advent of 1959's USS *Triton* (SSRN 586) was USS *Argonaut* (SM 1, later APS 1), commissioned in 1928 as a minelayer. She was lost to a fatal attack by Japanese destroyers south of New Britain during her third patrol in January 1943. Unable to help, U.S. Army Air Corps planes overhead could only witness her destruction—they were out of bombs! On an earlier patrol she had landed "Carlson's Raiders" on Makin in the Gilbert Islands.

Other 1943 losses to surface ships in the New Guinea and Solomons region were USS *Grampus* (SS 207) and USS *Triton* (SS 201). The latter downed eleven enemy ships including one in her sixth and final patrol and was already among the scoring leaders. Their loss, within ten days of each other, came during a critical phase of our turning back Japanese expansion into the Solomon Islands. Both were sunk by destroyers—*Grampus* with gunfire; *Triton*, with depth charges.

WWII SUBMARINE LOSSES

1941-1945

THE FINAL PATROL

"To those whose contribution meant the loss of sons, brothers or husbands in this war, I pay my most humble respect and extend my deepest sympathy. As to the 374 officers and 3131 men of the Submarine Force who gave their lives in the winning of this war, I can assure you that they went down fighting and that their brothers who survived them took a grim toll of our savage enemy to avenge their deaths. May God rest their gallant souls."

VICE ADMIRAL C.A. LOCKWOOD, JR.,
COMMANDER SUBMARINE FORCE, U.S. PACIFIC FLEET, 1943-1946

USS SEALION (SS 195)	USS GRAYBACK (SS 208)
USS S-36 (SS 141)	USS TROUT (SS 202)
USS S-26 (SS 131)	USS TULLIBEE (SS 284)
USS SHARK (SS 174)	USS GUDGEON (SS 211)
USS PERCH (SS 176)	USS HERRING (SS 233)
USS S-27 (SS 132)	USS GOLET (SS 361)
USS GRUNION (SS 216)	USS S-28 (SS 133)
USS S-39 (SS 144)	USS ROBALO (SS 273)
USS ARGONAUT (SS 166)	USS FLIER (SS 250)
USS AMBERJACK (SS 219)	USS HARDER (SS 257)
USS GRAMPUS (SS 207)	USS SEAWOLF (SS 197)
USS TRITON (SS 201)	USS ESCOLAR (SS 294)
USS PICKEREL (SS 177)	USS DARTER (SS 227)
USS GRENADIER (SS 210)	USS SHARK (SS 314)
USS RUNNER (SS 275)	USS TANG (SS 306)
USS R-12 (SS 89)	USS ALBACORE (SS 218)
USS POMPANO (SS 181)	USS GROWLER (SS 215)
USS GRAYLING (SS 209)	USS SCAMP (SS 277)
USS CISCO (SS 290)	USS SWORDFISH (SS 193)
USS S-44 (SS 155)	USS BARBEL (SS 316)
USS WAHOO (SS 238)	USS KETE (SS 369)
USS DORADO (SS 248)	USS TRIGGER (SS 237)
USS CORVINA (SS 226)	USS SNOOK (SS 279)
USS SCULPIN (SS 191)	USS LAGARTO (SS 371)
USS CAPELIN (SS 289)	USS BONEFISH (SS 223)
USS SCORPION (SS 278)	USS BULLHEAD (SS 332)

Preparatory to the late 1943 invasion of Tarawa, most famous of the Gilbert Islands, USS *Sculpin* (SS 191) was assigned to intercept convoys from Truk. She did exactly that. Preparing to surface and chase a convoy that had just passed, *Sculpin* inadvertently broached near a trailing "sleeper" destroyer. Attempting to go deep, she became the focus of an 18-depth-charge pattern, which put her nearly out of commission. Unable to remain submerged, *Sculpin* surfaced to fight it out. The under-gunned *Sculpin* was no match for the destroyer. Abandoning a severely damaged ship with a dead commanding officer was the only course left. Captain John Cromwell, division commander, who was on board to form and lead a "wolf pack" later, knew too much about the planned invasion of Tarawa to risk capture. Therefore, courageously he rode the boat to a watery grave rather than expose himself to torture and possible revelation of the imminent operation. The posthumous award of the Medal of Honor marks him as one of the war's most selfless heroes. A total of forty-one *Sculpin*

Above: *USS* Sculpin *(SS 191) is shown in San Francisco Bay, after being overhauled in May 1943. In November she was forced to the surface by a Japanese destroyer and scuttled after being riddled by gunfire. Twenty-one crewmen survived the war.*

Right: *This oil painting captures some of the action seen in the conning tower during battlestations. ("Up Periscope," Thomas Hart Benton, Navy Combat Art Collection)*

Above: *This photograph shows the control room of USS* Capelin *(SS 289) in August 1943. On the left is the diving officer overseeing the planesmen.* Capelin *was lost only two months later. It is likely these men went with her.*

USS Capelin *(SS 289) departed Darwin, Australia, in November 1943 and did not return. Enemy minefields are now known to have been placed along the north coast of Celebes in* Capelin's *patrol area, and she may have been lost to a mine explosion.*

crewmembers were pulled from the water by the Japanese. Two weeks later, twenty of the twenty-one *Sculpin* survivors embarked in a Japanese aircraft carrier bound for the Home Islands died when IJNS *Chuyo* was sunk by USS *Sailfish* (SS 192). Ironically, *Sailfish* was the raised and renamed USS *Squalus*—a victim of accidental sinking during sea trials off the New Hampshire coast some four years earlier. *Sculpin* had located *Squalus* on the bottom and stood by during crew rescue operations in 1939. To round out the dramatic story of *Sculpin*, *Chuyo* was the first Japanese aircraft carrier sunk by a U.S. submarine!

The second Shark *(SS 314) joined the Pacific War in 1944. She was lost on her third war patrol. The Japanese recorded depth charging a submarine, now thought to be* Shark, *on 24 October 1944, and having seen "bubbles and heavy oil, clothes, cork, etc." This attack is considered the most probable cause of* Shark's *loss. No one survived.*

Shallow waters in the East Indies saw, and may have contributed to, loss of USS *Capelin* (SS 289) and USS *Lagarto* (SS 371), each on her second patrol. Both had previous successful patrols. The former went down off Celebes in late 1943. Eighteen months later, the latter encountered a convoy in the outer Gulf of Siam. One of the escorts was *Hatsutaka*, a modern fast minelayer with a new, powerful radar. Her depth charges sank *Lagarto* in 180 feet of water.

As the Japanese Empire shrank from inexorable U.S. pressure, more war patrols were conducted closer to the Home Islands. Somewhat surprisingly, only three of the sixteen losses to surface attack alone occurred "up close and personal" to the major islands. Nearly or actually in sight of Honshu, the trio fell to local antisubmarine vessels operating very close to their bases. USS *Pickerel* (SS 177), a six-patrol veteran, sank off a lighthouse at Honshu's northern tip in the spring of 1943. Not far away, USS *Golet* (SS 361) was destroyed on her second patrol in June 1944. One year later, west of the island, USS *Bonefish* (SS 223) met the same fate, but not before having sunk more than 62,000 tons of shipping on seven prior runs. With the end of the war just weeks away, she was a member of one of three 3-ship wolfpacks to enter the Sea of Japan on the same day. Safety in numbers does not apply in every case.

USS *Trout* (SS 202), USS *Harder* (SS 257), and USS *Shark* (SS 314) were lost in the vicinity of the Philippines, all in 1944. *Trout* had first come to that area in early 1942, carrying ammunition to Corregidor in Manila Bay. She returned to Pearl Harbor with 20 tons of Philippine government gold and silver, sinking two targets of opportunity on the way home. One of the first to operate close to Japan in 1942, *Trout* met her

April Fool's Day in 1944 saw USS Harder *(SS 257) off the island of Woleai in the western part of the Carolines. A radio call indicated that a U.S. aviator was down on a small island just to the west.* Harder *moved in to effect a rescue. In a tremendous feat of seamanship, Commander Dealey put the bow of the boat against the reef only 1,200 yards off the beach and held it there against the surf by working both screws and rudder to prevent broaching. Three strong swimmers were selected to take the rubber boat ashore by swimming with it through the coral, surf, and sniper fire to pluck the airman off the island. Five months later,* Harder's *luck ran short, and she died with her crew near Caiman Point, Luzon.*

Above: *Shell splashes from USS* Bonefish*'s deck gun shower a Japanese ship and direct hits set her aflame. This photo, taken on the boat's fifth patrol, shows how U.S. submarines engaged the enemy close aboard. On her eighth patrol, she obtained permission to make an offensive patrol in Toyoma Wan, a bay on the west coast of Honshu. The merchant ship* Konzan Maru *was sunk nearby on 20 June 1945. Japanese records indicate that a depth charge attack was made shortly thereafter on a submerged submarine in the vicinity. It is reported that the attack brought up oil, air, and splintered wood.* Bonefish *had made her last dive.*

end while savaging a convoy northeast of Luzon on her eleventh and final patrol. *Harder*, under the command of Medal of Honor awardee Samuel Dealey, was sunk by a Japanese surface escort off the west coast of Luzon. Known as "The Destroyer Killer," Dealey had sunk at least four destroyers—a submarine's greatest nemesis—among the sixteen ships he sent to the bottom during five prior patrols. The details of the last moments of *Shark II* are as sketchy as those relating to the end of the earlier ship whose name she bore. It is certain, however, that surface ships depth-charged her at the western end of the Luzon Strait on 24 October 1944, the very day of history's last great encounter between battleships on the other side of the Philippines.

In the 1940s one might have thought that a magic combination of the traditional surface enemy with the brand-new airborne threat would certainly eliminate submersibles dependent daily upon the earth's atmosphere. One would have been very wrong. Only six of U.S. losses were attributable to that combination, and only three of them occurred in waters where one would expect Japanese air power to prevail fully.

In the outer empire, when the Solomons campaign was still undecided in early 1943, the urgent need for submarines shortened USS *Amberjack*'s (SS 219) refit period between her second and third patrols to a scant twelve days. Mid-February found her three weeks into the patrol lining up for an attack on a convoy east of New Guinea. An escorting aircraft attacked and evidently inflicted severe damage. A sub-chaser and a torpedo boat completed the assault with a fatal 9-depth-charge attack. USS

Cisco (SS 290), however, lost in the Sulu Sea west of Mindoro in the Philippines in September of that year, may have been detected and attacked by an aircraft that spotted a tell-tale oil trail. Antisubmarine surface ships joined to finish the job. One day into her first patrol out of Port Darwin, Australia, Cisco had to return to repair a significant hydraulic system casualty. It is possible that a recurrence contributed to the initial oil detection. Stepped-up antisubmarine activity by the Japanese in the Mariana Islands contributed to the loss of twelve-patrol veteran USS Gudgeon (SS 211) in the spring of 1944. A Japanese army plane scored a direct bomb hit and surface ship depth charges completed her destruction. She had sunk 79,000 tons of shipping during her long career.

Closer to the homeland, in the Ryukyus chain east of Okinawa, USS Grayback (SS 208) suffered a direct hit by an aircraft bomb. Surface ships depth-charged the spot where she submerged, ensuring the kill. The Japanese were beginning to recognize the increasing submarine threat and slightly imitated the American system of convoy defense in the Atlantic using carrier air groups. Grayback had accounted for 64,000 tons of shipping flying the Rising Sun flag. The eighth patrol of USS Scamp (SS 277) took her to an area just east of Tokyo and included lifeguard duties for Saipan-based B-29 Super Fortresses bombing the Japanese capital. In November 1944, an antisubmarine aircraft dropped near-miss bombs, and coast defense ships provided a 90-depth-charge barrage for the coup de grace. The last loss to an air-surface combination was USS Trigger (SS 237) in March 1945, also near the Ryukyus. Eight separate bombing attacks and

Above: *Gathered on the deck of USS* Snook *(SS 279) with its battle flag are members of her communications division. From left to right: Ensign E. H. Clark, II; Seaman First Class J. E. McGahan*; Radio Technician Second Class R. K. Burdick*; Quartermaster First Class Hall; Chief Radioman Conover; Radioman Third Class J. S. Parker*; Quartermaster Second Class Kloog; Chief Pharmacist's Mate Mann, Yeoman Second Class Stetson; Radioman Third Class B. A. Branum, Jr.,*; Radio Technician Second Class Will; Radioman Second Class Green; Lieutenant May. This photo probably was taken by Seaman First Class V. P. Mlynek* after her fifth patrol in March of 1944. After completing an overhaul at Hunter's Point, she made three more patrols ranging from the Kurile Islands in the North Pacific to the South China Sea. On her ninth patrol somewhere north of the Luzon Strait, she was lost without a trace and of causes unknown, taking with her eighty-four men, including those marked with an asterisk.*

Opposite, bottom: *USS* Shark *(SS 174) transported Admiral Hart and other officials from Manila to Surabaya in December 1941 on her first patrol. She was lost (with all hands) on the second patrol, probably to a depth charge attack, in February 1942.*

Above: *USS* Grayback's *(SS 208) Commander John A. "Johnny" Moore became one of the top skippers in World War II, standing twenty-first in tonnage sunk, after only three patrols. His and* Grayback's *luck ran out in February 1944, when a Japanese aircraft caught* Grayback *on the surface and scored a direct hit with a bomb. Japanese surface combatants rained depth charges on the oil slick and air bubbles rising to the surface to ensure her destruction.*

Above: *USS* Barbel *(SS 316) had a short life. Commissioned on 3 April 1944, she was sunk with all hands on 4 February 1945 by two bombs from a Japanese aircraft. The crew pictured here, most of whom went down with her, shows off her battle flag in November 1944. Postwar analysis gives* Barbel *credit for sinking seven ships.*

USS Bullhead *(SS 332) brings home a wounded pilot rescued while on patrol in early 1945. In August 1945 she was to transit Lombok Strait on her way to her patrol area near Java. She was bombed and sunk near the northern end of the strait on 6 August 1945. USS* Sealion *(SS 195) was the first of the fifty-two submarines lost in World War II.* Bullhead *was the last.*

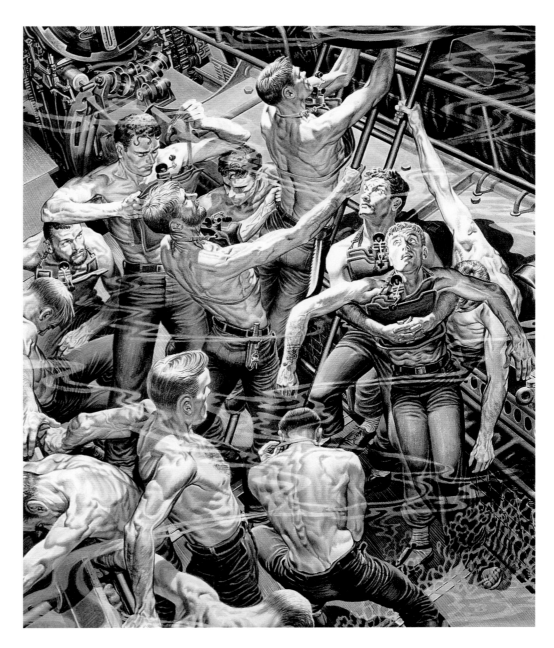

a working-over by surface ships ended a long and illustrious career that officially recorded eighteen enemy ships sunk in her twelve patrols.

"The best defense against submarines is other submarines." These are not the words of some cold warrior, but those of Brigadier General William A. ("Billy") Mitchell, the air power prophet of the 1920s. USS *Corvina* (SS 226), on her first patrol, was our only known loss to an enemy submarine. IJNS *I-176* delivered two torpedo hits when she caught *Corvina* on the surface on 16 November 1943, southwest of the huge enemy base at Truk. This loss was to the submarine that *Corvina* had been sent to sink!

The axiom might be said to have applicability on the other side of the fence: a whopping twenty-three Axis submarines, including two German U-Boats, were sunk by our own undersea forces in the Pacific. No other opposing ship types could claim an exchange ratio of that magnitude.

The 18 percent loss rate of U.S. combatant submarines to all causes was higher than that of any other ship type during World War II. Personnel losses were nearly 22 percent—375 officers; 3,131 enlisted men—higher than other branches of the services. Still, as navies go, U.S. submarines gave far more than they received. Comprising only 2 percent of the forces engaged, the submarine force accounted for 55 percent of all Japanese ships sunk—more than 1,300 vessels totaling over 5 million tons.

Finding My Father —Jeanine McKenzie Allen

*T*he submarine USS Triton *(SS 201) was lost on 15 March 1943, during her sixth war patrol. Triton was depth-charged by three Japanese destroyers in the Caroline Basin, northwest of the Admiralty Islands and to the north of New Guinea. She sank in 18,000 feet of water, taking with her a crew of seventy-four. One of those lost that day was my father, Chief Torpedoman's Mate Lloyd Charles McKenzie. He was but one of the 3,620 submariners who gave their lives during World War II and, with his fallen shipmates, remains on eternal patrol in the enduring memories of those who remember and honor these gallant men. For me, the memories were difficult and confusing but eventually took me on a journey to learn more about my father and his service to our country.*

It began at an early age, with me constantly wondering what had happened to my father. I remember holding my father's hand and pulling my wagon at the home he'd bought for us in San Diego, California, and I remember playing and laughing with him. All else about his last visit seems vague. I remember well the day, seven months later, when the telegram came, and how devastated my mother was. Only my 2 1/2-year-old sister and I were with her, and I felt so helpless trying to console my mother, rocking her body back and forth, trying to get her to tell me what was wrong. I begged, until she told me that I wouldn't understand. Then my goal, still rocking her from side to side the best I could, was to tell her I would understand! When she finally told me, through her sobs, that she thought my father was dead, I remember realizing with my 3 1/2-year-old mind, that she was right in thinking that I did not understand.

Everyone began to visit and told us to keep up hope, so we did, but gradually through a series of events, the understanding came to me that he might not be coming home. The last occurred while standing at the school window one day in early 1946, thinking my dad might be the next father running up the walk with my mother for

one of the glorious reunions our class had witnessed so joyfully for months. As men trickled home, some who had been missing in action came straight to the school to see their children. I kept going to the window to sharpen my pencil, just so I could be watching when they came. One day, the teacher said, "Jeanine, turn around. Class, Jeanine's father gave his life for our country. Let's give them a hand." It was a shock that I did not want, and suddenly I felt as if ballast had been taken from me, but I did begin to accept more the possibility that he might not come home.

Through the years, it was a subject that, if mentioned at all, was hushed immediately with an "Oh." If his name was mentioned, we'd talk about him a minute or so, and we'd usually hear that he was a wonderful, kind, and fun-loving person, then the subject was changed to something "happier." I remember once asking my father's mother to tell me about my dad. She smiled, but her eyes were so full of hurt, and she remained quiet as tears rolled gently down her cheeks. My dad's sister came in and said, "Who's upset Grandma?" I felt ashamed and sorry and never asked her again. The feeling of "ownership" of my dad seemed constantly elusive, and I craved and fell silent at any chance of hearing about him.

I never cried and never felt that he had truly died, until about 1986, when fathers of friends began to pass

Above: My father is 28 years old in this photograph. This was his last trip home. He was with us for ten days not having been home for fifteen months, during which time *Triton* had sunk the most tonnage of all submarines operating out of Pearl Harbor. This was September 1942, after *Triton*'s fourth war patrol. My sister Gayle is almost two years old here. I (Jeanine), the tallest, am almost 3 years old here. I remember playing with my father and holding his hand, as I pulled my red wagon to buy grass seed for the yard of this new home he had bought for us.

away from normal causes associated with aging. It was then that I experienced a tremendous sense of loss—sadness over never really having had the chance to know him better— and more profoundly an urgency to make certain that the world knew that he had existed and that he had done something for the world. I called Arlington National Cemetery, found that nothing commemorated the submariners lost in World War II, and asked how I could go about helping to create a memorial for all.

I was surprised to be told that a memorial plaque commemorating all submariners lost in World War II could not be placed at Arlington, but that each family could request a regulation stone for the hillside of the missing, so I presented plans for one to my mother and my aunt, listing my father as a torpedoman's mate first class. My aunt said, "He was made chief before he was killed." My mother argued that he was killed first, though he was supposed to have been made chief. My aunt pulled me aside and said, "Don't put up the stone until you can prove that he was promoted to chief."

The search that ensued led to many exciting discoveries. I attended a World War II Submarine Veterans convention and could not get enough of what these wonderful men were willing to take time to tell me about submarine life! I learned that my father had been part of a group called "Spritz's Navy," who underwent rigorous and exacting training to become submariners, in Groton, Connecticut, in early 1940. Only one in ten men who applied were accepted for this training, and one-third of those were quietly "let go" before training was completed. I bought a roster and was astounded to learn that Triton's original deck logs are at the National Archives. Reading them was fascinating, and I copied every page, plus the muster rolls, war patrol reports, action reports, and all of the message traffic

that I could find. I began to learn more than I had ever thought possible, from men whose names were found in the deck logs. John Deane, the Connecticut State Commander of the Submarine Veterans of World War II, and his wife Vivian, provided a wonderful last photo of Triton's crew.

Mr. Willard Devling, a Triton crewmember, who gave up his place on that fateful sixth war patrol to another who asked the favor, remembers my dad's on-deck promotion to chief petty officer and seeing him wearing his chief's hat, on board the submarine moored in Brisbane, Australia, prior to the last patrol. Mr. Devling also told me of helping celebrate the promotion by ceremoniously throwing my father into the Brisbane River, a common practice among submariners of the day.

Captain George Whiting, my father's boss on board Triton for the first three patrols, responding to a letter I'd written, said he'd lived next to and felt very close to my dad for 2 1/2 years. He told me of my dad's ability and place in battle, saying "Mac was the first loader on the deck gun crew that sank the first enemy ship by gunfire from a U.S. submarine in World War II. I was very proud of that gun crew." Captain Whiting later honored us by speaking of my father at the Arlington ceremony.

Mr. William Turbeville and Mr. Richard George told me about Triton and my father, as well. Mr. George explained that my dad was a helpful person and a mentor of sorts to the other men. They were on board as was Mr. Devling for Triton's fifth war patrol, when she served as the radio beacon and rescue team for our bombers' first land-based attack of Japanese-held territory, Wake Island on 23 December 1942. Following this, she sank a Japanese tanker, underwent depth-charging, and celebrated Christmas! I've found that Triton's fifth patrol was the subject of a "Silent Service" episode on television in the 1950s.

These dear gentlemen not only brought my father alive for me, but listening to them, plus reading the Archives records and books about submarines in World War II, made me aware of the intensity with which these men served and the extent to which they sacrificed. It has been an astounding revelation!

These were marvelous surprises, and more have surfaced as I've followed other leads in my ongoing search. We learned of and attended the ceremonies by Submarine Veterans of World War II, September 1995, in Groton, Connecticut, to dedicate the Submarine Wall of Honor listing each submariner lost in World War II. The wall is a block from where we lived on Spicer Avenue in 1940, while my father was training to become a submariner—it was the first time we'd returned in over fifty-five years.

In essence, these and many other wonderful submariner veterans, and the research that I have been privileged to do, have given my father to me, and I feel a great sense of pride and gladness. Also appreciated very much is the involvement of our present-day submarine force in maintaining and honoring its heritage. In April 1996, the Submarine Warfare Division at the Pentagon, the Submarine Veterans of World War II, and the U.S. Naval Submarine League provided a very meaningful ceremony for the dedication of my father's memorial stone at Arlington National Cemetery, at which time a chief's shadow box was presented to our family by the U.S. Naval Submarine League. I am so amazed by and proud of our submarine force today and the service it has given through the years.

In-depth research of message traffic for the sixth patrol revealed Triton's being praised for having sunk four of a convoy of five Japanese cargo ships and damaged the fifth over a two-day period, before her own loss. Early in the patrol, Triton tells of making an emergency dive to avoid her own circular-run torpedo. According to information found in John Alden's study and book, U.S. Submarine Attacks During World War II, Triton sank a total of nineteen Japanese vessels and damaged seven, during the first fifteen months of World War II. Those sunk included enemy tankers, transports, a destroyer, and a submarine.

Finally, in 1994, we inherited letters my father wrote to his parents and sisters. In one of the last, he wrote of how he missed all of us. He told his family not to worry, with one of his last sentences being, "This war is a hard and dirty life, but when it's over, nothing will ever be too difficult again."

Opposite: Chief Torpedoman's Mate Lloyd Charles McKenzie (shown here in a torpedoman's mate's first class uniform) is the father for whom Mrs. Jeanine Allen has searched over the years. Lovingly remembered by his daughter (she was three years old when they last saw each other), he and his shipmates were lost with USS *Triton* (SS 201) during its sixth war patrol.

Above: This photograph was sent to Ms. Allen by Mrs. John Deane, wife of the former Connecticut State Commander for the Submarine Veterans, World War II. Mrs. Deane (Vivian) is the widow of Adrian Fricke, as well, who is the third man from the right, in the middle row. He left *Triton* just before her last patrol and marked with an "X" all men who remained and were lost with *Triton*. This photograph was taken at the Royal Hawaiian Hotel, Pearl Harbor, mid-October 1942, before *Triton*'s fifth war patrol. Ms. Allen writes: "My father, 6 feet 2 inches, is the tall man in the center, to the right of two officers."

Uncommon Valor

Robert A. Hamilton, *New London Day*—Military Editor

Commander Howard Gilmore is a legend in the Submarine Force because of three short words—"Take her down!" Gilmore was the commanding officer of USS *Growler* (SS 215). On 7 February 1943, while making a night surface attack on what appeared to be a small gunboat, *Growler* collided with the target ship. The Japanese vessel immediately sprayed the submarine's bridge with machine gun fire, killing the officer-of-the-deck and one lookout and wounding three other men including the captain. Commander Gilmore gave the order to clear the bridge. As

Left: The Medal of Honor is the nation's highest decoration for valor in combat. It is sometimes called the Congressional Medal of Honor because it must be authorized by Congress and is frequently presented by the President. Unlike any other American military decoration, the medal is worn as a pendant on a ribbon around the neck.

Above: Commander Howard W. Gilmore, severely wounded by Japanese machine gun fire, gives his last order, "Take her down," to the officer of the deck of USS Growler *(SS 215) as the ship submerges beneath him. By diving rapidly,* Growler *was able to escape from the Japanese attack and return to Brisbane, Australia, where the ship was restored to its full combat capability after receiving an entirely new bow. (Fred Freeman)*

Opposite: Illuminated by explosions from a sinking Japanese ammunition ship, USS Barb *(SS 220) under Commander Eugene B. Fluckey retires at record speed on the surface in uncharted, mined, rock-strewn waters only 5 fathoms deep following a daring nighttime raid into the protected harbor of Namkwan, China, on 23 January 1945. Commander Fluckey was awarded the Medal of Honor, and* Barb *received the Presidential Unit Citation for this remarkable combat achievement. Among the most decorated combat veterans in American history, Commander Fluckey also received four awards of the Navy Cross, second in precedence only to the Medal of Honor, for four other highly productive patrols as captain of* Barb. *("The Galloping Ghost of the China Coast," Ted Wilbur, U.S. Naval Institute)*

Left: Mrs. Howard W. Gilmore shakes hands with Rear Admiral Andrew C. Bennett, Commandant of the Eighth Naval District, following the posthumous award of the Medal of Honor presented to her on behalf of her late husband. He had courageously sacrificed his own life to save his ship and his shipmates during an engagement at close quarters following a collision with a Japanese naval auxiliary. Their son, Howard, Jr., and daughter, Vernon Jeanne, stand at their mother's side.

MEDAL OF HONOR CITATION FOR COMMANDER HOWARD W. GILMORE:

For distinguished gallantry and valor above and beyond the call of duty as commanding officer of the U.S.S. Growler *during her fourth war patrol in the Southwest Pacific from 10 January to 7 February 1943. Boldly striking at the enemy in spite of continuous hostile air and antisubmarine patrols, Commander Gilmore sank one Japanese freighter and damaged another by torpedo fire, successfully evading severe depth charges following each attack. In the darkness of night on 7 February, an enemy gunboat closed range and prepared to ram the* Growler. *Commander Gilmore daringly maneuvered to avoid the crash and rammed the attacker instead, ripping into her port side at 11 knots and bursting wide her plates. In the terrific fire of the sinking gunboat's heavy machineguns, Commander Gilmore calmly gave the order to clear the bridge, and refusing safety for himself, remained on deck while his men preceded him below. Struck down by the fusillade of bullets and having done his utmost against the enemy, in his final living moments, Commander Gilmore gave his last order to the officer of the deck, "Take her down." The* Growler *dived; seriously damaged but under control, she was brought safely to port by her well-trained crew inspired by the courageous fighting spirit of their dead captain.*

Above: *USS* Growler *(SS 215) alongside the submarine tender USS* Fulton *(AS 11) in Brisbane, Australia, with its bow bent sideways like a broken nose following the collision with a Japanese naval auxiliary.*

the last of his men disappeared down the hatch, he realized that he could not get there himself. He gave his last order: "Take her down!"

Gilmore received the Medal of Honor posthumously for his actions. He was the first of seven men from more than 400 who commanded submarines during the war to earn the nation's top award for valor.

Lawson P. ("Red") Ramage earned the Medal of Honor for his actions on board USS *Parche* (SS 384) in the Pacific. But he wasted no time reflecting on any personal glory it conveyed. Instead, the 35-year-old Navy commander quickly put pen to paper to convey these sentiments to his crew:

> *"The captain wishes to emphasize the fact that the Medal of Honor was accepted from the President of the United States as the nation's tribute to a fighting ship and her courageous crew. He feels that every officer and man whose loyal cooperation and*

Mrs. Gilmore transfers the Medal of Honor awarded to her late husband to their son, Howard, Jr., as his sister, Vernon Jeanne, and Rear Admiral Bennett observe.

able assistance contributed to the success of the Parche *has an equal share in this award which he holds in trust for you. With great pride and respect, sincerely, L. P. Ramage."*

Eugene Fluckey, who was awarded the Medal of Honor for his deeds while commanding USS *Barb* (SS 220), has often said that he was prouder that all of his men came home without so much as a Purple Heart. Submarine skippers forged a reputation that bordered on reckless when it came to engaging the enemy because it was necessary. The best submarine skippers, including the seven who were awarded the Medal of Honor for their actions in the Pacific, shared one trait—selflessness.

By their words and deeds, the submariners who received the nation's

MEDAL OF HONOR CITATION FOR COMMANDER LAWSON P. RAMAGE:

For conspicuous gallantry and intrepidity at the risk of his life above and beyond the call of duty as commanding officer of the U.S.S. Parche *in a predawn attack on a Japanese convoy, 31 July 1944. Boldly penetrating the screen of a heavily escorted convoy, Commander Ramage launched a perilous surface attack by delivering a crippling stern shot into a freighter and quickly following up with a series of bow and stern torpedoes to sink the leading tanker and damage the second one. Exposed by the light of bursting flares and bravely defiant of terrific shellfire passing close overhead, he struck again, sinking a transport by two forward reloads. In the mounting fury of fire from the damaged and sinking tanker, he calmly ordered his men below, remaining on the bridge to fight it out with an enemy now disorganized and confused. Swift to act as a fast transport closed in to ram, Commander Ramage daringly swung the stern of the speeding* Parche *as she crossed the bow of the onrushing ship, clearing by less than fifty feet but placing his submarine in a deadly crossfire from escorts on all sides and with the transport dead ahead. Undaunted, he sent three smashing, "down the throat" bow shots to stop the target, then scored a killing hit as a climax to forty-six minutes of violent action with the* Parche *and her valiant fighting company retiring victorious and unscathed.*

Above: *The officers and crew of USS* Barb *(SS 220) display the ship's battle flag, with the commanding officer, Commander Eugene B. Fluckey, in the center of the front row. Each item on the battle flag represents a combat achievement of the ship or of an individual. The light blue ribbon with white stars just below Commander Fluckey represents his Medal of Honor and the ship's Presidential Unit Citation is to its immediate left. The train at the bottom center is unique among submarine battle flags. Japanese shipping had almost come to a complete standstill as a result of the stranglehold by U.S. Navy submarines. With characteristic initiative and aggressive leadership, Commander Fluckey continued to find targets—including putting a team of sailors ashore on Karafuto, Japan, to blow up a train by using one of the explosive charges designed to scuttle the submarine in an emergency. This raiding party was the only U.S. force to set foot on a Japanese home island during World War II.*

Right: *Commander Eugene B. Fluckey's wife, Marjorie, attaches the ribbon clasp as he receives the Medal of Honor from Secretary of the Navy James Forrestal for his performance in command of USS* Barb *(SS 220), while Fleet Admiral Ernest J. King observes. President Roosevelt's poor health prevented him from attending the ceremony.*

top honor for valor praised the crews who brought the boats through the dreadful poundings of depth charge attacks and withstood the terror of running gun battles on the surface. These submarine skippers had to take their men into harm's way to win the war, but when necessary they gave up their own lives to protect their men. When the bullets stopped and the last torpedo was fired, they did what they could to get for their men good liberty, back pay, and the recognition they deserved.

MEDAL OF HONOR CITATION FOR COMMANDER EUGENE FLUCKEY:

For conspicuous gallantry and intrepidity in action at the risk of his life above and beyond the call of duty as command-ing officer of the U.S.S. **Barb** *during her eleventh war patrol along the east coast of China from 19 December 1944 to 15 February 1945. After sinking a large enemy ammunition ship and damaging additional tonnage during a running two-hour night battle on 8 January, Commander Fluckey, in an exceptional feat of brilliant deduction and bold tracking, on 23 January, located a concentration of more than thirty enemy ships in the lower reaches of Nankuan Chiang (Nam-kwan Harbor). Fully aware that a safe retirement would necessitate an hour's run at full speed through the uncharted, mined, and rock-obstructed waters, he bravely ordered, "Battle stations—torpedoes!" In a daring penetration of the heavy enemy screen, and riding in five fathoms of water, he launched the* **Barb's** *last forward torpedoes at 3,000-yard range. Quickly bringing the ship's stern tubes to bear, he turned loose four more torpedoes into the enemy, obtaining eight direct hits on six of the main targets to explode a large ammunition ship and cause inestimable damage by the resultant flying shells and other pyrotechnics. Clearing the treacherous area at high speed, he brought the* **Barb** *through to safety and four days later sank a large Japanese freighter to complete a record of heroic combat achievement, reflecting the highest credit upon Commander Fluckey, his gallant officers and men, and the U.S. Naval Service.*

Seven submarine commanders received the Medal of Honor—three posthumously. They came from big cities like Dallas and Washington, D.C., and little-known towns like Monroe Bridge, Massachusetts, and Henry, Illinois. All graduated from the U.S. Naval Academy at Annapolis, Maryland. Some were standouts in their class, but others were not—one man "bilged out" because of poor grades in his freshman year, though he later won reinstatement and was graduated. These Medal of Honor recipients were from 32 to 42 years of age at the time of their storied exploits, and most continued to amass other medals as well. By the time of his death in 1944, Commander Samuel David Dealey had been awarded not only the Medal of Honor but four Navy Crosses, a Silver Star Medal, the Distinguished Service Cross, and a Purple Heart. By war's end Commander George Levick Street, III, had a Navy Cross and two Silver Star Medals.

It was a force where the most esteemed decorations were almost commonplace. Officers and men on *Barb*, where Fluckey earned his Medal of Honor, brought home a combined six Navy Crosses, twenty-three Silver Star Medals, and twenty-three Bronze Star Medals.

All the Medal of Honor recipients who survived the war continued to serve their nation for many years after the war. Fluckey retired as a rear admiral in 1972. He later wrote the best-selling book *Thunder Below.* Richard O'Kane, who won his own Medal of Honor in October 1944, wrote the equally well-received *Clear the Bridge* and *Wahoo.* Ramage retired as a vice admiral after commanding the U.S. First Fleet during the first years of the Vietnam War.

So far, five of the seven have had Navy ships named after them—the guided-missile destroyer USS *Ramage* (DDG 61) and USS *O'Kane* (DDG 77) are among the Navy's front-line surface combatants today. Earlier the destroyer escorts USS *Dealey* (DE 1006) and USS *Cromwell* (DE 1014)

Barb had raised such a ruckus that the Japanese reported an entire new U.S. fleet was operating close to the homeland. Fluckey's crew designed a flag to celebrate their success and flew it from the high attack periscope without Fluckey's knowledge as they got underway from Pearl Harbor for Fluckey's last war patrol. He began to suspect something when every ship in the harbor commenced signaling good luck, but when Admiral Halsey signaled "Good Luck Barb and Fluckey—Good Hunting and Give Them Hell—Halsey." He knew that something was amiss. Noting the crew on deck and the look-outs snickering, he looked for a reason and saw the flag high above his head. After the flag came down, the harbor returned to nor-mal, but Barb's crew still thought of them-selves as a fleet and not a lone submarine, skulking around Japan.

MEDAL OF HONOR CITATION FOR COMMANDER RICHARD HETHERINGTON O'KANE:

For conspicuous gallantry and intrepidity at the risk of his life above and beyond the call of duty as commanding officer of U.S.S. Tang *operating against two enemy Japanese convoys on 23 and 24 October 1944, during her fifth and last war patrol. Boldly maneuvering on the surface into the midst of a heavily escorted convoy, Commander O'Kane stood in the fusillade of bullets and shells from all directions to launch smashing hits on three tankers, coolly swung his ship to fire at a freighter, and, in a split-second decision, shot out of the path of an onrushing transport, missing it by inches. Boxed in by blazing tankers, a freighter, transport, and several destroyers, he blasted two of the targets with his remaining torpedoes, and, with pyrotechnics bursting on all sides, cleared the area. Twenty-four hours later, he again made contact with a heavily escorted convoy steaming to support the Leyte campaign with reinforcements and supplies and with crated planes piled high on each unit. In defiance of the enemy's relentless fire, he closed the concentration of ships and in quick succession sent two torpedoes each into the first and second transport and an adjacent tanker, finding his mark with each torpedo in a series of violent explosions at less than 1,000-yard range. With ships bearing down from all sides, he charged the enemy at high speed, exploding the tanker in a burst of flame, smashing the transport dead in the water, and blasting the destroyer with a mighty roar that rocked the* Tang *from stem to stern. Expending his last two torpedoes into the remnants of a once powerful convoy before his own ship went down, Commander. O'Kane, aided by his gallant command, achieved an illustrious record of heroism in combat, enhancing the finest traditions of the U.S. Naval Service.*

President Truman presents the Medal of Honor to Commander O'Kane on the White House lawn.

Tang *returns to Pearl Harbor after her second patrol. On deck are the twenty-two aviators rescued by her from the waters around Truk in April 1944.*

served with distinction. In addition, USS *Howard W. Gilmore* (AS 16), a submarine tender, was named for Commander Gilmore.

Though they were an elite group entitled to wear that prestigious blue ribbon with the gold star, they never held themselves out as special, never had any kind of reunion, or formed any sort of association of submarine Medal of Honor winners.

"During your active duty career, the Navy tends to keep you pretty widely separated, and I went out a lot later than the others," Rear Admiral Fluckey recalls. "For whatever reason, we never had any special meeting for ourselves."

Submarines got a slow start in the hero business during World War II because of several factors, most notably that the torpedoes used in the opening months of the war were notoriously defective. Stories of torpedo problems continued until near the end of the war. O'Kane's boat, USS *Tang* (SS 306), sank nearly 94,000 tons of enemy shipping before a circular run by one of its own torpedoes struck *Tang*'s stern sending her to the bottom of the Formosa Strait. Taken prisoner with eight of his shipmates, O'Kane endured ten months of beatings and a near-starvation diet in prison camps before he was freed at war's end.

Another problem for the force was that the tactical handbook had to be discarded, and a new one written under the pressure of combat. Before the war, submarines had trained to act as scouts, or a forward guard, for the surface fleet. They were there to protect the crown jewels of the Navy—the battleships that with their mighty guns ruled the high seas. Few in the U.S. Navy considered submarines much of an offensive weapon, and their prewar tactical employment reflected that point of view.

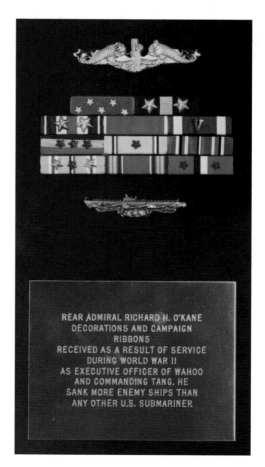

That changed on 7 December 1941, when the Japanese struck at Pearl Harbor. The battleships were smoking ruins, and the burden of protecting our interests in the Pacific fell to submarines. Old habits are tough to change, however, and for more than a year submarines were restricted to hit-and-run missions. It was not until 1943 that the Navy began to deploy submarines into heavily traveled shipping lanes.

It was a significant transition for the commanding officers as well. Before the war submariners relied on sonar that was largely ineffective to locate a target. Many commanding officers were replaced with younger, more aggressive submariners who would come to periscope depth and risk discovery—and death—to find the enemy. These younger submariners began to have an effect. Until 1943 the Japanese shipped 1.5 million barrels of oil a month through the Luzon Straits—a supply line vital to their war effort. By the end of 1944, shipments were down 80 percent.

The exploits of the Medal of Honor recipients were later depicted on television and in the movies, but celluloid can hardly capture the kind of audacity they displayed. Shallow water is anathema to submariners, because submarines on the surface are exceptionally vulnerable. Still, when Rear Admiral Fluckey spotted by radar a mass of Japanese ships

Displayed are Commander Richard O'Kane's ribbons, recognizing his prowess as one of the most successful submarine commanders of World War II.

Above: *Commander Samuel D. Dealey compiled an awesome war record. He was awarded four Navy Crosses, the Navy's highest award, and the Medal of Honor, the nations highest award. Well liked, the loss of Commander Dealey and his crew was keenly felt throughout the Submarine Force.*

Commander Gillette, USNR, Mayor of Santa Monica, California, presents the Medal of Honor to Mrs. Samuel Dealey. Mrs. Dealey had elected not to travel to Washington, D.C., to receive the award from President Truman. (Courtesy of David Dealey)

at anchor twenty-six miles inside the 20-fathom curve, he brought *Barb* in on the surface. He ran in through a black night for more than an hour, through uncharted rocks and past mines waiting to kill an unwary boat. When he finally brought *Barb* into attack position, he fired eight torpedoes into the mass of anchored ships scoring eight hits on six large targets, including an ammunition ship. Then, with two frigates pursuing on the way out, *Barb* broke the fleet submarine speed record by hitting 21.8 knots in a mad dash for deep water.

Street showed similar daring in April 1945 while in command of USS *Tirante* (SS 420) during its first war patrol. By that time submarines and aircraft had taken such a toll on enemy shipping that fewer than 30 percent of the submarines on patrols were reporting any contact with the enemy, and the captain deduced that the Japanese merchant ships must be hugging the shore and spending nights in sheltered harbors. A likely spot was the landward side of Quelpart Island off the coast of Korea, where the water was treacherously shallow, and where vigilant ship and shore radars would make it difficult to sneak in on the surface. Street brought *Tirante* to within 1,200 feet of the piers, to send an ammunition ship, frigate, and a third warship to the bottom.

He was awarded the Medal of Honor for that attack, but used the tactic effectively on other occasions as well, recalled his executive officer, retired Captain Edward L. "Ned" Beach, now a noted naval author:

> *Creeping into Nagasaki Harbor on* Tirante's *second patrol, he torpedoed several ships and burned a number of sailing craft to the waterline.*
>
> *There used to be a magnetic board at Pacific Submarine Force headquarters (SUBPAC), filled with little silhouettes of*

submarines in their operating areas, with a little Japanese flag attached to the silhouette for each confirmed kill. It was near the end of the war and there weren't a lot of targets, so most of the submarines had none or one. But Tirante *was covered with them—we had seven.*

Captain John Phillip Cromwell faced a grievous choice of action. As a Navy captain, Cromwell knew that the United States was deciphering encrypted Japanese military transmissions through its "ULTRA" codebreaking program. He was also part of the planning for Operation *Galvanic*, the planned invasion of the Gilbert Islands.

Captain Cromwell was on board USS *Sculpin* (SS 191) commanding a three-boat wolfpack attack group off Truk Island in November 1943 when *Sculpin* was depth charged to the surface by a destroyer. *Sculpin's* captain, executive officer, and gunnery officer all were killed. The lieutenant who was next in seniority gave the order to abandon the heavily damaged ship. As the chief of the boat opened valves to scuttle the ship, and others began to don life jackets, Cromwell said that he would go down with the ship rather than risk the intelligence loss the Navy might suffer if he were captured. Eleven of *Sculpin's* crew stayed with him.

"Captain Cromwell's selfless act of personal sacrifice represents what our Submarine Force is all about," Vice Admiral Charles Lockwood, the Submarine Force commander, said later. "It stands for dedication, courage, and honor in face of adversity. John Cromwell is a true American hero."

Admiral Fluckey summed up the philosophy of all his men in an article he wrote during the submarine centennial in 2000 for *Undersea*

When USS Sculpin *(SS 191) was forced to surface amid Japanese depth charges, the sub was scuttled, and its Commodore, Captain Cromwell, went down with the ship.*

Above: *Admiral Richard S. Edwards, commander of Western Sea Frontier, presents the Congressional Medal of Honor to John Philip Cromwell, Jr. The nation's highest honor to a hero was given to his father, John Cromwell, posthumously. Looking on from the left are Ann Cromwell, daughter, and Margaret Cromwell, wife of John Cromwell. (Courtesy of Henry Illinois Public Library)*

MEDAL OF HONOR CITATION FOR CAPTAIN JOHN PHILLIP CROMWELL:

For conspicuous gallantry and intrepidity at the risk of his life above and beyond the call of duty as commander of a Submarine Coordinated Attack Group with Flag in the U.S.S. Sculpin, *during the ninth war patrol of that vessel in enemy-controlled waters off Truk Island, 19 November 1943. Undertaking this patrol prior to the launching of our first large-scale offensive in the Pacific, Captain Cromwell, alone of the entire Task Group, possessed secret intelligence information of our submarine strategy and tactics, scheduled Fleet movements and specific attack plans. Constantly vigilant and precise in carrying out his secret orders, he moved his underseas flotilla inexorably forward despite savage opposition and established a line of submarines to southeastward of the main Japanese stronghold at Truk. Cool and undaunted, as the submarine, rocked and battered by Japanese depth charges, sustained terrific battle damage and sank to an excessive depth, he authorized the* Sculpin *to surface and engage the enemy in a gunfight, thereby providing an opportunity for the crew to abandon ship. Determined to sacrifice himself rather than risk capture and subsequent danger of revealing plans under Japanese torture or use of drugs, he stoically remained aboard the mortally wounded vessel as she plunged to her death. Preserving the security of his mission, at the cost of his own life, he had served his country as he had served the Navy, with deep integrity and an uncompromising devotion to duty. His great moral courage in the face of certain death adds new luster to the traditions of the U.S. Naval Service. He gallantly gave his life for his country.*

MEDAL OF HONOR CITATION FOR COMMANDER GEORGE LEVICK STREET, III:

For conspicuous gallantry and intrepidity at the risk of his life above and beyond the call of duty as commanding officer of the U.S.S. Tirante *during the first war patrol of that vessel against enemy Japanese surface forces in the harbor of Quelpart Island, off the coast of Korea, on 14 April 1945. With the crew at surface battle stations, Commander (then Lieutenant Commander) Street approached the hostile anchorage from the south within 1,200 yards of the coast to complete a reconnoitering circuit of the island. Leaving the 10-fathom curve far behind he penetrated the mined and shoal-obstructed waters of the restricted harbor despite numerous patrolling vessels and in defiance of five shore-based radar stations and menacing aircraft. Prepared to fight it out on the surface if attacked, Commander Street went into action, sending two torpedoes with deadly accuracy into a large Japanese ammunition ship and exploding the target in a mountainous and blinding glare of white flames. With the* Tirante *instantly spotted by the enemy as she stood out plainly in the flare of light, he ordered the torpedo data computer set up while retiring and fired his last two torpedoes to disintegrate in quick succession the leading frigate and a similar flanking vessel. Clearing the gutted harbor at emergency full speed ahead, he slipped undetected along the shoreline, diving deep as a pursuing patrol dropped a pattern of depth charges at the point of submergence. His illustrious record of combat achievement during the first war patrol of the* Tirante *characterizes Commander Street as a daring and skilled leader and reflects the highest credit upon himself, his valiant command, and the U.S. Naval Service.*

Above: *Commander Street is shown wearing the Medal of Honor following the presentation by President Truman.*

Right: *Commander George L. Street III brought USS* Tirante *(SS 420) back from the war zone to Washington, D.C., after the end of the war. He was awarded the Medal of Honor by President Truman for his first patrol in command of* Tirante, *and the ship received the Presidential Unit Citation for a daring surface raid into the shallow Japanese-held harbor of Quelpart Island. During the same visit to Washington, Commander Street received the Navy Cross from Secretary of the Navy James Forrestal for* Tirante's *second patrol, which included a shallow water attack near Nagasaki harbor. The photograph of* Tirante's *insignia on her superstructure was taken during the Washington visit in October 1945.*

Warfare, the official publication of the Navy's Director of Submarine Warfare. He said: "Serve your country well. Put more into life than you expect to get out of it. Drive yourself and lead others. Make others feel good about themselves—they will outperform your expectations."

Submariners outperformed everyone's expectations in World War II. Naval analysts say submarines so strangled Japanese industry that the country could no longer wage war. The seven who were singled out for special recognition epitomize what it was that made the undersea force so effective.

Above: *USS* Tirante *returns to Pearl Harbor passing sunken ships en route to the submarine base.*

Left: *Lieutenant Commander Street at* Tirante's *periscope. (Fred Freeman)*

VALOR— *Captain Harry H. Caldwell, USN (Ret)*

While a high percentage of military decorations was awarded to officers, heroism by enlisted submariners also received recognition. USS Cuttlefish *(SS 171) conducted its third war patrol in the archipelago south of Japan. Shortly after midnight on 14 August 1942, during a period of poor visibility, a Japanese destroyer loomed out of the dark, closing the range rapidly.* Cuttlefish *turned away to line up for a stern shot but was spotted by the destroyer, which turned to attack.* Cuttlefish *submerged.*

Quartermaster First Class Richard Breckenridge was positioned beneath the upper conning tower hatch, which led to the bridge. His job was to pull the hatch shut and tighten it down after the last man came down from the bridge. This time when he pulled the hatch shut, he found that the hatch wheel interlock was jammed, making it impossible to shut the hatch tightly. As water gushed in around the lip of the hatch, the conning tower started to fill and was ordered to be abandoned. All hands except Breckenridge dropped below and the lower conning tower hatch was quickly sealed to avoid flooding the control room. Breckenridge continued to struggle with the jammed handwheel until finally it broke free.

The citation that accompanied his award of the Navy Cross stated:

With the lower conning tower hatch closed and with water coming through the upper hatch, Quartermaster First Class Breckenridge cooly remained at his station and by his skill and determination succeeded in freeing the handwheel and securing the hatch before flooding of the conning tower reached the floor plates. By this act of heroism valuable instruments were saved and the submarine was able to continue on a successful patrol.

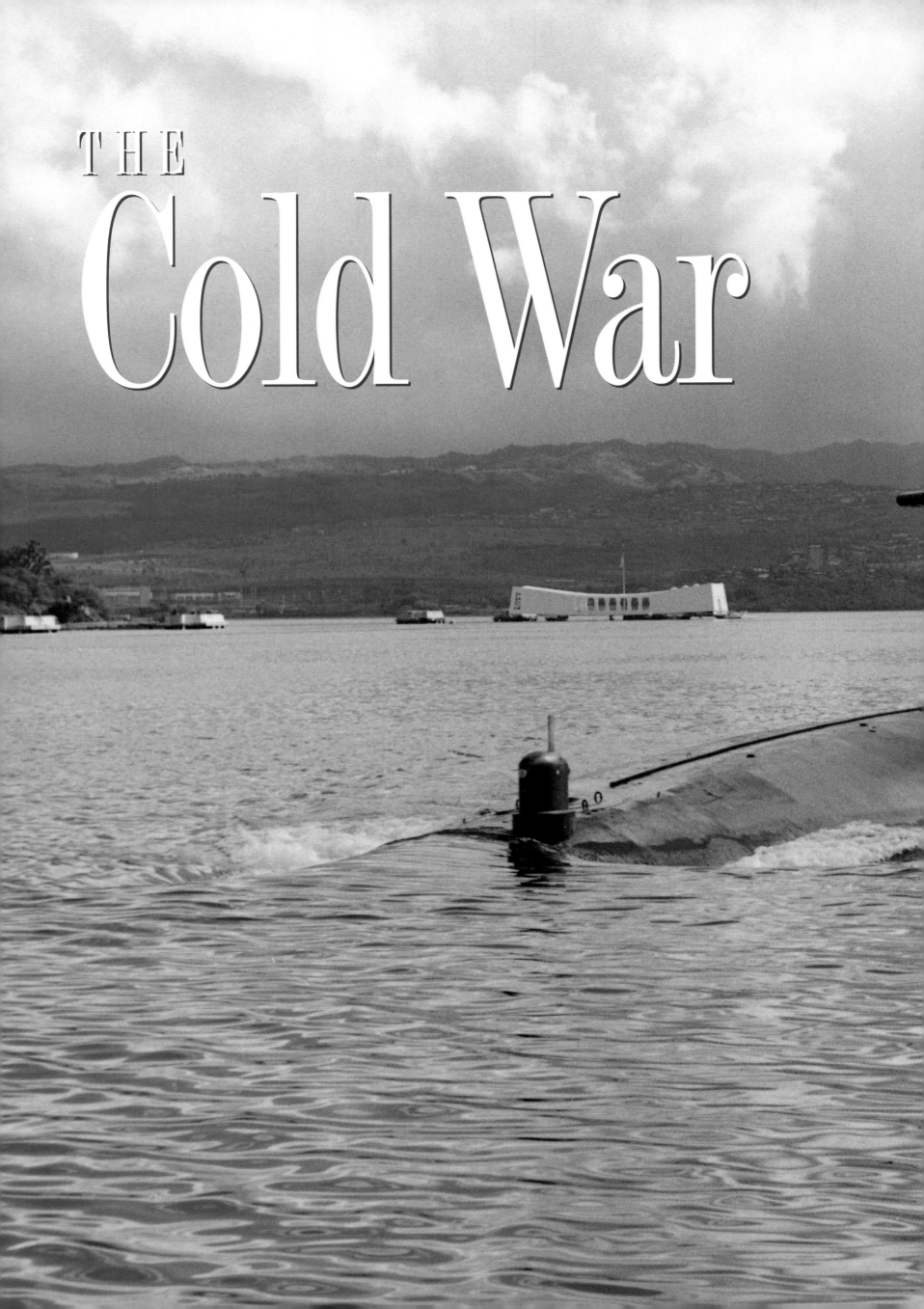

THE Cold War

POST WORLD WAR II
The Years of Innovation

Captain Raymond D. Woolrich, USN (Ret)

USS Flying Fish *(SS 229), USS* Spadefish *(SS411), USS* Tinosa *(SS 283), and USS* Bowfin *(SS 287) returning to Pearl Harbor in 1945, following raids in the Sea of Japan. USS* Bowfin *still proudly stands the watch at the USS* Bowfin *Museum and Park, adjacent to the* Arizona *Memorial visitor's center in Pearl Harbor, Hawaii.*

The war was over!!

More than ten million servicemen and women, including nearly 15,000 submariners, turned their minds and hearts back home. They counted "points" (the numeric values assigned based on length and difficulty of wartime service) to see who could return first.

Their thoughts focused on building a normal life—a life free from war—a life where the hard work and determination they used to forge victory from the ashes of destruction would mean security and prosperity for them and the families they would start—a life where the fear of death no longer accompanied them everywhere they went. No more ration cards! No more reveille!

This generation of warriors—perhaps more than any before or since, tempered in the Great Depression and plucked, sometimes voluntarily, sometimes by the draft—was called to fight a war in lands about which many had only read. They knew what they wanted when they returned. Never again would they or their children go to war. Never again would their nation be caught so woefully unprepared.

Most returned to convert wartime production lines into consumer product lines to feed the demands of a country hungry for them after years of rationing, and a world trying desperately to rebuild. Many took advantage of the GI bill to further their education. These veterans brought a gritty practical determination with them to American campuses. They knew the value of an education and had seen how powerfully technology could be applied. The foresight of President Franklin D. Roosevelt and the generosity of a nation trying to repay its returning sons and daughters, while avoiding the mistakes made following the return of the veterans from

Returning GIs crowd in to sign up for college courses following World War II. The GI bill was one of the most productive investments the United States has ever made. It enabled large numbers of servicemen and service-women to obtain a college education, adding immeasurably to the wealth of talent and ability that was, and is, the nation's true capital. (Photo: Bettmann/CORBIS)

Fleet Admiral Chester W. Nimitz (center) speaking at ceremonies in which he was relieved by Admiral Raymond Spruance (just to the right of Fleet Admiral Nimitz) as Commander-in-Chief, Pacific, on board USS Menhaden *(SS 377) on 24 Nov 1945.*

Page 150–151: *During the height of the Cold War, USS* George Washington *(SSBN 598) passes the USS* Arizona *Memorial as she departs Pearl Harbor, Hawaii.* George Washington, *lead ship of the U.S. ballistic missile submarine force, had been con-ducting deterrent patrols for more than a dozen years prior to an interfleet transfer to begin Polaris A-3 patrols in the Pacific. Submarines of the strategic submarine force remain ever vigilant.*

USS R-6 *(SS 83) served as a test platform for the first U.S. experimental snorkel in 1945. The snorkel mast and head valve can be seen on the main deck forward of the conning tower. The snorkel is an extendable pipe that enables a submarine to operate its diesel engine when submerged, by providing a conduit for air from the surface. The snorkel head valve is designed to shut automatically when under water, thus protecting the submarine from flooding if depth control is lost. The snorkel system contributes to the submarine's stealth as the head valve provides a much smaller visual and radar target than does the surfaced submarine. On the other hand, a snorkeling submarine is more readily detectable by sonar and also lacks the protection afforded by topside lookouts.*

U-3008 was one of two Type XXI submarines brought to the United States for study after World War II. Thorough testing of the latest German technology took place off Key West in the late 1940s. Lessons learned were used in the Guppy conversion program and heavily influenced the design of the new construction Tang *class.*

World War I, would pay handsome dividends in the latter half of the twentieth century. Life would be good!

However, the Soviet Union, one of America's key allies in the war against Nazi Germany, had delayed withdrawal from Eastern Europe. It imposed what Winston Churchill called during his famous 1946 speech at Westminster College, in Fulton, Missouri, an "iron curtain" around its neighbors with the steel of its powerful armed forces, and would soon challenge the West with a blockade of Berlin. With the threat from Japan gone, China disintegrated into a civil war that would eventually be won by the Communist forces of Mao Tse-tung.

In 1945 the U.S. Naval Technical Mission sent by the Navy Department to uncover German wartime secrets discovered the astonishing details of the Type XXI U-boat. It quickly became clear that had the Type XXI submarine become truly operational it would have had a major impact on the Battle of the Atlantic.

After the war, two of the Type XXI U-boats (*U-2513* and *U-3008*) were brought to the United States for study. Ominously, twelve of them were taken to the Soviet Union, where they would become the basis for the Soviet Whiskey-class diesel submarine that was mass-produced for the Soviet navy as it entered the Cold War.

While most of the nation's citizen soldiers demobilized as quickly as they could after the war ended, the cadre of Submarine Force leaders—both military and civilian that remained—was extraordinary. They were the innovators who had learned to live on the meager budgets of the depression years. Boat by boat and submarine class by submarine class they had evolved their small, gasoline-powered coastal "torpedo boats" from the ungainly fleet scouting and coastal boats of World War I into the graceful, wide-ranging, and deadly fleet submarines that carried the war so effectively to Japan's home waters after the Pacific battle line had been laid to waste in Pearl Harbor.

Drs. Maurice Ewing and J. Lamar Worzel at Woods Hole Oceanographic Institute had begun the studies that would lead to the Navy's understanding of sound propagation in the deep ocean. Their work would

Aerial view of the New London Submarine Base, circa 1950, showing World War II fleet boats laid up ("mothballed") following the war. The submarine tenders USS Apollo *and USS* Anthedon, *shown in the center, assisted in the preservation work. Buildings in the background are the Submarine School campus and enlisted barracks.*

eventually lead to the development of long-range submarine sonar systems and ultimately to the powerful underwater sound surveillance system (SOSUS). At the Naval Research Laboratory in Washington, D.C., the vision of Drs. Ross Gunn and Phillip H. Abelson, key researchers in the process necessary to produce the atomic bomb, laid the intellectual groundwork for submarine nuclear propulsion. They proposed parallel development of both the hull form and land-based reactors to test this radical concept. When responsibility for nuclear development was turned over to the Atomic Energy Commission (AEC) from the Manhattan Project, the Navy's Bureau of Ships (BUSHIPS) worked with the AEC to develop a nuclear propulsion plant. Over the objections of his staff, Vice Admiral Earle Mills, BUSHIPS director, selected an obscure but highly effective engineering duty officer, Captain Hyman Rickover, from the BUSHIPS electrical section to head the team studying nuclear power at Oak Ridge, Tennessee.

Captain Rickover forged an important alliance with the Electric Boat Company at Groton, Connecticut. In view of the paucity of contracts for new construction submarines, Electric Boat, under the enthusiastic and

USS Perch *(ASSP 313), seen here in pancake ice off the coast of Alaska in July 1950, was converted to meet a Marine Corps requirement for stealthy transport of commandos.*

The pregnant Perch. *After completing seven successful war patrols in World War II, USS* Perch *(SS 313) was converted to a troop carrier submarine transport (ASSP 313). In September 1950, she carried sixty British Royal Marine commandos through a known mined area for a daring raid on the northeast coast of Korea, west of Tanchon. Their target was a train tunnel on the main north-south supply line. The commandos fought their way back to* Perch, *who was there for them despite the entire area becoming a virtual hornets' nest of activity.* Perch *officers and crew were awarded the Submarine Combat Pin for this successful raid.*

visionary leadership of John Jay Hopkins, was trying to convert its superb record of wartime production into peacetime product lines—from bowling alley pinsetters to offset printing presses. With the purchase of Canadair in 1947, Electric Boat was on its way to becoming General Dynamics Corporation. Along the way it would build the world's first nuclear submarine and a large portion of the post-World War II submarine fleet.

Spurred on by the realization that the Soviet Union, which already possessed an enormous submarine fleet, would challenge the western democracies around the globe, U.S. Navy planners took steps to respond. Innovation was the key. A nation still staggering under the weight of wartime debt would not tolerate large budgets to build new submarines, particularly with a relatively new wartime fleet still being decommissioned.

But the threat truly *had* changed. The Soviets were projected to be building more than 300 submarines that evolved from the German Type XXI. With a submarine fleet like that they could rule the sea-lanes to Europe and cut off any support from the United States. Communism would be free to dominate the Eurasian continent at will. The Soviet Union was a land power that would not be crippled by U.S. fleet submarines as the island nation of Japan had been during World War II.

The United States had to counter the Soviet threat. We needed sonars to take advantage of the new understanding of underwater sound

Top: *USS* Pomodon *(SS 486) was a prototype Guppy conversion. Fitted with a double-sized battery (504 cells) and with her topside streamlined,* Pomodon *could accelerate to 18.2 knots submerged for a short time. Gone from topside are guns, antennas, mooring cleats, and lifelines. Note that the sail area covers only mast supports. The snorkel was added in a later conversion.*

Middle, left: *USS* Ronquil *(SS 396) is seen off Mare Island following her Guppy IIA conversion in 1953. This Guppy variant had number 2 main engine removed with the space used by auxiliary machinery (such as air conditioning plants). In addition, considerable attention was paid to the use of sound isolation techniques to reduce the submarine's radiated noise output.*

Left: *USS* Clamagore *(SS 343) in 1962 shortly after her upgrading from a Guppy II to a Guppy III. Among other improvements, this conversion added 15 badly needed feet to the boat's length, making space for more modern sonar, noise quieting improvements and equipment, as well as improved habitability.*

propagation. We needed torpedoes that could detect, outrun, and destroy submarines hiding beneath the ocean's thermal layers. We needed submarines that were quiet, fast, and deep diving to seek out the hidden Soviet submarine fleet. Given that antisubmarine warfare (ASW) had never been a mission envisioned for the U.S. Submarine Force, could it respond to this challenge?

The first practical efforts following World War II focused on modifying the existing fleet submarines into boats that could approach the performance of the Type XXI. The Guppy (for Greater Underwater Propulsion Power) modifications resulted. These conversions replaced the original pair of 126 cell batteries with four higher capacity, lightweight batteries, and streamlined the topside fittings. The deck guns were removed, and a faired superstructure (later called the "sail") enclosed the conning tower. Finally a snorkel system was added to allow the Guppies to recharge batteries submerged. In all, fifty fleet submarines were converted for service in the U.S. fleet in five versions: I, IA, II, IIA, and III. They were capable of 14 to 17 knots submerged and became the backbone of the post-World War II submarine fleet until eclipsed by the nuclear submarine early in the 1960s. It was good, but not good enough.

Meanwhile, at Portsmouth Naval Shipyard, design work began for the first submarine built from the keel up to match the Type XXI. The *Tang*

Launched in September 1955, the 49-foot X-1 *(SSX 1) experimented with a unique diesel propulsion system. It used hydrogen peroxide instead of air as an oxidant. This enabled the mini-submarine to operate her diesel engine to recharge the batteries, while fully submerged, which was a huge advantage for diesel-powered submarines. Unfortunately, in 1957, a leak of the highly unstable hydrogen peroxide onto a pipe created a violent chemical reaction and the boat "blew up." It was later refitted with a diesel electric propulsion system and used for submarine research and development.*

SUBMARINE TECHNOLOGY CHANGES— *CAPTAIN HARRY JACKSON, USN (RET)*

Just after World War II a major change in submarine technology came about with the development of USS Albacore *(AGSS 569). She was the brainchild of Rear Admiral Charles B. Momsen, USN, a brilliant submarine officer who made many distinguished contributions to the submarine service. Among these were the development of deep diving suits, tactics for employment of submarines in a wolf pack, the Momsen lung, and the McCann rescue chamber that was used to rescue the thirty-three survivors from USS* Squalus *(SS 192), which sank during builders trials in 1939. At the end of World War II, Rear Admiral Momsen was ordered to the Office of the Chief of Naval Operations as head of the newly formed submarine desk (OpNav 31). While serving as commander of a submarine squadron, he had thought hard about submarine operations after the war. He came to believe that a submarine should fly like a plane or a bird.*

Shortly after he joined OpNav, he visited the National Science Foundation, which established the Committee on Undersea Warfare. Professor K. Davidson of Stevens Institute headed this committee with members Vice Admiral E. L. Cochrane, USN (Ret), Rear Admiral P. F. Lee, USN (Ret), and Rear Admiral A. I. McKee, USN (Ret). The naval officers had been members of the Construction Corps when the Bureau of Aeronautics was formed. They had passed on to the fledgling bureau some techniques of ship design, many of which were directly applicable to the new airplanes and dirigibles that were being designed and built. When design of USS Albacore *was being considered, it was payback time. Much research was done in the wind tunnel, and more flow data was obtained by flying a quarter scale model under a blimp.*

After many debates it was decided to design a submarine with a length to diameter ratio of about 7. This gave the minimum resistance at the expected maximum submerged speed. In order to obtain this ratio, the pressure hull had to be 2 feet larger in diameter and the engines had to be the same General Motors "pancake" diesels as those in the Tang *class. Also, to obtain a match of the buoyancy and the weight it was necessary to construct the hull from a new stronger alloy known as special treated high-yield (HY) steel. This became the forerunner of HY-80, the hull material of choice for USS* Skipjack *(SSN 585) and all subsequent submarines for the next thirty-five years.*

USS *Albacore's* (AGSS 569) hull form was developed in part from blimp designs and tested in wind tunnels by David Taylor Model Basin scientists.

class was born. Although evolutionary rather than revolutionary, *Tang* was capable of operating at depths to 700 feet, speeds to 17.5 knots, and carried twenty-six torpedoes. Unfortunately, the class suffered significantly from an unreliable power plant, when a new compact "pancake" diesel engine was installed to keep its length as short as possible. But the shorter, broader hull form provided a proven concept in which to install the nuclear propulsion plants under development by BUSHIPS and the AEC.

Now the innovators began to bubble toward the surface. The revolution in nuclear power was an obvious breakthrough. But the ultimate

AGSS569

SS563 CLASS

GUPPY 1A

FLEET TYPE

dazzling success of the nuclear submarine depended on far more than the engineering marvel of its power plant. Submariners understood the implications of the experiments at Woods Hole Oceanographic Institute and the naval laboratories in underwater sound propagation. Perhaps ASW really

Above: The evolution of the post-WWII diesel submarine, from the fleet boat, to the Guppy, to the Tang *(SS 563), to the revolutionary* Albacore *(AGSS 569). (Courtesy of Harry Jackson)*

Left: USS K1 *(SSK 1) (later named* Barracuda*) was the lead ship of what was expected to be a large class of small submarines configured specifically for ASW. While K-1 carried torpedoes, its principal weapon was the BQR-4 sonar, a low frequency, long range passive set that could detect and classify snorkeling submarines at great range. Note the large sonar dome on the bow. The design suffered from low propulsion power, and after only three K-boats, was replaced by a class of SSKs converted from World War II fleet boats. By 1959 the SSK designator was dropped and all attack submarines took on ASW as a primary mission.*

Opposite, bottom: USS Tang *(SS 563) is launched at Portsmouth Naval Shipyard in Kittery, Maine, in 1951. Tang was sponsored by Ernestine O'Kane, whose husband Dick was awarded the Medal of Honor for his heroic actions in the original World War II Tang. The post-World War II Tang-class submarine was the first class of U.S. submarines designed from the keel up to take advantage of the improvements gleaned from the German Type XXI submarines acquired after World War II.*

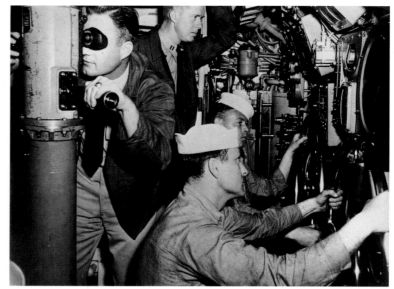

Top, left: *USS* Pickerel *(SS 524), one of four submarines laid down at the Boston Navy Yard near the end of World War II, was completed as a Guppy II in 1949. This public affairs event makes a dramatic picture.* Pickerel *was too late for World War II, but she was one of the first submarines to enter the Korean conflict. She made three patrols in Korean waters and was one of two submarines awarded the Submarine Combat Pin in that conflict.*

Top, right: *Lieutenant James L. Carter, Jr., later thirty-ninth President of the United States, has the dive on K-1 and concentrates on keeping the submarine at periscope depth.*

Below: *USS* Spinax *(SSR 489) was completed as a radar picket submarine designed to detect, track, and identify aircraft approaching a task force. In this quarter view, height-finding and search radar antennas are seen on the main deck aft. They took a terrible beating from the sea, and in later SSRs were elevated to masts just aft of the conning tower.*

could become a Submarine Force mission. Powerful sonars, carried by quiet submarines, or laid in strategic areas along the ocean bottom, could make the snorkeling diesel submarine and the noisy early nuclear submarines vulnerable to detection and attack.

U.S. engineers developed the AN/BQR-4 passive sonar from the German Gruppen Horch Geraeten (GHG) sonar, for employment on board a new class of small hunter-killer submarines, the SSK. The SSKs were intended to be mass-produced as a class of inexpensive, very quiet submarines with a powerful long-range sonar. Mass production, it was believed, would allow nearly 1,000 of them to be deployed to bottle up the rapidly growing Soviet Northern and Pacific fleets in their ports. Although the SSK's BQR-4 sonar system and quieting improvements provided much needed advances, the small boat proved no match for the northern Atlantic or Pacific oceans, and only three were produced. The small SSKs were replaced by converting wartime veterans such as USS *Bashaw*

Above: *USS* Carbonero *(SS 337) with a Loon missile on the launcher positioned for a test firing in 1949. USS* Cusk *(SS 348), configured similarly, performed the first submarine launch of a cruise missile—a Loon—in 1947. The Loon missile was soon replaced by the Regulus I missile, and by 1959 the system was deployed to the Western Pacific with four "birds" programmed to strike strategic targets in the Soviet Union. USS* Tunny *(SSG 282), USS* Barbero *(SSG 317), USS* Grayback *(SSG 574), USS* Growler *(SSG 577), and USS* Halibut *(SSGN 587) took turns keeping the watch through a total of forty-one Regulus patrols.* Polaris *submarines replaced them in 1964.*

Left: *Innovation is not without its risks. This submarine-launched Loon cruise missile (modeled after the World War II German V-1 missile) exploded on the deck of USS* Cusk *(SSG 348) as she conducted a test firing off Point Mugu, California.* Cusk *submerged to put out the fire.*

Above: *Pictured here is a modern sonar sphere fastened to what will become the forward elliptical bulkhead of the submarine. Once the thousand-plus transducers that both transmit and receive sound are installed, the bulkhead will be welded to the cylindrical hull section forming the forward pressure hull boundary. A thin unpressurized nose section will then be used to enclose the sphere and form the streamlined bow of the ship. The multitude of cables in the foreground will connect the transducers to the sophisticated sonar electronic suite.*

Left: *A Loon test cruise missile blasts off from* Carbonero *during a series of 1949 flight tests.*

(SS 241), USS *Bluegill* (SS 242), and USS *Bream* (SS 243) in the Pacific and USS *Angler* (SS 240), USS *Cavalla* (SS 244), and USS *Croaker* (SS 246) in the Atlantic into hunter-killer submarines. With the BQR-4 sonar installed, they became effective ASW units against snorkeling submarines.

But innovations were still growing out of World War II. Some worked; some did not, but all taught lessons that would continue to foster growth. The idea for a radar picket submarine to accompany battle fleets grew out of the heavy losses suffered by surface radar pickets from kamikaze attacks off Okinawa. Called Project Migraine, ten submarines were modified as, and USS *Triton* (SSRN 586) initially built as, fast carrier group escorts that would operate their air search radars to warn the carrier task force of an impending air attack, then submerge to escape detection. When all-weather carrier early-warning aircraft were developed in the late 1950s, the submarine radar picket mission was dropped.

The fleet submarine USS *Cusk* (SS 348) was modified in 1946 to launch a Loon cruise missile (a U.S.-engineered version of the German V-1 missile) on the surface. Not only did this experiment echo USS *Barb*'s (SS 220) rocket attacks on the coast of northern Japan during World War II, but it proved that submarines could launch missiles, presaging the Regulus, Harpoon, and Tomahawk cruise missile systems to follow, and, ultimately, the Polaris, Poseidon, and Trident strategic missile systems.

In 1946, Dr. Gaylord P. Harnwell from the University of California Division of War Research contacted Rear Admiral Harold Bowen at the Office of Naval Research (ONR) and suggested the formation of the Committee on Undersea Warfare (CUW). Composed of some of the greatest

Below: *Rear Admiral R. S. Benson, USN, was an aggressive, innovative, and successful submarine skipper during World War II. When it became necessary to evaluate the submarine's capability to detect, classify, and track other submarines, Admiral Benson was chosen to run the initial tests. As the first Commander, Submarine Development Group TWO, he set the tone and the agenda for submarine versus submarine strategy and tactics.*

minds in the wartime research effort, this committee was intended to retain the outstanding relationship between the research community, industry, and government that had been so successful in solving the undersea warfare problems of World War II. The recommendations of this committee would have far-reaching impact on the development of submarine propulsion systems, sonar systems, sound silencing, and hull design.

At about the same time the Chief of Naval Operations (CNO) was considering how to counter the looming Soviet submarine threat, and in January 1949 he directed the commanders of the Atlantic and Pacific Submarine Forces to establish one submarine division in each fleet to explore the feasibility and tactics of submarine-versus-submarine ASW against a Guppy-type submarine or better. As a result of this direction, Submarine Development Group TWO (SUBDEVGRU TWO) (later Submarine Development Squadron TWELVE) in New London was formed under Captain Roy Benson. Taking two SUBDEVGRU TWO submarines to Bermuda in 1949, Commodore Benson proved beyond a doubt the feasibility of submarine-versus-submarine ASW, just as had been predicted by the scientists at Woods Hole and the Naval Laboratories in New London and San Diego. From that day until today the Development Squadron has continued to play a pivotal role in the evolution of our nation's submarine warfare systems and tactics.

CUW was busy in other areas as well. In 1948 it proposed building a single screw submarine from high-tensile strength steel and with a body of revolution hull form to maximize submerged performance. The result was USS *Albacore* (AGSS 569), whose design was based on years of model testing, called Series 58, at the David Taylor Model Basin. *Albacore* was designed as a full-scale experimental vehicle, without armament, so that it would be used exclusively to test advanced hull concepts. Of particular concern were problems surrounding control of submarines at high submerged speeds that had been observed in the Type XXIs and the Guppies. As tests would show, the body of revolution hull form was much more hydrodynamically stable at high speeds than conventionally designed submarines. During her lifetime *Albacore* would be rebuilt in four major design phases,

USS Seawolf *(SSN 575), the Navy's second nuclear-powered ship, used liquid sodium instead of pure water as a reactor coolant. While this design offered more efficient heat transfer and other desirable characteristics, an inadvertent mixing of the sodium and water would create a violent reaction. For this and many other reasons, the sodium-cooled reactor design was abandoned. After operating for two years,* Seawolf's *reactor was replaced with a pressurized water system.*

Commander Richard B. Laning, USS Seawolf *(SSN 575) commanding officer, and President Eisenhower are photographed on board* Seawolf. *The President embarked in* Seawolf *for a short indoctrination cruise in September 1957.*

Left: *Rear Admiral J. R. Redman (left) accompanies Fleet Admiral Chester W. Nimitz (right) during Fleet Admiral Nimitz's first cruise on board USS* Nautilus *(SSN 571). The officer of the deck is Lieutenant Ken Carr, future COMSUBLANT.*

163

A crewmember services a Mk 48 torpedo on board the nuclear-powered attack submarine USS Oklahoma City (SSN 723).

Opposite: USS Grayback (SSG 574) on 1 July 1957, one day before launch. The two unfinished missile hangars are visible on the bow. Grayback was the first submarine to be completely designed and built by the Mare Island Naval Shipyard, and was originally designed to be the lead ship in an improved Tang-class. In January 1956, with construction over 80 percent complete, work was stopped and she was cut in two just aft of the forward torpedo room to accommodate forty feet of additional hull for Regulus I and II missile equipment. The added length also allowed the twin Regulus missile hangars to be faired into a more efficient hydrodynamic form.

proving the effectiveness of many novel ideas, including the cruciform control surface configuration and locating control surfaces forward of the propeller rather than aft of it, as called for in standard ship design practice. Three diesel-powered militarized versions of Albacore were constructed in the late 1950s and were known as the Barbel class.

By the time Albacore was commissioned in 1953, USS Nautilus (SSN 571) was well into its construction using a modified Tang hull form. The follow-on USS Seawolf (SSN 575) and Skate (SSN 578) class nuclear submarines were built along the same lines. However, when Albacore demonstrated her speed and agility, there was little question that a marriage of the two technologies would produce a submarine with unprecedented capabilities, and plans were laid down for the Skipjack class in 1956.

In 1955 the CNO again asked the CUW to study ASW, now assuming that the Soviets would soon produce an equivalent to USS Nautilus (they did so with the November-class SSN in 1958). The result was the Nobska Report, named after the estate near Woods Hole where the committee held its meetings. This report focused Navy attention on the threat posed by high-performance nuclear submarines and offered some solutions. A high-speed submarine could easily outrun existing homing torpedoes, like the Mk 37. Until a homing torpedo with a conventional warhead capable of 45 knots or better could be developed, nuclear ASW weapons like the Mk 45 Astor wire-guided torpedo and the torpedo tube launched submarine rocket (SUBROC) would need to be deployed to fill the gap. Nobska sparked a torpedo development program called RETORC

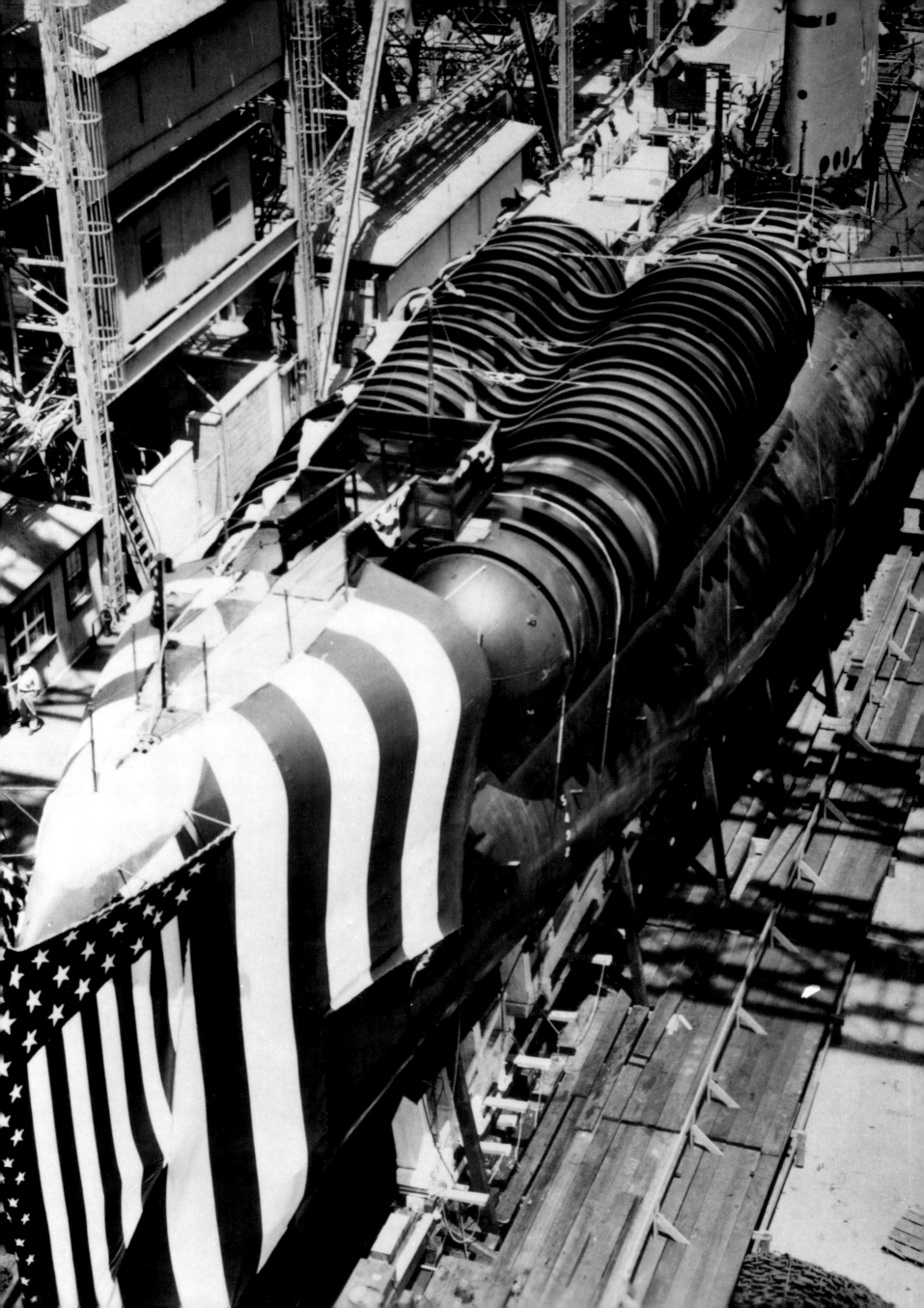

Above: *USS* Skipjack *(SSN 585) on builders trials in 1959. Skipjack was the first nuclear-powered submarine with a teardrop-shaped hull. Other features included a single propeller instead of two and the relocation of the forward diving planes to the sail instead of the bow. These features provided unprecedented high submerged speed and maneuverability. Notice, however, that when steaming on the surface the decks were normally awash, which is not considered a problem since nuclear submarines generally remain submerged except for entering and leaving port.*

Right: *In this 1986 scene by Commander Gerald Levey, a retired submariner, USS* Groton *(SSN 694) is shown getting underway from the submarine base in Groton, Connecticut. The submarine escape training tower, once a base landmark, since removed, is in the background.*

(Research Torpedo Configuration) that eventually produced the Mk 46 and Mk 48 torpedoes in the early 1970s. The Nobska Report also suggested that one way to counter the Soviet submarine threat would be to put nuclear-tipped missiles to sea on board submarines, compounding the Soviet ASW problem and forcing the Soviets themselves to concentrate on open-ocean ASW to protect their homeland, rather than offensive submarine operations.

When Arleigh Burke became CNO in 1955, he ordered parallel development of an intermediate range ballistic missile (IRBM) program alongside the more mature cruise missile program, then represented by the Regulus missile and both nuclear (like USS *Halibut* (SSGN 587)) and diesel (like USS *Grayback* (SSG 574)) submarine platforms. The Navy's Bureau of

FROM FICTION TO FACT

USS NAUTILUS
20,000 LEAGUES

Aeronautics (BUAER) and Bureau of Ordnance (BUORD) began competing over who should control the IRBM program. Admiral Burke resolved the squabble by assigning responsibility for the IRBM program to the newly created Special Projects Office, headed by Rear Admiral W. F. Raborn.

Admiral Burke had some tough decisions to make. Though the Navy wanted to build more Regulus SSGNs, he recognized that such a decision would destroy the blossoming ASW program. The decision was made to pursue the ASW program, and abandon the Regulus program in favor of the IRBM program, now called Polaris. The Special Projects Office asked Commander Harry Jackson at BUSHIPS to develop design plans for a Polaris submarine carrying sixteen missiles, and the third *Skipjack*-class SSN, USS *Scorpion* (SSN 589), which was already being built at Electric Boat Shipyard in Groton, was ordered cut in two to add a missile section. She would re-emerge in 1959 as USS *George Washington* (SSBN 598). The risks were enormous, and BUSHIPS, Special Projects Office, and Electric Boat fully appreciated them. But they also understood the tremendous potential that existed. They understood the national treasure they commanded in the post-World War II leadership of the Navy, the business and scientific communities, and the men and women who had won the war and returned home to work in the defense industry or study under the GI bill. With the trust, flexibility, and responsiveness that existed in the naval-industrial-scientific complex, nothing was impossible!

And so the stage was set. From the successes of the Submarine Force in the Pacific, the shock of the discoveries from German wartime submarines, the application of far-reaching scientific principles, the testing and stumbling inherent in new technologies and concepts, the budget battles, and the inter-service rivalries emerged a totally new Submarine Force. This Submarine Force could not only carry out the sea denial mission it executed so superbly in World War II but was also poised for dominance in the dual roles of ASW and strategic deterrence. The path was becoming clear and there was a national commitment to take it. However, even Jules Verne would have had difficulty imagining the journey from the first *Holland* to here—and what a journey it was!

This 1962 photograph shows USS Seadragon *(SSN 584) returning to its homeport in Pearl Harbor, Hawaii, having completed its voyage to rendezvous with USS* Skate *(SSN 578) at the North Pole.* Seadragon *and* Skate *conducted various scientific experiments and antisubmarine exercises in the Arctic during that expedition. In the background is the famous Hawaiian landmark, Diamond Head.*

Opposite, top: *On 16 September 1958 USS* Grayback *(SSG 574) successfully conducted the only launch of a Regulus II missile from a submarine. While it appears that the missile is launching directly over the bow, in reality it is already clear of the starboard side of* Grayback. *The Regulus II program was canceled shortly thereafter.*

167

Rickover

Admiral James D. Watkins, USN (Ret)
Captain Edward L. Beach, USN (Ret)

In attendance for the March 1974 dedication ceremony of Rickover Hall at the U.S. Naval Academy were Mrs. Rickover in her commander's uniform and then Secretary of the Navy, John Warner. Before the ceremony, Admiral Rickover personally welded his initials into a plate on a column of the hall. This can be seen over his right shoulder.

Above: *Rickover Hall opened for classes in the fall of 1976 as the principal engineering building at the U.S. Naval Academy. On 29 March 1974, Admiral Rickover came to the Academy and had lunch with the midshipmen in his four-star uniform, which was reportedly the only time he wore this uniform.*

A dmiral Hyman Rickover had the most powerful impact on the U.S. Submarine Force of any individual since John P. Holland. His nature was complex and multidimensional. Slight of physique, he was an intellectual heavyweight with a strong will who influenced every aspect of the submarine community.

In this chapter we present two quite different assessments of Admiral Rickover—both by naval officers who were closely associated with his program. Admiral James D. Watkins, U.S. Navy (Ret), a nuclear-trained submarine officer, when in the rank of commander served for two years in the Division of Naval Reactors, Bureau of Ships, Admiral Rickover's bailiwick. In 1983, when Admiral Rickover was honored by having a submarine named for him during his lifetime, Admiral Watkins, by then the Chief of Naval Operations, was the guest speaker at the launching of USS *Hyman G. Rickover* (SSN 709). This article is a slightly modified version of his remarks.

In our second article Captain Edward L. Beach, U.S. Navy (Ret) views Admiral Rickover from another perspective. Captain Beach was one of the first officers chosen by the Admiral to command a nuclear submarine. Besides his reputation as a top-flight author, Captain Beach is well remembered for taking the submerged USS *Triton* (SSRN 586) around the world, following the route of Magellan. Captain Beach's article is adapted from his foreword to the book, *Rickover and the Nuclear Navy*, by Francis Duncan, published by the Naval Institute Press.

—THE EDITORS

Above: *Bust of Admiral Rickover in Rickover Hall at the U.S. Naval Academy, Annapolis, Maryland. Some of the bronze used to make the bust was taken from USS* Nautilus *(SSN 571).*

Top, left: *Admiral James D. Watkins, Chief of Naval Operations, with Admiral and Mrs. Rickover on 27 August 1983, when Mrs. Rickover christened USS* Hyman G. Rickover *(SSN 709).*

Top, right: *USS* Hyman G. Rickover *(SSN 709) slides down the ways on 27 August 1983. Naming a ship for a living naval officer is a rare honor.*

Above: *Lieutenant Rickover served in submarines from 1929 to 1933 on board USS S-9 and USS S-48. He qualified to command submarines in 1931.*

Opposite, bottom: *USS* Nautilus *is shown in the East River, New York City, after her polar transit. Jubilant New Yorkers welcomed the* Nautilus *home with a three-day celebration. Admiral Rickover joined the tickertape parade, wearing his white uniform. The mayor provided a cavalcade of jeeps for the parade. At the start there were three sailors in each jeep, but a number of female New Yorkers joined the young sailors as they proceeded—it was a grand parade. Tickets to Broadway shows, parties, and presentations made it an event never to be forgotten.*

Admiral Rickover's Chosen Course of Excellence

Admiral James D. Watkins, USN (Ret)

To introduce this extraordinary Naval officer, I would like to share with you a story of an ancient philosopher who came to a city, determined to save its inhabitants from sin and wickedness. Night and day the philosopher walked streets and haunted marketplaces. He preached against greed and envy; against falsehood and indifference. At first people listened and smiled. Later they turned away; for he no longer amused them. Finally, a child asked, "Why do you go on? Do you not see it is hopeless?"

The man answered, "In the beginning, I thought I would change men. If I still shout, it is to prevent men from changing me."

This is a story that Admiral Rickover used to tell and used in many speeches. It is the timeless story of a visionary who perseveres, who does what he knows is right; the story of a teacher, who desires to impart his knowledge to others; a story of courage, the search for excellence, the use of every skill and God-given capability that one man possesses; it is the Admiral Rickover story.

I speak from personal experience, for I am one of his students. Military and civilian—active duty and retired—students of Admiral Rickover came from the ranks of the former Atomic Energy Commission, Naval Reactors Directorate, both houses of Congress, and from the nation's scientific and engineering communities. While their backgrounds varied, they shared one thing in common—they all became better human beings because he taught them to strive for excellence and not settle for mediocrity. They knew, because he taught them; intellectual integrity, technical honesty, sound analysis, and courageous decisions are essential ingredients in managing the development of technology.

These are the qualities often overlooked by the sensationalist or gossiper who watched the Admiral from afar—who had no direct linkage; who spoke of personal-interview folklore; who fed on and reproduced rumor ever more exaggerated with each one-sided source input. These people missed the mark. They did not begin to understand the depth of this brilliant American, his dedication to American ideals, his quest for excellence in himself and others, and his undaunted spirit.

Even biographical summaries found in the libraries of the world only tell part of the Admiral Rickover story. While properly crediting Admiral Rickover as the father of the nuclear submarine, these accounts still miss the mark. An engineer, educator, patriot, and critic, Admiral Rickover's range of interests and knowledgeable teachings have run from conservation of our natural resources to the study of ethics and morality.

Admiral Rickover has said that "one must learn to reach out, not to struggle for that which is just beyond, but to grasp at results which seem almost infinite." Reaching for the infinite—that aptly describes much of Admiral Rickover's work as a teacher. Fifty years ago, the Admiral reached for the infinite when he envisioned the warfighting potential of the nuclear submarine. Because of his perseverance, and despite many others who were doubting and narrow-in-vision, our Navy is the world's foremost source of knowledge in design, construction, and safe, efficient operation of nuclear power plants.

Some time ago I had the chance to visit USS *Nautilus*, then being readied at Mare Island Naval Shipyard for delivery to her memorial home in Groton, Connecticut. As I walked through the submarine, I was reminded of how revolutionary she was back in 1954. With *Nautilus*, we slipped the confines of having to surface frequently to recharge our batteries and refresh our air supply. We were able to stay submerged and run at high

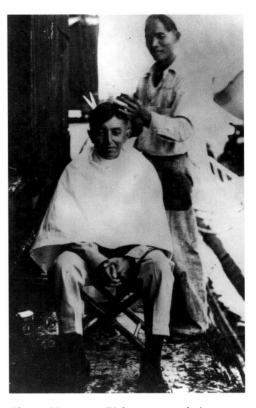

Above: *Lieutenant Rickover gets a haircut on board the USS* S-48. *Barbers are not a submarine billet, but every submarine has someone on board who volunteers to cut hair. Admiral Rickover never missed a chance to get a free haircut during a visit to a ship. He often conducted meetings while his hair was being cut—giving the barber a moving target unless the sailor was bold enough to place a hand firmly on the admiral's head to hold it steady.*

This official photograph of Rear Admiral Rickover was taken in 1955, the year Nautilus *signaled, "Underway on nuclear power." In 1972, Admiral Rickover wrote a book entitled* Eminent Americans—Namesakes of the Polaris Submarine Fleet. *He dedicated the book to his first wife with the following inscription:*
This book is a memorial to my wife, Ruth Masters Rickover, who gave me unmeasurable assistance in preparing the text. She was at once the most human and intelligent person I ever knew, the greatest influence on my life and work. To borrow from Tibullus, "Tu mihi curarum requies, tu nocte vel atra lumen, et in solis tu mihi turba locis."

The guided missile cruiser USS Port Royal *(CG 73) and the nuclear-powered submarine USS* Annapolis *(SSN 760) steam in formation with the nuclear-powered aircraft carrier USS* Nimitz *(CVN 68).* Nimitz's *battle group was deployed to the North Persian Gulf in support of Operation Southern Watch.*

speeds almost indefinitely. That marked a watershed in submarine development and the beginning of a revolution in strategy and tactics. USS *Nautilus* was the first true submarine.

This success story goes back even farther, to the 1940s, when few were enthusiastic about nuclear power and many thought it outright impossible. So it took a visionary to circumvent the ever-present naysayers and get this program going. Against all odds, Admiral Rickover proved that nuclear power could be safely used—both in shipboard propulsion and civilian power-generation applications.

Admiral Rickover knew that investments in proper design, quality control in manufacturing, and excellence in training were prerequisites for safety and success. He recognized that if you pay now for quality assurance and environmental protection, you avoid paying later in potential environmental damage, tragic loss of life, and prohibitive remedial costs. While others looked for short-cuts, Admiral Rickover insisted upon establishing his standards of performance—with checks and balances, concern and quality, and extra care that have become the hallmark of our Navy's nuclear power program.

From the very beginning, Admiral Rickover was particularly concerned about safety; it was a fundamental consideration in every facet of his program. The Admiral has testified repeatedly, "Where radiation is involved, we are dealing not just with the lives of present-day individuals, but with the genetic future of mankind." From the beginning he designed each nuclear ship with the thought that his own son would be a member of the crew.

Long before environmental impact statements were even thought of, Admiral Rickover was concerned about man's ability to properly use new technologies, hailed as advancements, and what long-range effect they might have on our environment and our children's children. The teacher also knew that the vital link in any technological advancement was the human element—could people be trained to safely operate and use what scientists and engineers produced?

Many others failed to understand what Admiral Rickover already knew—the quality of people makes the difference. An engineering system could be designed perfectly, but still it could be made to fail, if those required to operate it did not understand and respect every theoretical and practical aspect of what they were doing.

Because the Admiral understood human significance in the equation, he did not produce technocrats alone. Instead he developed the Navy's nuclear power program around a solid core of dedicated individuals who showed the same care, understanding, and quest for excellence. This philosophy led the Admiral's searching mind to question the very capability of our national education system to give him the raw material he needed to successfully operate the nuclear power program. When he saw just how weak our nation's educational standards were, he put his energy and drive toward correcting the discovered inadequacies. Not only did he build his own schools and trainers in the Navy to do what had to be done, he embarked on a one-man campaign to improve the educational system throughout the country.

Left: *Admiral Rickover is shown on board* Nautilus. *Standing silently by himself with a pleased expression on his face, the admiral must be enjoying a great sense of accomplishment. His dream had become a reality. He could feel the ship vibrate as she charged through the water using a source of power that would revolutionize naval warfare—and he was responsible for making it happen.*

Bottom, left: *Cruising deep in the Atlantic in the nuclear submarine* Skipjack, *Vice Admiral Rickover briefs Senators Anderson and Jackson on new developments in the country's naval reactors program.* Skipjack *set world underwater speed records during an overnight cruise with seven members of the Joint Congressional Committee on Atomic Energy on board.*

Bottom, right: *Admiral Rickover carried his quest for improving national education standards to the highest level. Education was one of the primary topics in this discussion with President Kennedy in February 1963.*

173

First Lady Jackie Kennedy christens USS
Lafayette *(SSBN 616). Jackie, in her famous
"pill box" hat, was at her effervescent best for
the launching of* Lafayette. *General Dynamics
President John J. Hopkins is on the right. A
large number of dignitaries from France and
Washington, D.C., joined the throng celebrating this tribute to the Marquis de Lafayette,
who came to America and served as a general
in George Washington's Continental Army.*

To quote Admiral Rickover: We need "to develop to the utmost our human resources—the minds of our young people. They will need far more highly trained minds than the ones we now get by with in order to cope with the poorer and more crowded world we are bequeathing to them." Written by the admiral over forty years ago, it still encapsulates a driving motivation in his life which may well surpass all others in intensity—the proper education and training of our young people.

Admiral Rickover also wanted each of his students to make full use of their God-given talents to do the job right. He knew that all too often the mediocre and status quo were the world's standards of performance—not the exceptional and the excellent. He acknowledged that success was only possible with hard work and heavy sweat, reminding his students that the hard-fought is the sweetest victory of all.

Individual responsibility for excellence was a central philosophy of his life. He incorporated this belief into the very organization of the Naval Reactors Directorate, which he founded. When the rest of the Navy—and government—were rushing off to reorganize and build large bureaucracies, he fenced off his own organization to ensure against obfuscation of individual responsibility and accountability. He always was fully accountable for his actions, first and foremost, to himself—the toughest judge of all.

He also championed the cause of not cheating the taxpayer out of his tax dollar, long before "fraud, waste, and abuse" became Washington buzzwords. He was concerned not only with blatant subterfuge and outright evasion of the law by industry, appointed officials, and government employees, but also with attempts to circumvent established practices of responsible behavior. He did not subscribe to the Roman maxim *caveat emptor*, let the buyer beware, but believed that everyone had a moral and technical responsibility to provide a quality product—whether it was a piece of equipment from a manufacturer or the day-to-day performance of an employee, nobody should cheat the taxpayer. His efforts in this area were recognized early by some of the military's toughest critics, like Senator William Proxmire, who called Admiral Rickover a "National Treasure" because of his tireless protection "of the taxpayer."

Admiral Rickover's visionary teachings and leadership set the tone and pace for a wide variety of vital initiatives, which improved the quality of our Navy's overall warfighting capabilities. Many of the Admiral's doctrines, first strongly opposed, are now accepted standards throughout the Navy. Why? Because they work and they're the right thing to do.

The legacy of superb performance continues today. Since *Nautilus* first put to sea in 1955, twenty-eight years ago, our nuclear-powered ships have steamed over 55 million miles and have accumulated over 2,600 reactor-years of operation. Further, in the thirty years since the *Nautilus* land prototype first operated—and with 127 nuclear submarines, 4 nuclear carriers, 9 nuclear cruisers, a total of 170 reactors in operation today (1983—*Editors*)—there has never been an accident involving a nuclear reactor, nor has there been any release of radioactivity, which has had a significant effect on our environment. To date, almost sixty thousand officers and enlisted men have been trained in this program, all striving to meet that Rickover mark of personal excellence.

USS Hyman G. Rickover *(SSN 709) ship's patch.*

The admiral often spoke about the proper utilization of our limited national resources—human, financial, and natural. It was appropriate then, as he left active duty, to name a submarine after the admiral; for his teachings of properly using our resources to the fullest were embodied in this submarine and her sisters. This was the most quiet—most "stealthy"—most sophisticated submarine of the day; this submarine was the result of applied knowledge, which produced solid, well-designed, and tested engineering systems; this submarine showed the admiral's concern for system reliability, redundancy, and simplicity, built in as standard equipment, not as options; and the crew of this submarine continues to reflect the admiral's reliance upon well-trained people who use their full potential.

USS *Hyman G. Rickover* (SSN 709) and the fine crew that took her to sea are symbolic of a much larger group of submarines that already bear that unique mark of Rickover excellence. They will be the principal determinant of victory during any protracted war at sea.

It is difficult to properly honor Admiral Rickover for what he has accomplished. This same problem confronted the admiral's headquarters staff at Naval Reactors, at the time of his retirement. They wondered, what type of recognition do you give a man whose service performance has transcended all others? How do you honor a man after sixty-four years of active duty service who already has fifteen honorary degrees? Who has won over sixty different awards, including a Presidential Medal of Freedom and a Congressional gold medal?

What you give him is a special, very personal gift that shows your respect for the man. To do that, they chose to support Eleanore Rickover's work as a member of the Board of Hospice of Northern Virginia. Eleanore was not only a Hospice board member, but also an active volunteer, caring for the terminally ill in the hospice, as well as in their own homes. The staff raised over five thousand dollars for the hospice. This loyalty, commitment, and compassion in his staff tells more about Admiral Rickover and his life's accomplishments than any other biographical footnote. This honored him and his wife better than any other type of special award or recognition.

It is an "Admiral Rickover Story" such as this, which best tells about the man and his life. This is a story about undaunted spirit, Diogenes-like intellect, an untiring man who sought excellence and took individual responsibility for each and every action. It is a story of a patriot; the story of a winner who values the proper development and education of our young people because he knows that each American can only be a full partner in citizenship if he or she has the knowledge and determination to seek such a partnership. That was the real Admiral H. G. Rickover this fine submarine represents.

It was the admiral's demanding leadership; his technical wisdom and engineering foresight; his frank and knowledgeable discussions with our nation's elected leaders; and his consuming pursuit of a strict adherence to standards of excellence that gave this nation a nuclear navy second to none. Without this man's contributions, *Nautilus'* famous "Underway on Nuclear Power" would probably still be an unfulfilled "Jules Verne vision."

Admiral Rickover had a wry sense of humor. His retort to a question at a gathering for USS Los Angeles *(SSN 688) brings a laugh from President Jimmy Carter and the gathered crowd.*

President Richard M. Nixon congratulates Rickover on his promotion to the rank of Admiral. Rickover, still wearing the gold stripes of a Vice Admiral on his sleeve, was only the second engineering duty officer to be promoted to four star rank.

This inter-office memorandum testifies to a waggish sense of fun that Admiral Rickover could display when he wanted to.

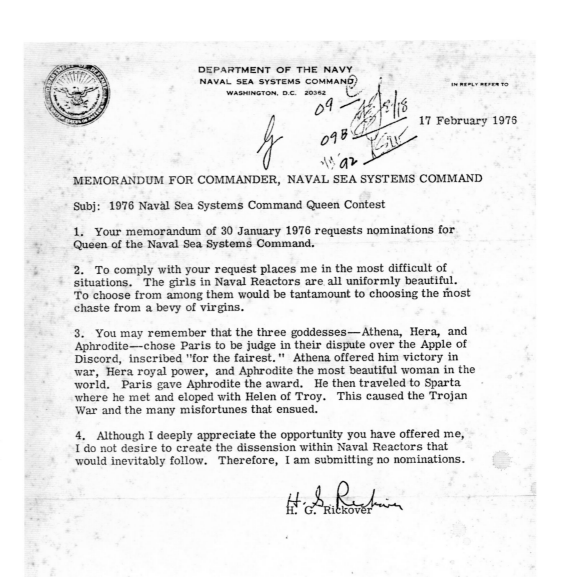

DEPARTMENT OF THE NAVY
NAVAL SEA SYSTEMS COMMAND
WASHINGTON, D.C. 20362

IN REPLY REFER TO

17 February 1976

MEMORANDUM FOR COMMANDER, NAVAL SEA SYSTEMS COMMAND

Subj: 1976 Naval Sea Systems Command Queen Contest

1. Your memorandum of 30 January 1976 requests nominations for Queen of the Naval Sea Systems Command.

2. To comply with your request places me in the most difficult of situations. The girls in Naval Reactors are all uniformly beautiful. To choose from among them would be tantamount to choosing the most chaste from a bevy of virgins.

3. You may remember that the three goddesses—Athena, Hera, and Aphrodite—chose Paris to be judge in their dispute over the Apple of Discord, inscribed "for the fairest." Athena offered him victory in war, Hera royal power, and Aphrodite the most beautiful woman in the world. Paris gave Aphrodite the award. He then traveled to Sparta where he met and eloped with Helen of Troy. This caused the Trojan War and the many misfortunes that ensued.

4. Although I deeply appreciate the opportunity you have offered me, I do not desire to create the dissension within Naval Reactors that would inevitably follow. Therefore, I am submitting no nominations.

H. G. Rickover

Midshipman Rickover's academic prowess was noted in remarks with his graduating picture in the 1922 Naval Academy yearbook. "Neither a star on the gridiron nor a terror in the pool, yet did he loom large through the chalk screens."

First Lady Mamie Eisenhower christens USS Nautilus *(SSN 571), the world's first nuclear ship. President Eisenhower's naval aide, Commander Ned Beach, and General Dynamics President, John Jay Hopkins, assist.*

Admiral Rickover and the Nuclear Navy
Captain Edward L. Beach, USN (Ret)

No one in 1918, surveying that year's entering class at the U.S. Naval Academy in Annapolis, would have picked the diminutive Hyman George Rickover as the only one in that group of aspiring youths who would achieve the rank of Admiral (four stars), remain on active duty the longest (nearly sixty-four years), and attain international fame on an unprecedented scale. All this would happen through his development of an entirely new discipline not yet thought of by man. He would never participate in combat, the Navy's ostensible mission, and yet he would be in some sort of battle all his life, accomplishing everything through a species of infighting never before seen in Navy annals.

He created, and remained in charge of, the most significant naval engineering program of all time, and yet even this tremendous advance in our Navy's capabilities was, at least initially, accomplished against opposition from the U.S. Navy and virtually all other authorities in the land as well. He gained success because his machinery worked superlatively well, with extraordinary dependability, and because Congress and the press would not accept the notion that the Navy bureaucracy, geared as it was to rotation for the sake of combat effectiveness (and its own sake as well), could maintain the engineering drive he was demonstrating.

Admiral Rickover (far right) is photographed at sea on board USS Sculpin *(SSN 590). He rode every new construction submarine on first sea trials to ensure that the nuclear power plant performed to his specifications.*

In short, the Navy was (and is) automatically opposed to the creation of any "empires" within its arena of concern, no matter how good the result. Thus, Rickover's methods were (and are still, and rightly so) an anathema to it. But Congress did not care about this. It had faith in him and his brand of leadership where his peers and superiors in the Navy did not. And his immediate subordinates, the relatively few in his inner circle, served him with a rare fanaticism. The press loved him, because his continual challenge to "the establishment" (much of it fully justified) was unfailing good copy. And he was adept at bringing forward, for the delight of the media, the numerous instances of his unfair treatment at the hands of the Navy hierarchy.

On the other hand, civilian industry felt his difficult iconoclastic personality and domineering methods more than any other segment of the nation, and here as in the Navy, with but few exceptions, he was feared and to a large degree hated by those who had to deal with him. Feared because he personally controlled huge sums of money in the shape of contracts for nuclear research, engineering, or construction, and through this he wielded tremendous power, destructively as well as constructively, upon individuals and institutions alike. Hated because his form of leadership, undeniably successful, was demeaning in the extreme to his subordinates, often forcing them to servility to help their company or themselves. To the membership of Congress, however, the real source of his power, he

showed an entirely different side of his personality. To say he was obsequious might be too strong, but he was invariably deferential in ways the Navy and industry never saw.

His peers in the Navy's engineering branch thought to get rid of him through failure of promotion above captain. This would entail automatic retirement at the thirty-year mark. But someone made the case to the U.S. Senate, charged by the Constitution with formal confirmation of military promotions. In that year, 1953, two years before *Nautilus* first went to sea, the Senate failed to give its usual perfunctory approval of the Navy's admiral promotion list, and the press was outraged because Rickover's name was not on it. The situation was at an impasse. Without Senate approval nobody could be promoted. Ultimately an enlightened Secretary of the Navy, Robert B. Anderson, ordered a special selection board to sit. With some shuffling of feet it did what it had been ordered to do, and neither Congress nor the press cared that the Navy's carefully created promotion system had been violated.

Rickover personally interviewed every officer candidate for nuclear power training, and those interviews, numbering in the thousands, are legendary for their invective, unfairness, and personal destructiveness. He was one of the most senior officers in the Navy, as much as sixty years older than some of the interviewees, who were usually midshipmen, ensigns, or junior-grade lieutenants, all of them literally quaking at the thought of the career-determining confrontation ahead.

Tales of these interviews are legion in the U.S. Navy. Some have been retold by the press, but in no other situation, except perhaps in court circles of the Middle Ages, has it been customary to condone, even to praise, such offensive performances by the autocrat in charge. In no other instance has the press of this country invariably portrayed an arrogant, overbearing superior (especially in one of the military services) as acting disinterestedly, with only the best interest of the country at heart, whereas the anxious applicant is depicted as supercilious, shallow, even arrogant. Portrayed as the admiral's means of personally ensuring selection of the

best candidates for nuclear power training, these interviews have long been known in the Navy as his method of asserting personal dominance from the beginning. That they were intended for this purpose alone is obvious from their capricious context. Seldom, if ever, was anything related to nuclear engineering discussed or even mentioned. As usual, the Navy surrendered, for there was no other choice. Only good candidates, already vetted by preliminary staff interview and benefited by a rather considerable degree of surreptitious coaching, were sent to the admiral for final interrogation. Those accepted were top caliber, as were those he rejected.

For an unprecedented thirty-six years he was czar of nuclear power in the U.S. Navy, a law unto himself, becoming more irascible and unpredictable every year. Like other tyrants, he took no account of his own gradually failing powers; his displacement, at age 82, came at the hands of a Secretary of the Navy half his age, and he died at the age of 86.

Hyman Rickover was also the creator of *Nautilus*, unquestionably the greatest engineering advance ever experienced by warships. The U.S. Navy cannot stand many men like Rickover in a single generation, but once in a great while, in a situation of transcendent importance, such a person is needed. Even Rickover's faults, great as they actually were, were useful to his objectives. No personal, financial, or extracurricular excess of any kind for him! None of the capital's social life—certainly no "wine, women, and song"—but as for his work, excess was the norm. Increasingly better machinery for nuclear energy was his one obsession, begun with the submarine but later extending to surface ships and power plants on shore. Personal dominance, power, invective, and fear were his tools, and he used them exclusively to further nuclear power. Nothing else mattered. It would be equally correct to say that he used them also in a self-serving way, but he and nuclear power were indissolubly intertwined.

It has been said somewhere that "you always have to take the whole man. You can't take only part of him. He comes as he is, with all his faults and warts." In Rickover's case, even his warts, like them or not, somehow contributed to the extraordinary success of what he accomplished.

Above: *Former President Jimmy Carter chats with the Director, Naval Nuclear Propulsion, Admiral Frank L. Bowman atop the sail of the nuclear attack submarine USS* Seawolf (SSN 21). *President Carter visited* Seawolf, *then the Navy's newest fast-attack submarine, following the Secretary of the Navy's announcement in 1998 naming the third submarine of this class in his honor.*

A Cold War Retrospective

Vice Admiral Joe Williams, Jr., USN (Ret)

Above: *USS* Bushnell *(AS 15) and four submarines are tied up at the repair base in San Diego, California, on 11 February 1946. These submarines and others became the raw material for the Submarine Force to update, modify, and improve for use at the dawn of the Cold War as no new submarines were built and commissioned until 1951.*

Opposite, top: *The first submarine of new design to be commissioned following World War II was USS K-1 (SSK 1), later renamed USS* Barracuda. *The "killer" designation was a reflection of her designed role as an antisubmarine platform, and she joined Submarine Development Group TWO to research antisubmarine issues and to develop antisubmarine tactics. Her sister ship, K-2 (later renamed Bass), pictured here, shows the enormous BQR-4 sonar array installed in the SSKs.*

J oseph Stalin, ruthless dictator of the Soviet Union, started the Cold War in 1945 when he swept the countries of eastern Europe and East Germany behind his Iron Curtain. He threatened to do the same with Greece and Turkey, announced his intent to spread his brand of communism throughout the world, and predicted war with the West by the mid-1950s. Essential to his success were:

- A blue-water Navy with which he could wrest control of the seas from the West.

- A capability to destroy our strategic bombers, which, from their bases in the U.S., could deliver nuclear bombs worldwide.

Unknown to us, the Soviets had also succeeded in building an atomic bomb and were developing intercontinental ballistic missiles (ICBMs) with which to destroy our bombers and their bases, leaving us without a retaliatory capability. Capitalizing on captured German technology and German experts, they had also embarked on a rapid modernization of about 350 diesel-electric submarines and had commenced building submarines of advanced design. Their obvious intent was to do to us what our submarines had done to the Japanese in World War II. For those who may have forgotten, our submarines, operating submerged and on the surface in Japan's home waters, sank almost all of their merchant ships and many of their warships including those of the antisubmarine warfare (ASW) forces escorting their convoys. We lost fifty-two submarines but in the end we prevailed.

As for Japanese submarines, our submarines could sink only those that were caught on the surface. We simply had no capability in those days to detect or destroy submerged submarines. You can imagine then the surprise of our Submarine Force commanders when in 1946 they were directed by the fleet commander to prepare for the conduct of ASW in the event of war with the Soviet Union. The assets the force commanders had to accomplish that mission included:

- About 100 very reliable, long-legged, diesel-electric submarines along with about 10,000 veteran submariners who had used them to defeat Japan.

Vice Admiral Joe Williams, Jr., (shown center and above) is one of those exceptional individuals who does the Navy proud. His rise from apprentice seaman to vice admiral, climbing through every rate and rank, is a tribute both to the Navy and to him. He fought World War II in the surface Navy, destroyers in the Atlantic, and amphibious forces in the Pacific. He fought the Cold War in submarines, including command of three submarines and was the Deputy Director, Special Projects Office—the organization responsible for Polaris and Poseidon weapon systems. Vice Admiral Williams finished his career with three years as Commander, Submarine Force U.S. Atlantic Fleet, and Commander, Submarine Forces NATO—thirty-seven years of service to Navy and country.—THE EDITORS

Taken from remarks given at the dedication of the Submarine Force Library and Museum's new wing on 28 April 2000 at Groton, Connecticut.

■ A professional core of naval architects and designers who had just finished designing the new *Tang*-class diesel-electric attack submarine, then building at Electric Boat and Portsmouth Naval Shipyard. These new boats were faster submerged, deeper diving, quieter, and equipped with better sonar and attack computers than our World War II leftovers—thus the beginning of submarine ASW capability.

■ The best submarine constructors in the world.

Fortunately, there also remained a group of scientists and engineers, not yet demobilized, who, working in our Navy laboratories, had invented, developed, and produced the equipment and systems used by our surface and air ASW units to win the Battle of the Atlantic against the German U-boat. In 1944 with that battle won, they had turned their attention to submarine requirements such as active sonars for mine detection, an underwater telephone, large arrays for long-range detection of noisy targets, smaller arrays for obtaining an accurate target bearing, and a small torpedo that could "home in" on the noise of a target. Many of them were persuaded to stay on and accelerate their work on submarine detection devices and better weapons. Little did they know they would still be at it thirty years later.

Immediately on receipt of this new ASW mission, Commander Submarine Force Pacific (COMSUBPAC) formed a division of four submarines in San Diego devoted to evaluation of equipment and tactics to be used in coordinated Hunter-Killer operations with surface and air ASW forces. Their supporting technical team was comprised of scientists and engineers from Scripps Institute of La Jolla, California, and the Navy Electronics Laboratory in San Diego, California.

The Atlantic Submarine Force commander's response was to form the Submarine Development Group in New London, Connecticut, and provide it with submarines dedicated to the mission of ASW. The group commander was directed to work closely with the scientists, engineers, naval architects, designers, and constructors in the development; at-sea testing; and production of new equipment, systems, concepts, and tactics. This organization would be staffed on a continuing basis with first-rate imaginative officers and men with a flair for technology and analysis.

That was the start of the team approach with the Naval Underwater Systems Center (NUSC), now Naval Undersea Warfare Center

Above: *Submarine Development Group TWO (later Submarine Development Squadron TWELVE) was established on 9 May 1949 and charged with a broad but straightforward charter: "to solve the problem of using submarines to defeat and destroy enemy submarines." This charter was later expanded to support the full range of submarine missions including arctic warfare, antisubmarine warfare, antisurface ship warfare, mine warfare, and tactical strike warfare. As the tactical development agent for the submarine force, Atlantic and Pacific, DEVGRU TWO/DEVRON TWELVE excelled under the dynamic leadership of thirty-one squadron commanders (many of whom attained flag rank) during its first half century of service to the force.*

Left: *Hunter-Killer (HUK) operational tactics and procedures were developed and tested by groups such as Task Group ALFA shown here during exercises in the Atlantic in 1959 with the Secretary of the Navy, William B. Franke, on board. Task Group ALFA included USS Valley Forge (CVS 45), seven destroyers, and two submarines. Airborne units included S2F tracker patrol planes and HSS-1 Seabat helicopters from the carrier's air group, as well as land-based P2V Neptune ASW patrol planes.*

USS Pickerel *(SS 524) illustrates the submarines that were available to conduct reconnaissance and intelligence collection in the early 1950s. Construction of* Pickerel *began in 1944; however, when World War II ended, construction was interrupted and not completed until 1949, when* Pickerel *was completed as a Guppy II submarine, then later converted to a Guppy III. "Guppy" is an acronym for Greater Underwater Propulsion Power. The modified designs of these submarines called for improved propulsion and snorkel systems. They also incorporated improved radar and sonar sensors, many of which were based on German technology or design.*

The Submarine School plays an essential role in the safe operation of submarines. Trainers and simulators are used to teach everything from maintenance to operation to casualty control. One of the first trainers installed after World War II was a ship-handling trainer used to teach docking and mooring of a submarine. Docks, slips, and mooring buoys could be rearranged to simulate specific harbors or docking areas. Pumps and fans created currents, even eddies, and winds that would be encountered at various locations around the world. The model was a scaled replica of an operational submarine and was remotely controlled to answer course and speed orders.

(NUWC) laboratories still in use today. It has produced extraordinary warfighting systems in a steady stream for over four decades. Many of those systems are on display here today. If a system on today's submarines has anything to do with warfighting, this team invented, developed, and produced it, or provided management and technical oversight of the industrial entity that did.

The team effort for submarine modernization and accelerated development of sensors and weapons, capitalizing on German technology, had by 1950 provided the Submarine Force with a modest ASW capability against a snorkeling submarine. Therefore, when the Korean War started in 1950 our submarines were ready to conduct reconnaissance and intelligence collecting patrols in Soviet operating areas. The officers and men of our Submarine Force, augmented by World War II veterans recalled to the Korean War, took their boats into Soviet home waters for a confrontation with Soviet submarines and antisubmarine forces which continued at a level of intensity unrivaled even in World War II. In that war the detection, closing, and sinking of a target was an intense and risky effort, but the average time span of the encounter was relatively short. In the Cold War the continual close observation could extend over a period of sixty days or more with maneuvering, data taking, and decision making being accomplished by watchsection personnel. This intensity of effort and concentration became a way of life. Over the years, it worsened as submarines—theirs and ours—became faster, deeper diving, quieter, and equipped with better detection equipment. Close became closer, intensity more intense, and risk riskier.

The dedicated supporting scientists and engineers, though not facing the same risks, pursued their tasks with similar intensity. They worked long hours in laboratories inventing, designing, and producing better equipment which they then took to sea on submarines for long days of testing and data gathering, cat naps on a mattress between torpedoes, and then back to the laboratories for analysis of data and resolution of problems. They worked to send their submarine teammates to sea equipped to do a better job with less risk. It was a stressful way of life with frequent absences from home that became the norm for most of the laboratory technicians.

Led by Captain H. G. Rickover, a second group of scientists and engineers, destined to become the Naval Reactors Branch of BuShips, also labored long hours, studying, conducting basic and advanced research, inventing, developing, and constructing a nuclear ship propulsion plant. Finally, in 1955, USS *Nautilus* (SSN 571), the world's first true submarine, was ready for sea. Rickover's group, always training, teaching, and working hand-in-hand with the operators, was responsible for the nuclear Navy we possess today. They and the designers and constructors of the Naval Sea Systems Command provided us with ever faster, quieter, and deeper-diving submarines. The submarines of today possess a very sophisticated warfighting capability and fantastic endurance.

In 1957, when the Soviets launched Sputnik into orbit, the existence of a Soviet ICBM that was capable of carrying a nuclear warhead was confirmed. We, the West, were behind in the race for space, and a survivable ballistic missile/nuclear weapon system capability became the nation's top priority overnight. Out of that necessity was born a team effort, the scale and complexity of which were mind-boggling; the feverish pace at which its objective would be pursued had never before been seen. The Navy's Special Projects Office, reporting directly to the Secretary of the Navy, was formed in 1955 with then Rear Admiral "Red" Raborn its director and Captain Levering Smith its technical director. Their mission was to build a survivable sea-based missile system that, with nuclear warheads, could strike Soviet targets; not to wage nuclear warfare, but to "deter" nuclear war. The team included naval architects, engineers, and operators working with industry leaders of Lockheed, General Electric, Westinghouse, Rockwell, Sperry, Litton, and others; each of whom was willing to sacrifice recognition for attainment of the goal. By 1960 over 50,000 contractors, directed and coordinated by fewer than 150 naval officers, scientists, and engineers of the Special Projects Office, had, in partnership with the Naval Reactors team, put the 5,900-ton nuclear-propelled USS *George Washington* to sea carrying sixteen Polaris A-1 missiles. Powered by a solid propellant rocket fuel they had invented, the Polaris A-1 could hurl a nuclear warhead 1,100 miles from the undetectable submerged submarine. Each missile's payload comprised more explosive power than all the bombs dropped by both sides in World War II including the nuclear bombs dropped on Nagasaki and Hiroshima. Forty submarines so equipped would follow the *George Washington* to sea by 1967—a mighty feat. Ever longer-range, more accurate missiles with heavier payloads would follow. Today we have eighteen, 18,000-ton super-quiet, invulnerable *Ohio*-class submarines each carrying twenty-four missiles which can strike targets more than 4,000 miles away. This Trident system that evolved from the Polaris system is but the latest

Top and above: *This picture (top) of Vice Admiral Hyman G. Rickover visiting the USS* Nautilus *(SSN 571) is often compared to a similar photo (above) taken of John P. Holland, designer of the first submarine commissioned in the U.S. Navy. While Holland is often credited with being the father of the U.S. Submarine Force, Admiral Rickover is similarly looked upon as the father of the U.S. nuclear Navy.*

Page 186: *From her launch in 1955, USS* Nautilus *(SSN 571) broke performance and endurance record after record and dominated essentially every naval exercise in which she took part. Probably the world's best-known submarine,* Nautilus *was hailed and welcomed wherever she went.* Nautilus *is shown on one of her several visits to New York City—this one in January 1962.* Nautilus *is currently the star attraction at the Submarine Force Library and Museum in Groton, Connecticut.*

Page 187, bottom: *To accommodate the ambitious schedule established to deploy a ballistic missile submarine, the submarine* Scorpion *under construction at the General Dynamics Electric Boat shipyard in Groton, Connecticut, was cut in two and a missile compartment added for sixteen Polaris A-1 missiles. This submarine, commissioned USS* George Washington *(SSBN 598), became the lead ship for its class, as well as the first of a fleet of forty-one ballistic missile submarines known as the "Forty-one for Freedom."*

model of a nuclear deterrent system that has ensured over the past fifty-five years that no nuclear war would occur. The name of the team has been changed to Strategic Systems Project Office, and that team and Naval Reactors are still going strong.

Two crews, the Blue and the Gold, were provided for each of the forty-one Polaris/Poseidon submarines and the eighteen Tridents to maximize the "on patrol" time for each submarine. The crews alternated every three months between functioning as operating "on-crew," or as "off-crew" in training. The operating cycle began when the submarine returned from patrol. One month of maintenance and repair was conducted at a feverish pace to meet the departure date for the next patrol with all systems operating properly.

The ensuing sixty-day undetected patrol required an intense around-the-clock effort to ensure that all vessels operating in the area were detected and avoided. In addition, were the requirements to maintain uninterrupted receipt of National Command radio communications, and constant readiness to launch their first missile within fifteen minutes of receipt of the strike message.

The crews were away from home six months of the year during which four months were spent submerged and out of contact with family.

As of October 1991, 2,427 Polaris and Poseidon patrols had been conducted over thirty-two years of the Cold War with an impressive level of reliability.

The eighteen Trident submarines, with two crews each, operate and conduct maintenance in homeports with patrols of about seventy-five days. On average, each crew spends five months submerged on patrol with seven months in homeport. Intensity remains high today.

Over the years, the Soviets worked hard and spent vast sums trying to catch up with the United States. With the help of data stolen from the United States, they built submarines with nuclear propulsion and put ballistic missiles on big submarines, but the quality was never there.

Right: *Six open missile tubes can be seen here on USS* Abraham Lincoln *(SSBN 602) (with the missile tracking ship USS* Observation Island *(EAG 154) in the background) at Patrick Air Force Base, Florida, in April 1961. As originally built, each of these tubes consisted of a large tube, over 6 feet in diameter, which by hydraulic shock absorbers supported a smaller inner tube that could be removed to accommodate the larger missile then under development.*

Above: *SSNs, such as USS* Finback *(SSN 670), are built to operate submerged. High speed on the surface results in a wet bridge.*

During any significant operation, a submarine control room is a crowded and busy place. It would not be unusual to have between fifteen and twenty people in this space, which is also crammed with equipment and occupies no more floor space than a large room in an average home. Shown here is the control room of a Sturgeon-*class submarine with both periscopes raised and manned. Having both periscopes raised at the same time is unusual and would seldom occur in a tactical situation.*

They were always vulnerable because of technology lag; the unreliability of their systems; the high noise levels of their submarines; and lack of enough educated, well-trained, men and officers.

The United States always had an accurate understanding of Soviet capabilities and shortcomings because we monitored them closely. To illustrate, in 1976, Commander Glenn Arthur had command of USS *William H. Bates* (SSN 680). He was preparing to go on patrol in the Barents Sea when we received word from one of our boats that the first of the Soviet's new Delta-class submarines, carrying missiles with a range of 4,000 miles, had gone to sea. Since Delta could hit targets in the U.S. from the Greenland Sea, we thought Delta might patrol there instead of the Atlantic. I asked Glenn to detour into the Greenland Sea on his way to the Barents to test that theory. A few weeks later on Christmas I received a message from Glenn saying, "In trail of Delta in Greenland Sea. Merry Christmas." One of the products that Glenn brought home was Delta's radiated noise profile. We had the Soviet's number and they knew it. They had to assume that one of our submarines was always watching them conduct training in their operating area and, for each Soviet submarine on

Above: *The 18,000-ton* Ohio-*class SSBNs out-fitted with twenty-four Trident missiles are more than three times larger than their George Washington-class predecessors and many times quieter. Later Ohio-class SSBNs were updated to carry the Trident D-5 missiles with significantly larger payloads and more than five times the range of the Polaris A-1s carried to sea on* George Washington's *first deterrent patrol in November 1960.*

Left: *Shown are missile tubes on USS* Ohio *(SSBN 726) configured to launch the Trident C-4 missile. Although Polaris missile tubes were large, Trident D-5 missile tubes would dwarf them by comparison. The Polaris missile tube had to accommodate a missile 32.3 feet long and 54 inches in diameter weighing 28,000 pounds. Trident D-5 tubes are required to launch a 44-foot missile that is 83 inches in diameter with a prelaunch weight of 130,000 pounds.*

The Trident D-5 missile employs an extendable aerospike on its nose to improve aerodynamic performance of the missile, which increases its range.

deployment, there was one of our submarines close by—ready to destroy their submarine if we chose to do so.

The Soviet hierarchy could not use their land-based ballistic missile force for a devastating first strike against our land-based missiles and bombers because we could destroy their country at a time of our choosing with missiles launched from our survivable ballistic missile-carrying submarines. They could not count on their blue-water attack submarines to gain control of the seas because our nuclear attack submarines, with or without the support of other ASW forces, would surely destroy them.

The coup de grace was the deployment of the Tomahawk missile on our submarines. It could, with pinpoint accuracy, destroy ships and fleet

Left: *USS* William H. Bates *(SSN 680) was a long hull (300 feet versus 292 feet for a short hull) Sturgeon-class submarine. Built at Ingalls Shipyard in Pascagoula, Mississippi, she was commissioned on 5 May 1973. It is interesting to note that* William H. Bates *was the first modern attack submarine in the U.S. Navy to be named after a person. This break in tradition occurred to honor U.S. Representative William H. Bates of Massachusetts. Representative Bates was devoted to the vital importance of U.S. seapower. He served in the Navy for ten years and as a representative from 1950 to 1969, becoming the senior Republican member of the House Armed Services Committee and the second ranking House member of the Joint Atomic Energy Committee. To the traditionalists who objected to the departure from naming submarines for fish, Admiral Rickover said, "Fish can't vote."*

Above: *Underway deep in the Pacific Ocean, sonar technicians man their watchstations at the sonar consoles on board the* Los Angeles-*class nuclear-powered attack submarine, USS* La Jolla *(SSN 701).*

Far left: *Trailing operations are grueling enough but are even more difficult against a new class of submarine about which little acoustic or tactical information is known. For such operations to be successful, each watchstander throughout the submarine must pay careful attention to his watchstation duties and take care not to make noise to give away his own ship's presence or to miss or misinterpret tactical information from the opposition submarine. Perhaps the burden is heaviest on the sonar watchstanders, one of whom is shown here trying to identify the class of ship emitting the sound detected.*

Left: *Shown here is USS* Billfish *(SSN 676) in drydock. The rounded hull and paucity of hull protuberances, with extensive sound quieting and sophisticated sonar and fire control systems, made* Billfish *and the other Sturgeon-class submarines particularly well-suited for Cold War operations.*

191

In addition to Tomahawk cruise missiles that could be carried in a torpedo room in lieu of torpedoes, some Los Angeles-class submarines were outfitted with twelve vertical launch tubes in the bow to significantly increase the firepower of these submarines. Shown here is USS Santa Fe (SSN 763) with the doors to the Mk 36 vertical launch system (VLS) tubes in the open position.

Opposite: With its multiple variants—the Tomahawk land attack missile with a conventional or nuclear warhead (TLAM and TLAM-N), or the Tomahawk antiship missile (TASM)—the Tomahawk missile has significantly increased the firepower and versatility of nuclear attack submarines.

support facilities at ranges up to 1,000 miles. Following President Reagan's announced intent to build an antimissile defense force, unable to build a credible missile defense and with their economy bankrupt, the Soviets threw in the towel.

You can see displays of the wondrous weapon systems I've referred to as you tour the museum. They are remarkable, but most remarkable are the people who produced and used them. Much honor goes to the operators who confronted the Soviets day after day for forty-plus years. There were three and one-half generations of them; often the father after a career in the force handed the task to his son who, after a career, passed it off to his son who is probably at sea today on "peace patrol."

Our operators are represented by the officers and crew of *Nautilus* paraded here before us. They "have been there"—and are here on well-deserved shore-duty. Certainly, much honor is due them, their shipmates at sea today, and those operators who have gone before them. No less honor is due to the scientists, engineers, and construction workers who have kept the operators provided with the wherewithal to get the job done. I see many of them in the audience. Just inside the museum entrance behind me is the Cold War Leadership Wall. There you will see the names of many of the operators, scientists, and engineers who led the teams during those hot years. Many of them are still at it. Maybe some of them are your unpretentious neighbors about whose exploits you have never heard.

Operation Evening Star: The Cold War Under the Sea

Rear Admiral Thomas W. Evans, USN (Ret)

In this article, Rear Admiral Thomas W. Evans, USN (Ret), recounts his experiences as commanding officer of the nuclear-powered fast attack submarine USS *Batfish* (SSN 681) in 1978 during a recently declassified operation. Then Commander Evans and his crew silently located, followed, and tracked a Soviet nuclear-powered ballistic missile submarine patrolling submerged off the East Coast of the United States for almost two months. In the process, they gathered invaluable intelligence information on Soviet missile submarine operating patterns and patrol areas, and provided continuous opportunity for early indication of any potential surprise attack on the United States.

*S*ilently patrolling deep in the cold, dark waters of the *Norwegian Sea hundreds of miles north of Iceland, the nuclear-powered attack submarine USS* Batfish *waited for a Soviet submarine to arrive. It was 17 March 1978. A Soviet nuclear-powered ballistic missile submarine was expected to emerge from Russian home waters in the frozen Barents Sea bordering the Arctic Ocean and proceed into the Atlantic Ocean to commence*

its patrol—targeting cities and military installations in the United States. The American submariners would not have long to wait. The Soviet nuclear-powered missile submarine that would be their constant, unsuspecting companion during its 9,000-mile undersea journey over the next fifty days arrived right on schedule.

Late in the afternoon, the officers and enlisted men on watch in the Batfish *command attack center heard the electrifying initial report over the intercom system from the sonar watch supervisor in the sonar room: "Conn, Sonar. Sonar Contact Bearing Zero-Five-Four. Classified Possible Soviet Submarine!" Unique sounds and machinery noise coming from the Soviet nuclear submarine had been detected on the sensitive sonar sensors in* Batfish, *on a bearing line toward the northeast. This was what they had been waiting for. Operation Evening Star was now underway.*

Batfish *was extremely quiet compared to the Soviet submarines of that era. This significant difference in*

sound silencing design, plus the accuracy and sensitivity of our passive sonar listening devices, gave us a substantial tactical advantage over our opponents. But it was the men who served in these ships that really made the difference. Just as they are today, these highly intelligent, dedicated, and industrious young men were the mainstays of the submarine force during the Cold War and were our finest assets.

Batfish *had departed her homeport of Charleston, South Carolina, on 2 March. The U.S. Atlantic Fleet Commander's orders were clear and concise:*

> **"USS Batfish (SSN 681) is directed to proceed to the Norwegian Sea . . . locate, follow, and track the next Soviet nuclear-powered missile submarine to exit Russian home waters proceeding to patrol station . . . maintain continuous contact on the submarine for its entire patrol . . . gather detailed intelligence on the Soviet crew's tactics, methods of operation and patrol areas . . . remain undetected."**

The mission details were classified Top Secret. The mission was assigned the unclassified designation "Operation Evening Star."

We got down to the business of tracking the Soviet submarine immediately after making initial contact on 17 March. Our first major task was to establish an effective trailing position well behind the Soviet submarine at a distance that would be a compromise between getting close enough to hear the noises emitted by their machinery and propeller amidst the other noises in the sea, yet

Opposite, right: Operating below periscope depth and "rigged for quiet running," a submarine such as *Batfish* with a well-trained crew was an extremely stealthy and capable platform, one which could readily operate outside the counterdetection envelope of even the best Soviet submarines operating in the late 1970s. Using information garnered from operations such as the Walker spy ring, the Soviets significantly improved the performance and tactical employment of their submarines in the 1980s. Significantly upgraded combat suites and platforms, as well as ever-evolving tactics by U.S. laboratories, industry, and the Submarine Force, however, allowed the U.S. Submarine Force to retain a considerable tactical advantage through the end of the Cold War.

Above: USS *Batfish* (SSN 681), a long-hull *Sturgeon*-class nuclear-powered attack submarine commissioned in 1972, was more than a match for the Soviet Yankee-class nuclear-powered ballistic missile submarine that *Batfish* was assigned to detect and track in the spring of 1978.

far enough away to avoid being detected. In many ways this undersea duel was very similar to a silent chess match between two highly skilled opponents.

A submarine tracking another submerged submarine cannot visually see its target. However, when our sonar sound operators could not actually hear the contact, classified as a Soviet Yankee-class submarine, on their sonar earphones, they could "see" the Yankee on the video screens of their computer-driven sonar equipment as it processed and displayed the target's unique sounds. This involved separating the target's sonar signature from the other sounds of the sea created by wind, waves, and the abundant marine life that surrounded us at all times. Fish, porpoises, whales, and "snapping shrimp" produced a shrill chorus of clicks, chirps, pops, and groans as the two submarines passed in single file through their domain.

Each submarine emits a set of sounds called a "sound signature" that is unique to that class of ship. With the passage of time while tracking a particular submarine such as the Yankee, the unique sound signature can be determined and recorded. This information is updated frequently and used repeatedly as a tactical tool. Throughout all of this, the sonar analysis team manning the sensor consoles in the sonar room observed the bearing to the target and passed the information to the tactical analysis team in the command attack center. The tactical analysis team in turn used computer and graphical plotting techniques to determine the target range and bearing drift and computed target course and speed to predict the next movements of the Yankee.

The first several days of the mission were the toughest of all. From 18 March to 20 March the weather became

Top: Although the sonar control room depicted is that on board USS *Louisville* (SSN 724), the sonar room on board USS *Batfish* was equally crowded with watchstanders and the earlier generation AN/BQQ-2 sonar suite.

Left: USS *Batfish* (SSN 681) is shown underway on the surface.

Opposite, top: The Soviet Yankee-class nuclear-powered ballistic missile submarine trailed by *Batfish* in 1978 was modeled after and closely resembled U.S. SSBNs. The Yankee-class submarine, pictured here in 1986, suffered an internal liquid missile propellant explosion and had to surface. The crew could not save the ship, and three days later she sank in 18,000 feet of water.

"our enemy." A storm building in the North Atlantic crossed over Iceland and blanketed the lower Norwegian Sea with gale force winds and heavy rain, creating severe background noise that masked the Yankee's sound signature. We were hanging on with increasing difficulty, passively tracking the target under these arduous conditions.

After a period of intermittent contact, Batfish repositioned south to the strait between Iceland and the Faeroe Islands where the weather was better. Key relocating information on the Yankee was provided by the U.S. Navy's ocean submarine surveillance system and Navy P-3 Orion antisubmarine patrol aircraft operating out of air bases in Iceland. By the evening of 21 March, we had regained solid contact and were firmly in trail of the Yankee as we both moved out into the North Atlantic.

The Yankee turned south on 25 March, and began running along the underwater shelf region 100 miles west of Ireland. We began to encounter other ships and fishing boats operating on the surface in this very busy commercial shipping corridor. Batfish operated deep to stay well below the Yankee and the surface traffic. Tracking our target through the maze of interfering contact noises penetrating the sea was an enormous challenge. The undersea bottom in this deep area is very rugged. Underwater sounds careened off the rocky masses in every direction, and we endured many anxious hours during this phase of the transit.

The Soviet crew made our lives even more exciting by periodically turning their submarine around to check their rear, a tactic known as "clearing baffles." This allowed the Soviets to listen on their sonar pointed toward the blind spot astern previously masked by their propeller noise prior to the maneuver. We had learned to expect this ploy, dubbed the "Crazy Ivan" by U.S. submariners, several times a day during the transit to their ultimate patrol area. Constant vigilance was the watchword. Although we began to discern a pattern in the timing of these excursions, we were never exactly certain when they would occur or how long they would last. At times the Yankee would reverse course and come rumbling back down the previous track. On other occasions, the Soviet watch officer would execute a complicated series of turns and spirals over a period of one or two hours, treating us to an intricate underwater ballet.

A typical Crazy Ivan maneuver would begin with the Yankee slowing down and starting a turn to the left or right. We would frequently lose all sonar contact as target aspect changed. Our response would be to slow as well and commence a slight turn to fade away from the known direction of the Yankee. As the problem unfolded, we would commence analyzing the new target course and speed, and try to predict what would happen next. Sometimes we guessed right and sometimes we did not.

On and on we went. At midnight on 28 March, the Yankee conducted a lengthy baffle clearing maneuver that kept us on edge; then he changed course to the southwest and headed for a broad area west of the Azores Islands in the central Atlantic. It was becoming apparent that the Soviet alert patrol area would probably be situated several hundred miles due east of Washington, D.C.

On 2 April, the Yankee slowed and the pattern of maneuvers became more complex. Analysis of our position revealed that the Soviet submarine was now near enough to our shores for his 1,600-mile range missiles to reach our heavily populated eastern seaboard. The critical phase of the mission was now at hand. For the next three weeks, the Soviet crew would be on constant alert to launch missiles against cities in the United States. And they would be far more vigilant than they had been in their transit to this patrol station. At this new slower speed of operation, the Yankee's radiated noise was now much less audible than during the transit, and sonar tracking by our operators became even more difficult.

Our life on board Batfish revolved completely around the Yankee's daily schedule. We organized ship operations personnel into three rotating watch teams throughout the ship. Each watch period lasted six hours, followed by twelve hours off for regular shipboard duties, equipment maintenance, training, meals, recreation such as movies and card games, and finally—sleep. On Sunday mornings, religious services were conducted by lay leaders in the crew's dining area of the operations compartment.

The busiest and most complicated evolutions of each day were the separate excursions up to periscope depth by both the Yankee and Batfish from our respective cruising depths. When the Yankee went up to periscope depth twice a day to obtain an electronic navigational position, receive radio messages, and conduct what are known as "housekeeping" chores—blowing sanitary refuse tanks overboard to sea with air and ejecting trash and garbage through a pressurized tube—we normally stayed deep and listened to the show. Frequently we heard bottles on their way to the bottom popping as the deep ocean pressure crushed them.

Following these events, the Yankee would conduct a long series of baffle clearing maneuvers. Our rotating watch teams in the attack center became very adept at predicting what would happen next. Our control room watch officers claimed that they could tell which Soviet officer was on watch on board the Yankee by the type of Crazy Ivan maneuver he selected.

Then it was our turn to go up. Once the Yankee was back at patrol depth and had settled in, we would select the optimum moment to proceed to periscope depth to get our own operations completed. Our procedure was very disciplined. We started the preparations up to an hour ahead of time. I appointed our communications officer, Lieutenant (jg) (later Rear Admiral) Kirk Donald to be the periscope depth operations coordinator. He stationed additional equipment operators who were called up to supplement the regular watch team. Telephone headsets were manned throughout the ship. Everything was coordinated to the minute, and each evolution was conducted with the utmost precision to avoid making unnecessary noise.

On 21 April, the Yankee began to stir from the slow and cautious posture that we had observed over the past three weeks. New noisy machinery operations were heard, and the overall speed of advance began to increase as we both began to move back toward the northeast. By midnight, it was clear that the Soviet crew was heading home. Our orders were to continue in trail until the Yankee was back in the Norwegian Sea and about to enter home waters. This phase of the operation was very important in order to learn which route would be used on the return leg of the journey and which security tactics would be employed in the process.

The passage of the Faeroe-Shetland gap, as the strait is called, was an ordeal. Hundreds of fishing boats dotted the area with engines

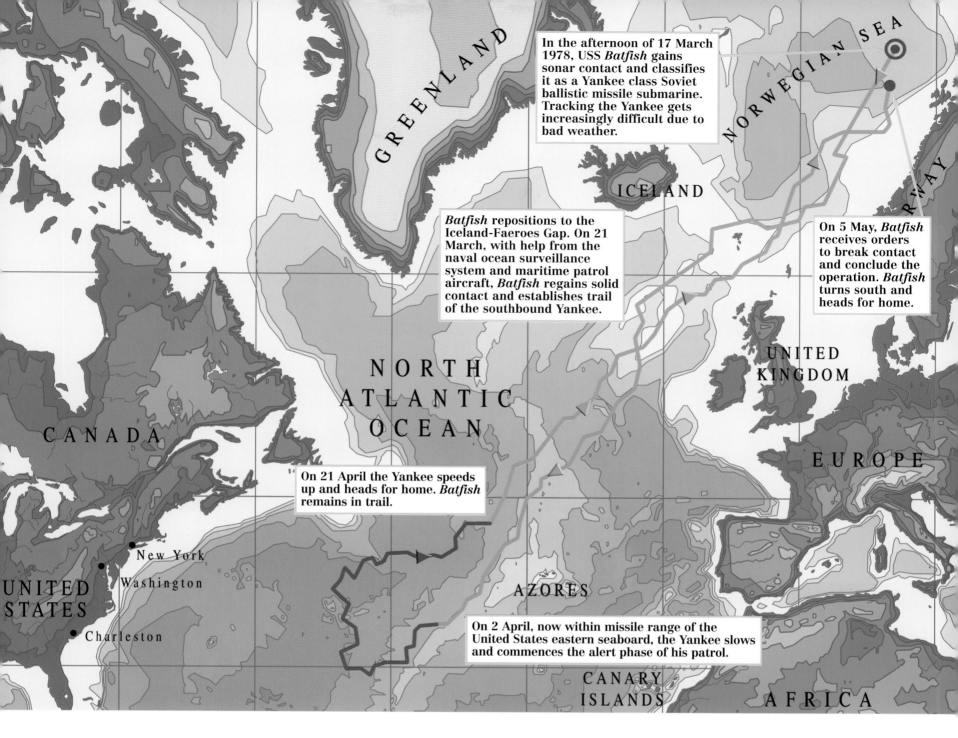

In the afternoon of 17 March 1978, USS *Batfish* gains sonar contact and classifies it as a Yankee class Soviet ballistic missile submarine. Tracking the Yankee gets increasingly difficult due to bad weather.

Batfish repositions to the Iceland-Faeroes Gap. On 21 March, with help from the naval ocean surveillance system and maritime patrol aircraft, *Batfish* regains solid contact and establishes trail of the southbound Yankee.

On 5 May, *Batfish* receives orders to break contact and conclude the operation. *Batfish* turns south and heads for home.

On 21 April the Yankee speeds up and heads for home. *Batfish* remains in trail.

On 2 April, now within missile range of the United States eastern seaboard, the Yankee slows and commences the alert phase of his patrol.

GREENLAND

NORWEGIAN SEA

ICELAND

NORWAY

UNITED KINGDOM

NORTH ATLANTIC OCEAN

CANADA

EUROPE

New York

Washington

UNITED STATES

Charleston

AZORES

CANARY ISLANDS

AFRICA

rumbling and trawls scraping the bottom. All the while, schools of sea creatures squealed, whistled, and snapped in raucous protest to these rude intrusions. To make matters worse, several survey ships were in the area, setting off explosive charges every few minutes as they probed the earth's crust beneath the sea in the relentless search for new petroleum reserves. These blasts sounded like depth charges, blanked the sonar screens, and deafened the unlucky sonar operator who failed to anticipate the next boom and did not remove his headphones. It would take over half an hour before his ears stopped ringing, and he could resume his watchstation. Tracking the Yankee through this chaos was a testimonial to the skill and determination of the sonar division.

On 5 May off the coast of Norway, Batfish received a message from the Atlantic Fleet Commander in Norfolk to break contact with the Yankee and conclude the operation. We bade a silent farewell to the Soviet submarine and her crew and turned south for home. The crew was exhilarated but relieved that Operation Evening Star was over. We had successfully accomplished everything that had been demanded of us.

Opposite, top: Land-based antisubmarine patrol aircraft such as this P-3 Orion, which dropped sonar buoys to detect and relay acoustic information for analysis and tracking purposes, frequently worked hand-in-glove with submarines to establish and maintain track on Soviet submarines during the Cold War. This photograph of a P-3 aircraft with one propeller feathered was taken through a submarine periscope. As many as 20,000 buoys have been dropped over a sixty-day coordinated P-3/SSN trail of a Soviet submarine.

Opposite, bottom left: Training, meals, movies, card games, study, and even religious services often take place in the same place—the crew's dinette, which is the only space large enough to accommodate many crewmen. The photograph shows an awards presentation on board USS *Pasadena* (SSN 752).

Opposite, bottom right: Commanding USS *Batfish* was Commander (later Rear Admiral) Thomas W. Evans. President Carter awarded the Navy Distinguished Service Medal to Commander Evans for his exceptional performance and leadership during Operation Evening Star, and *Batfish* received the Navy Unit Commendation for a hard job well done.

Above: The track of the Yankee-class Soviet nuclear-powered ballistic missile submarine trailed by USS *Batfish* (SSN 681) is pictured above. *Batfish* detected *Yankee* in the Norwegian Sea, shadowed him to his patrol area several hundred miles east of Washington, D.C., monitored his patrol routine, and gave him a silent escort out of the Atlantic.

Submarine Confrontation

Captain James C. Hay, USN (Ret)

T here are three main points about the Cold War, which together set it apart from all the other conflicts the world has known. At its very core, the Cold War was a nuclear confrontation with Armageddon-like potential. It concluded without any direct combat between the two major competitors. It lasted forty years, during which massive technological change occurred. It also was very much a "Submarine War."

Submarines had the unique ability to provide adversarial proximity while avoiding public provocation from the beginning of the Cold War and continued to do so for the duration. The former was required by the nuclear nature of the conflict. It was absolutely necessary to maintain contact for observation of developments and familiarity with capabilities during a period in which miscalculation carried grave risks. The latter was vital to reduce the odds of direct combat, and thus any escalation leading to nuclear war. The third element of Cold War character was the length of the confrontation coupled with the breadth of technological advancement. The great leaps of capability during this time arguably affected submarines more than any other force type. Just as convincingly, the step changes in undersea warfare put submarines into place as one of the Cold War's deciding factors.

The national strategy of the United States during the Cold War was two-pronged. It called for containment of Soviet expansion and deterrence of Soviet aggression. The supporting naval strategy, therefore, was a classic application of sea control. The strategy against which the U.S. Navy had to be competing was one of Soviet sea denial.

At the beginning of the Cold War, the Soviets had hundreds of diesel-electric submarines, more than all the North Atlantic Treaty Organization (NATO) navies combined, and they maintained a numerical superiority for the entire duration. The advent and introduction of nuclear-powered attack submarines, first by the Americans then by the Soviets, heightened the emphasis on antisubmarine warfare (ASW) by the United States. As the Soviet navy became more of a blue water force, both in sea experience and ship construction, the problem expanded from one of monitoring and being able to control the "chokepoints" to meet deployments from Soviet home waters, to considering engagements in the mid-Atlantic, Pacific, and Mediterranean. Concurrent with the growing sophistication of the tactical naval picture, and the emerging importance of the SSN as the leading instrument of *sea control*, the submarine launched ballistic missile (SLBM) brought a new dimension to naval warfare and to submarine strategy.

Deterrence was the central strategic military theme for the NATO allies during the Cold War. That meant that they had to have a credible capability to either stop aggression by the Warsaw Pact or to punish that aggression by destroying vital national resources within the Pact nations' homelands. For this plan to be an effective deterrent, the Soviet leadership had to be convinced that they could not win, and any attempt to do so would cost them dearly.

With the advent of the longer range Trident missiles carried on Ohio-*class SSBNs, the need for overseas basing of SSBNs was obviated, resulting in only one West Coast (Bangor, Washington) and one East Coast (Kings Bay, Georgia) ballistic missile submarine base. Shown here are docking activities at the magnetic silencing facility at the Bangor submarine base, which is used for degaussing the submarine.*

One of the primary ASW platforms throughout much of the Cold War was the Sturgeon-*class nuclear submarine. USS* Pogy *(SSN 647) is shown alongside the November Pier at the submarine base in San Diego, California. These submarines not only conducted reconnaissance and intelligence-gathering operations against the Soviet Union but also detected Soviet SSBNs and conducted long-duration tracking operations against them.*

Although the SLBM and SSBN (fleet ballistic missile submarine) combination became the primary element of the U.S. structure of strategic deterrence, it was not the only submarine contribution to the strategic force side of the Cold War. Each side had to prepare for a campaign by the opposition's attack submarines against one's own ballistic missile submarines. Strategic ASW is much different than other operations against strategic nuclear forces. For instance, if either the Soviet Union or the United States had wished to knock out the other's land-based, intercontinental ballistic missiles (ICBMs), they would have to use their own ICBMs in a preemptive nuclear strike. If either had wanted to knock out the other's submarine missile force, they could have used their attack submarines to find the enemy's strategic submarines and sink them with conventional torpedoes. In such a strategic war submarine interchange, the winner will be the nation with the hardest-to-find strategic submarines. If that same nation also has the attack submarines capable of finding and neutralizing the enemy's strategic submarines, the enemy will be deterred from starting a war in which the final step is predetermined.

Each side in the Cold War had a strong force of ballistic missile firing nuclear-powered submarines. The U.S. provided for the survivability of its SSBN forces by deploying them over vast ocean areas—making significant detections by an enemy extremely difficult. The Soviets went to a bastion defense. In that strategy, their SSBNs deployed to waters close to home, which could be defended by main fleet and air forces.

That opposition of two very different visions of submarine strategies created a fortunate opportunity for the West. By concentrating their strategic (SSBN) and tactical (SSN) submarines in their bastions, the Soviets ceded the fight against U.S. SSBNs and also focused the effort of Western attack submarines against the Soviet SSBNs.

In this final analysis, it was the competence of Western attack submarines that spelled the end of the competition. With each submarine-vs-submarine engagement—a one-on-one, may-the-best-man-win confrontation—the excellence of boat, equipment, and crew was decisive, rather than mass of forces.

As the most survivable leg of the strategic triad (air-based, land-based, and sea-based assets), nuclear-powered ballistic missile firing submarines were one of the mainstays of United States ballistic missile deterrent forces throughout much of the Cold War. In this photograph, President Kennedy shows his excitement following his look through the periscope of USS Thomas A. Edison *(SSBN 610) on 14 April 1962.*

The Los Angeles-*class submarines were originally designed as high-speed escorts for high-value units such as carriers. In this photograph from May 1977, President Jimmy Carter cruises atop the sail of USS* Los Angeles *(SSN 688) while conversing with the ship's commanding officer, Commander John E. Christensen, USN.*

The Polaris base in Holy Loch, Scotland. Because of the short range of the early ballistic missiles and the desire to maximize missile alert coverage of the Soviet Union, Polaris submarines were supported by forward-based submarine tenders in Holy Loch, Scotland; Rota, Spain; and the island of Guam in the Pacific.

The Commanders

Commander David Randall Hinkle, USN (Ret)

The Submarine Force may be small in numbers, but this elite force has produced six Chiefs of Naval Operations (CNOs), a Chairman of the Joint Chiefs of Staff, and a President. James Earl "Jimmy" Carter, Jr., graduated from the United States Naval Academy in 1946. He later did graduate work in nuclear physics at Union College. During his naval career, he served as a submariner in both the Atlantic and Pacific fleets and advanced to the rank of lieutenant, working under Admiral Hyman Rickover in the development of the nuclear submarine program. He later became the thirty-ninth President of the United States. In celebrating the submarine centennial, he spoke eloquently of the "silent service" and its distinguished service, sacrifice, and success in both war and peace.

"The year 2000 marked the 100th anniversary of the U.S. Naval Submarine Force. Those 100 years were filled with a proud history of remarkable technological development and extraordinary service to our country by the members of our Submarine Force and the industrial base that supported them.

Many of us are well aware of the incredible self-sacrifice and success of our Submarine Force during World War II. As a former Commander in Chief of our armed forces and a former submariner myself, I can assure you that our Submarine Force distinguished itself in times of relative peace as well. Undergoing long deployments around the world, around the clock, surrounded by danger and separated from family and friends, our submariners have been and continue to be a national asset of which we can all be proud.

Thank you to all those submariners, and especially their families, who, along with the staffs, industrial engineers, scientists, and managers all contributed to making our Submarine Force the most formidable defender of freedom in the world. Thank you, and God bless."

PRESIDENT JAMES EARL CARTER, JR.

Left: Ensign Jimmy and Rosalynn Carter on their wedding day 7 July 1946. (Courtesy of Carter Library)

ADMIRAL WILLIAM J. CROWE, JR.

Left: Admiral William J. Crowe, Jr., commanded the submarine *Trout* and went on to become eleventh Chairman of the Joint Chiefs of Staff, the nation's senior military officer and the principal military advisor to the President from 1985 to 1989. He also served as the Chairman of the President's Foreign Intelligence Advisory Board (1993 to 1994) and was the U.S. Ambassador to the United Kingdom of Great Britain and Northern Ireland (1994 to 1997). During an illustrious military career he gained a reputation as a political military specialist, served as commander of riverine forces in Vietnam, commanded NATO Forces Southern Europe, and was Commander-in-Chief, Pacific.

Admiral William J. Crowe, Jr., USN, served as the Chairman of the Joint Chiefs of Staff, the nations highest ranking military officer, responsible to the President for our national defense from 1985 to 1989. He played an important personal role in defusing the tensions between the Soviet Union and the United States—helping to bring the Cold War to an end.

The submarine service came of age in World War II and produced two great leaders. The first, Fleet Admiral Ernest J. King, took over as CNO shortly after the devastating attack on Pearl Harbor by the Imperial Japanese Navy. He served in that capacity throughout the war. The CNO is the principal naval advisor to the President and is responsible for all naval operations. Although Admiral King never qualified in submarines, he attended submarine school; commanded Submarine Flotilla, Atlantic Fleet, Submarine Divisions 3 and 11; the Submarine Base at New London; and was the commander in charge of the rescue and salvage of two sunken submarines, USS S-51 in 1925 and USS S-4 in 1927. His

Right: Fleet Admiral Chester W. Nimitz, USN, CNO 1945 to 1947. "We, who survived World War II and were privileged to rejoin our loved ones at home, salute those gallant officers and men of our submarines who lost their lives in that long struggle. We shall never forget that it was our submariners that held the lines against the enemy while our fleets replaced losses and repaired wounds." (McClelland Barclay)

intimate familiarity with submarines and their capabilities made him a strong supporter of the submarine war in the Pacific.

Fleet Admiral Nimitz was a more traditional submariner. He made his first dive in the Navy's first submarine, Holland, *as a midshipman. He served as skipper of* Plunger (A-1), Snapper (C-5), Narwhal (D-1), *and* Skipjack (E-1). *He commanded Submarine Division 14 in Pearl Harbor and the Atlantic Submarine Flotilla.*

FLEET ADMIRAL CHESTER W. NIMITZ

ADMIRAL LOUIS E. DENFELD **ADMIRAL JAMES D. WATKINS**

In December 1941, he was designated Commander in Chief, Pacific Fleet, hoisting his flag in the submarine Grayling *amid the devastation that was Pearl Harbor. He used the submarine force to stem the Japanese tide until the Fleet could be rebuilt and take the offensive, and then to starve the Japanese home islands.*

Fleet Admiral Nimitz signed for the United States in the formal surrender ceremony on board the battleship Missouri *in Tokyo Bay. Later that year he relieved Fleet Admiral King as CNO. He was relieved in 1947 by another qualified submariner, Admiral Louis E. Denfeld. Admiral Denfeld's term as CNO was cut short by his support of the "Admirals' Revolt." He was retired in 1949 for protesting the Air Force's insistence that strategic bombing was their private domain.*

Submariners again rose to prominence during the Cold War. Admiral James D. Watkins was appointed CNO in 1982. He was relieved by Admiral Carlisle A. H. Trost in 1986. Admiral Kelso relieved Trost in 1990 and served until 1994. Thus, submariners held the top Navy job for a period of twelve consecutive

years and played a major role in ending the Cold War. Unlike their predecessors who served in submarines early in their careers and then turned to other branches of the Navy, the Cold War CNOs served long distinguished careers in submarine billets prior to fleet commands and selection as the senior naval military advisor to the President of the United States.

In addition to the six CNOs, the top job in the Navy, a number of other submariners were Cold War leaders. Admiral Henry "Hank" Chiles, Jr., was the first naval

Top, left: Admiral Louis E. Denfeld, CNO 1947 to 1949. "The entire Navy … is gravely concerned whether it will have modern weapons, in quality and quantity, to do the job expected of the Navy at the outbreak of a future war. We have real misgivings over the reductions that are taking place in the Navy today." Statement by Admiral Denfeld before the House Armed Services Committee (October 1949). (Alicia Rhett)

Top, right: Admiral James D. Watkins commanded USS *Snook* (SSN 592) from 1964 to 1966 and became the twenty-second CNO, from 1982 to 1986. While at the head of the Navy, he took a leading role in articulating the morality of the military profession and placing the issue of nuclear deterrence within that context. He also authored the first unclassified version of the U.S. Maritime Strategy, in which he made clear that the Soviet seaborne strategic deterrent force was at risk. His leadership in making that effort both credible and perceptible to the Soviet Union served as an effective deterrent during the last decade of the Cold War. Another strategic effort, which is little known, was his introduction into the national security process and subsequent effective advocacy of the Strategic Defense Initiatives.

ADMIRAL CARLISLE A. H. TROST

ADMIRAL FRANK B. KELSO II

ADMIRAL HENRY G. CHILES, JR.

officer named Commander in Chief of the U.S. Strategic Command. As such he was responsible for all the U.S. strategic forces, submarines (FBM), land-based intercontinental missiles (ICBMs), and strategic long-range bombers (former SAC). Admiral William Arthur Owens served as Vice-Chairman, Joint Chiefs of Staff—the number two position in the U.S. armed forces. Admiral Harold E. Shear served as Vice Chief of Naval Operations (VCNO)—the number two position in the Navy. He retired and was appointed the U.S. Maritime Administrator responsible for all U.S. flag merchant shipping. Admiral Bernard "Chick" A. Clarey also served as VCNO and was a Commander in Chief, U.S. Pacific Fleet (CINCPACFLT).

Admiral John Sidney "Jack" McCain, Jr., the son of an aviator admiral and the father of the Senator from Arizona, John S. McCain, III, was CINCPAC during the Vietnam War. CINCPAC commands all U.S. forces (Air Force, Army, and Navy) in the Pacific theater. The command includes the Indian Ocean and extends from the West Coast of the United States to the east coast of Africa, covering over 50 percent of the earth's surface. Admiral McCain had the added burden of prosecuting an unpopular war while his son, a naval aviator who was shot down while on an air

mission over North Vietnam, suffered in a cruel prisoner of war camp. Admiral Robert L. J. Long also served as CINCPAC and as VCNO.

These are only a few of the many submariners who held positions of great national responsibility and authority during the past century.

Above, left to right:

Admiral Carlisle A. H. Trost commanded the Blue Crew of USS *Sam Rayburn* (SSBN 635). He became the twenty-third CNO and served from 1986 to 1990. While in that position, he stressed the relationship between naval personnel and the senior leadership of the Navy. He worked to improve the Navy's relations with U.S. allies and also with the Soviets. A critical achievement in quality of life for Navy personnel was his stabilization of deployment schedules. He was particularly effective in taking the lead in the various arms control issues of the day. He continued the strong work in naval strategy he had shown both as a senior OPNAV staff officer and as a fleet commander, and directed the U.S. Navy's efforts effectively as the Cold War ended.

Admiral Frank B. Kelso II commanded both USS *Finback* (SSN 670) and USS *Bluefish* (SSN 675). He served as the twenty-fourth Chief of Naval Operations from June 1990 until May 1994. A brilliant administrator, his reorganization of the central staff of the Navy was aimed at sharpening the focus of decision-making at a higher level. In the complex security environment of the immediate post-Cold War period, he emphasized the Navy's role in projecting power *from the sea* to influence conflict on the land. During that same time, he managed, without disruption of naval personnel, the overall drastic drawdown in naval forces.

Admiral Henry G. Chiles, Jr. was the first naval officer named Commander in Chief of the U.S. Strategic Command. As such, he was responsible for the entire U.S. strategic triad, which included the Navy's sea-based fleet ballistic missile (FBM) submarines and the Air Force's land-based intercontinental ballistic missile (ICBM) system, as well as strategic air long-range bomber aircraft. Admiral Chiles was also the chairman of the Submarine Centennial Committee and organized a year-long celebration of the first century of the Submarine Force.

Submarines
in Strategic Deterrence

Captain Richard T. Wright, USN (Ret)

After the end of the Cold War, General Colin Powell, Chairman of the Joint Chiefs of Staff, said that "no one has done more to prevent conflict—no one has made a greater sacrifice for peace—than you, America's proud missile submarine family. You stand tall among our heroes of the Cold War." General Powell's statement came almost forty years after the conception of the fleet ballistic missile (FBM) submarine and almost fifty years after the initial concept of placing nuclear-tipped cruise missiles on diesel-electric submarines. Both concepts involved targeting those nuclear missiles at land-based enemy targets in a deterrent role.

Libraries of books have been written about strategic deterrence in the nuclear age. Simply stated, the purpose of strategic deterrence is to prevent a potential enemy, such as our prime adversary during the Cold War, the Soviet Union, from calculating that by striking first with nuclear weapons it could achieve its strategic objectives. Strategic deterrence serves to convince a potential enemy that should it strike first; it would be powerless to prevent a devastating nuclear response against everything it holds dear. To achieve such a goal, the deterrent must above all be credible to the enemy. Several qualities are indispensable to that credibility. First and foremost is survivability. The enemy must be convinced that it cannot possibly eliminate the deterrent before, during, or after a first strike. Second, the deterrent must be perceived as reliable. Third, the deterrent must be perceived as effective. Finally, the deterrent should be seen as responsive, and the enemy must be convinced that its adversary has the political will to use it.

The most obvious advantage of the submarine in the strategic deterrent role is its stealth. Remaining undetected, the submarine is inherently survivable. Nuclear power makes submarines more mobile than ever, adds greatly to their stealth and endurance, and thereby significantly enhances their survivability. Another advantage of the nuclear submarine is that the entire weapon system can be tested in the real-world environment, and its

Above and below: On 18 February 1947, USS Cusk *(SS 348) launched an LTV-N-2 Loon missile. The Loon, based on the German V-1 missile that wrought terror on the British Isles in the latter part of World War II, was fired from a rail launcher mounted topside, so* Cusk *initially had to remain on the surface until the missile was fired. Subsequently, a missile container (see below) that could hold one Loon with the wings detached was added to the deck so the submarine could submerge on its transit to the launch point. Over the six-year life of the program,* Cusk *and her sister ship, USS* Carbonero *(SS 337), conducted many Loon firings in exercises that confirmed the value of submarine stealth in missile operations and led to great advances in sea-borne missile guidance capability. (Photo: Dzikowski Collection)*

Opposite: Trident submarine USS Alaska *(SSBN 732) picks her way toward the fog-shrouded Golden Gate.* Alaska *is one of eighteen U.S. behemoths that roam the sea in the further-ance of their mission to deter aggression against the United States and its allies.*

The nuclear-powered guided missile submarine USS Halibut (SSGN 587) sends a Regulus I missile skyward. The sleek, jet-powered missile packed a nuclear warhead. Five submarines—two World War II retrofits (Tunny and Barbero), and two new-construction diesels (Grayback and Growler), and finally the nuclear-powered Halibut—comprised the Submarine Force's initial strategic deterrent force.

USS Grayback (SSG 574) enters port with a Regulus I missile in launch position. Originally designed to be an improved Tang-class SS, she was cut in two during construction to insert a 40-foot section just aft of the forward torpedo room for Regulus missiles. She carried four Regulus I or two Regulus II missiles. From September 1959, when Grayback deployed on her first strategic deterrent patrol, until July 1964, when USS Halibut (SSGN 587) returned from her last patrol, the five Regulus submarines conducted forty-one strategic deterrent patrols.

reliability, effectiveness, and responsiveness can be demonstrated to friend and foe alike. Because its credibility has been demonstrated over many years, the U.S. Fleet Ballistic Missile Force became the most important leg of our strategic TRIAD, a three-pronged strategic force comprised of land-based missiles, long-range bombers, and FBM submarines.

The FBM submarine was not the first submarine missile program. Earlier submarine missile programs began shortly after the end of World War II. During that war, German scientists developed the deadly V-1 and V-2 missiles that bombarded British cities throughout the last years of the war. The V-1 was an air-breathing cruise missile, essentially an unmanned jet aircraft, with a range of about 150 miles. The V-2, a rocket-propelled ballistic missile, had a longer range and higher speed. Fortunately, the Germans never developed a nuclear weapon with which to arm their missiles.

After World War II, scientists knowledgeable of German missile and rocket technology were brought to the United States. The combination of nuclear warhead and long-range missile was recognized as a revolutionary advance in firepower. Many platforms including submarines were considered for these new weapons. The diesel submarine was considered a good candidate because of its stealth. What evolved was the submarine-based Loon missile program, which started in March 1946 with the 150-mile V-1 as its prototype. The first launch of a submarine cruise missile was a Loon from USS Cusk (SS 348) in February 1947. Later that year, the Navy missile program began a transition to Regulus. The first submarine flight test of the Regulus I missile was from USS Tunny (SSG 282) in July 1953, and in 1956 the first submarine deployment with Regulus occurred. Two diesel submarines were retrofitted to carry two Regulus missiles each—USS *Tunny* and USS *Barbero* (SSG 317). Two additional diesel submarines were built to carry four of these missiles, USS *Grayback* (SSG 574) and USS *Growler* (SSG 577). Finally, a nuclear submarine, USS *Halibut* (SSGN 587), was built to carry five Regulus I missiles. Because Regulus missiles needed to be guided to their distant targets by an external controller, additional submarines were configured as Regulus control ships.

Beginning in October 1959, while the Polaris missile was being developed and tested, the five SSG/SSGNs carrying Regulus missiles conducted regular deterrent patrols in the Pacific and were integrated into the national strategic targeting system. Regulus deterrent patrols continued until late 1964. After forty-one successful patrols, the submarine Regulus program was terminated in favor of the Polaris FBM submarines that started patrolling in the Pacific in 1964. Polaris represented a substantial quantitative and qualitative advance in submarine strategic deterrence.

The concept of marrying a nuclear-armed ballistic missile that required no external control to the nuclear submarine had emerged sometime in the early 1950s. This early concept evolved into the development of the Polaris FBM. In 1955 the Navy's ballistic missile program commenced as part of the Joint Army-Navy Jupiter Program. The Special Projects Office, which now operates as the Strategic Systems Project Office (SSPO), was established in November of 1955 to support the program. In December 1956, the Navy under Admiral Arleigh Burke, the Chief of Naval Operations (CNO), received approval to initiate its own Polaris FBM Program and terminate its involvement in the joint liquid-fuel Jupiter Missile Program. Polaris was to be a smaller solid-fuel missile that could be adapted to submarine use, replacing the larger Jupiter. Because the Polaris program competed directly with other submarine and Navy programs for an essentially fixed pot of money, the program did not initially enjoy overwhelming Navy or submarine support, particularly in the Pentagon. Fortunately, a few visionaries such as Admiral Burke and Rear Admiral William F. "Red" Raborn, the director

Above: *An FBM submarine on patrol. Strategic deterrence must be credible to the enemy. In order to be credible, the deterrent force must be survivable. The inherent stealth of a submarine when it submerges and the unknown whereabouts of the nuclear-powered submarine provided by its unlimited submerged endurance make the FBM the most credible deterrent in America's strategic arsenal.*

Above and below: *USS* Theodore Roosevelt *(SSBN 600) (above), a George Washington-class SSBN, is shown leaving Mare Island on sea trials. The temporary device on her bow is for the trials. The urgency of getting the Polaris force operational did not permit waiting for a "keel-up" design, so designers took the plan of the* Skipjack *class, cut it aft of the sail, and inserted a missile section. Compared to later SSBNs (like USS* Benjamin Franklin *(SSBN 640), below) in which the missile section is faired into an integrated design, the five ships of the* George Washington *class look distinctly unstreamlined.*

USS Daniel Webster *(SSBN 626) is shown in a floating drydock in Holy Loch, Scotland. The relatively short ranges of the first Polaris missiles made forward-basing necessary. These bases in Holy Loch; Rota, Spain; and Guam had floating drydocks and fleet ballistic missile (FBM) tenders rather than an all-permanent support infrastructure. (Photo: Yogi Kaufman)*

Vice Admiral "Red" Raborn, the director of the Special Projects Office, and Commander Jim Osborn, the first skipper of USS George Washington *(SSBN 598), get a pat on the back from the Chief of Naval Operations, Admiral Arleigh Burke. You can tell from the smiles that everyone is quite happy about the success of the Polaris missile program.*

of Special Projects Office, an aviator, understood the need for a viable sea-based strategic deterrent. Polaris needed to be operational at the earliest opportunity because the national security situation vis-à-vis the Soviet Union was perceived to be shifting against the United States as the famous "missile gap" emerged.

As they say, "the rest is history." The first two U.S. FBM submarines, designated as SSBNs, USS *George Washington* (SSBN 598) and USS *Patrick Henry* (SSBN 599), were designed, built, equipped, manned, tested, and on patrol by the end of 1960. Completed over a period of four years, a technical and managerial feat rarely achieved even in wartime.

In retrospect, the number of management, operational, command and control, logistic, and technical issues that had to be resolved to make that achievement possible is breathtaking. There was first the question of time and resources. How were we to develop such a weapons system in such a short time? Admiral Burke gave the Special Projects Office the highest priority in the Navy, essentially a "hunting license," for resources and personnel and maintained his unwavering support for the program. The planners and managers also had to determine how many SSBNs were to be built. The Navy's study indicated a required force of forty-five. Admiral Burke reduced that to forty-one and that was how many Polaris SSBNs were built by 1967. Next there were also operational and logistics questions to be answered.

Who was to command this national strategic asset? This was a controversial issue. The USAF argued that it should be under the command of

the Strategic Air Command (SAC), a USAF specified command that also commanded the land-based missiles (ICBMs) and long-range bombers. The Navy prevailed and command was vested in the three unified commanders (CINCLANT, CINCPAC, and USCINCEUR) and submariners performed day-to-day operational control. To justify their enormous expense and take advantage of their inherent survivability, these submarines had to maximize their time at sea, operating submerged and undetected. In order to be responsive to a launch order, they needed to be operated forward in range of targets in the Soviet Union. As national strategic weapons, their targeting had to be coordinated with other strategic assets in the Single Integrated Operational Plan (SIOP) developed by the Joint Strategic Targeting Planning Staff (JSTPS) at Omaha, Nebraska. Because of the relatively short ranges of the first two Polaris missiles, to maximize target coverage, forward basing was deemed necessary, and bases were established at Holy Loch, Scotland, in 1961 and at Rota, Spain, and at Guam in the Western Pacific in 1964. To support the submarines at these sites, the decision was made to create mobile rather than fixed bases for the SSBNs. As a result, new submarine tenders were required. The first FBM tender, USS *Proteus* (AS 19), was retrofitted to support the FBM weapon system, and four more were built as FBM tenders from the keel up. Floating drydocks were also required at the forward bases, as were replenishment ships to supply those bases. Special missile transport ships were also required.

The question of how these submarines should be manned was another controversial issue. To take full advantage of these valuable strate-

The first FBM tender, USS Proteus *(AS 19), was converted from a World War II submarine tender to handle the special requirements of the FBM submarine. This picture of* Proteus *and USS* Patrick Henry *(SSBN 599) transferring a Polaris A-1 missile was taken in the first overseas refit of an SSBN in Holy Loch, Scotland, in 1961. The white tube-like object being lifted by* Proteus's *missile crane is the missile handler, which was fitted and locked onto the submarine during missile transfer so that ships' motions did not affect alignment of the missile into or out of the tube. The missile handler contained an internal hoist that actually raised or lowered the missile.*

Deterrent Patrol Insignia.

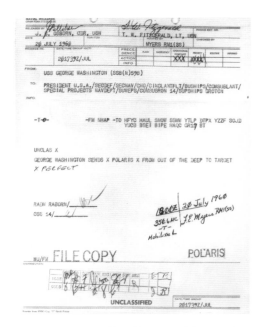

Special Projects Office file copy of the naval message from Commander J. B. Osborn, Blue crew captain of USS George Washington, *to President Eisenhower and other officials announcing the first successful Polaris launch.*

Realizing that a liquid-fueled missile was inherently dangerous and cumbersome prompted the decision to design the Polaris *with a solid propellant. This is a photograph of an early static motor test to determine the true performance data of the new solid fuel. Literally hundreds of propellant formula combinations and heat-resistant metal alloys were explored before flight tests could be justified.*

Opposite: *The first successful launch of a Polaris A-1 missile was from the submerged USS* George Washington *(SSBN 598) off Cape Canaveral. Senator John F. Kennedy, then running for President, witnessed the launch. He stated: "It is still incredible to me that a missile can be successfully and accurately fired from beneath the sea. Once one has seen a Polaris firing, the efficacy of this weapons system as a deterrent is not debatable." Polaris submarines at sea during the Cuban missile crisis two years later were credited as President Kennedy's trump card in Khruschev's decision to back down.*

gic assets, they needed to spend more time at sea than other submarines normally did. To solve this dilemma, the two-crew concept was adopted—a radical concept that was a complete break with several thousand years of naval tradition. Thus came into being the alternating Blue and Gold crews for SSBNs. To maximize efficiency and minimize the need for crews to be away from home when in an off-crew status, it was decided to build off-crew training sites at New London, Connecticut; Charleston, South Carolina; and Pearl Harbor, Hawaii, and to "home port" the crews at those sites.

Finally there was the question of naming these new submarines, a seemingly trivial question, but one of considerable symbolic importance. Traditionally, submarines had been named for fish. To underscore their importance as capital ships and their unique nature, it was decided to name the first forty-one SSBNs after great American patriots, starting with the "father of his country," George Washington, and ending with Will Rogers.

The technical challenges confronting the Navy in putting a submarine-launched ballistic missile (SLBM) to sea in four years were even more daunting than the nontechnical issues. So much that needed to be developed had never been done before, was at the cutting edge of technology, and all had to be done concurrently and quickly. To help solve these technical challenges, Rear Admiral Raborn brought on board Captain Levering Smith as Technical Director of SSPO and formed a team of some of the best companies in the U.S. defense industry. The primary challenges were in six areas: the missile, missile guidance, ship navigation, the fire control system, missile launchers, and the ship itself.

Development of the missile followed from a realization by the Navy's Special Projects Office that a liquid-fueled missile was too large and inherently more cumbersome and dangerous than a missile with solid propellant. This realization prompted the decision to design the Polaris missile with a solid propellant. At the time solid propellants were being developed for intercontinental ballistic missiles (ICBMs), but it was not a mature technology. In spite of some inevitable missile failures during the compressed flight test program, the Polaris A-1 missile developed by Lockheed with solid propellant rocket motors developed by Aerojet General was successfully launched from the submerged *George Washington* on 20 July 1960. The first Polaris SSBN was ready for her first patrol on 15 November 1960.

Several methods of missile guidance were being developed at that time. All involved guidance systems too large for the relatively small Polaris A-1 missile. Scientists under the direction of Dr. Draper at the Massachusetts Institute of Technology (MIT) working with those at General Electric succeeded in designing, fabricating, and testing miniaturized inertial components that could be integrated successfully to create a guidance system that met the demanding specifications set by the Navy.

To successfully guide a ballistic missile over 1,000 miles and hit a target, the launching submarine's position must be known with considerable accuracy—greater accuracy than was possible using traditional means of navigation. To be able to launch missiles at any time also requires knowing the ship's position continuously between fixes. Knowing the direction or azimuth of the target accurately is a third requirement for an FBM navigation system. These three navigation problems had never been pursued

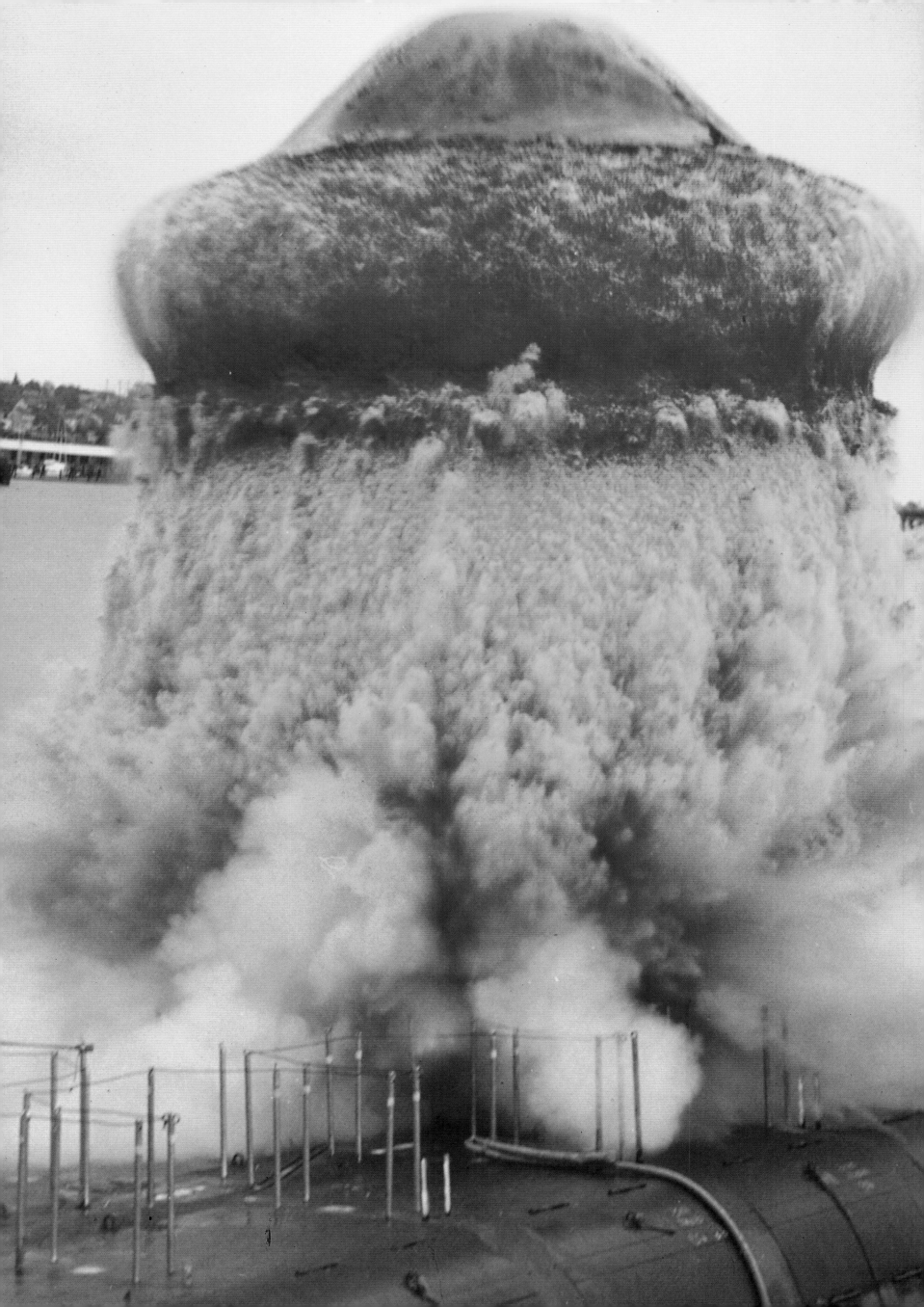

FAMILY GRAMS— *Captain Richard T. Wright, USN (Ret)*

It was recognized early on that "routine" SSBN patrols (sixty to seventy days at sea, mostly submerged, and out of touch with home) could become a morale problem in peacetime (the Cold War was technically peacetime). This was particularly true for married crew members (who were generally in the majority in most submarine crews of the time) if there wasn't an easy, routine way for the families to send messages to their loved ones at sea.

Someone came up with the idea of a "family gram" to solve this problem. The family gram was a cryptic, brief communication similar to a telegram that a spouse or other family member could compose and have sent by the Navy to the submarine at sea. Because SSBNs observed strict radio silence, there could be no response to these family grams. At first, crew members were allowed three very brief family grams each patrol. Needless to say, family grams were a major morale booster for crews on patrol.

Family grams were a conduit for both good and bad news from home. Bad news often brought unhappiness or even grief to a sailor, but at least he knew that he was being kept informed of developments on the home front. Good news helped keep spirits up, and no news was usually considered good news.

USS WILL ROGERS SSBN-659

FAMILYGRAM!

FOR: LT LAFORCE

MESSAGE

PIPES FROZEN- CALLED PLUMBER. MAY REMOVE WALL TO
REACH PIPES. HURRY HOME AND BRING HEAT WITH YOU. LOVE,
KAREN.

At the end of one of the early patrols, some officers were planning a celebration in nearby Glasgow. One of them received some good and bad news when a family gram from his wife arrived toward the end of patrol announcing her intention to meet the ship on its return to Scotland, "Forget the banquet, your ham sandwich is on the way!"

Family grams from home were always a welcome break in the routine of a strategic deterrent patrol. No matter how welcome they were, these short messages from family and friends connected submariners with the outside world and sometimes contained only a part of the whole story. In this case, the frozen pipes and warm affectionate thought didn't provide any clues as to how the pipes became frozen. A more detailed story when the officer returned home after patrol revealed that one of the couple's sons left a basement door ajar to allow a pet cat to come and go as it pleased. Cold New England air followed the cat and produced the frozen pipes. In the end, shutting the basement door allowed the pipes to thaw, and a visit from the plumber was not needed.

before for long-range sea-going weapon systems. Under the direction of the two prime contractors, Sperry and North American Aviation, all of these technical issues were addressed. The contractors developed more accurate fixing techniques using radio navigation, bottom contour navigation, and, later, satellite navigation to fix the submarine's position. They also developed an accurate dead-reckoning system in the form of the ship's inertial navigation system (SINS) that provides continuous, accurate position information between navigation fixes. Finally, the contractors provided an improved method of heading determination based on the observation of celestial bodies using a new Type XI periscope. The required navigation systems were developed, tested, and ready for deployment in 1960.

A reliable fire control system for taking digital and optical-alignment data from the navigation system, calculating the necessary data to enable the missiles to fly from the ship's current position to the assigned targets, and transmitting that data to the missile guidance systems in a few seconds had to be developed. The fire control prime contractor, General Electric, designed, developed, constructed, and tested the digital Mk 80 fire control system that successfully solved the basic ballistic missile fire control problem.

In the design and development of the missile launcher system, several challenges faced Westinghouse, the prime contractor. Vertical,

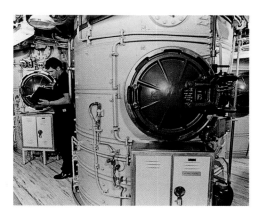

Above: *Torpedoman's Mate Robert McClelland makes a systems check in the missile compartment on board USS* John Adams *(SSBN 620). The missile compartment, commonly referred to as Sherwood Forest, was a spacious area by submarine standards and served as exercise room, barber shop, and storeroom, among other things, for crew members on patrol.*

Opposite: *This mushroom-like surge of water from a Polaris missile tube is part of a dockside test of missile launch pressures. (Photo: PHOTRI-Microstock)*

Above: *Admiral Galantin watches as crew-members are drilled in the techniques of operating one of the many complex instrument consoles that seem to fill every cubic inch of usable space. The fire control console is continuously feeding up-to-the-minute instructions to the guidance capsules of the sixteen Polaris missiles.*

Top, right: *After more than three months of separation, both the SSBN crewmen and their families were excited to see the end of patrol and looked forward to the three month off-crew period when the other crew had the ship. After being converted to the longer range Trident I (C-4), some of the SSBNs operated out of the continental United States (CONUS) ports instead of forward bases. This meant families could actually meet their loved ones on a ship coming in rather than on a bus bringing the crew from the airport where the crew flight had landed. This picture shows some of the crowd welcoming USS* Ohio *(SSBN 726) to the Trident Refit Facility in Bangor, Washington.*

Right: *The high state of readiness of our strategic missile deterrent force is maintained by continuous monitoring and periodic diagnostic testing. In this photograph a crewman checks the internal systems of missiles in the missile diagnostic center of USS* Georgia *(SSBN 729).*

Above: *President Dwight D. Eisenhower thoroughly enjoys his cruise on board USS* Patrick Henry *(SSBN 599). He is seated at one of the two diving and steering control stations maneuvering the ship.*

"submerged" launch of a ballistic missile had never before been contemplated. Propelling the missile through the water while keeping it dry was no small feat. A method of ejecting the missile through a frangible diaphragm using compressed air was developed. The diaphragm kept the missile dry when the launch tube muzzle hatch was opened during a launch. Once launched, the missile was kept dry by an envelope of air as the missile moved to the ocean surface. Concurrently, a method was developed for almost hovering while quickly compensating the ship for weight changes after each missile launch to enable the ship to remain submerged at or near launch depth. Because the first missile launch would compromise the submarine's position, a rapid firing rate of the remaining missiles was required. The launcher system, as well as the fire control and navigation systems, had to be designed to sustain the rapid firing rate.

The final technical hurdle was the ship. The challenge was to design, build, and test a submarine of revolutionary design in less than four years.

A number of questions required resolution. How many missile tubes should there be and where should they be located? Should there be an entirely new design for the ship? In the interest of time, it was decided to use the design of a modified *Skipjack*-class attack submarine hull for the first five SSBNs and develop a new design for the next five. For the first SSBN, it was decided to use the hull of USS *Scorpion* on the building ways at Electric Boat by literally cutting it in half and inserting a 130-foot missile compartment containing sixteen vertical launch tubes—thus was born USS *George Washington*. The following four SSBNs, USS *Patrick Henry*, USS *Robert E. Lee* (SSBN 601), USS *Theodore Roosevelt* (SSBN 600), and USS *Abraham Lincoln* (SSBN 602), were built from the keel up as modified *Skipjack*-class submarines.

The role of the initial FBM crews must also be recognized in meeting these daunting challenges. The first ten skippers—Erb, From, Long, Miller, Osborn, Perry, Shear, Sims, Williams, and Woodall—and their officers and crews made significant contributions to the FBM program and got SSBNs to sea and on patrol years earlier than originally thought possible.

To capitalize on the unique characteristics of the SSBN and to optimize its role as a strategic deterrent, it became obvious to the early FBM planners that these submarines should be manned, operated, and controlled very differently from other submarines and other strategic assets. What evolved was a modus operandi that maximized the SSBN's ability to

Top: *USS* Patrick Henry *(SSBN 599) with Commander Harold Shear in command approaches USS* Proteus *(AS 19) for the first FBM upkeep in Holy Loch, Scotland. Holy Loch was used as a support base for SSBNs from 1961 to 1992. Commander Shear had a most successful naval career, advancing to the grade of Admiral and serving as the Vice-Chief of Naval Operations and Commander of the NATO Southern Command.*

Above: *USS* Henry Clay *(SSBN 625) conducts a rare surfaced test launch of a Polaris A-1 missile. While the system is designed for launching missiles from the surface as well as when submerged, the latter mode was normal. Note the list to port carried by the submarine. This is to preclude the possibility that the weapon would fall back on the ship if the propellant failed to ignite.*

The Naval Submarine Base at Kings Bay, Georgia, was commissioned in 1978 to be homeport to Submarine Squadron SIXTEEN, the Rota, Spain-based FBM squadron. In 1982, it was designated as the East Coast homeport of the Trident submarine fleet. Construction of this base was the largest peacetime construction program ever undertaken by the U.S. Navy. The Trident Refit Facility, shown under construction in this 1989 photograph, has the largest covered drydock in the western hemisphere.

remain undetected by foe and friend alike while remaining ready to respond to a launch order from the National Command Authority (NCA), functionally the President, on very short notice—a condition called "ALERT" status. Implied in this ALERT status is a requirement that the SSBN remain within range of assigned targets and maintain a continuous watch on the FBM broadcast (radio frequencies) over which a launch order would be received.

This concept was initially implemented by designing an SSBN patrol rotation from the advanced base at Holy Loch. Each SSBN spent about thirty days in refit and trials, then about sixty days on patrol with the Blue crew, followed by a similar period with the Gold crew. A brief turnover period occurred at the end of each patrol, after which the off-going crew flew home for just under ninety days. While off crew, about 20 percent of the crew was shifted to other duties, leave was granted, and rigorous individual and team training was conducted. The rotation was designed so that about the same number of SSBNs were on patrol at all times. Numerous minor modifications to this concept have been made over the years, but the basic Blue/Gold rotation continues to this day.

SSBNs in port are not inherently survivable, but in an emergency they can usually put to sea and become survivable in short order. For example, the in-port SSBNs were scrambled within forty-eight hours during the Cuban Missile Crisis in 1962 and again during the Yom Kippur War in 1973—another tribute to the SSBN crews.

In 1973, the U.S. Navy announced its intention to build the homeport for the first squadron of Trident submarines at the site of its ammunition depot at Bangor, Washington. Construction began in October 1974, and the base was activated in early 1977. The base is in a beautiful geographic location on the Kitsap Peninsula and the Hood Canal. This photograph shows a Trident submarine in the Magnetic Silencing (degaussing) Facility at the Trident Refit Facility, Bangor.

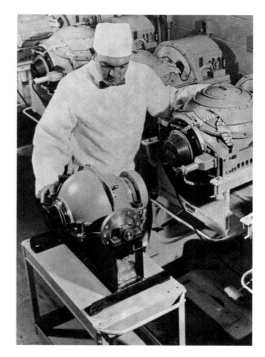

Above: *The development of a much smaller and lighter Mk 2 inertial guidance system helped extend the range of Polaris missiles to 2,500 nautical miles. A refinement of earlier inertial systems (shown in background), the compact, self-contained Mk 2 consists of precise gyroscopes, accelerometers, computers, and associated servos and power supplies.*

After the initial five SSBNs of the USS *George Washington* class came five SSBNs of the larger USS *Ethan Allen* (SSBN 608) class, then thirty-one SSBNs of the still larger USS *Lafayette* (SSBN 616) class. These Polaris submarines were sometimes called "Boomers" and collectively nicknamed "Forty-one for Freedom." The last of the original forty-one SSBNs was commissioned in April of 1967, roughly seven and a half years after *George Washington*. These ships provided the backbone of the FBM force and of the U.S. national strategic deterrent during most of the Cold War. Subsequently eighteen much larger Trident SSBNs of the USS *Ohio* (SSBN 726) class were built, each carrying twenty-four missile tubes. These successive classes deployed with improved missiles as they became operational—*Ethan Allen*, the 1,500 nautical mile A-2; *Lafayette*, the 2,500 nautical mile A-3; *Ohio*, the 4,000 nautical mile C-4; and later 5,000 nautical mile D-5. The earlier SSBNs were then backfitted with various improved missiles.

To support the first forty-one SSBNs were five SSBN tenders, the retrofitted *Proteus* (AS 19) and the specially designed USS *Hunley* (AS 31), *Holland* (AS 32), *Simon Lake* (AS 33), and *Canopus* (AS 34). The tenders were positioned at four sites: Holy Loch, Scotland, from 1961 to1992; Rota, Spain, from 1964 to 1979; Guam in the Mariana Islands from 1964 to 1981; and Charleston, South Carolina, from 1965 to 1994. To support the eighteen SSBNs of the *Ohio* class, shore bases were built at Bangor, Washington, and Kings Bay, Georgia.

Page 222, top: *Although the FBM program has been remarkable for its successes, there have been occasional mishaps. This spectacular photo shows an aborted Trident II (D-5) launched from USS* Tennessee *(SSBN 734) off Cape Canaveral in March 1989. (Photo: U.S. Air Force)*

Right: *The first fleet ballistic missile, Polaris A-1, an "interim capability" missile with a range of 1,100 nautical miles (nm), first went to sea on USS* George Washington *(SSBN 598) in 1960. The A-2, with a range of 1,500 nm, entered service in April 1962. With the introduction of the 2,500 nm A-3, available sea space for patrol areas was vastly increased although forward basing was still necessary. The Poseidon C-3 missile employed the multiple independently targetable re-entry vehicle (MIRV) technology that permitted a single missile to cover several targets. Because the 616 class and later SSBNs were designed with spacers inside their missile tubes when carrying Polaris missiles, they could be backfitted with the larger diameter (74 vice 54 inches) Poseidon when that became operational. The Trident I (C-4) missile had a range in excess of 4,000 nm and was backfitted to some of the* Lafayette- *and* Benjamin Franklin-*class SSBNs. The Trident II (D-5) is 10 feet longer than the Trident I and has a range of 5,000 nm. This range permits easy access to targets all over the world while operating from CONUS ports. (Graphic: Mark Patnode/Sonalysts)*

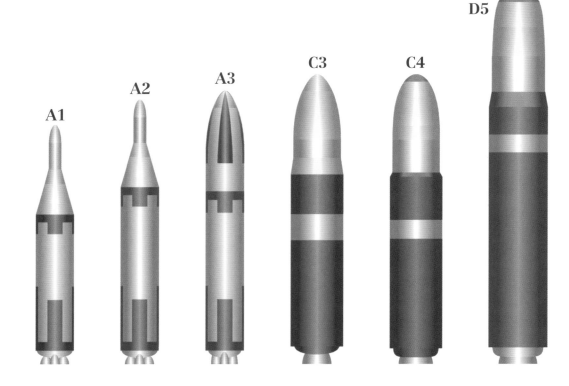

Much has changed in the FBM weapon system since *George Washington* went on patrol on 15 November 1960. Many of the changes occurred under the direction of Rear Admiral Levering Smith, the original technical director of the Special Projects Office and one of Vice Admiral Raborn's successors as Director of Special Projects. The missiles have become much larger, longer range, more accurate, and more reliable as they evolved from Polaris A-1, A-2, (1962) and A-3 (1964) to Poseidon C-3

Above: Even though Trident submarines conduct their refits at Kings Bay or Bangor, the possibility of needing to be served away from their homeport remains. Trial runs with SSN tenders serving Tridents included this situation in July 1987 in Seward, Alaska, where USS Alaska *(SSBN 732) is shown alongside USS* McKee *(AS 41).* McKee *is in full dress ship for Independence Day.*

Left: USS John Marshall, *commissioned in 1962 as SSBN 611, was converted in 1985 to an SSN and fitted to carry swimmer delivery vehicles. The missile tube area was modified as berthing space for special operations forces troops.* John Marshall *was finally decommissioned in 1992.*

Page 224: The massive size of the Trident submarine compared to the 688-class SSN is apparent at the launching of USS Phoenix *(SSN 702) at Electric Boat in Groton, Connecticut, in December 1979. The first Trident submarine, USS* Ohio *(SSBN 726), is in wet dock and USS* Michigan *(SSBN 727) is on the ways, with some of her twenty-four missile tubes clearly visible.*

Page 225, bottom: The FBM submarines are manned by two crews (Blue and Gold). Each year an FBM conducts about four patrols, each about two months in duration. In between each patrol a one-month maintenance upkeep is conducted, and the ship is turned over to the other crew. The pace of a Trident submarine upkeep can be quite hectic for the crew. The seals, however, find the bow of USS Ohio *a serene spot at the Trident Refit Facility, in Bangor, Washington.*

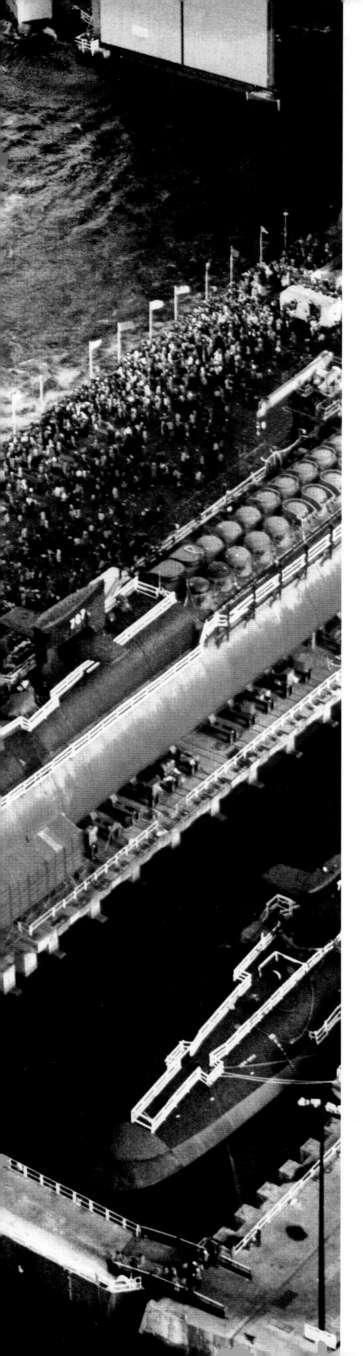

(1971), and finally to Trident C-4 (1979) and D-5 (1990). They also evolved from the single warhead A-1 and A-2 to the multiple warhead A-3 to the multiple independently targeted vehicle (MIRV) technology of the C-3, C-4, and D-5. With longer-range missiles, SSBNs are able to patrol in much larger ocean areas making them even less vulnerable to antisubmarine warfare (ASW) threats. Missile guidance components have become miniaturized and missile accuracy has been improved, even at much longer ranges, thanks to improvements in inertial components and computer-chip technology, as well as the advent of technology that allows a missile in powered flight to make a mid-course correction that nullifies much of the original navigation error.

The navigation system has become more accurate because of improved satellite navigation, the introduction of the Global Positioning System (GPS), and the use of monitor gyroscopes on the SINS to establish an accurate heading reference. Much longer intervals between fixes are now made possible by significant improvements in the inertial components of the SINS and by development of the Electrostatic Gyro Navigation (ESGN) system. The fire control system has become smaller, faster, and more automated while eliminating the need to optically align the missile guidance systems. The launch tubes are larger. Many years ago reliable gas generators replaced compressed air for launching. Trident missiles can be launched from deeper depths, which somewhat mitigates the depth control problem. Finally, advancements in communications technology have enabled SSBNs to patrol deeper and faster while continuing to copy the radio broadcast.

After the 598 and 608 classes of SSBNs were retired from FBM service in the 1980s, relieved by the new *Ohio*-class ships carrying C-4 missiles, five of them were unloaded and reclassified as SSNs. Later, USS *Kamehameha* (SSBN 642) and USS *James K. Polk* (SSBN 645) were unloaded and reconfigured as Sea Air and Land (SEAL) carrying submarines with removable dry-deck shelters designed to allow SEAL teams to depart and enter the submarine while submerged and deploy on a variety of special warfare operations. Two SSBNs, USS *Sam Rayburn* (SSBN 635) and USS *Daniel Webster* (SSBN 626), were retired and

Three trident submarines nesting at Delta Pier, Trident Refit Facility in Bangor, Washington.

Opposite: *When she returned from operational patrol to Bangor, Washington, on 25 May 2001, USS* Florida *(SSBN 728) completed the 3,500th strategic deterrent patrol conducted by the U.S. Navy's FBM Submarine Force. Since USS* George Washington *(SSBN 598) deployed on her first patrol on 15 November 1960, the FBM force has been on virtually continuous patrol for more than forty years, conducting 1,245 Polaris, 1,182 Poseidon, 826 Trident I, and 247 (and counting) Trident II patrols. This totals more than 245,000 mission days (more than 670 years) of combined service on patrol.*

converted to moored training ships to provide nuclear power training to new submariners. In 1994, as a result of ongoing strategic arms limitation talks, the decision was made to reduce the number of active SSBNs from eighteen to fourteen, each to eventually carry twenty-four Trident II D-5 missiles. Until this reduction occurs, the future employment of the four *Ohio*-class submarines not needed as SSBNs will remain undetermined. Possible uses include conversion to SSGNs, carrying Tomahawk cruise missiles, and as special warfare submarines, equipped to deliver SEALs and other special forces to areas of conflict.

Today there are eighteen *Ohio*-class SSBNs equipped with C-4 and D-5 missiles operating from Bangor and Kings Bay. They continue to be operated alternately by Blue and Gold crews so that part of the force is at sea and survivable at all times, just as they have been for over forty years. More than 3,500 strategic deterrent patrols have been conducted by fifty-nine different SSBNs. While the Cold War may be over, any nation that would contemplate a nuclear strike against the United States must reckon with that survivable component of the FBM force that is on patrol where it has been for so many years. It continues to provide our country the ultimate strategic deterrent to nuclear war. To reiterate General Powell's message—America's proud missile submariners continue to "stand tall."

CREW FLIGHTS— *CAPTAIN RICHARD T. WRIGHT, USN (RET)*

When the first SSBNs started making patrols from Holy Loch, Scotland, the crews were shuttled between McGuire Air Force Base in New Jersey and Prestwick, Scotland. Later they departed from Quonset Point Naval Air Station in Rhode Island. At first the crews were flown by the Military Air Transport Service (MATS). A little later, they were transported on commercial flights chartered by MATS.

Fortunately no crew flight was ever lost, but there were some exciting trips in the early days. It seemed that rarely did a flight (MATS or chartered) ever cross the Atlantic without losing at least one of four engines; sometimes two pro-pellers were feathered on arrival! Delays, particularly coming home, were common, and many crews had to spend an extra night at the bar or playing cards in Prestwick or in Gander, Newfoundland, where the flights often stopped to refuel.

Particularly unsettling for the Blue crew of USS Patrick Henry *(SSBN 599) was their first chartered flight from Quonset Point on Overseas National Airways. First, the three chartered aircraft were late arriving, then the flight crews appeared, unshaven and unkempt, looking as though they had just flown the Berlin Air Lift. Finally, in a display of supreme self-confidence, the flight crew lined up to buy flight insurance from coin-operated machines! The apprehensive submarine sailors, never particularly confident above the surface, and always alert to danger, were in line immediate-ly after the flight crews! Fortunately, it was money wasted, and the crew made it to Scotland, even if a little late.*

Fleet Ballistic Missile submarine crews were flown to and from advanced bases in Holy Loch, Scotland, Rota, Spain, and Guam, and home bases in Groton, Connecticut, Charleston, South Carolina, and Pearl Harbor, Hawaii. Often these flights were flown on unheard of airlines, which generated numerous comical (and some not so comical) sea stories. One of the two crews assigned to USS *Lewis and Clark* (SSBN 644) boards their crew flight at Prestwick, Scotland, on their way home to Charleston in January of 1988. The crew had been relieved by the second crew and had traveled by launch from Holy Loch to Glasgow, and then by double-decker bus from Glasgow to the airport at Prestwick to board the flight for home. (Courtesy of Terry Scott)

Special Projects: FBM Pioneers

Vice Admiral Joe Williams, Jr., U.S. Navy (Ret)

Admiral Arleigh Burke, the father of the Polaris submarine launched ballistic missile (SLBM), was a famous World War II hero. The press nicknamed him "31 knot Burke" because his destroyer squadron rushed to intercept Japanese fleets at "flank speed."

Foremost among Admiral Arleigh Burke's goals as CNO was to develop and deploy a fleet ballistic missile system. Admiral Burke was convinced that sending missiles to sea on the trackless oceans, covering nearly three-fourths of the earth's surface would be a powerful deterrent to the launching of a "first-strike" by any enemy. To stop a squabble between the Bureaus of Aeronautics (it flies) and Ordnance (it's ballistic) as to who would develop such a system, Burke established the Special Projects Office. Its director would report directly to the Secretary of the Navy.

As director, Burke picked a newly promoted Rear Admiral, William F. "Red" Raborn, a carrier pilot, and a pioneer in developing the Navy's air launched missiles.

Admiral Burke offered Raborn the pick of any forty officers and civil servants from anywhere within the Navy Department except those working on nuclear propulsion for Admiral Rickover.

Raborn rapidly welded together a Navy-industry team and put them on a wartime footing. One of the key people picked by Admiral Raborn was Captain Levering Smith, an ordnance specialist and combat veteran, who had a strong knowledge of rocket propellants and a rare gift for organization and management.

High on Captain Smith's agenda when he joined the Office was the development of a solid propellant capable of meeting the requirements of a submarine launched missile, and by September 1956 a high-impulse solid propellant had been proofed. Raborn had elected to discontinue work on the large, dangerous liquid-fueled Jupiter and to proceed rapidly on a smaller missile—Polaris.

In August 1957 the Soviets launched their first intercontinental ballistic missile (ICBM) followed by the sizeable satellite Sputnik-1 on 4 October. Shortly thereafter the larger Sputnik-2 carrying a dog was in orbit. The media sounded off in alarm. Congress and the public feared the Soviets would be capable of nuclear blackmail, and President Eisenhower made radio broadcasts calculated to calm the public's fears while the military sought a solution.

Admirals Burke and Raborn proposed accelerating the nuclear deterrent system, Polaris, to achieve an operational date in 1960 vice 1963. Such could be realized by using existing attack boat hulls already designed or under construction and inserting a 130-foot section amidships to house the missiles rather than waiting for hulls to be designed uniquely for

Polaris. While the Air Force scoffed, Special Projects shifted their Navy-industry team into high gear.

True to their word, USS George Washington *(SSBN 598) and USS* Patrick Henry *(SSBN 599) sailed in 1960 for the first nuclear deterrent patrols. Three more Polaris submarines became operational in 1961. By 1967 forty-one SSBNs would be on the line.*

"Red" Raborn, "31-knot" Burke and Levering Smith, none of whom had ever served in submarines, created a mobile survivable submarine strategic deterrent system that saved the world from nuclear blackmail.

Left: Vice Admiral "Red" Raborn, the first Director of the Special Projects Office, was instrumental in creating the world's predominant strategic weapon system.

Opposite, left: Rear Admiral William F. "Red" Raborn, Director of the Special Projects Office (SPO), and Admiral Arleigh Burke, Chief of Naval Operations, examine a model of USS *George Washington* (SSBN 598) in July 1959. The progress of the Soviet missile and space program heightened the sense of urgency in getting a nuclear deterrent program operational. Under Rear Admiral Raborn's leadership, the SPO advanced the program by almost three years from its scheduled mid-1963 operational deployment when *George Washington* deployed in November 1960 on her first strategic deterrent patrol.

Opposite, right: Captain Levering Smith was drafted by Rear Admiral Raborn from the Naval Ordnance Missile Test Facility at White Sands, New Mexico, to become technical director of the Special Projects Office (SPO) because of his reputation as the Navy's pre-eminent expert on rockets and solid propellants. Later promoted to rear admiral, then vice admiral, Smith took over as director of SPO in 1965. Due to his modest nature and low-key style, Vice Admiral Smith received little public notice, but within the Navy his essential role was unquestioned.

Below: USS *Henry M. Jackson* (SSBN 730) steams in a beautiful sunset en route to her Trident deterrent patrol.

Saturdays, Sundays & Nights (SSNs)

Captain F. T. Jones, USN (Ret)

The "attack boats" of the U.S. Navy are now all nuclear-powered and so labeled SSNs. Many are deployed to the far reaches of the world ready to respond to emergent crises. They may be called upon to covertly execute a variety of missions such as coastal or maritime reconnaissance and land attack missile strikes, many times unexpectedly. Hence many submariners say that SSN stands for "Saturdays, Sundays, and Nights." ("Fast Attack, Fast Dive," John C. Roach)

An "attack" submarine is really a multipurpose/multimission platform. To use the aircraft analogy, it would probably be more correct to refer to it as a "fighter/attack" submarine. In the postwar years, until being phased out in the 1970s, diesel-powered "attack" submarines (designated SS) operated in all the oceans of the world, performing every mission that the Cold War demanded, but they were limited in speed and endurance by their diesel-electric propulsion plants. With the advent of nuclear propulsion, the general-purpose submarine (now designated SSN) enjoyed a quantum improvement in military capability based on a major increase in submerged speed and endurance.

Following the launching of USS *Nautilus* (SSN 571) on 21 January 1954, the first nuclear-powered "fast attack," a succession of submarines emerged that were not very different in hull form from diesel submarines of the same period. Several of these were one-of-a-kind ships, each making an advance in the sophistication of the nuclear propulsion plant or being a test bed for a different nuclear reactor, engine room, or hull design. This period of development produced USS *Seawolf* (SSN 575), launched 21 July 1955; USS *Triton* (SSRN 586), launched 19 August 1958; USS *Halibut* (SSGN 587), launched 9 January 1959; and USS *Tullibee* (SSN 597), launched 27 April 1960.

In parallel with these developments, the first class of nuclear-powered "fast attack" submarines was being built. This was the *Skate* class, which consisted of four sister ships, all launched between 16 May 1957 and 16 August 1958. Smaller than *Nautilus*—52 feet shorter and with 1,300 tons less displacement—these ships soon became the workhorses of the Atlantic and Pacific Submarine Forces. Although their combat systems and sensors were no more advanced than the conventional

Conventional submarines made valuable contributions to the Cold War, the Korean conflict, and in Vietnam. USS Salmon *(SS 573), shown here prior to beginning a regular overhaul at Hunters Point, California, in 1967, had seen two Vietnam tours. For their operations in Southeast Asia,* Salmon's *crew was awarded the Vietnam Service Medal.*

USS Tullibee *(SSN 597), launched in 1960, was the first nuclear submarine designed specifically for antisubmarine warfare (ASW). She was the first submarine to be equipped with a large spherical sonar array mounted in the bow. To minimize self-noise in the vicinity of the sonar, torpedo tubes were installed amidships, rather than in the bow. To further reduce radiated noise, she had a turbo-electric propulsion plant rather than the conventional drive with its noisier gearing. Initially manned with only six officers and fifty enlisted men, it was quickly learned that this pioneer in advanced ASW needed additional crew and the complement was increased.*

USS Albacore *(AGSS 569) was the test bed for hull design and control surface concepts. Many* Albacore *design features became standard in later submarines.*

Here USS Sargo *(SSN 583), the third American submarine to reach the North Pole, is shown surfaced through the Arctic ice pack on 9 February 1960.*

submarines of the day, the *Skate*-class submarine had speed and endurance never before achieved. The limits of endurance were no longer determined by how much fuel or water could be carried on board. In fact, the practical limiting factor of endurance became the amount of food that could be carried.

Another significant development in submarine design was the *Albacore* hull form. No longer would the submarine hull be designed for surface operations, as had been the case for conventional submarines. For the first time, it would be optimized for submerged running, with top submerged speeds greater than could be achieved on the surface.

Marrying the advances in nuclear propulsion with the *Albacore* hull form, the *Skipjack* class was the high-performance sports car of submarines. Having only a single screw (propeller), displacing 3,513 tons, and with a length of only 252 feet, the six submarines in the class were exceptionally fast and easy to maneuver.

The propulsion plant that went to sea for the first time in *Skipjack* was well laid out and would prove to be so reliable that, with only minor changes and with steady increases in reactor core life, it would be used in ninety-nine submarines (*Skipjack*, *Permit*, *George Washington*, *Ethan*

Allen, *Lafayette*, *Franklin*, *Sturgeon*, and *Lipscomb* classes) over a period of sixteen years. This provided the added benefits of fewer refuelings plus standardizing repair parts, maintenance procedures, operating procedures, and training and qualification for submarine propulsion plants.

At the same time that engineering advances were changing the capabilities of the submarine, the changing role of the submarine in the Cold War was requiring other technological advances. Increasingly, anti-

The sleek "tear-drop" hull form of USS Skipjack *(SSN 585) and later classes of nuclear attack submarines is evident in this view of USS* Scorpion *(SSN 589) launching on 19 December 1959. Note the narrow sail structure and the diving control planes mounted on the sail.*

A Permit-*class submarine, USS* Haddo *(SSN 604), is underway. The modern fast attack submarine is well designed to be fast submerged; however, while on the surface, it rides low in the water and in any seaway or with moderate speed, the bow wave washes over the foredeck to the sail.* Permit-*class boats had a small sail with the sail planes placed higher than in the later* Sturgeon *class.*

submarine warfare (ASW) became the most important mission of the submarine force. This required improved ship quieting, acoustic sensors, combat systems, and ASW weapons. These attributes were the design drivers for the USS *Permit* (SSN 594) class. With a 22 percent increase in submerged displacement but no increase in propulsion power, the resulting decrease in maximum speed was considered acceptable to make more room for sound isolation of machinery, state-of-the-art sonar and combat systems, and an increased weapon load.

Tullibee excepted, submarines constructed before the *Permit* class had relatively small cylindrical-array sonars for search and tracking. Bow-mounted cylindrical arrays did not preclude the placement of the torpedo tubes in the bow of the ship, so the torpedo room was the forward-most compartment, and the torpedo tubes were installed parallel to the centerline of the ship. In *Permit* and later submarines, a large spherical array became the primary search and tracking sonar. This larger array made it possible to achieve greater sensitivity and accuracy for both active and passive sonar, but the size of the spherical array did not leave enough room for the torpedo tubes to remain in the bow as well. The solution was to move the torpedo room aft to the middle of the ship and to cant the torpedo tubes outward.

The USS *Sturgeon* (SSN 637) class was a redesign of the *Permit* class to improve mission capability, maintainability, and habitability. With an increase of slightly more than 11 percent in submerged displacement compared to the *Permit* class (again with no increase in propulsion power), the

Above: *Torpedoman's Mate Third Class Greg Culbreath operates a rammer while he and other torpedo gang members backhaul a Mk 48 torpedo on board the* Los Angeles-*class submarine, USS* Norfolk *(SSN 714). The torpedomen on board a fast attack submarine are adept at moving these heavy weapons around the confined space of the torpedo room quickly and efficiently. In addition, their skills extend to electrical and fluid systems that relate not only to the torpedo, but to the launch tube, fire control systems, and the launching support systems. Torpedomen are some of the best all-around technicians on board the boat.*

Opposite: *Senior Chief Machinist's Mate Robert McCoy, left, chief of the boat, watches as Torpedoman's Mate First Class Michael Munz, leading torpedoman, inspects a torpedo tube of the nuclear-powered submarine USS* Los Angeles *(SSN 688).*

Above: *USS* Glenard P. Lipscomb *(SSN 685) underway on the surface. Some of the Sturgeon-class hulls were used to test other concepts. Lipscomb was equipped with a turbo-electric main power plant instead of the standard turbine reduction gear drive. This made it possible to eliminate the reduction gears, thereby removing a major source of noise in other Sturgeon-class submarines.*

This painting shows a fast attack submarine firing a torpedo while at periscope depth. ("Hot and True," John Roach)

Sturgeon-class submarines were easier to maintain because of improved access to equipment and improved auxiliary systems and more livable because of the increased space. *Sturgeon*-class submarines were designed to operate under the pack ice of the Arctic Ocean and to be able to surface through the ice. (This was possible because of a hardened [strengthened] sail, and fairwater planes that could rotate through a 90-degree angle to allow them to pass vertically through the ice.) Once again the changes meant a decrease in speed.

By the late 1960s, the Navy determined that it needed a high-speed nuclear submarine to perform escort duties for the carrier battle groups and regain a tactical speed advantage vis à vis the Soviet submarines. This reflected the importance placed on dealing with the ASW threat in the Cold War. Conceptually, the new submarine would be powered by the nuclear reactor already designed for use in a destroyer, mated to a submarine engine room. The hull design would be new, but whenever trade-offs were required, they would be made in favor of increased speed and reduced cost. As a result, the new class of submarines would not dive as deep, or carry as much surveillance equipment as the *Sturgeon*-class ships, and could not surface through the ice. The resulting submarine design, which became the *Los Angeles* (or 688) class, named for the lead ship, was the fastest and quietest that the United States had built.

By the mid-1980s, the early *Sturgeon*-class submarines were twenty years old, and it became obvious that there was a need to replace those very capable, multimission boats with something more than just a high-speed, carrier escort submarine. Although there had been evolutionary improvements in the *Los Angeles* class over the dozen years in which they had been operational, USS *San Juan* (SSN 751) marked the beginning of

Sailors still join the Navy to see the world. Here USS Archerfish *(SSN-678) leaves the tender USS* Orion *(AS 18) in La Maddalena, Italy, for operations in the Mediterranean Sea. (Photo: Steve Kaufman)*

USS Narwhal *(SSN 671) was a Sturgeon-class boat whose design was altered to test a quieter propulsion system. She was equipped with a natural circulation reactor plant, which obviated the need to operate the noisy main circulating water pumps. A modified form of this plant powers the* Los Angeles *and* Ohio *classes.*

Computer Submarine Simulations

Neal Stevens

In 1869, Jules Verne took readers where no technology could—twenty thousand leagues under the sea. His fantastic tale of the submarine Nautilus foreshadowed a popular fascination with submarines. The allure of three-dimensional sailing and the peculiar set of risks and tactics associated with submarine warfare create a compelling environment for entertainment mediums such as novels, films, and computer games.

Unlike a movie or novel, a computer submarine simulation (subsim) is wholly interactive. A subsim player is not merely being told a story; he is an active participant in the action as it unfolds on his monitor. The player is virtually transported to the control room of a U-boat or Los Angeles-class attack submarine.

Within the genre of submarine simulations two distinct branches exist—World War II and nuclear submarine warfare. World War II subsims re-enact the war of attrition that saw submarines as commerce raiders. A nuke subsim mirrors the operating environment of its counterpart by replicating target motion analysis (TMA), fire control, sonar waterfall, and other electronic screens.

Submarine simulations first surfaced with the advent of the personal computer in the 1980s. Gato (1983), set in World War II, gave the player command of a U.S. fleet boat. With graphics limited to sixteen colors and ships depicted as basic silhouettes, Gato was the "Pong" of subsims. Moving ahead to the 1990s, Silent Service II contained 256 color graphics, digitized speech, and a war-spanning dynamic campaign.

The complexity and variety of subsims improved with Wolfpack (1992), which offered command of either Allied surface ships or German U-boats, a mission editor, and a mouse-oriented interface. Seawolf SSN-21 (1994) allowed the player to receive his crew reports with video clip inserts. One of the most highly regarded subsims was Aces of the Deep (1995). Aces featured U-boats in World War II complete with a dynamic campaign and a rolling, white-capped ocean. Players still testify to Aces of the Deep's immersive gameplay.

The 1996 subsim Silent Hunter presented U.S. submarines in the Pacific during World War II. The graphics were crisper than Aces of the Deep and even included coastal cities. Stalking Japanese ships within sight of the home islands conveys the stark reality faced by such intrepid and heroic commanders as Fluckey and O'Kane.

The most recent title, Jane's 688(I) (1997), featured ship characteristics so realistic it caused some concern over security. The first Internet multiplay subsim, 688(I), was a commercial and critical success that spawned numerous "virtual fleets" with thousands of players prowling the depths of cyberspace.

For those who served on board submarines deep inside enemy lines in the Pacific War or under the desolate ice caps in the Cold War, survival was no game. Computer submarine simulations are as close to undersea warfare as most people will ever reach.

Above: Shown are three of the immensely popular, and increasingly sophisticated, computer submarine simulations: "Silent Service II" (1991), "Silent Hunter" (1996), and "Jane's 688(I): Hunter Killer" (1997).

Above: *A floating drydock, USS* Shippingport *(ARDM 4) at the Submarine Base, Groton, Connecticut, holds a* Los Angeles-*class submarine. The green fabric covers the giant screw that can propel the submarine at speeds well in excess of 20 knots. The size of the submarine is more evident when in drydock. When in the water alongside a pier, over two-thirds of the boat is hidden underwater. As a matter of scale, the distance from the water to the top of the dock wall is the same as a four story building.*

Left: *An artistic rendering of a* Permit-*class submarine transiting on the surface with a moderate sea running. (*"Dace Under Way at Morning Light," *John Roach)*

the improved *Los Angeles* class (or 688I class as it is usually called). The most noticeable change was the relocation of the forward control surfaces from the sail to the bow. The use of bow planes, which could be rigged in so as not to protrude beyond the hull, and the strengthening of the sail gave the 688I boats the ability to surface through ice. Improved electronics for surveillance and reconnaissance were developed and also backfitted into the earlier *Los Angeles*-class ships.

Also by the mid-1980s, it became obvious that the Soviet submarine force had made great strides in quieting their submarines of all classes. The Soviet Union continued to produce new designs of attack, cruise missile, and ballistic missile submarines at an alarming rate, to say nothing of the

The Mk 117 was the first all-digital U.S. submarine fire control system. It used a UYK-7 computer and was linked to the BQQ-5 sonar system. The operator's consoles, seen here, are a series of computer displays on which may be shown various elements of the torpedo or missile fire control problem. The digital computer has allowed the optimization of target motion analysis and passive sonar tracking of multiple targets.

quiet conventional submarines that they were building for their own use and for export. In order to stay "ahead of the curve" (the projected rate of submarine quieting that the Soviets were demonstrating), the United States would need an entirely new submarine design. This submarine would need to be quieter than a *Los Angeles*-class submarine, able to search with its sonar while traveling at a higher speed, and carry more weapons to take the battle to the enemy and not have to return to port for reloads as often. The product of the resulting design competition was USS *Seawolf* (SSN 21).

A naval tradition hundreds of years old is the plotting of the ship's position on a paper map called a chart. Here, Quartermaster Second Class Blackburn plots the position of the USS Asheville *(SSN 758) off San Diego, California. The plotting on modern fast attacks of the later* Los Angeles-*class,* Seawolf-*class, and* Virginia-*class boats is becoming more a matter of computer displays than paper and pencil, and the quartermaster rate has been melded with electronic technicians.*

Seawolf is big, quiet, fast, and expensive. Also, it was overtaken by events. No one could have predicted the fall of the Berlin Wall and the end of the Cold War when the design effort began for the Seawolf program. However, by the time Seawolf was launched on 24 June 1995, Congress was looking for the "peace dividend," defense spending was on the decline, and the Navy had a hard time justifying the continuation of a class of $2 billion submarines. There were many competing needs in other Navy warfare communities, and no credible near-term threat scenario included an adversary with a submarine force that warranted the continuation of the class. Congress authorized three ships of the class, but that was probably driven by the need to keep the nuclear submarine building yards alive.

At this time, most Sturgeon-class submarines were at or approaching thirty years of age, and the early Los Angeles-class submarines were already twenty years old. The Navy, the Department of Defense, and Congress recognized that there still must be a submarine construction

The standard outfit of periscopes on a fast attack submarine consists of an attack scope (shown here) and an observation scope, seen on the right in this picture. The attack scope has a very narrow top and is designed to leave little to be seen above the surface. Because of its size, it sacrifices the light gathering and antenna space that characterize the larger observation scope.

program to meet the future submarine force-level requirements. Fiscal reality dictated that the per-ship cost had to be lower than the *Seawolf* class, but even if it were significantly lower, it was unlikely that the building rate would be able to sustain two competing building yards or a Submarine Force of Cold War size.

The effect of all of these factors was to bring about a collaborative design effort by the Electric Boat Division of General Dynamics and the Newport News Shipbuilding and Drydock Company. The program, begun as the New Attack Submarine and then the New SSN (or NSSN), became the design for the *Virginia* class. Reduced in size and cost compared to the *Seawolf* class, when the USS *Virginia* goes to sea in 2004, it will have *Seawolf* quieting, improved sensors, and state-of-the-art technology based on commercial-off-the-shelf (COTS) components. The move away from the procurement of components built to military specifications (MILSPECs) is intended to reduce the life cycle cost of the ships and to make it easier to upgrade systems by taking advantage of the rapid technological changes occurring in industry today.

It was the contribution of the Submarine Force in the Pacific during World War II that has become best known, having been captured and retold to the public through books and movies numerous times. Submarines attacked the logistic network of the Japanese empire, not only

Above: *A Mk 14 Mod 3 torpedo is being lowered down the skids through the forward torpedo room loading hatch on board a fleet type submarine. This torpedo was the mainstay torpedo during World War II and continued in service well into the 1970s. It was powered by an alcohol-fueled steam engine and had a range of 4500 yards at just over 46 knots carrying in its warhead over 600 pounds of torpex.*

by sinking thousands of tons of merchant shipping that were necessary to keep the Japanese military machine in operation, but also in sinking many of their naval vessels.

Although less well known to the public, the Submarine Force performed several other missions that were also essential to the war effort. These included: search and rescue (SAR); the insertion and recovery of

During much of the Cold War one of the weapons in the SSN arsenal was a nuclear-tipped ASW weapon called SUBROC—submarine rocket. The SUBROC was launched from a torpedo tube and rocket propelled for airborne delivery to the target. Here is a test launch of a SUBROC.

Left: *The end of the day on the Navy's underwater test range in the Tongue of the Ocean, Bahamas, is pictured. The Navy uses a deepwater three-dimensional instrumented range to conduct submarine interactions and test weapons. The official name of the range is the Atlantic Undersea Test and Evaluation Center (AUTEC).*

Above: *The Mk 48 (ADCAP) torpedo is the mainstay antiship weapon of the U.S. Navy's submarine force. It is capable of a speed of 55 knots for a distance of 13 nm or 40 knots out to 20 nm. The torpedo contains an active and passive sonar system, a wire guidance system, and has the ability to dive to over 2,000 feet. Here the torpedo is being loaded on board a submarine in 1987.*

special operations forces (SOF); indications and warning (I&W); intelligence, surveillance, and reconnaissance (ISR) and mining (MIW).

Only recently, since the end of the Cold War, has the role of the Submarine Force in that period of super-power competition been disclosed to the public. ASW became the primary mission for a number of reasons. First, the threat from Soviet submarines to carrier battle groups, surface action groups, and amphibious ready groups had to be countered if the United States and its allies were to be able to control the North Atlantic for the defense of Western Europe. SSNs could clear areas ahead of the advance of the surface ships. Second, a significant number of the Soviet strategic missiles were carried in ballistic missile submarines and a capable SSN force was a necessary counter to that threat. Finally, SSNs were needed to deal with the Soviet SSN threat to the ballistic missile submarines of the United States. There was concern that, prior to a Soviet first strike, the Soviets would try to remove the ability of the United States to retaliate with its submarine-launched ballistic missiles (SLBMs).

Also important during the Cold War was the ability of the West to monitor the movements of communist military forces throughout the world and to collect intelligence regarding their capabilities. Because of its stealth

Opposite, bottom: *USS Halibut (SSN 587) is photographed underway with a deep submergence rescue vehicle (DSRV) on deck aft. Some submarines are designed for one task but undergo changes during their lifetime and take on completely different roles. One such boat was Halibut. Originally built to carry the Regulus missile, the boat became a test bed for the DSRV and also took on secret special operations.*

Right: top, center, and bottom: *Throughout the Cold War SSNs routinely monitored Soviet naval exercises. By maintaining close-up surveillance of exercise participants, extraordinary insight into Soviet naval capabilities and tactics was gained. These clandestine photographs taken through the periscope are of a Bear F ASW aircraft, an Echo II nuclear-powered guided missile submarine, and a Kanin-class destroyer. (Unclassified U.S. Navy photograph)*

Above: *Submarines are ideally suited to conduct covert coastal reconnaissance and intelligence gathering. They can observe and photograph shore installations and associated activity through the periscope. With their sophisticated electronic sensor suites, they can intercept, record and analyze radio communications, radar, fire control, and other electronic transmissions. (Unclassified U.S. Navy photograph)*

Opposite, top: *As seen through the submarine's periscope, a BGM-109 Tomahawk land attack missile (TLAM) targeted on an Iraqi position is fired from a vertical launch tube on board the nuclear-powered attack submarine USS* Pittsburgh *(SSN 720). Fast attack submarines of the* Los Angeles *class (Improved) can launch TLAMs from a submerged position over 1,000 nm from a selected target. The TLAM flies to its target using flight path terrain following and accurate global positioning systems. Its accuracy is measured to within a few feet. The concept that the launching submarine is undetectable makes this missile launch and targeting capability a very present and very real threat. The threat became a reality on 19 January 1991 when* Pittsburgh *launched this Tomahawk missile in the opening minutes of the Persian Gulf War.*

and ability to remain on station undetected for months if necessary, the SSN was an ideal platform to perform these missions.

In the post–Cold War world, many ethnic and religious conflicts that had been held in check by authoritarian central governments have erupted in the last decade. Because these conflicts frequently threaten the stability of a region, the United States has found itself involved militarily, either through the United Nations, through the North Atlantic Treaty Organization (NATO), or unilaterally because its own political and economic interests are threatened. The effect this has had on the armed forces of the United States has been to demand that they be more flexible —able to respond to any level of conflict in any part of the world on short notice. It has also meant that there are many more potential trouble spots to monitor on a nearly continuous basis.

For the Submarine Force, this change in the world's political-military climate has meant moving away from a singular focus on ASW and placing a new emphasis on multimission capability. Today's Submarine Force trains for all of the missions that their predecessors carried out; and it has added a very important new one—Strike Warfare.

The addition of cruise missiles to the submarine's arsenal has brought about a significant increase in mission capability. Originally introduced as an antiship cruise missile in the early to mid 1980s, Harpoon could be launched through the torpedo tubes and gave the SSN a weapon to use against surface forces at much greater range than a torpedo could reach.

Harpoon was soon followed by Tomahawk, a longer range cruise missile available in several variants that could be launched both from torpedo tubes and the vertical launch tubes that had been built into the bow of the *Los Angeles*-class submarines. By the mid to late 1980s, SSNs had the ability to strike targets at much longer ranges, giving them the ability to project power ashore for the first time. This capability was to prove significant in the decade of the 1990s as SSNs participated in fleet, joint and combined operations in the Arabian Gulf, the Adriatic Sea, and elsewhere. Improvements in connectivity make targeting and retargeting easier, weapon improvements make precision strike possible, and the ability of the SSN to remain on station with a significant number of weapons—completely undetected by the opposition force—make the submarine invaluable to the theater commander.

Below: *USS* Scranton *(SSN 756), a 688I class submarine, underway on sea trials off the Virginia Capes in December 1990. She shows the distinctive streamlined sail that resulted from shifting the sailplanes to the bow as part of the under-ice package for that class.*

SOVIET
UNION

SEA OF JAPAN

On the evening of 10 May
1972, USS *Guardfish* visually
detected a Soviet Echo II
missile submarine deploying
in response to the U.S. mining
of North Vietnamese harbors.

Vladivostok

During the next two
days *Guardfish* detected
two and possibly three
other Soviet submarines
heading south and
alerted her operational
commander.

Beijing

NORTH
KOREA

Seoul

SOUTH
KOREA

JAPAN

CHINA

YELLOW SEA

Guardfish abandoned her surveillance patrol in the Sea of Japan
to trail the Echo submarine that
they had visually detected.

Shanghai

On 15 May the Echo turned
southeast and entered the
Philippine Sea.

On 28 May after leaving
the South China Sea, the
Echo established a much
less threatening patrol
area in the Philippine Sea
south of Okinawa.

TAIWAN

On 6 June *Guardfish* was
detected and lost contact
with the Echo.

Hanoi

Hong Kong

Haiphong

On 26 May, two days after
Nixon and Brezhnev met in
Moscow, the Echo II departed
his holding area and headed
back for the Bashi Channel.

On 17 May after experiencing some
navigational difficulties, the Echo
transited the Bashi Channel and
entered the South China Sea.

PHILIPPINE SEA

NORTH
VIETNAM

Da Nang

SOUTH
VIETNAM

Between 18–26 May, the Echo
operated in a holding area between
Luzon and the Paracel Islands,
well out of his missile range to U.S.
forces on the Vietnamese coast

Manila

PHILIPPINES

Saigon

SOUTH CHINA

GUARDFISH Trails an Echo

Captain David C. Minton, III, USN (Ret)

During the summer of 1972 USS Guardfish (SSN 612) was deployed in the Sea of Japan when world events thrust her and her crew into the adventure of a lifetime. On 9 May the Vietnam War was heating up as the Paris peace talks had broken down, and our forces had commenced mining Haiphong and other major North Vietnamese harbors to deny the North Vietnamese army from being supplied by sea. Guardfish was alerted by message to the possibility of a Soviet naval response.

The world situation was tense. No one knew how the Soviet Union would react to the mining. Guardfish was positioned at periscope depth near the Soviet's largest Pacific naval base. Late on the evening of 10 May a surface contact was detected standing out the channel at high speed cutting across the normal channel boundaries and heading almost directly for the waiting Guardfish. As the contact closed, it was visually identified in the growing darkness as a Soviet Echo II-class missile submarine. This class displaced 5,000 tons, was powered by a nuclear reactor, and carried eight Shaddock surface-to-surface missiles that could hit targets up to 200 miles away. Guardfish followed. Soon Echo II submerged and headed southeast at high speed. Was this sortie in response to the mining of Haiphong?

During the next two days the Soviet submarine frequently slowed and spent long periods at periscope depth, probably receiving detailed orders from his naval commander. While listening for Echo II, Guardfish slowed, which significantly extended her sonar detection range. To the crew's surprise and alarm, they were able to detect at least two and possibly three other Soviet submarines in the area. One submarine is hard to trail—three or four is impossible! Therefore, Guardfish's tracking party focused all efforts on maintaining contact with the Echo II they had identified visually.

Opposite: Chart of USS *Guardfish*'s (SSN 612) trail of a Soviet Echo-class nuclear submarine. The Echo-class was specifically designed to counter U.S. aircraft carriers by launching long-range anti-surface ship missiles from a submarine.

Above: *Guardfish* was a member of the *Permit* class and a sister of the ill-fated USS *Thresher* (SSN 593). This submarine class pioneered many major improvements in submarine design, including increased operating depth, more capable sonar equipment, more sophisticated noise quieting, and the torpedo room moved from the bow to midships.

When Echo II *resumed its transit toward the southern exit of the Sea of Japan, as captain I had two important decisions to make. First, did the deployment of three, possibly four, Soviet submarines meet the requirement for breaking radio silence? The number one priority of all submarine surveillance operations was to provide an early warning of an unusual deployment of Soviet naval vessels. This type of report, called a "critic" report, had never been sent before. I determined that now was the time for* Guardfish *to break that silence and notified my operational commander of the situation. Second, should* Guardfish *abandon her surveillance mission in the Sea of Japan to continue the trail of the Soviet submarine? The operations order was silent on this count, but it made sense to me that our naval commander would want to know where the Soviets were going. Because I didn't have the luxury of time to wait for orders, I invoked the submarine commander's secret creed, "No guts—no hero ribbon." We were on our way!*

Trailing is a complex task. For a submarine to remain undetected a contact's position, course, and speed must be determined using passive sonar bearings. Passive ranging required Guardfish *to continually maneuver to generate a changing bearing to the contact. Too close and you could be detected—too far away and contact could be lost. These maneuvers were usually conducted in the baffle area of the contact, the blind spot astern.*

Echo II *turned to clear this baffle area almost hourly. Sometimes it was a very passive turn of 90 degrees so that his sonar could listen for anything behind him and at other times he aggressively turned*

180 degrees and raced back along his previous track right at Guardfish. *This maneuver was dangerous with a real possibility of collision. At the very least there was a chance he could detect* Guardfish's *presence as the range closed. When* Echo II *made a baffle clearing maneuver,* Guardfish *tried to anticipate which way he would turn so that* Guardfish *was slightly off of* Echo II's *track on the opposite side. Additionally,* Guardfish *slowed immediately to be as silent as possible and give more time and distance for* Echo II *to return to his previous course.*

Frequent status reports were needed in Washington to assess the threat and intent of the Soviet forces. President Nixon and his National Security Advisor were briefed daily. Because high-powered, high-frequency radio transmissions from Guardfish *were subject to detection and location by the Soviet electronic intercept network, an alternate method of communicating was established. Navy ASW P-3 aircraft flew covert missions over* Guardfish's *projected location and received status reports via short range ultra-high-frequency radio either directly from* Guardfish *at periscope depth or via slot buoys—small, expendable battery powered transmitters that could be programmed with a short message and shot out of the signal ejector while* Guardfish *remained at trail depth.*

During this period of the trail every available submarine in the Pacific was urgently being deployed to provide protection for our aircraft carriers operating off the Vietnamese coast and to search for the other Soviet submarines. This deployment created a mutual interference problem for both Guardfish *and the submarine operations staffs.* Guardfish *was committed to* going wherever the Soviet Echo II *went, and the staffs had to relocate the deploying submarines frequently to ensure that the much quieter U.S. submarines would not endanger each other or* Guardfish.

Once in the Philippine Sea, Echo II *turned southwest heading in the general direction of the Bashi Channel—the strait between Taiwan and the islands north of Luzon, Philippines. The Bashi is the usual northern entrance to the South China Sea and I was sure that it was the Soviet submarine's objective, but their track continued well south of the normal course. Then* Echo II *slowed, came to periscope depth, and went active on his fathometer on a short-scale, which was not suitable for the depth of water. He was lost! While at periscope depth he must have obtained a good navigational fix because he now went deep, turned toward the Bashi Channel, and increased speed to 16 knots. After reporting this rapid course correction by slot buoy,* Guardfish *rushed after him knowing that the repositioning of U.S. submarines would be nearly impossible on such short notice. As a precaution against collision with another U.S. submarine,* Guardfish *changed depth to 100 meters, a depth commonly used by Soviet submarines and one I knew U.S. submarines would avoid. My apprehension was justified when* Guardfish *detected a U.S. submarine clearing to the north at high speed.*

On 18 May Echo II *entered the South China Sea and transited to a point approximately 300 miles off the coast of Luzon. For eight days he established a*

slow-moving grid track that covered a rectangular patrol area approximately 700 miles from our carriers along the Vietnamese coast, well beyond the 200-mile range of his missiles.

While the tracking team struggled to main- *tain contact with the Soviet submarine, world events were moving in a more peaceful direction. After long negotiations President Nixon went to Moscow for his historic summit meeting with Soviet General Secretary Brezhnev. During the summit on 24 May, National Security Advisor Kissinger informed Brezhnev that the United States knew the Soviets had deployed submarines, and that their presence so close to the Vietnamese War Zone was provocative and extremely dangerous. Within two days of this confrontation, the Soviet* Echo II *submarine started north.*

After transiting the Bashi Channel Echo II *established a second patrol area in the Philippine Sea south of Okinawa. This area of the ocean had some of the worst possible acoustical properties. At night the biological noise and frequent rain showers were deafening to sonar. Maintaining contact became even harder than before, making it necessary for* Guardfish *to trail at closer and closer ranges.*

A lengthy procedure to transfer the trail to another U.S. submarine, just developed by the staff, was placed on the radio broadcast. While Guardfish *was at periscope depth copying this urgent message,* Echo II *unexpectedly came to periscope depth and visually detected* Guardfish. *The maneuvers that followed were violent and at high speed. Holding on to an alerted contact proved to be impossible and contact with* Echo II *was lost.*

When Guardfish *returned to Guam on 10 June, the crew had been underway submerged for 123 days with only an eight-day refit as a break; however,* Guardfish's *morale was sky high. The officers and crew were all justifiably proud of what they had accomplished.*

Opposite, left: Masts and antennas of the Echo-class submarine as seen through the periscope of *Guardfish.* (U.S. Navy photo courtesy of David Minton)

Opposite, right: Pictured here is an Echo II-class submarine of the type trailed by *Guardfish* in 1972 from the Sea of Japan to the South China Sea. *Echo* approached the area where U.S. aircraft carriers were operating off Vietnam, but stayed outside cruise missile range (about 200nm). The openings in the hull casing contain missile launchers and eight surface-launched anti-ship cruise missiles.

Left: Special recognition for completing an operation of great national significance was well deserved. In addition to other awards, Commander Minton was awarded the Distinguished Service Medal, and the ship received the Navy Unit Commendation.

Life on Board

Captain F. T. Jones, USN (Ret)

Without a doubt, life on a nuclear submarine is much better for the crew than it was on conventional submarines. That is not to say that it is not without its inconveniences and shortcomings, but to a submariner that's just part of the package that you get when you volunteer for this demanding, exciting duty.

Conventional submarines were notoriously unhygienic. Given the constant presence of diesel fuel and hydraulic fluid and the frequent absence of air conditioning or sufficient fresh water for laundry and bathing, a long patrol, especially in warm waters, could be a pretty smelly experience. No wonder nicknames such as "pig boats" were often attached to early submarines. With the advent of nuclear propulsion, plenty of electric power was available to run air conditioning plants (and they were necessary with the operation of a steam propulsion plant), there was much less use of diesel fuel, and there was sufficient fresh water created to allow for regular laundry and showers. Of course nuclear submariners are still expected to take water-saving "Navy showers," but at least the shower stalls are used for more than storing sacks of potatoes.

Life on a submarine at sea comes in six-hour segments. That is the length of a normal watch. Therefore, depending on the number of people available to stand the watch, a submariner's day may be based on twelve, eighteen, or twenty-four hour cycles. If only two people are qualified to stand a particular watch, that unfortunate situation is known as being "port and starboard." It means that an individual will stand a six-hour watch, have six hours off, stand a six-hour watch again, and have six hours off, continuously. In the time not on watch, the submariner has to eat, sleep, attend training, work on qualification, do administrative paperwork, and perform corrective and preventive maintenance. Showers and recreation are optional. This watch rotation isn't much fun even for short periods. The individual spends a few hours asleep before each watch but

The crew's mess is busy twenty-four hours a day. Four meals are served, but the space also serves as a lecture hall, a ceremonial center, recreational space, and as a desk for many crewmembers.

The crew's mess serves as the center of life in a submarine. Between meals it is in constant use. An honors ceremony is pictured here. The commanding officer is presenting an award to Sonar Technician Smith of the nuclear attack submarine William H. Bates *(SSN 680).*

Opposite: *On long patrols on board a fast attack submarine meals take on special significance. Good food has always been a hallmark of the Submarine Force. Cooks and messmen work long hours in cramped spaces to prepare and serve meals for over a hundred men. One of the special smells that can waft through a submarine is that of baking bread, or even more special, the night baker's large pans of sticky buns.*

Above: *With space at a premium, the issue of privacy takes on an importance not seen outside of submarines. The only place a crewman is truly in a private space is in his bunk. Just over 6 feet long and 30 inches wide, with barely 20 inches between the mattress top and the bottom of the bunk pan above, the space is cramped but serves as a retreat from the bustle of the other parts of the boat.*

The bridge watch on USS Louisiana *(SSBN 743) gets an unscheduled shower as the ship ploughs through 8-foot waves along the Florida coast. The submarine was near the fringes of 1998's Hurricane* Mitch *conducting predeployment sea trials.*

is perpetually tired. The remedy is to get more people qualified or to get the commanding officer to make an exception and allow the watch to rotate at longer intervals.

The one-in-three rotation is the most common and puts an individual in an eighteen-hour cycle with six hours on watch and twelve hours off. This is tolerable for long periods of time; however, it takes getting used to because the individual doesn't work or sleep the same hours every day.

The one-in-four rotation (six hours on watch and eighteen hours off) is about as good as it gets at sea. There just isn't enough room on board a submarine to carry four people qualified to stand every watch. The one-in-four rotation occurs for the more senior watchstations and is more common near the end of a deployment, when there has been a lot of at-sea time for training and watchstation qualification.

The meal schedule on a submarine is established to match the six-hour watch rotation. On-going watchstanders are allowed to eat first and then relieve the watch; off-going watchstanders then have time to eat before the meal is secured. So that there is food available for every watch change, submarines serve four meals a day—breakfast, lunch, dinner, and "midrats," or midnight rations, which is a less formal meal

Left: *On earlier fast attacks, the "yeoman's shack" consisted of a cramped space with a typewriter, a set of Navy Regulations and ship's manuals, and a few filing drawers. The more modern ship's office has to cope with the modern paperwork blizzard and modern communications. The typewriter has been replaced with computers and word processing programs. Although some regulations and instructions are kept in binders, more of these are on computer disks. Here on board USS* Norfolk *(SSN 714) Yeoman Third Class Clifton Williams works in the ship's office that is equipped with a fax machine and electronic copier and computer.*

Above: *This photograph, titled, "Are You Being Served" won Photographer's Mate Second Class Aaron Ansarov first place in the illustrative category of the 1999 Military Photographer of the Year competition. Petty Officer Ansarov's photograph shows Mess Management Specialist Yin Lau bringing food to the bridge watch on USS* Jefferson City *(SSN 759) on New Year's Day 1999.*

Above: *There is never enough room for crew or food when loading out for an extended cruise. Here in USS* Will Rogers *(SSBN 659), sacks of potatoes are hung from the overhead and a temporary bunk is placed beneath them. In a submarine—no space is unused. (Photo: Steve Kaufman)*

that might consist of soup, sandwiches, leftovers, pizza (especially on Saturday night), or other local favorites.

Submarines have long been known for serving good food in generous quantities. As partial compensation for the rigors of submarine life, some items in the Navy's supply system were not available to all shipboard messes but could be ordered by submarine supply officers. The tradition continues today. If there is any problem, it's eating *too* much when underway for a long time. With the ability to exercise somewhat restricted, it is easy to gain weight and find oneself outside the limits established by the Navy for physical fitness.

Loading and storing enough food for a crew for three months is a serious task, and for most nuclear submarines, a stores load is an all-hands evolution. Because space is always at a premium, as food is loaded, unneeded cardboard and other wrapping materials are removed and taken off the ship while still pierside. The total amount of food needed for a long deployment will exceed the volume of the freeze box, chill box, and dry storerooms, so it is common to have at least a single layer of cases of canned goods on all the walking decks at the beginning of a deployment, making it necessary to walk stooped over until the crew is able to "eat its way" down to the decks again.

When a submarine goes to sea, there may be 130 to 145 men on board. The actual number depends on how long the submarine will be gone, its mission, and whether additional "riders" are on board who are not part of the permanently assigned crew. A typical crew consists of about fourteen officers, about the same number of chiefs, senior chiefs, and master chiefs (E7 through E9) combined, and slightly over one hundred more junior enlisted men (E2 through E6). The Navy's intention is to man a submarine at about 10 percent above the number needed to operate it. That allows someone to stay ashore for leave or school without forcing the others to be in continuous "port and starboard" watch rotations.

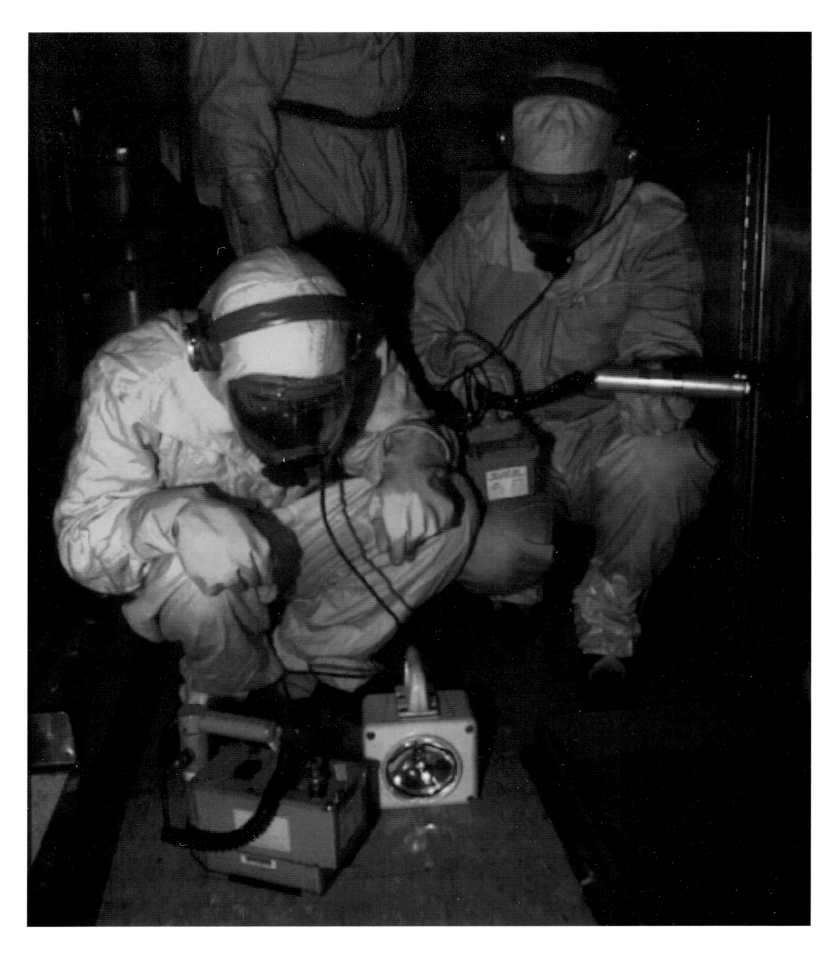

All aspects of submarine operations and safety are reviewed frequently. This photograph shows a nuclear radiation drill. (Courtesy of USS Alabama *SSBN 731)*

The number of men on board frequently exceeds the number of bunks (or sleeping berths) that were built into the ship. To mitigate this, boats often carry portable bunks that are installed in the torpedo room and may even have some air mattresses that are placed on the deck in out-of-the-way places; however, these are only used for short periods because of the lack of any personal storage space. If the number of people still exceeds the number of bunks, even with portable bunks and air mattresses, the solution is "hot bunking." Hot bunking is the practice of assigning two men to a

Above: *On submarines, everyone has a job to do, even the most junior people. Ensign Aaron Keffler updates a contact evaluation plot on board the nuclear attack submarine USS* Tucson *(SSN 770) during a 1998 deployment to the Persian Gulf.*

Above: *In Hampton Roads, Virginia, on 20 April 1994, crewmembers of the nuclear-powered attack submarine USS* Norfolk *(SSN 714) prepare to get underway for departure from their homeport at the Norfolk Naval Base.*

Crewmen studying in the mess deck on board the Los Angeles-*class nuclear-powered attack submarine USS* LaJolla *(SSN 701). Submariners are constantly studying. Everyone in a submarine, from captain to mess cook, devotes at least two hours a day to studying, training, and qualifying.*

bunk or three men to two bunks, requiring them to coordinate their schedules so that they get equal time in the rack. Typically this impacts the most junior, unqualified personnel, so that with time on board and satisfactory progress in qualification, a man can eventually get a bunk to call his own.

Submariners are constantly training. It involves everyone on board (including the commanding officer) and is so pervasive as to be the factor that drives the Plan of the Day. All-hands topics are covered in general military training (GMT) that is held once a week. Each department on board runs its own training program and holds a department training lecture weekly. Each division has a training program to cover in-rate (technical specialty) topics. In addition to these training programs, nuclear trained officers and senior enlisted personnel have weekly training in additional propulsion plant topics, and all officers meet to cover professional topics on a weekly basis. That's just the classroom-training portion of the program. To the extent permitted by the ship's operational demands, casualty drills are conducted for all hands on a weekly basis and the nuclear propulsion watchstanders are given drills on a watch-section basis (casualties that don't require an all-hands response). The ship control party can also be given minor casualties on a section basis, and the tracking party (those that follow contacts with the ship's sensors) can train with simulated contacts to hone their proficiency.

The qualification program is distinct from the ongoing training program. Submariners "qualify" in two ways. All hands must qualify in submarines, meaning that they must learn enough about all of the ship's systems and procedures to pass written and oral examinations. This process takes about a year from the time that a new man reports to his first submarine. Successful completion of submarine qualification is the basis for being awarded the submariner's breast insignia, the Dolphins. The second type of qualification is watchstation qualification. Each man, depending on his rating or specialty, is expected to complete qualification for a series of demanding watches. Different watches are required when the boat is at sea and when it is in port. The most senior of these watches

Above: *The crew's mess serves many functions. It is the primary entertainment center as well as a working space. Mess Management Specialist First Class Bryron Blackmon works on a laptop computer in the mess deck of the* USS Tucson *(SSN 770) during operations in the Persian Gulf. He is concentrating on his work, ignoring the movie being shown behind him and other shipmates, not in view, who are also working or watching the movie.*

Below: *A desk is where one can find a flat space. Machinist's Mate First Class Robert Ramos is shown using a work bench to write up the next quarter's preventive maintenance schedule on board the* USS Miami *(SSN 755).*

might not be completed until a man is serving on his second or third submarine because of the experience and knowledge required to safely stand the watch.

Submarining is not all work and no play. Recreational opportunities at sea include reading, playing cards or games, watching movies, and exercising. The ship's library is not extensive because of space constraints, but a good paperback book usually circulates as long as it holds together. Cribbage, long a favorite game of sea-going men, is still played, but today's submariner also can choose from a variety of board games or computer games played on the television in the crew's mess. The evening movie has also taken on a different character in recent years, since the Armed Forces Radio and Television Service shifted from 16mm films to video tapes. Nuclear submarines don't have a lot of room for exercise equipment, but submarine sailors have always found enough space to store free weights (perhaps made on board from garbage weights), and today's ships probably have a treadmill or an exercise bike installed somewhere on board. Swim call doesn't come often, but if the ship is in warm waters and schedules permit, a chance to go topside and dive in is a big morale booster. Finally, liberty call in interesting foreign ports has always been a unique aspect of going to sea. Although submariners may not spend much time in port, a long deployment normally includes a few chances to see the world.

Although awards ceremonies are usually held in port so that the families of the crew can attend, a submarine at sea has its ceremonies as well. The centuries-old traditions of holding initiation ceremonies upon crossing the Arctic Circle (Bluenose) and the Equator (Shellback) are still carried out with ingenuity and enthusiasm on submarines. Requiring less

preparation, but perhaps more important, are the ceremonies to award Dolphins to those who complete qualification in submarines. Not wanting to wait any longer than necessary once a man completes all requirements, these ceremonies may be as simple as the commanding officer picking up the 1MC announcing system microphone in the control room and announcing the name of the latest qualified submariner as he pins on the man's Dolphins. By pinning on a man's Dolphins, the man's commanding officer is certifying, for the world to see, that he and the man's shipmates place, with trust and confidence, their lives in the man's hands, knowing that he will do the right thing at all times and not jeopardize the safety of the ship or crew. This is a strong bond that ties all submariners together.

Submariners enjoy showing off their ship. Midshipmen from the U.S. Naval Academy receive a tour of the USS Norfolk (SSN 714) from Chief Fire Control Technician (FTC) Ricky Williams during a port call at Annapolis, Maryland. The gold hash marks on Chief Williams's left sleeve are for twelve years of exemplary service. One red stripe is awarded for each four years of such service. After the third award, all three hash marks switch to gold.

Above: *Submariners are great jokesters. Here, Santa Claus waves from the North Pole during USS Pogy's (SSN 647) scientific expedition into the Arctic.*

Left: *Finding room to exercise can be difficult on board a submarine, even on the Navy's newest nuclear-powered attack submarine USS Seawolf (SSN 21). Electrician's Mate First Class Carl Tilden takes advantage of the ship's exercise bike in a passageway lined with computer components.*

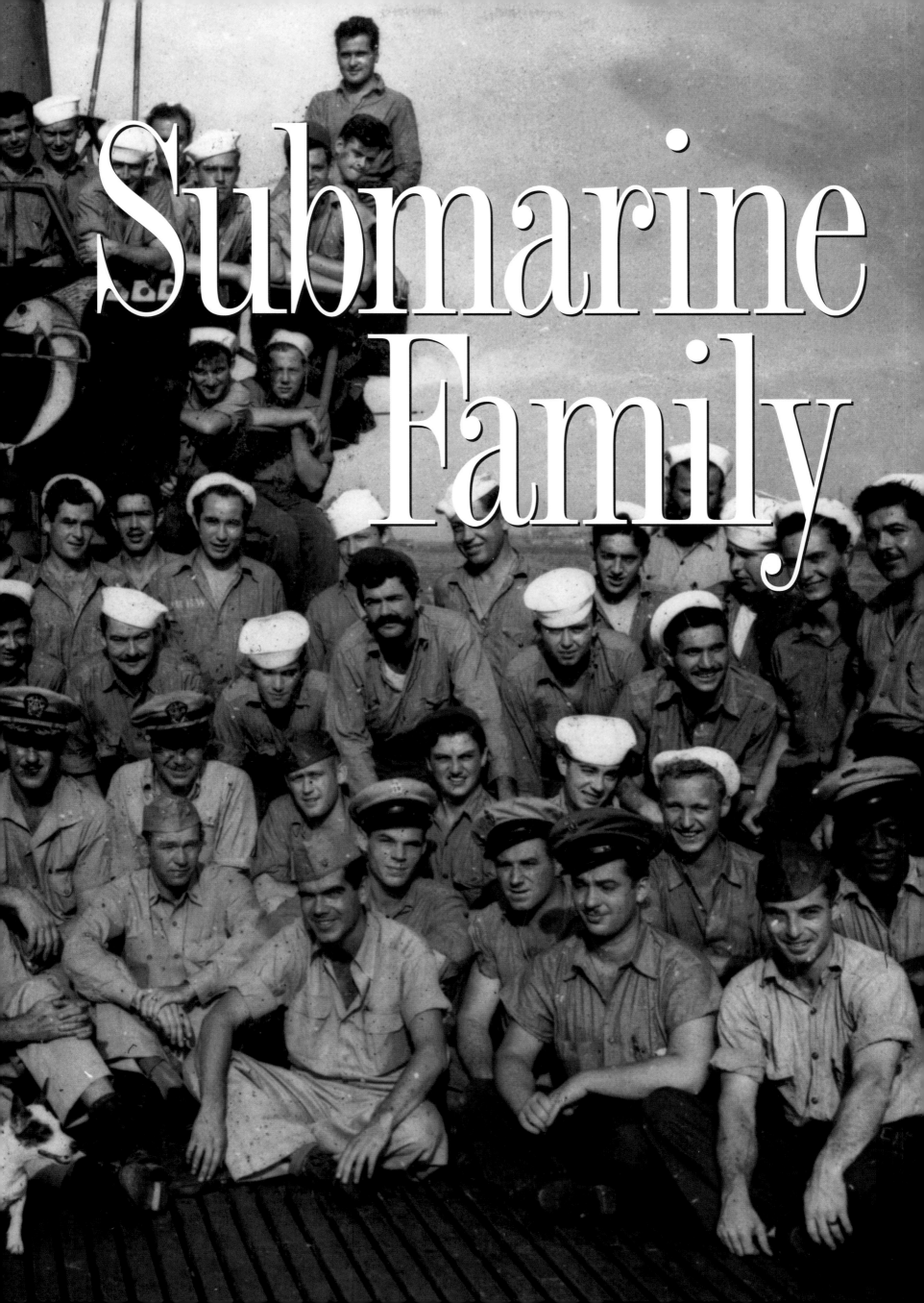

Submarine Family

Submariners AND THE Submarine Family

Lieutenant Commander Don C. LaForce, USN (Ret)

ride runs deep! These three words speak volumes about those
who form the heart and soul of the Submarine Force—the submariners. From its very beginnings in October of 1900, the U.S.
Navy Submarine Force has been blessed with extraordinary
people—people who have voluntarily given of themselves in service to
their country and who have demonstrated to their shipmates that they
can be counted on in any emergency and in the face of any enemy.

Being recognized as a submariner involves a rite of passage where
the individual demonstrates that he can perform as part of a crew. Submariners are required to be responsible to themselves as well as to each
other for the safe and effective operation of their submarine. They must
show that they can be trusted and that, when the going gets tough, they
have the knowledge and the initiative to help their shipmates through any
peril or crisis. When, and only when, an individual has shown that he can
do his job, perform as part of the crew, and understands the submarine's
intricate systems and equipment is that rite of passage complete. It is at
that point that the individual is designated as "qualified in submarines"
and becomes at once and for all times a submariner, earning the right to
wear the Dolphin insignia and add "SS" after his rate.

The process of qualification is demanding and difficult—a process that
culminates with a deep sense of pride. Pride runs deep among submariners

Above: *The ship's control party in the control
room on USS* Batfish *(SS 310) prepares to
submerge the submarine. The enlisted man
in the back operates the stern planes that
control the angle of the submarine, and the
man in the foreground takes charge of the
bow planes that are used to control depth.
Behind the two operators stands a junior officer assigned as the diving officer, who directs
the actions of the enlisted watchstanders.
The diving officer takes his orders from the
conning officer, who is standing watch in the
conning tower, located above the control room.*

Pages 260–261: *USS* Spadefish *(SS 411)
officers and crew pose with their battle flag
following a successful World War II patrol
in the Pacific. The all-volunteer officers and
crew, typical of the many who served on submarines during the war, left family, friends,
jobs, and home to go in harm's way and bring
victory in the Pacific.*

Opposite: *USS* Pasadena *(SSN 752), an
improved* Los Angeles-*class attack submarine
is in a floating drydock for maintenance and
repairs. Standing in front of the ship's bow is
part of her complement of officers, chief petty
officers, and enlisted men displaying a ship's
banner highlighted by the ship's patch on the
left and the Submarine Squadron ELEVEN
patch on the right.*

Top: *The crews on the earliest U.S. submarines were small. Living space was limited and cramped and the men knew little in the way of privacy or comfort. USS* Holland *visited the Naval Academy at Annapolis, Maryland, and frequently hosted visits by midshipmen, many of whom served in submarines after they graduated and became commissioned officers.*

Above: *This recruiting poster, used to attract young men into the Submarine Service and the Navy Nuclear Power Program, provided a recurring theme for those who served on submarines. "Pride Runs Deep" found its way onto bumper stickers and billboards and has become a phrase symbolic of how submariners view submarine duty.*

because they know that those who wear Dolphins have been tested and are accepted as part of a long line of submariners who have gone before them shaping the traditions that have set submariners apart since the earliest days. Submariners have learned from the beginning that they must not only know their jobs and their submarines, but they must also pass on their knowledge as well as their traditions to following generations.

The traditions started early in U.S. Submarine Force history. The first crew of the first submarine, USS *Holland*, commanded by Lieutenant Harry Caldwell, had essentially no experience with submarines. They drew on the experience and training that made them sailors and used that background, good common sense, and dedication to the task at hand to become submariners. It was from these humble beginnings that all U.S. submariners have joined this cadre of professionals.

Before placing *Holland* in commission, the commanding officer and his crew learned from the builders and engineers who were the only ones who knew how to operate the submarine. Together the crew learned the systems that made it dive and surface, became aware of its inherent dangers, and developed the techniques needed to operate it safely and effectively. This was no simple task. During this precommissioning period, Lieutenant Caldwell reported to his superiors at the Naval Torpedo Station at Newport, Rhode Island, concerning the requirements for submarine crews. He wrote:

> *The enlisted men in such a boat must be of the highest intelligence, steady of nerve, quick of resource, and implicitly obedient. The present crew fills these requirements. The officer in the turret cannot see what his men are doing and must be able to*

thoroughly rely on them, as the safety of the boat depends on the individual action of any one. It seems only fair that these men should receive extra compensation.

Lieutenant Caldwell could not have imagined the profound nature of his words. As the only commissioned officer assigned to the ship, he did not list the traits needed for the leaders of submarine crews. If he had, he might have observed that submarine crews take on the character and example of their leadership and noted that good crews help build strong leaders. Before long, submariners would receive extra pay as compensation

This artist's sketch, based on a drawing by H. Reuterdahl published in the September 1900 issue of Harper's Magazine, *illustrates Holland's Lieutenant Harry Caldwell's view that the submarine commander must be able to completely trust the men assigned to the ship, since neither could see the other in such circumstances. Directing the movement of the ship while standing erect in the turret, the officer must have confidence that the men below are properly carrying out his orders. (Mike Eagle)*

The first class of twenty-four officers at the Naval Submarine School in New London, Connecticut, began their studies to prepare for submarine duty in the summer of 1916. Twenty-two would graduate by Christmas of that same year, bound for assignments on submarines. Within a year, this first class of submarine officers, and those in classes that followed, were serving around the world as the United States entered World War I.

Above: *Line handlers stand by on board the attack submarine USS* Chicago *(SSN 721) as the submarine returns to San Diego following a deployment to the Persian Gulf. Handling the wet mooring lines is a sometimes dangerous chore but one that all submariners experience during their tour of duty.*

Right: *The commanding officer of the attack submarine USS* City of Corpus Christi *(SSN 705) along with the officer of the deck (OOD) and a lookout stand atop the sail. All the submarine's operations and evolutions are directed by the officer of the deck with guidance from the commanding officer. The OOD gives all orders needed to operate the ship safely—orders that are carefully carried out by watchstanders throughout the ship.*

Above: *USS* Sand Lance *(SS 381) is shown underway for a war patrol during World War II. The men on watch include the ship's OOD and several enlisted men assigned as lookouts, who are responsible for sighting and reporting any visual contacts as the ship runs along on the surface.*

for the risks and responsibilities inherent in submarine duty. The extra pay has continued and submariners—officer and enlisted—must still measure up to Caldwell's requirements.

Measuring up as a submariner involves a time-honored process of training and qualification that, for submariners, never ends. The process starts with the basics. All submariners are sailors first, submariners second, and thus share a common bond in learning about the Navy first. Whether they pass through enlisted boot camp, Officer Candidate School, the Naval Reserve Officer Training Corps program, or are graduates of the Naval Academy, they all learn the basics of being sailors and about life and service at sea. Technical schools where individual sailors learn a specific trade or skill often follow this basic training. Next comes Submarine School, which for nearly all submariners, marks the start of their life in the Submarine Force. This wasn't always the case.

When USS *Holland* was commissioned on 12 October 1900, there was no formal training process in place, and there was no submarine school in existence to teach the fundamentals. Until 1916, when the first officer course at the New London Submarine Base in Groton, Connecticut, began, the bulk of all submarine training was conducted on board individual submarines and tenders. Enlisted submarine school began in 1917. Establishment of the officer and enlisted courses ensured that each future submariner would begin his service only after he learned the basic concepts and principles he would need to start the process of submarine qualification. Training starts at the Submarine School and continues with assignment to an operational submarine for on-the-job training and qualification. This path is the same for both officers and enlisted men.

The chain of command on submarines parallels that for all Navy ships. The commanding officer is at the top of the chain, supported by an executive officer and a wardroom of department heads and division officers. In the enlisted ranks generally several chief petty officers and senior petty officers lead the various divisions. The divisions include groups of more junior petty officers and nonrated enlisted men. All submariners know and support this traditional chain of command; however, in submarines, assignment to higher responsibilities is also linked to experience and qualification. Submarine crews function not just as individuals but

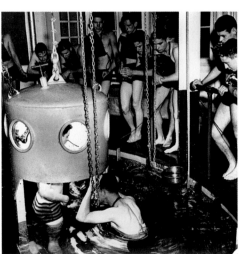

Top: *The enlisted courses at Naval Submarine School began in the winter of 1917 in a building located near the waterfront on the Naval Submarine Base. At Submarine School, submariners learn the basic principles of submarine operation, study ship's systems, and generally prepare for the process of qualification once they report to their first submarine.*

Above: *Students and instructors at Submarine School on the U.S. Submarine Base, conduct escape training using Momsen lungs. The training was given in a specially built escape training tank that allowed students to practice escape from depths of up to 100 feet.*

267

Above: *Submarine crews learn by practicing and conduct frequent drills to hone their skills, even in the most unusual places. Crew members of the nuclear submarine USS* Pogy *(SSN 647) don emergency breathing masks for a drill during a scientific expedition to the Arctic.*

Right: *During World War II, all U.S. submarines used diesel engines for producing power to drive the ship and generate needed electrical power. Trained operators were needed to run and repair these large engines. Training was given at the Submarine School in New London and followed up by intensive hands-on on-the-job training and qualifications on the individual submarines.*

On board the nuclear submarine USS Halibut *(SSGN 587) Hospital Corpsman First Class Patrick Cronan takes a radiation survey with a portable detector. Radiation checks are made frequently to ensure that the areas outside the ship's reactor compartment are virtually free from radiation. Although crewmembers receive less radiation than a person living ashore receives from the sun's rays, submariners rely on the checks by their shipmates to detect any problems.*

as well-drilled teams where the best and most experienced people are assigned the most critical jobs and lead both juniors and seniors in the tasks at hand. Proper respect for seniority is always apparent but is usually balanced with the understanding that experience trumps rank when the going gets tough.

Each submariner shares the common experience of reporting to his first "boat" or submarine and enduring the rigors of qualification in submarines, becoming integrated into the crew, and ultimately earning the trust of his shipmates. The task is not a simple one. Submarine qualification ensures that each individual is fully qualified to stand watches on the submarine focused on his rating or job specialty. The process also ensures that everyone is capable of effectively combating casualties occurring in the equipment he operates and within the spaces where he normally works and lives. Finally, submarine qualification ensures that the entire crew is capable of rendering effective damage control assistance in casualty situations anywhere in the ship.

DOLPHIN SCHOLARSHIP FOUNDATION

The Dolphin Scholarship Foundation (DSF) began modestly in 1961. The foundation was the brainchild of then Commander Submarine Force, U.S. Atlantic Fleet, Vice Admiral E. W. Grenfell and his wife Martha. Mrs. Grenfell was truly the driving force behind the idea. With the support of Submarine Officers Wives' Clubs throughout the Navy, the first Dolphin Scholarship, in the amount of $350, was awarded in the spring of 1961. Originally established to provide undergraduate college scholarships for the children of submarine officers, the program was extended in subsequent years to include the children or stepchildren of past or present members of the U.S. Submarine Force, officer or enlisted, who have either qualified in submarines or served in submarine support activities.

From the beginning, the search was on for creative ways to raise money. The generous nature of the submariners and their wives quickly became evident. The wives' clubs worked tirelessly to raise funds through bake sales, auctions, and other fundraising activities. The men contributed "dolphin dollars" during the April anniversary week of the U.S. Submarine Force. The foundation was off and running.

In 1990, under the leadership of the foundation directors and the advisory committee, the legal structure of the foundation and its affiliation with the Submarine Officers Wives' Clubs were thoroughly reviewed. As a result, the Dolphin Scholarship Foundation was incorporated on 19 November 1990 in the Commonwealth of Virginia as a nonstock corporation. By incorporating, the foundation was established as a legal entity all its own. Thus, the foundation and the wives' clubs are different and distinct legal entities, but bound legally in the nature of a parent and subsidiary corporations.

Since its inception, DSF has awarded in excess of $4 million dollars in scholarship assistance. DSF has had the extreme good fortune to be handled by a succession of presidents who all share a love for both the submarine family and education. Coupled with a superb group of decision-makers, the foundation has been able to grow and flourish. With the ongoing generosity of its supporters, the foundation will continue to meet the challenges of assisting deserving children in obtaining a college education.

Submarine qualification is certified by a series of oral and written examinations designed to test the individual's overall knowledge and understanding of the submarine. Qualified submariners run the program, give the examinations, and teach the prospective submariner the things he needs to know. The process is arduous but is the essential means that passes both the skill and the art of submarining from one generation to the next. Beginning submariners today are asked questions that have their origins in the early days of the submarine service—questions that are as valid and important today as they were throughout the history of the Submarine Force. For submariners, the process of qualification never ends. There is always a more advanced watch station, a new piece of equipment, or improved procedures to learn and each man wearing Dolphins is responsible for training the next generations. The never-ending process has a hidden benefit. Qualification in submarines marks the end of the initiation process for each person who completes the task. The newly qualified crew member becomes part of the "club," one of the elite—a valued and respected member of the submarine family.

Submariners are responsible for more than qualification. They also must run and maintain the ship, both in port and underway. They perform preventive and corrective maintenance on equipment and systems, stand watches to ensure the safe operation and security of the

Submariners qualify to stand a variety of specialized watches that require additional skills and training. Electronics Technician Third Class Donny Scroggins checks navigational charts on board USS Annapolis *(SSN 760) in preparation for a 1997 deployment to the Persian Gulf as part of a carrier battle group. Petty Officer Scroggin's job is to assist the ship's OOD in safely navigating the ship.*

A torpedoman's mate performs a maintenance routine on the breech door of one of his submarine's torpedo tubes. Behind the enlisted technician is the acoustic nose of a Mk 48 torpedo. A mistake by the crewman could render the tube useless, limiting the ability of the submarine to fire torpedoes and reducing its effectiveness in battle. On submarines, every task is important.

ship, and when needed, man assigned stations to take the ship into battle or perform a variety of other special evolutions. Each individual is also responsible for his own advancement and improvement and for his contribution to the ship and the Navy. It is always a source of wonder for those outside the Submarine Force to realize that all of this responsibility falls on a corps of comparatively young men. These same observers are also generally struck by the realization that all this occurs within the confines of the submarine—an environment that can test even the strongest and most adaptable under normal circumstances.

Above: *Maneuvering a submarine beneath the Arctic ice requires careful attention and teamwork from the submarine crew. The ship control party on USS* Pogy *(SSN 647) work together as they transit under the ice during a scientific expedition.*

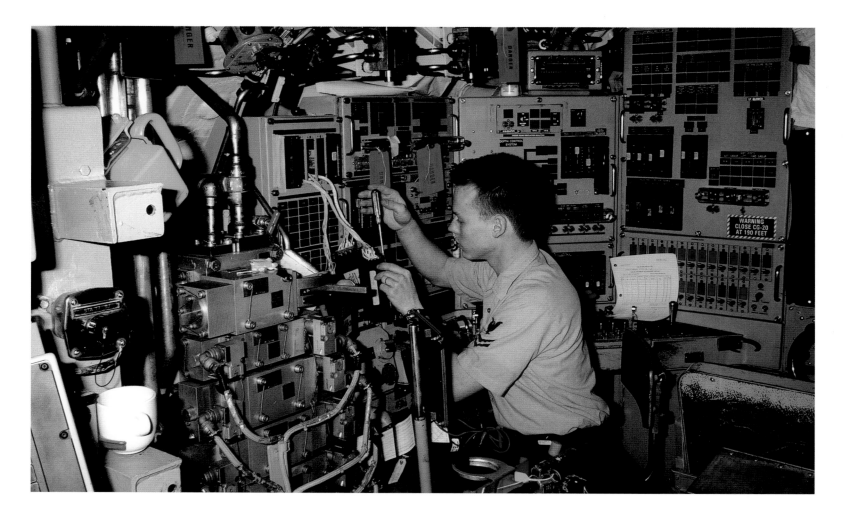

Submarines are warships and as warships their design and function revolve around their warfighting missions. The limited space on even the most modern submarines is thus allocated first to the ship and its systems and second to the crew. Bunk and locker space is minimal and privacy is limited. In some cases, the crew outnumbers the available bunk space and crewmembers either sleep in temporary bunks in the torpedo room or "hot-bunk" with one or two other crew members. "Hot-bunking" means that the crew members will rotate their time in the bunk to match their schedules for watches and other duties. Just when you're the most tired, it is the other guy's turn in the bunk.

Submarine equipment undergoes both preventive and corrective maintenance to ensure that the hundreds of vital systems operate correctly. Maintenance is performed by trained and qualified enlisted men who must understand not only how the equipment operates, but also how it relates to other equipment and systems. These technicians must be reliable and competent because the tasks they perform are important to the safety of the ship and crew.

Left: *Tucked snugly into his bunk on board USS* Pasadena *(SSN 752), Machinist's Mate Second Class (SS) Chris Fitchet enjoys some quiet time in the only space he can call private. There is little privacy for the crew on submarines and a submariner's bunk, no matter how small, is still an important amenity.*

Opposite, bottom: *Any fire in a submarine can create havoc for the crew and the ship's equipment. Every crew member must be trained to fight all types of fires to reduce the potential for injuries to their shipmates and to protect the ship and its essential systems. Submarine crews conduct frequent drills, much like the one shown here, where personnel on USS* Alabama *(SSBN 731) simulate extinguishing a hydraulic oil fire.*

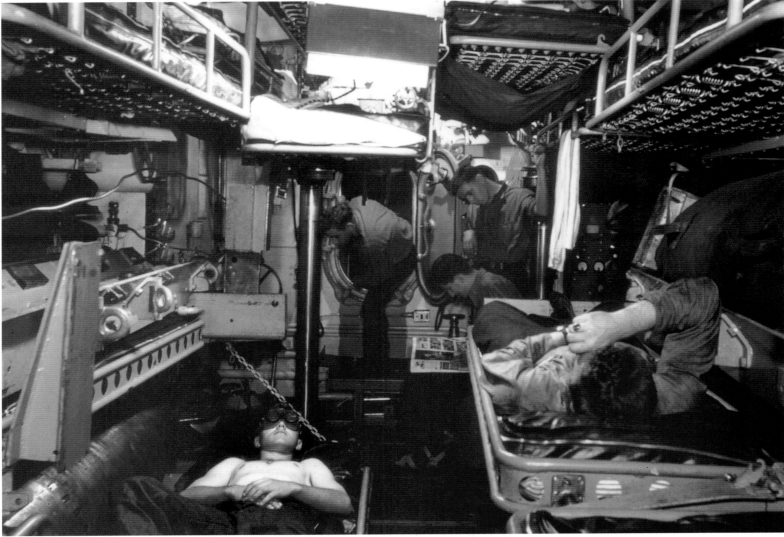

Personal hygiene isn't much easier. Bathrooms or "heads" are few in number and are shared with the rest of the crew. Officers and chief petty officers have things a little better, with slightly more storage space for their personal gear and a little more privacy. On modern submarines the commanding officer and executive officer enjoy private staterooms but often share a head. If this sounds almost tolerable, it is worth recognizing that on a typical modern *Los Angeles*-class attack submarine, about 125 or more officers and enlisted men eat, sleep, shower and shave, train, and enjoy what free time is available in a space only slightly larger than a three-story house. These living quarters are certainly not palatial, especially when that same three-story house contains the torpedo room, sonar room and equipment, the control room, and a myriad of other spaces and equipment. Nonetheless, compared to previous generations, modern submariners live in luxury.

Above: *Mess Management Specialist Second Class Wilbur Fifield prepares a dessert for the crew on board USS* Seawolf *(SSN 21). Often referred to as "fat pills" or "ge-dunks," submarine desserts and pastries are a favorite part of nearly every meal.*

Opposite, top: *The ship control party on USS* Seawolf *(SSN 21) guides the submarine through the ocean depths, controlling the depth, course, and speed of the submarine. The two enlisted men actually operating the controls are among the youngest and newest members of the crew, yet they are given the responsibility for controlling the movements of a 9,000-ton submarine.*

Opposite, bottom: *Submariners relax in their bunks in the torpedo room of a World War II submarine. Space is at a premium and shared with torpedoes and other equipment. The watertight door at center leads to the forward battery compartment, or "officers country," where the ship's officers sleep and eat.*

Left: *On board modern submarines, the crew's mess provides the space for the crew to eat its meals, conduct training, and enjoy a variety of recreational activities. At sea, the crew eats in shifts, scheduled to match the watch rotation. The food is rated among the best in the Navy.*

Page 274: *All submarines have limited space and facilities for personal hygiene. World War II submarines also suffered with a limited capacity to distill fresh water, reducing the number of times the crew could shower and shave. This S-44 crewman might be trimming his beard or he might be shaving it off, having waited weeks for water.*

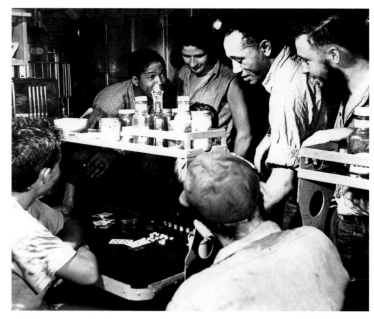

From the beginning, submariners have been called on to live and work in the harshest of surroundings, facing dangers as a normal part of their service. Chief Gunner's Mate William H. Reader, the first chief of the boat on USS *Holland*, wrote about conditions on the Navy's first submarine, "The only place where one could stand straight was in the conning tower and in the forward portion of the engine room. There were no accommodations for eating or sleeping."

What Chief Reader didn't write is almost as revealing. *Holland* had limited ventilation and certainly no air conditioning. Sanitation was almost nonexistent, consisting only of a throne-like water closet, and there

Above, left: *Submarine life is not all work and no play. Submariners find many ways to enjoy a little free time. Some play cards like these USS* Tucson *(SSN 770) crewmembers enjoying a friendly game of poker, while others watch a movie, read a book, or play a computer game.*

Above, right: *Although space was more limited, sailors on World War II submarines, like these on USS* Sea Dog *(SS 401), always seemed to find enough room and time for a card game, such as poker, cribbage, or pinochle or board games like checkers, chess, and the ever-popular "Acey-Deucey" or backgammon.*

Above: USS Holland *consisted of a single compartment so that everyone on board was exposed to the noise of the engine and the resulting gasoline and exhaust fumes. The interior of the submarine provided limited headroom and only the minimum of open space. This drawing is based on H. Reuterdahl's illustration published in* Harper's Magazine *September 1900 issue. (Mike Eagle)*

Left: *World War II diesel submarines were designed with larger engine rooms and much larger diesel engines. Communications were difficult and watchstanders developed a system of hand signals to ease the minute-to-minute tasks of operating the engines.*

Above: *The earliest submarines were basically dimly lit sealed tubes with little ventilation and no air conditioning. The crew would seek relief by gathering topside whenever they could to enjoy a bit of fresh air and sunshine. (Courtesy of Andrew Feindt)*

Above, right: *The crew's mess and galley on World War II vintage submarines were quite small. Meal preparation required using all available space, including the dining tables. On USS* Bullhead *(SS 332), food service personnel prepare vegetables while chatting with a war correspondent on board for a war patrol.*

Bottom, left and right: *Submarine endurance is affected by the amount of fuel and provisions that can be stored on board prior to departing for a patrol. Loading needed stores of food became a normal routine for submarines preparing for a voyage. Sailors from USS* Bream *(SS 243) delve into boxes of fresh fruit during a stores load. Fresh provisions don't last long on submarines, in part because they are quickly used and because there is limited refrigeration space to preserve them.*

were no "creature-comforts" to ease the strain of a day at sea. Crew comfort was limited to a stool at each station. The interior was damp and clammy, and the air was a foul mixture where the stench of gasoline and engine exhaust fumes competed with the acrid smell of battery electrolyte. The noise of the engine drowned out any attempts at conversation. Throughout the early years of the U.S. Submarine Force, improvements in submarines as warfighting machines didn't always carry over to improvement in living conditions, but over the years, things have gotten better. Installation of electronics systems created a need for air conditioning with the added benefit of cooling an otherwise sweaty crew and the need for longer-range submarines produced larger boats with slightly more space for people.

The advent of nuclear power allowed for an increased capacity to distill water and generate electricity, both necessary utilities to improve otherwise Spartan living conditions. Submarines have always had a

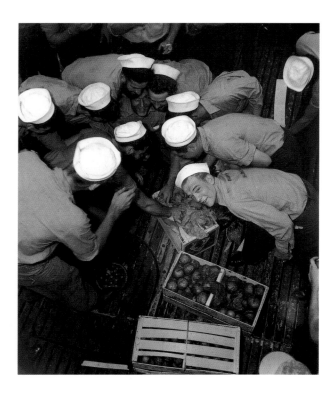

VOLUNTEERS ALL

Submariners have enjoyed the support of their wives or sweethearts, sons and daughters, parents, extended families, and friends. For many, this support extends far beyond their immediate families. They volunteer to help at Navy and Marine Corps Relief Centers, at local charities, places of worship, schools, youth sports teams, and as Scout leaders.

One way that some help is by becoming American Red Cross volunteers, better known as the "Gray Ladies." Founded in 1918 at Walter Reed Hospital in Washington, D.C., the Gray Lady Service provided nonmedical assistance in Army and Navy hospitals during the First World War and served in veterans' hospitals after the war ended. These volunteers wore long gray aprons (with long sleeves) buttoned down the back over a white dress. The uniform had large red crosses on it. Long gray veils completed the uniforms. The wounded sailors and soldiers for whom the Gray Ladies provided aid originated the name of the service, referring to the women as "my Monday Gray Lady," or "my Wednesday Gray Lady." The gray motif was modernized to blue pinstripes during the 1960s, but the fond reference to these dedicated volunteers as Gray Ladies has remained.

Submarine wives proudly serve as Gray Ladies at submarine bases on both coasts. Mrs. Joan White's experience as a Gray Lady is typical of the dedication many submarine wives devote to caring for the submarine family. Her recollection of her experiences speaks volumes, not just for her role, but for the many submarine family members who served so well:

In 1965, having been retrained as a hospital volunteer in San Diego, I was assigned to wards holding troops wounded in Vietnam. I brought them books and magazines and sometimes read to them or helped them send cards and letters home. Some just needed someone to talk to or perhaps simply listen. In 1966, after a move to the Submarine Base, New London, as soon as our offspring were settled in school and the boxes unpacked, I was ready to go to work in the clinic. There were two wooden buildings that comprised the outpatient clinic and another that served as the women's ward—all attached to the brick hospital building by covered ramps. There were Navy doctors and nurses, and male hospital corpsmen, and lots of "Gray Ladies" in our blue and white pinstriped uniforms with a Red Cross volunteer badge.

This was a new type of job for me, with less ward visiting but plenty of "hands-on" work at Family Sick Call where I kept busy handling charts, taking temperatures, and logging patients into the clinic. Then the OB/GYN clinic needed more help. I learned to stand by during the examinations and other medical procedures. There was a full complement of Navy nurses for the inpatient wards but only one nurse for the outpatient clinics. She trained us all, as the patient load was large and there was only one paid female aide assigned to the clinic. Every department had Gray Ladies—emergency room, pharmacy, pediatrics—and virtually every outpatient clinic relied on the volunteers to help out.

I believe that we all enjoyed our work. For us, being a volunteer is more than just helping out. We were all military wives, active duty or retired, and knew well what stresses were involved in the health of our patients. We tried to make getting medical care a little less frustrating, hopefully easing the strain in some small way.

I'm still a Gray Lady and I still enjoy it. People have asked me if we are paid for our work. I usually answer, "Yes. In smiles . . ."

Mrs. Joan White (front row center) presents a new group of volunteers for a capping and pin ceremony. The cap and pin presentation was the culmination of many hours of volunteer service, completion of the probation period and the recommendation of the Area Red Cross representative, the head nurse of the hospital, and the chairman of volunteers. Affectionately known as "Gray Ladies," volunteers like these represent the thousands of wives and family members of submariners who give freely of their time.

Right, top and bottom: *A favorite treat for submariners is homemade pizza. Some crews devise contests to see which department, division, or individual can concoct the best pizza. These competitions can be fierce, and the winners get the dubious honor of making pizza for the crew again and again. No matter who wins the fixing part, nearly everyone seems to like the eating part that follows. On board USS* Pasadena *(SSN 752) (bottom) Yeoman Al Gregory (left) and Mess Management Specialist Jeffery Smith (right) prepare pizza for the crew. On USS* La Jolla *(SSN 701) (top), lucky crew members sample similar results from their ship's galley.*

Opposite, top: *Coffee is a staple on submarines as shown in this view of two World War II submariners enjoying a cup drawn from the large urn in the background. On many submarines, having fresh coffee reached high enough importance that the procedure became part of submarine qualification. If you couldn't make a pot of coffee, you didn't pass the qualification process.*

reputation for serving the best food in the Navy. On nuclear submarines, food becomes the limiting factor in the ship's endurance, and on all submarines, the quality of the "chow" impacts crew morale. Submariners learn to gauge how long they have been at sea by the menu. Limited cold storage and short shelf life make fresh fruit and vegetables disappear quickly. In spite of the shortfalls, submarine food is varied, plentiful, and good.

Most submariners have a special memory of submarine food. For some the memory of fresh-baked bread on the midnight watch brings a smile. For others the thought of pizza on Friday night is the fondest. And for many, it's something as simple as the coffee. Whether it's brewed in the restaurant-style urns installed on older submarines, or the espresso and cappuccino machines on the latest boats, submariners have always liked their coffee. In recent years, the traditional coffee has been supplemented with soft drink machines, hot chocolate packets, and a variety of fruit drinks commonly referred to as "bug juice." On submarines, food and drink are strong morale builders.

From where do submariners come? This is best answered in the general sense. They are the kid next door, your old friend from high

school or college, or that quiet man at the end of the church pew. They come from all walks of life and from every corner of the country. They have been and are an integral part of the community and share the common bond of all Americans—as citizens. As members of the community, submariners give of their free time to coach Little League teams, volunteer for service projects too numerous to list, and raise families. They act as mentors in schools near submarine homeports and help out in soup kitchens and shelters. In foreign ports they often find ways to contribute their time and talents to the local townspeople and villagers. They proudly share their experience and attitude with parents, brothers and sisters, friends, and sweethearts. They volunteer and those around them volunteer, too. Submariners and their extended families and friends can be counted on to do their share—whatever the need.

A crowd of family members and friends waits on the pier as the nuclear attack submarine USS Louisville *(SSN 724) returns to San Diego following a Gulf War deployment to the Persian Gulf. Homecomings are always filled with emotion, which is heightened whenever the returning ship has been in a wartime operation.*

279

Opposite, and top left: *Another traditional way for submariners to relax is to surface the submarine, stop the engines, and hold "swim call." With rifle-bearing shark watches standing by to warn the swimmers of approaching danger, the crew don swim trunks and dive in to cool off. On diesel submarines, the swimmers jumped from the topside deck much like these sailors on USS* Cero *(SS 225) during a training cruise. On more modern submarines, like USS* William H. Bates *(SSN 680), would-be platform divers leap from the fairwater planes that protrude from the sail or fairwater.*

Top, right: *A sailor in the torpedo room on board USS* Batfish *(SS 310) fastens battle flags to a line. The flags will be flown when the ship returns home at the end of its war patrol as a symbol of pride felt not only by the young submariner working on the display, but also by every man on board.*

Center: *The bridge watch on board USS* Kentucky *(SSBN 737) is responsible for making sure the submarine conducts a safe transit on the surface. The rest of the crew depends on them to maintain a vigilant watch to keep the ship out of harm's way.*

Left: *Symbolic of the volunteer spirit shown by submariners, personnel from the pre-commissioning unit for the attack submarine USS* Montpelier *(SSN 765) help clean up the ship's namesake city of Montpelier, Vermont, after a 1992 flood. Members of the crew are shown helping remove debris from the basement of a local business. Other submarine crews, including men from USS* Oklahoma City *(SSN 723) who traveled to Oklahoma from the East Coast following the terrorist bomb attack in 1995, have provided similar help.*

YOGI KAUFMAN: ONE TOUGH SUBMARINER— Commander David Randall Hinkle, USN (Ret)

War or peace, submarines go in harm's way. Covert missions place crews under extreme stress for long periods. They stay physically fit so they can operate at peak efficiency for days under the most stressful conditions. But all submariners recognize that Yogi Kaufman stood alone when it came to physical fitness.

Yogi could do one-arm pull-ups with either arm all day and then do one-arm push-ups with either arm and someone sitting on his back. On departure for a long patrol he would challenge his crew to form two-man teams. Any team that together could do more total push-ups, chin-ups, and sit-ups at the end of the run than Yogi would get a three-day pass at any port of their choosing. Only once did he have to pay off. He would also challenge anyone to race him the length of the submarine, about 110 yards. The chiefs made some money betting young sailors that they couldn't outrun the "old man."

In 1968 Yogi, then a Navy captain in his early forties, was in Washington, D.C., on temporary duty. Yogi was staying with his mother-in-law. There was a lot of unrest in D.C. that summer and some rioting, but Yogi considered the neighborhood safe. Late one night, he wrote a letter to his wife Lucille and went to post it at the nearest corner box at about one a.m. It was warm, so he wore just slacks, T-shirt, and bedroom slippers. He ignored a car that passed and stopped at the intersection. His first inkling of danger was someone grabbing his rear pocket to get at his wallet. Spinning around, he was confronted by four armed hoodlums. One had a two-by-four; another, a chain. Yogi grabbed one thug and rammed him into a tree trunk. He said he could hear bones break and considered that one out of action. A hard right to the chin disposed of a second one. He grabbed the biggest thug, who was slashing him with a chain, and wrestled him to the ground and began working him over. At this time the hoodlums decided it was time to disengage and managed to escape, leaving Yogi bloodied, but victorious. They must have been the most surprised people in the District of Columbia. What had looked like easy pickings—a little, baldheaded man in bedroom slippers—turned out to be a barracuda in disguise. Yogi was the welterweight boxing champion of his class at the Naval Academy. He never made better use of his training.

Following a distinguished naval career, which took him to the rank of Vice Admiral, Yogi Kaufman became a professional photographer. He is recognized as one of the best in the world. His photographs have been widely published and several appear in this book.

After a full and rewarding thirty-eight-year submarine career in the U.S. Navy, Vice Admiral "Yogi" Kaufman launched a second career as a photographer and writer. His work appears in numerous magazines and books worldwide. Well known for his writing and photos on submarines and aircraft carriers, Yogi's real joy is photographing wildlife and natural history.

Opposite, top and left: News from home is very important to all U.S. sailors, and submariners are no exception. Often isolated for months at a time, mail calls are rare events during long deployments. In recent times, submarines sometimes get a "special delivery" like the one enjoyed by the crew of USS Scranton *(SSN 756) with a mail drop from an SH-60 Seahawk from Helicopter Anti-Submarine Squadron Five (HS-5). For submarines serving in World War II, mail was usually held until the ship returned from patrol. Then crews pored over the sacks of letters and packages like kids at Christmas, much like the sailors serving on USS* Bream *(SS 243) are doing as they arrived home after a war patrol.*

A frequently seen slogan, emblazoned on commissary shopping bags and bumper stickers declares, "Navy wife—the toughest job in the Navy." This is particularly true for wives of submariners. Submarine deployments are usually of about the same length as those of other Navy ships. What sets submarines apart is the long periods of isolation when there is little or no communication from the submarine. Contact with home is limited to a few short "family-grams," telegram-like messages that families can send, knowing that they will get no response. Wives and families must function on their own, with no input from afar for months at a time. It is a tough job and those who do it rarely get the credit they deserve. It is always an emotional moment when submariners retire from the Navy and during the ceremony take time to recognize their families and the sacrifices each has made.

The reasons for becoming a submariner are more elusive. For many, the motive is a complex blend of a desire to have a high degree of

responsibility, belong to an elite group, seek adventure, and earn extra pay. The basis for volunteering is as varied as the individuals who become submariners. Whatever the reason, the Submarine Force has always been fortunate to attract good people. It is also notable that, throughout the history of the U.S. Submarine Force, submariners have been able to keep pace with profound advances in technology. Nuclear propulsion, sophisticated strategic and tactical weapon systems, and complex sonar and computer systems all require smart operators and technicians. Lieutenant Caldwell's remarks concerning the requirements for submarine crews are as true today as they were when he first made them.

Above, right: *Taking a submarine to sea always carries the possibility of hostile action. When the crew is called to "battle stations" all the lessons learned from training, qualification, and drills are applied to the task the ship was designed to perform—warfighting. Crewmen of the Trident missile submarine USS* Ohio *(SSBN 726) man battle stations in the missile control center as they practice a simulated missile launch.*

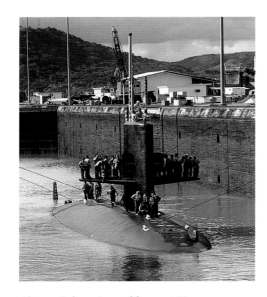

Above: *Submariners, like most Navy personnel, get a chance to travel, see new places, and experience different cultures. Submarines are sometimes moved from one ocean to the other for operations or as part of a change of homeport. Crewmembers crowd the decks and diving planes on USS* Shark *(SSN 591) as the submarine is towed through the Panama Canal, en route to the Pacific Ocean.*

Above: *During homecoming ceremonies, a submariner assigned to the attack submarine USS* Louisville *(SSN 724) proudly displays a Louisville Slugger baseball bat commemorating the submarine's role in the Persian Gulf war.* Louisville *successfully launched Tomahawk land attack missiles against Iraq while supporting Operation Desert Shield and Desert Storm.*

Right: *A submarine crew stands tall during an awards ceremony following World War II combat action. Awards can recognize the continued fidelity, zeal, and obedience of an individual sailor, detail the heroic deeds of a few, or acknowledge the dedicated and meritorious service of an entire crew. All submariners present at these events carry a sense of pride and the knowledge that they are part of something larger than themselves—the Submarine Service.*

Opposite: *The best part of any successful deployment is coming home. Wives, children, family, and friends gather on the pier, their ranks swelled by other submariners, bands, and well-wishers to welcome the crew home. Here the nuclear fast attack submarine USS* Pogy *(SSN 647) returns to San Diego, California, from the North Pole in November of 1996 following a scientific exercise.* Pogy *spent fifty days beneath the Arctic ice and managed to bring Santa Claus along for an early holiday celebration.*

As part of the Submarine Force tradition, submariners honor their fellow submariners through demonstrated loyalty, trust, and reliability so that each submariner knows that he can depend on his shipmates for the safe operation, and survival of the ship. The respect for tradition also involves learning and applying the lessons of the past and passing on the "art" of submarining. Submariners know that only by learning from mistakes as well as success can they ensure that submarines will continue to make a strong contribution in times of peace as well as in times of conflict.

Duty at sea on a submarine requires people who know and understand the fundamental risks of such business. The sea is a harsh master in any case—operating beneath the waves where the crush of the ocean can flood the inside of a submarine in a few seconds is a simple, often unrecognized act of bravery. Compound that inherent danger with the various threats of armed conflict and a picture of a higher level of bravery emerges. As volunteers, submariners accept those dangers and risks and rarely consider that they are involved in an act of bravery or courage. Submariners know the history of the U.S. Submarine Force and the stories of brave acts by the heroes of World War II, and the losses suffered by those who wore the Dolphins. Throughout history, submariners have faced the perils of the sea, confronted the enemy in hot and cold wars, and spent endless hours away from family and friends to do the job they volunteered to do. For submariners, perhaps the bravest act is the simplest one—they volunteered. Submariners know what is expected of them, and voluntarily give more than they take. They care about their ship, their shipmates, and their country. They are made of the stuff that ensures the rest of us can sleep well knowing that dedicated and committed people are keeping watch under the world's oceans.

Chief of the Boat

Lieutenant Commander Don C. LaForce, USN (Ret)

From the beginning, the U.S. Submarine Force has assigned a senior enlisted crew member as the chief of the boat. Known to the crew and officers as the "COB," this one man acts as the principal enlisted advisor to the commanding officer and also serves as the administrative assistant to the executive officer. The chief of the boat's basic function is to keep the command aware of situations, procedures, and practices that affect the welfare, morale, job satisfaction, and utilization of the crew, but his responsibilities reach much further.

The COB is expected to instill leadership in the crew and promote effectiveness and efficiency throughout the chain of command. He must act as counselor and problem solver, arbitrator and mentor, advisor, and critic. Individuals selected to serve as the chief of the boat must lead effectively, manage efficiently, and provide a strong example to all. This has been the role of the COB since the beginning.

When the Navy commissioned USS Holland, its first submarine, Chief Gunner's Mate William H. Reader served as the U.S. Navy's first chief of the boat. With only one commissioned officer assigned as the commanding officer, it was essential that Holland have a senior enlisted man to direct the activities of the crew. The position was unique for the U.S. Navy and has remained so throughout the history of the U.S. Submarine Force. Submarines have been blessed with thousands of such men who have followed Chief Reader's example. It is a rare submariner who doesn't recall the COBs he has served with and the contributions they have made along the way.

These men, charged with immense responsibility, armed with substantial authority, and held to the highest standards of accountability, command the respect and admiration of submarine crews despite differences in leadership style. Each COB develops his own sense of what works to act as friend, drill sergeant, teacher, and boss all rolled into one. COBs "cut their teeth"

serving on submarines with plenty of knowledge
gained at the feet of those who served before them.
Over time, submarine crews have learned that the COB
watches out for them and works hard to keep things
on an even keel. Nonetheless, the chief of the boat's job
is both a constant challenge and an unsolved puzzle.
The challenge is easily understood but the puzzle may
never be solved—where does the Submarine Force find
such amazing men?

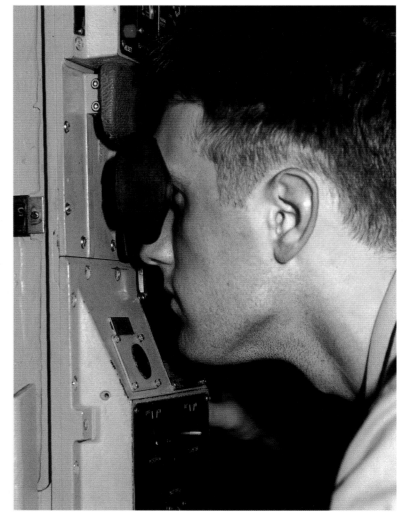

Top: Electronics Technician Master Chief Wesley C. Harper, chief of the
boat (COB) for USS *Tucson* (SSN 770), demonstrates both his knowledge
of submarines and his diplomatic skills as he guides former Japanese
secretary of defense, the honorable Masatka Suzuki, through a series
of maneuvers near Yokosuka, Japan.

Right: COB, Senior Chief Sonar Technician Peter Manias takes a turn
at the periscope during operations on USS *Norfolk* (SSN 714). The
COB keeps a watchful eye on the submarine's crew and acts as a key
assistant to the ship's commanding officer and executive officer.

Opposite: The U.S. Submarine Force's first COB, Chief Gunner's Mate
W. H. Reader (center) is sitting on the edge of USS *Holland*'s (SS 1) turret
surrounded by the enlisted crew. *Holland* was in port in Newport, Rhode
Island, when the photograph was taken.

History of the Naval Submarine School

Captain Arnold O. Lotring, USN

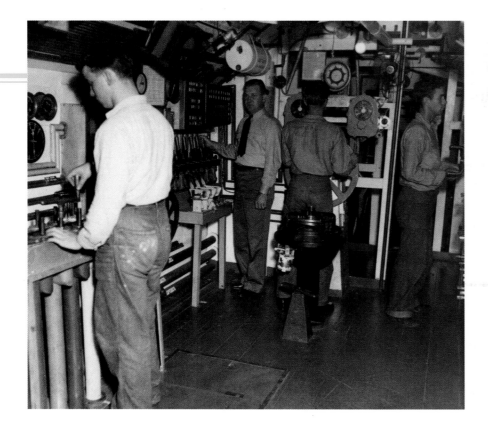

A great tragedy in the Submarine Force resulted in the creation of a school dedicated to teaching the art of submarine warfare. The sinking of the submarine *F-4* off the coast of Hawaii with the loss of all hands in 1915 caused the Secretary of the Navy to direct the establishment of a formal school to instruct submariners in the operation and maintenance of these specialized boats. The commanding officer of the Submarine Base in New London, Connecticut, was directed to establish the Naval Submarine School, which began operation on 1 July 1916. After six months of training, the first officer class graduated on 23 December 1916. The first enlisted class graduated one year later.

Originally, the Naval Submarine School was established in Building Three on the Lower Base with only lecture rooms and a small amount of submarine training equipment. Late in 1918, the school purchased and put into operation its first attack teacher, a trainer used to practice approach tactics. In 1930, a submarine escape training tank was built and put into service to train all submariners in basic escape and survival skills. During its first twenty-two years of service, the school's four departments—Electrical, Diesel Operations and Maintenance, Communications, and Administration—remained within the area of the waterfront piers in two buildings.

World War II brought dramatic changes to the submarine school. The reliance on submarines to take the offensive against Japan required the school to train large numbers of recruits to man the rapidly expanding submarine force. Along with new buildings and modernized facilities, the training emphasis shifted from the theoretical to the practical. Practical hands-on training enabled graduates to man a battle station the day they reported on board.

During the six-week basic enlisted course every student received personalized instruction in the basic elements of submarining. A three-story building was provided for this purpose. New classes with as many as 170 men started at the building's top deck and worked their way down to the lower deck, spending two weeks on each deck. Throughout the six-week period, students would conduct drills on board USS *Gloryhole*, a mockup of a submarine that was located in the basement of the building. Students

Above, left: *During World War II, new basic enlisted classes with as many as 170 men started each week. Throughout the six-week course, students would conduct drills on board USS* Gloryhole, *a mockup of a submarine located in the basement of the building. The highly structured drills and rotation of trainees through all watchstations ensured that each student became familiar with all the stations necessary to man a submarine.*

Above, right: *Students on board the SS* Lookout *train to search for planes and surface contacts and to report contact data using proper terminology.*

Opposite: *During the school's early years, the curriculum was largely theoretical and few training aids were used. With the advent of World War II, a great push was made to modernize the curriculum and training facilities. The new training aids are clearly evident in this picture of a World War II electrical controls class.*

Above: *This 1960s-era attack teacher relied on scale models moving on a floor replicating the earth's curvature to provide realistic antishipping attack scenarios. Computer technology has enabled the latest trainers to simulate sophisticated attack centers and provide realistic team training for a multitude of submarine missions using actual fire control and sonar system hardware.*

Above: *This Polaris navigation trainer was one of the first trainers developed to support the FBMs going on patrol in the 1960s. The trainer can imitate every navigational situation a Polaris submarine could meet anywhere at sea, in any kind of weather, day or night. Here the crewmen take a star fix—one checking the star-finder chart, another locking on the star through the periscope, and a third punching the information into a navigation computer console.*

practiced interior communications, rigging for dive, the diving procedure, firing torpedoes, rigging for depth charge attack, and surfacing. The highly structured drills and rotation of trainees through all watchstations ensured that each student became familiar with all the stations necessary to man a submarine and operate as a team.

Additionally, every three days during the basic course students embarked for a day of underway shipboard training. Submarine School had firmly established the teaching tenet of theoretical knowledge reinforced with hands-on training and practice. Following basic submarine training, enlisted men received training in their designated rate. These courses included: Quartermasters and Signalmen, Gunner's Mates, Torpedomen, Radiomen, Electrician's Mates, and Engineers.

For officer training, an eighteen-week course included three weeks of underway operations. Officers attended lectures and then spent numerous hours devoted to practical work using training aids. Many hours were spent in the Askania training device, a rudimentary dive trainer purchased from Germany in 1936. As part of the underway period that followed the classroom and practical training, all students were required to fire torpedoes. Officers also received instruction in code and cipher devices and the basic operation of diesel engines and electrical equipment.

The size and scope of the school changed dramatically in support of the war effort. Instructors with war experience returned to the school to prepare new crews, and top performing skippers returned to instruct their reliefs. Captain F. B. "Fearless Freddy" Warder, a highly decorated World War II submarine commanding officer, was officer in charge from October 1944 to July 1946.

The submarine school established a short advanced course for prospective commanding officers (PCOs). The purpose of the course was to "increase knowledge of approach and attack methods by study and discussion, and technique by actual practice by experienced submarine officers who are slated to become commanding officers or to hold senior positions on board submarines." The first PCO class convened on 15 March 1941. Many notable submariners, including Congressional Medal of Honor winner Rear Admiral R. H. O'Kane, have served as PCO instructors for the course.

During World War II, the Naval Submarine School trained an average of 75 officers and 500 enlisted men per month. The wartime maximum capacity was 1,550 enlisted students at one time consisting of 150 students per class, with new classes forming every week. During the course of the war only 2,000 officers and 22,000 enlisted men graduated from the Naval Submarine School of the 250,000 men who applied.

The post-World War II period brought new challenges to the school. The introduction of nuclear-powered submarines, nuclear weapons, and the proliferation of computerized and electronic systems required both in-depth theoretical instruction and hands-on training.

As the mission of antisubmarine warfare became preeminent during the Cold War, the Submarine School grew in size and stature as it trained tens of thousands of submariners. Submarine School instructors developed the first navigation and piloting trainer using an obsolete attack teacher and an improvised model of Pearl Harbor. The trainer became a mainstay of navigation training for submarines in overhaul and fleet ballistic missile (FBM) crews during the off-crew period.

The development of the two-crew concept of the FBM submarine, coupled with the inherent complexity of the Polaris weapon systems created the demand for two new training departments. The Fleet Ballistic Missile Training Department provided training on Polaris weapon systems and navigation system maintenance, as well as operational team training for SSBN crews. The realistic simulators used for team training in English and Fife Halls consisted of SSBN weapon subsystems, controlled by digital and analog computers. Students also conducted hands-on training using a Polaris training missile.

The Fleet Ballistic Missile Propulsion Maintenance Department enabled the nuclear personnel to maintain their proficiency in nuclear operations and propulsion equipment repairs. Additionally, the school instituted a revised five-week prospective commanding officer and executive officer course specifically tailored to the unique issues of commanding an FBM submarine.

By 1963 the school had implemented a new advanced dive trainer known as the Universal Submarine Simulator. This device incorporated the exact ship controls and surfaced and submerged handling characteristics (rolling as well as pitching motion) of the latest submarines. While students studied submerged ship handling on the universal simulator, the maneuver and docking trainer enabled students to learn basic surfaced ship handling skills by directing radio-controlled drone submarines.

Naval Submarine School changed status from an activity to a command on 1 July 1968. At this time, the school was the largest educational institution in southeastern Connecticut, housed in twenty-seven buildings, and boasting a variety of trainers ranging from sonar and escape trainers to docking and attack trainers.

Advancements in computer technology led to improvements across a wide range of trainers. The attack teachers had developed into sophisticated attack centers providing concentrated team tactical training using actual fire control and sonar system hardware. These innovations enabled submarine school instructors to provide basic ship refresher training and advanced pre-deployment training, as well as the more traditional training historically given at the school for junior officers, department heads, and prospective executive and commanding officers.

By the 1980s, Submarine School had grown into an institution training 65,000 students annually in 379 different courses. Its elite staff of 110 officers, 875 enlisted, and 30 civilians taught in nineteen buildings and forty major trainers—facilities representing an investment of more than $1.4 billion.

With the end of the Cold War, Naval Submarine School shifted to the new priorities of supporting the fleet across a wider range of missions and areas of engagement. The employment of cruise missiles, delivery of special operating forces, and operations in shallow coastal areas required the development of new trainers and curricula. Electronic classrooms, interactive software, distance learning, and virtual reality training devices will assist the Submarine School in meeting these challenges. It is, however, the teachers, working with future submariners as they did in 1916, that will enable the school to remain as a premier training and education warfare center.

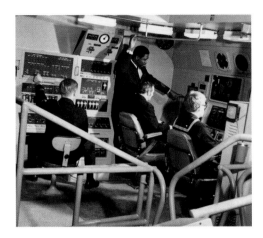

Above: *Submarine exercises too dangerous to practice at sea can be simulated in ship control trainers.*

Above: *Crew members attach a temporary patch to a leaking pipe in a submarine simulator during a damage control exercise.*

Four USS Ohio *(SSBN 726) crewmembers participate in a simulated missile firing in the Missile Control Center (MCC) during precommissioning activities. The precommissioning period is marked by extensive testing to ensure that the ship and all of its systems and equipment perform as designed.*

Opposite, bottom: *The realistic simulators used for team training in English and Fife Halls consisted of SSBN weapon subsystems that were controlled by digital and analog computers.*

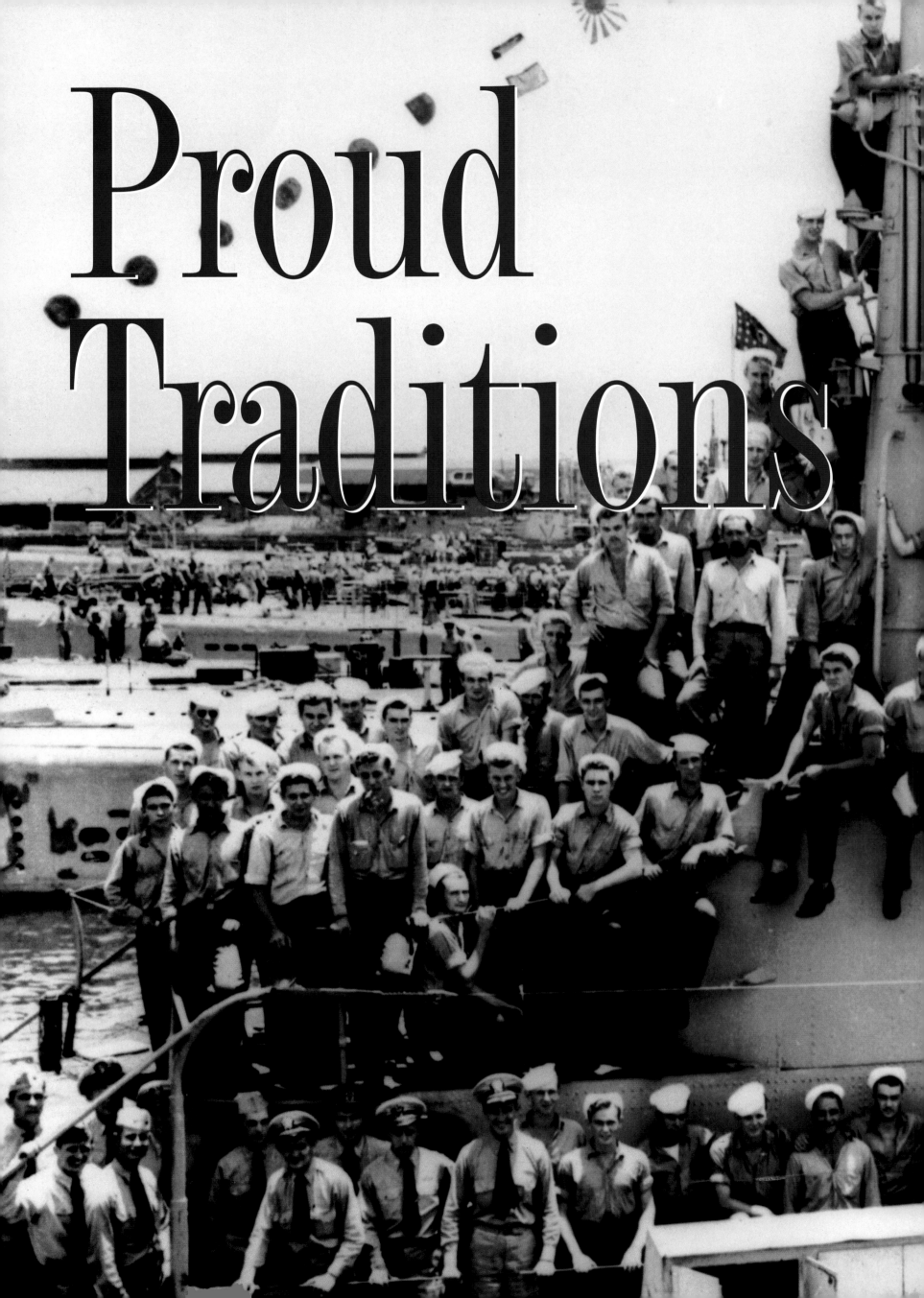

Proud Traditions

Insignia & Decorations

Wendy S. Gulley, Archivist, Submarine Force Museum

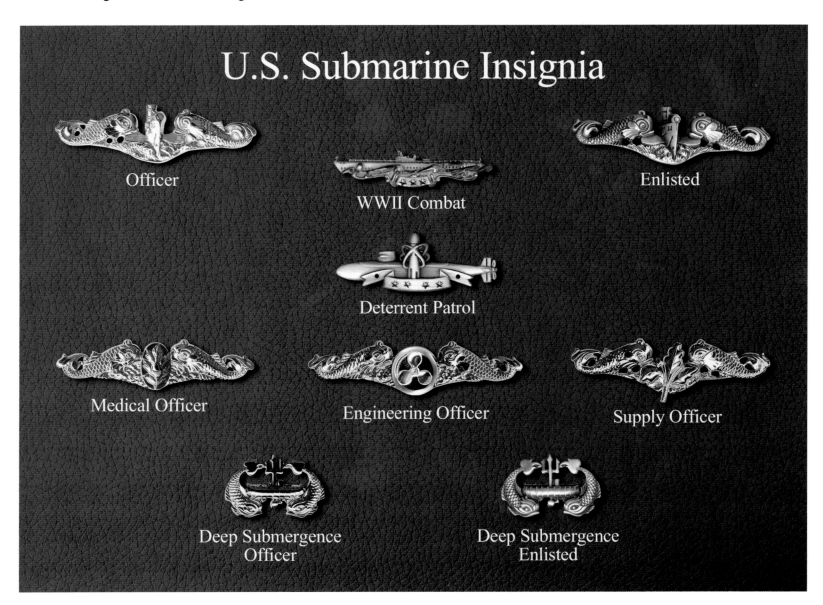

U.S. Submarine Insignia

Officer

WWII Combat

Enlisted

Deterrent Patrol

Medical Officer

Engineering Officer

Supply Officer

Deep Submergence
Officer

Deep Submergence
Enlisted

Submarine Dolphins of the World

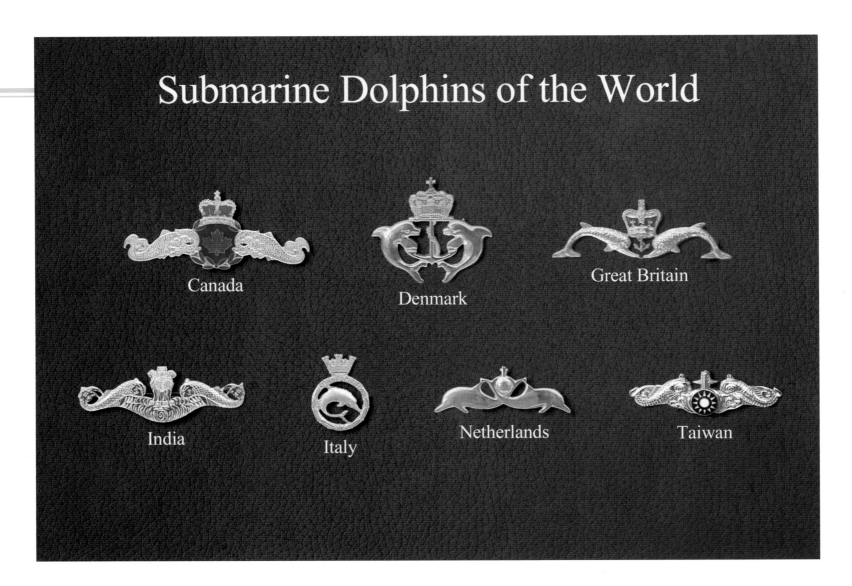

Canada

Denmark

Great Britain

India

Italy

Netherlands

Taiwan

Badges of Honor:
Emblems of the Silent Service

From a very early date many navies have awarded a unique badge or insignia to denote service in submarines. Many of the designs feature the dolphin, the traditional attendant of Poseidon, Greek god of the sea and patron deity of sailors; therefore, it has become common to refer to the device as the submariner's "Dolphins."

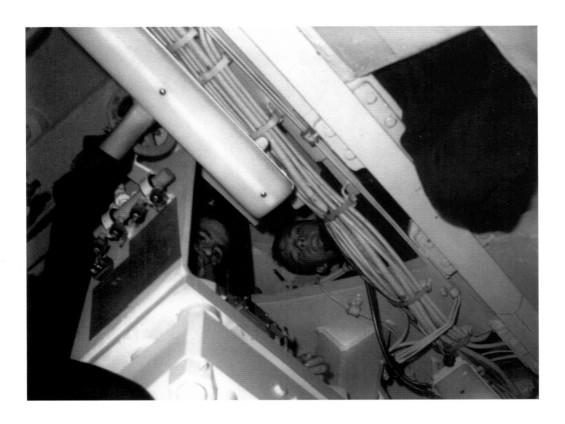

Above: The U.S. Navy is not alone in awarding the dolphin insignia to its qualified submariners. Many nations have chosen the dolphin—traditional attendant of Poseidon, Greek god of the sea—as a symbol of their submarine forces.

Opposite: Although different U.S. submarine insignia exist, each requires extended periods at sea in submarines to satisfy qualification requirements. They are worn with great pride because they represent the respect and trust placed in the wearer by their peers and shipmates. (Insignia courtesy of Hilborn-Hamburger)

Page 292–293: The crew of USS Bowfin *triumphantly gathered on her decks at the submarine base in Pearl Harbor. This photo was taken on 4 July 1945 as* Bowfin *returned to port after a historic patrol during World War II.* Bowfin *is the centerpiece of the USS* Bowfin *Submarine Museum and Park in Pearl Harbor, Hawaii.*

Left: Submariners crawl the ship in order to be familiar with every system and be able to fight fire, flooding, or system failure in any location within the submarine. Here two crewmen are tracing a system in the overhead. The orange pipe with four fittings provides air for emergency air breathing masks. The manifolds are located throughout the ship. One drill is to move from one end of the ship to the other wearing an air breathing mask, transferring to new air outlets as one moves through the ship.

Above: *During his qualification process, the would-be submariner will study each of the major systems in the submarine, visually tracing them out inch-by-inch, learning the location of each pipe, switch, valve, and operating station, until he understands how the system works and can draw it from memory.*

Right: *Enlisted personnel, as well as officers assigned to nuclear submarines, must "Qualify in Submarines" within their first year on board. This qualification is accomplished by completion of a Qualification Checkout Card itemizing each system and watch station that the sailor must learn. The qualifier will be tested twice on each item and then must make a walk through the boat with a final qualification board, before he can wear the Dolphin insignia.*

The origin of the U.S. Navy Submarine Insignia dates back to June 1923, when Captain Ernest J. King, later to become fleet admiral, and at that time Commander Submarine Division THREE, suggested to the Secretary of the Navy that a distinguishing device for qualified submariners be adopted.

U. S. S. PATRICK HENRY (SSBN 599)

SUBMARINE QUALIFICATION CARD

Date Reported: *15 DECEMBER 1961*

Name: *MEADER*	Rate: *EN 2(SS)*	Dept: *AUXILIARY*		Req. Date:
Ship's Organization Manual and Instructions	Date:	Division Officer		
Ship's Indoctrination	Date:	Examining P.O.		

	Date	Petty Off.	Date	Division Off.
Bridge & Topside				
Missile Compartment				
Reactor Compartment				
Torpedo Room				
Operations Compt. (1st level)				
Operations Compt. (2nd level)				
Operations Compt. (3rd level)	*2-14-62*			
Machinery Space				
Engine Room				
Trim and Drain	*1-8-62*			
Fresh Water	*1-12-62*			
High Pressure Air/MBT Blow	*1-15-62*			
Hull Ventilation	*1-22-62*			
Sanitary	*1-22-62*			
Snorkel Induction & Exhaust	*7-9-62*			
Piping				
Service Air	*1-3-62*			
Low Pressure Blow	*1-7-61*			
Main, Vital & Lead Hydraulics	*2-4-62*			
External Hydraulics	*2-1-62*			
Oxygen/Air Bleeding Emergency Breathing	*1-1-62*			
Magazine Flooding	*1-7-62*			
Basic Electrical	*2-1-62*			
F.O. Trans. & Compensating	*1-19-62*			
Telephone and MC				
Escape Trunks				
Air Conditioning & Heating				
Main Propulsion	*1-19-62*			
External Salvage				
Ballast Control Panel				
Missile Compensation				
Battery Ventilation				

Submariners live and work in an inhospitable and unforgiving environment. Their warships are among the most technologically advanced machines ever built, requiring a tremendous amount of skill and knowledge to operate. At sea, submerged for months at a time, the submarine is a world unto itself. Each man is totally dependent upon the skill of every other man in the crew, not only for top performance but also for actual survival. Because this is so, the submarine world depends on rigid and exacting qualifications with qualified men. Regardless of their specialty, each crew member must learn how everything on the boat works and how to respond in an emergency in order to become "qualified in submarines" and earn the right to wear the coveted dolphins.

The intense qualification process in place today has evolved from a matter of informal custom to formal regulation beginning in the year 1900 with the first submarine USS *Holland*. The knowledge her crew acquired and refined through experience was handed down to the next generation of submariners who, in turn, passed on that original foundation of knowledge to those who followed and so on until the outbreak of World War I. By then submarines had grown significantly in complexity and capability.

Officers and men alike needed special skills requiring formalized training. In 1914 the Navy Bureau of Navigation approved a formal system of qualification in submarines. Two years later the Submarine School at New London began to take form. By the 1920s a systematic training establishment existed and stringent criteria for qualification were established.

In 1923 Captain Ernest J. King, later to be named fleet admiral, recognized an important facet in the human aspect of submarining. As Commander Submarine Division THREE, he realized the significance and effort involved in becoming "qualified in submarines." To Captain King these were "picked men who are carefully trained in work, which is of extra-hazardous character," and they deserved to be rewarded "with a distinguishing badge that would infuse in them a deep sense of pride in their accomplishment." In June 1923 Captain King sent his recommendation along with a pen-and-ink sketch of his proposed insignia up the chain of command to the Secretary of the Navy.

At each level Captain King's suggestion was strongly endorsed. With the final approval of the Secretary of the Navy, the Bureau of Navigation began soliciting designs. Suggestions ranged from matched seahorses, to a diver's helmet, to a variety of submarine and dolphin motifs. One submariner stationed on board USS *S-1* went against the emerging dolphin trend and submitted a submarine and shark design. He argued that "the dolphin idea is all right, but I think a good, lively, vicious-looking tiger shark would be more apropos, since it is well known that we submariners are a fearlessly resolute bunch." In the end, dolphins were by far the most

Top: *By the end of World War I the foundation of today's rigid submarine qualification process was in place. Prospective submariners were first given basic instruction at the newly established submarine school and then assigned to a boat where they completed a formal qualification program.*

Above: *These are a few of the numerous proposed designs for the submarine insignia. Captain Ernest King's original 1923 design appears on top.*

Above and above, right: *Newly qualified sub-mariners are awarded their silver dolphins in a traditional pinning ceremony. In honor of this significant day their first set of dolphins have been purchased for them by the members of their division and engraved with the date. Here, Machinist's Mate Nathan Heitzman, wearing his new dolphins, cheerfully displays the newly earned submarine qualification certificate. Signed by his commanding officer, the certificate tells of his accomplishment. "Having successfully completed the rigorous professional requirements for qualification in submarines, having gained a thorough knowledge of submarine construction and operation, having demonstrated his reliability under stress, and having my full confidence and trust, I hereby certify that he is 'Qualified in Submarines.'"* (Courtesy of USS Philadelphia SSN 690)

Right: *Young sailors on USS* Columbus (SSN 762) *proudly show off their newly awarded dolphins.*

The original design for the U.S. Submarine Force insignia approved in 1924 by Theodore Roosevelt, Jr., Acting Secretary of the Navy, is still in use today.

popular choice to symbolize the Submarine Force. The same Philadelphia jewelry firm that had designed the naval aviator insignia was selected to refine the design. Theodore Roosevelt, Jr., acting Secretary of the Navy, approved the design in March 1924. The final design, a bow view of a submarine proceeding on the surface with bow planes rigged for diving, flanked by dolphins with their heads resting on the upper edge of the bow planes, is still in use today.

The officer's insignia is a gold metal pin worn centered above the left breast pocket and above the ribbons or medals. At first, enlisted men wore an embroidered insignia, in white on blue for blue clothing and blue on white for white clothing. This was sewn on the outside of the right sleeve, midway between the wrist and elbow. In 1950, silver metal dolphins, to be worn above the left breast pocket, were approved for enlisted men. Over the years a series of similar "dolphin" badges would be created to recognize some of the specialized talents unique to the complex and highly technical world of submarine warfare.

In May 1943 the first specialized submarine officer pin was authorized for submarine medical officers. The insignia, which features the

familiar line officers' dolphins on either side of the oak leaf and acorns symbol of the Navy Medical Corps, is awarded to medical officers who specialize in the study and treatment of submarine personnel.

In 1950 a special dolphin insignia was authorized for the engineering duty officer who specialized in submarines. As a general rule these officers are assigned to a nuclear shipyard or Supervisor of Shipbuilding office and have significant experience in the design, acquisition, or maintenance of submarines. Once he has completed a thirteen-week indoctrination period on board an operational submarine, the officer is awarded a gold metal insignia with two dolphins facing a silver circular center inscribed with a three-bladed propeller.

In 1964 the U.S. Navy created a third submarine specialty when it recognized the importance of proper logistic support to keep its submarine

Above: Although not practiced today, "dunking" was once a cherished tradition in the submarine service. Men who had qualified for their dolphins were enthusiastically grabbed and tossed into the drink at the conclusion of the ceremony. For many years, submariners believed that new dolphins should not be pinned on a dry shirt.

Right: *A nuclear fast attack submarine is re-supplied while underway on deployment. Without critical supplies and repair parts available when needed, a submarine could easily sacrifice its mission. The Supply Officer's Insignia was created to designate the officer on board responsible for this crucial role. (Courtesy of USS* Philadelphia *SSN 690)*

Projecting power ashore from the sea, a developing mission for the submarine force is illustrated by the brooms flying from the periscopes of USS Miami *(SSN 755), indicating a clean sweep of enemy forces well inland from the sea. Miami's performance in Iraq and Kosovo earned combat decorations for the ship and crew. Commander James Ransom was awarded the Silver Star Medal and the ship was awarded two Navy Unit Commendations.*

The woman in this World War II recruiting poster admires her beau's submarine combat insignia. This coveted badge was awarded to each crewmember when a submarine completed a successful patrol against the enemy. The gold stars on the sailor's pin indicate three additional successful patrols.

fleets operating and authorized a special insignia for Supply Corps officers serving as the submarine supply officer. This resembles the line officer's badge, but the central device now took the shape of the Supply Corps oak leaves and acorns. As a permanently assigned member of a submarine crew, the submarine supply officer must be proficient in supply matters and must also qualify in key watchstanding stations.

Two decades later, as the Navy expanded its undersea missions to include deep-sea research and recovery, it became necessary to recognize one additional group of submarine specialists. In 1981 the Deep Submergence Insignia was approved to recognize the crews of the Navy's bathyscaphes and research submersibles. The badge depicts a deep submergence vehicle in front of an upright trident flanked by two diving dolphins.

In addition to their Dolphins many submariners wear one of two submarine patrol pins. The older of these two pins, the Submarine Combat Insignia, was first issued in 1943. This insignia was awarded to officers and men when a submarine completed a war patrol during which at least one ship was sunk, one U.S. aviator was recovered, or a special mission was accomplished successfully. The badge alone, which depicts a broadside view of a submarine proceeding on the surface, represented one successful patrol. Stars appearing on a scroll below the submarine note additional successful patrols.

Successor to the Combat Insignia is the device known as the Deterrent Patrol Insignia. It is awarded to crews in ballistic missile submarines (SSBNs) who complete one or more deterrent patrols. The criteria were recently expanded to include the five Regulus guided missile submarines deployed on forty-one deterrent patrols over the course of five years from 1959 to 1964. The device is silver and depicts a *Lafayette*-class submarine with superimposed Polaris missile and electron rings that signify the armament and nuclear-powered characteristics of the boats. A scroll beneath the submarine holds stars for each patrol after the first. A gold deterrent pin, known as the Neptune Award, is presented to the sailor on active duty, officer or enlisted, with the most deterrent patrols.

A fleet ballistic missile submarine and her crew depart their home base and head into the sunset to begin their two-month submerged deterrent patrol. The Deterrent Patrol Badge (inset) was created in 1969 to recognize the sacrifice and hard work that goes into maintaining nuclear-powered ballistic missile submarines on almost constant patrol.

Pyramid of Honor:
Symbols of a Nation's Gratitude

Over the years the awards system of the United States has evolved into a structured hierarchy known as the "pyramid of honor." The system is designed to recognize service ranging from heroism in battle to superior performance of noncombat duties. At the top of the "pyramid" and taking precedence over all other awards is the Medal of Honor, followed by the remainder of the category of awards known as "decorations." These awards are conferred on an individual for acts of valor or meritorious service and the medals come in distinctive shapes such as crosses, stars, or geometric designs.

Second only to the Medal of Honor is the decoration known as the Navy Cross. It is awarded for extraordinary heroism in the presence of great danger or at great personal risk. Instituted in 1919, this award was originally given both for heroism in combat and for other distinguished noncombat service. Although a majority of the early awards were for service in World War I, a number of Navy Crosses were conferred for heroism

Above: *Second only to the Medal of Honor, the Navy Cross is awarded for extraordinary heroism in the presence of great danger or at great personal risk. The most Navy Crosses awarded to one individual (five) in World War II went to a submariner. The color blue in the ribbon bar alludes to Navy service, and the white represents the purity of selflessness.*

Left: *Ribbons from a submariner's uniform are arranged in a hierarchy that has come to be known as the Pyramid of Honor. These ribbons proudly tell their tales of valor, service, and loyalty to a cause. Beginning at the top from left to right: Silver Star, Bronze Star (with combat V), Purple Heart, Good Conduct, American Defense, American Campaign, Asiatic Pacific Campaign, and World War II Victory.*

Above: *Admiral Chester W. Nimitz, Commander-in-Chief of the Pacific Fleet and qualified submariner himself, presents the Navy Cross to Lieutenant Commander Richard O'Kane, commanding USS Tang (SS 306). Lieutenant Commander O'Kane had previously been awarded the Presidential Unit Citation Ribbon and Silver Star with one star representing a second award. Before the war was over, he received the Legion of Merit, and our nation's highest award—the Medal of Honor.*

Above: *In World War I submarine captains and crews took their boats on dangerous and unprecedented voyages across the ocean to battle the Germans. Lieutenant Eric Barr (pictured) made the first crossing in the oldest and smallest of all the boats, USS E-1 (SS 24). Both Captain Barr and his Chief Gunner's Mate W. Elmore received the Navy Cross for extraordinary heroism. Chief Gunner's Mate Elmore, in the middle of the Atlantic in heavy seas, selflessly leapt overboard to clear a line fouled in the propeller.*

Opposite, bottom: *In the 1930s, Captain Charles B. Momsen was renowned for developing the submarine escape device known as the Momsen lung. Momsen received renewed attention during World War II when he was awarded the Navy Cross and the Legion of Merit for commanding the U.S. Navy's first submarine wolf pack.*

in rescue and salvage operations during submarine disasters. A World War II submarine captain, Commander Roy Davenport, received the most Navy Crosses ever awarded to one individual—five. Six more submarine captains received four each and although enlisted men were rarely in a position to earn this decoration, several enlisted submariners also received the Navy Cross.

Ranking third in order of precedence in the Navy pyramid of honor is the Distinguished Service Medal. Like the Navy Cross this award was also established in World War I and was instituted for the purpose of recognizing individuals who distinguish themselves by exceptionally meritorious service in a duty of great responsibility. In general the Distinguished Service Medal is awarded only to those officers in principal commands at sea whose service contributes materially to the success of a major command or project. For their significant contributions to the excellent performance of U.S. submarines in World War II as commanders of the Pacific Fleet, Atlantic Fleet, and Southwest Pacific submarines, Admirals Lockwood, Daubin, Wilkes, Christie, and Fife were each awarded the Distinguished Service Medal.

The Silver Star Medal joined the Naval pyramid of honor in 1942. The medal recognizes "gallantry in action that renders an individual conspicuous and well above the standard expected." The first awards of Silver Star medals to submariners went to the crew of USS *Trout* (SS 202), who, in early February 1942, came to the aid of American forces pinned down and under attack on the island of Corregidor. After resupplying the troops with vital antiaircraft ammunition the crew of *Trout* then loaded on board and evacuated 20 tons of Philippine gold and silver removed from Manila banks for safekeeping. President Roosevelt was so relieved to hear of the positive outcome of *Trout*'s mission, at a time when good news was so desperately needed, that he personally directed the commanding officer be awarded the Distinguished Service Cross and everyone else on board receive the Army Silver Star Medal.

Instituted at the request of President Franklin D. Roosevelt the Legion of Merit, with or without the combat "V," is one of the most prestigious awards a sailor can receive. Those who wear it are recognized as having made a significant contribution to the mission of the U.S. Navy. In World War II this prestigious award was received by both high-ranking officers such as Captain Charles Momsen, who organized the first submarine wolfpack, and enlisted men such as Torpedoman's Mate First Class Vincent Dallessandro, who was instrumental in the sinking of an enemy destroyer, the reconnaissance of an enemy base, the shelling of a hostile airstrip, and the rescue of a naval aviator while under concentrated enemy fire. With the advent of nuclear power, submarine captains with names such as Anderson (USS *Nautilus*), Beach (USS *Triton*), and Osborn (USS *George Washington*) would be awarded the Legion of Merit for pioneering new submarine missions. These missions included the first submarine voyage to the North Pole, the first submerged circumnavigation of the globe, and the successful deployment of the first nuclear ballistic missile submarine.

In order to recognize a different category of meritorious service, the Navy and Marine Corps Medal was established in 1942. This highly

Top, left: *World War II saw over 4,000 combat awards for valor made to enlisted dolphin wearers alone. Seven of them (and one officer), crew members of USS* Barb *(SS 220), were awarded the Silver Star for their participation in a daring raid that went ashore and blew up a Japanese train. Chief of the Boat Paul Saunders (kneeling on the left) was one of the most highly decorated enlisted submariners in the war, earning a Silver Star Medal, Bronze Star Medal, and several Commendation Ribbons.*

Top, right: *Following World War I a series of tragic accidents required many submariners to rise to unexpected heights under intense pressure. Chief Torpedoman's Mate Francis G. Smith, seen here being lowered to the sunken submarine USS* S-51 *(SS 162), received one of the few Navy Crosses awarded in peacetime for his efforts in making possible the salvage of the submarine. While blasting a tunnel 30 feet long and 10 feet deep in the sand beneath the submarine, the tunnel caved in behind him burying him beneath the submarine. Not willing to risk another life to dig him out, Smith passed the nozzle of his air hose back between his legs, and guiding it with his feet, washed his way back out.*

Left: *Crewmembers of USS* Trout *unload 20 tons of Philippine gold and silver safely evacuated from the Philippines in February 1942. Each member of the crew was awarded the Silver Star Medal.*

prized medal rewards noncombat heroism such as acts of lifesaving performed at the risk of one's own life. Although the most famous recipient of this award, World War II PT boat commander Lieutenant (jg) John F. Kennedy, was a surface sailor, over sixty World War II submarine officers and more than 130 enlisted submariners also were awarded this honored symbol of courage and devotion to duty.

Top: *Captain Edward Beach, commander of the nuclear submarine* Triton *(SSRN 586), having just completed a 36,000 mile submerged circumnavigation of the world, is being airlifted from his submarine to be flown directly to the White House. There President Dwight Eisenhower conferred on him the Legion of Merit.* Triton *also received the Presidential Unit Citation for this unprecedented voyage.*

Above: *Part of the collections of the Submarine Force Museum, these medals belonged to Master Chief Samuel Bledsoe who earned the Bronze Star (far left) in the last submarine attack of the war for his expert firing of the torpedoes and quick reloads. Due in part to Bledsoe's efforts, a freighter was damaged and her two escorts were sunk. Today a training facility at the Naval Submarine School bears Bledsoe's name.*

The Bronze Star Medal, another creation of World War II, recognizes sailors who distinguish themselves by heroic or meritorious achievement or service. A bronze "V" (valor) on the ribbon denotes heroism in combat against an armed enemy. Over 420 submarine officers and 450 enlisted submariners were awarded the Bronze Star from the start of World War II up to and including the last torpedo shot of the war.

Considered of equal precedence to the Bronze Star, the Meritorious Service Medal is for the recognition of noncombat service comparable to that required for the Legion of Merit but in a duty of lesser responsibility. The Meritorious Service Medal is awarded to individuals who have contributed notably to the effectiveness of their units.

Established with the intent to recognize the service, achievements, and contributions of officers and enlisted personnel, the Navy Commendation Medal has its roots in World War II when the Commendation Ribbon was authorized. Later a medal was designed to accompany this award designated for sailors who distinguish themselves in one of three ways—through acts of heroism, outstanding achievement, or meritorious service. The Navy Achievement Medal, often considered a junior version of the Commendation Medal, is awarded for either professional or leadership achievements. When awarded for combat actions a "V" device is authorized for both the Navy Commendation and Navy Achievement Medals.

Following the military decorations in the pyramid of honor are the "unit awards." These awards are part of a system by which an entire unit, such as a submarine, can be recognized for outstanding performance

Left: *By the end of World War II submariners had become one of the most decorated groups of servicemen in the war. The original Navy caption accompanying this photograph makes the point: "Though highly-prized, awards are an old story to veteran submariners. Note how most of the men on board the other subs go about their activities with scarcely a second glance at the presentation ceremony held on the vessel at the left."*

Above: *USS* Philadelphia *(SSN 690) pulls into Port Everglades, Florida, for a celebration honoring all who served in Operation Desert Storm. Displayed on the sail is a ribbon board denoting the unit awards the boat has received. These awards, given to the submarine for superior performance of her mission and participation in various campaigns, include the Navy Unit Commendation, Meritorious Unit Commendation, Battle "E," and the Navy Expeditionary Medal.* Philadelphia *was awarded the Southwest Asia Campaign Ribbon.*

of her missions. The award takes the form of a burgee-shaped pennant to be displayed by the unit receiving it, as well as a ribbon to be worn permanently on the uniform by those who were members of the unit at the time of recognition.

The first formal unit award for combat services, the Presidential Unit Citation (PUC), was introduced in 1942. This award is given in the name of the President to a unit that distinguishes itself by action comparable to that which would merit the award of a Navy Cross to an individual. Thirty-four submarines were awarded the PUC during World War II. Two submarines, USS *Tang* (SS 306) and USS *Guardfish* (SS 217), received the award twice. USS *Nautilus* (SSN 571) had the distinction of receiving the first peacetime award for its trip to the North Pole in 1958. Two years later USS *Triton* (SSRN 586) was awarded the citation for completing the first submerged circumnavigation of the globe. Four more submarines were awarded the PUC for completing highly classified and dangerous intelligence gathering missions during the Cold War. USS *Parche* (SSN 683), operating under a veil of secrecy unusual even for the close-mouthed submarine service, has been awarded an unprecedented five Presidential Unit Citations.

Following the Presidential Unit Citation in precedence are the Navy Unit Commendation (NUC) and the Meritorious Unit Commendation (MUC). Established in 1944, NUC is conferred on a submarine for outstanding heroism or extremely meritorious service (combat or noncombat) in support of military operations. To justify this award, the unit must have performed service comparable to that for which an individual would receive either the Silver Star Medal or Legion of Merit. Thirty-nine submarines received the NUC for combat actions in World War II. Since the war numerous submarines have been awarded the NUC for noncombat actions that were vital to our national interests. In the

Five enlisted men of the crew of USS Guardfish *(SS 217) are shown on the deck of their submarine just having been decorated by the Commander of Allied Naval Forces. The submarine was presented with the Presidential Unit Citation in the same ceremony.* Guardfish *was one of only two submarines to receive this highly respected award twice during the war.*

In the year 2000, USS Miami *(SSN 755) received two Navy Unit Commendations for actual combat operations. In a single deployment* Miami *delivered many Tomahawk cruise missiles to Iraqi targets in the opening hours of Operation Desert Fox, suppressing air defenses and allowing U.S. planes and ships to operate near the coast. After reloading in the Mediterranean, she repeated this operation in Kosovo a few months later.*

Right: *A submarine commanding officer poses for his official portrait. His gold officer dolphins are pinned above his left pocket. Beneath his medals is a Deep Submergence badge indicating qualification in a deep submergence vessel. The gold star worn above his right pocket indicates that he is presently in command of a Navy ship. The first two medals on his left pocket are decorations for personal merit and come in distinctive shapes. The remaining three circular medals are service awards given to him for participation in specific campaigns. On his right pocket he displays the unit awards received by boats on which he served.*

Far right: *Facing 15- to 25-foot waves in the middle of a typhoon, USS* Barb *(SSN 596) rescued four crew members of a downed B-52 bomber off the coast of Guam.* Barb *was awarded a Meritorious Unit Commendation, and several submariners who played perilous roles topside received individual commendations.*

1990s, U.S. submarines were once again being awarded the NUC for combat actions after several submarines were called on to launch Tomahawk cruise missiles against targets in Iraq and Bosnia.

The Meritorious Unit Commendation (MUC), established in 1967, recognizes units whose performance in combat or noncombat situations renders the unit outstanding compared to other units performing similar service. It is considered the unit equivalent of the Bronze Star Medal.

Distinguishable from decorations by their circular shape, service medals are awarded for participation in specific battles or campaigns, and are often known as the "I was there" medals. In addition to participating in each of our nation's major conflicts, members of the submarine service have also intervened in brief and little known operations around the world, seldom gaining notoriety. The Armed Forces Expeditionary Medal and Navy Expeditionary Medal are the nation's method of recognizing submariners' actions. The medals have been awarded to crew members whose submarines were in danger of hostile action by foreign armed forces or that operated under circumstances that merit special recognition. Operations off the coast of Grenada during the 1983 invasion

and recent participation in Operation Southern Watch in the Arabian Gulf have earned U.S. submarines the Armed Forces Expeditionary Medal. Submarines operating in the Arabian Gulf during the Iranian Hostage Crisis, and off the coast of Libya during the period of military skirmishes in 1986, were awarded the Navy Expeditionary Medal.

In each of our nation's major conflicts and in the intervening periods of peace, U.S. Navy submariners have consistently demonstrated that special quality that sets some apart from the rest. The colorful ribbons worn below the dolphins on a submariner's uniform paint a vivid picture of his dedication, devotion to duty, and of the sacrifices he has made in the service to his country.

Above: *Our nation's most highly decorated submarine, USS* Parche *(SSN 683), is entitled to fly the distinctive blue, yellow, and red pennant representing the Presidential Unit Citation, adorned with four stars—the highest award given to a submarine for valor.* Parche *received five separate awards—the citations that describe* Parche's *specific actions are classified.*

Left: *Among the awards given to submarines is the Navy Efficiency Award. This award known as the battle "E" is won in competition with other submarines. Each year the boat in each squadron that best exhibits excellence in all areas of submarine operations is given this award. The winning boat is entitled to display a large white E on its sail, giving it bragging rights on the waterfront.*

Page 308: *USS* Gurnard *(SSN 662) surfaced at the North Pole. Throughout the Cold War submariners conducted daring and critical tasking, often taking extraordinary risks in highly classified missions. As the Cold War progressed, U.S. submarines began to expand their focus to Arctic warfare, where Soviet submarines, including ballistic missile submarines, were expected to operate in the event of war.*

Patches and Flags

Captain Michael G. Riegel, USN (Ret), and Commander John D. Alden, USN (Ret)

The colorful jacket patches illustrated throughout this book are found today everywhere in the U.S. Submarine Force and in most other Navy units as well. The exact circumstances of their origin are shrouded in the mists of time.

As U.S. submariners began to prepare for World War II, someone decided that the boats should have distinctive emblems. A design based on the creature for which the boat was named, riding or firing a torpedo, was an obvious choice for many early logos. Frequently the artwork was done by prominent illustrators like Walt Disney, whose company ultimately provided some 1,200 logos for naval vessels during the war years. Some

designs were originated by crew members and painted by local artists.

The original drawing for a new boat was often signed by the members of the commissioning crew— the plank owners—framed and hung in the crew's mess or wardroom. It was a simple next step to paint the insignia on the conning tower superstructure or on a sailor's working jacket. In the case of USS Scamp *(SS 277) the emblem was designed by two members of the crew, who took advantage of the popularity of a brand of ladies' panties called "scamps." The logo featured a young woman resembling Marilyn Monroe with skirt aloft, holding a fuzzy puppy on a leash. Another use*

With flags and insignia displayed, USS *Dace* (SS 247) is mooring at the New London Submarine Base in late October 1945 after a long trip from Saipan at war's end. The battle flag is strung up between the 40mm gun barrel and the radar mast. At the foot of the mast, partly obscured by an antenna insulator is the ship's insignia. Near the top of the mast support the commissioning pennant can be seen fluttering above the Navy Unit Commendation pennant. The fourteen small Japanese flags strung from the periscope shears to the foc'sle represent the ships that *Dace* sank or damaged during seven war patrols.

for a boat's emblem was on its battle flag. USS *Raton* (SS 270) showed its Mickey Mouse logo on its flag in a 1944 photo.

Jacket patches began to appear more often only after many of the wartime boats had been decommissioned. Sometimes when a boat was being recommissioned the crew would design a different logo. USS *Archerfish* (SS 311) came up with one in 1952 that showed a fish shooting a torpedo from a bow. It turned out, apparently unintentionally, to be quite similar to the wartime Disney emblem used on the submarine's battle flag, although the boat's name was then spelled (incorrectly) *Archer-Fish*.

When nuclear power entered the Submarine Force with USS *Nautilus* (SSN 571) in 1954, many patches continued to be based on the fish motif, often with additional atomic symbols or some reference to the boat's wartime namesake.

The advent of the Polaris boats, which were named after famous men, stimulated an entirely different type of

Top row, left: USS *Raton* (SS 270). Walt Disney produced the original design for this interesting patch. The open-mouthed toothy snarl and eyes on the torpedo were added later.

Top row, center: Several variants of USS *Cusk*'s (SS 348) patch exist. Early versions featured a toothy fish, wearing a sailor hat, steering a torpedo. This colorful patch shows that the fish has endured but is now carrying a torpedo-wielding King Neptune on its back. The figure in the upper left represents the V-1 type rockets carried by *Cusk* in her post-wartime role.

Top row, right: The World War II USS *Blackfin* (SS 322) patch, shown here, features a fish dressed as a "Keystone Cop" twirling a baton, which was actually a torpedo.

Middle row, left: USS *Harder* (SS 257) was lost with all hands on her sixth war patrol in late August 1944. SS 568 was also named *Harder* in honor of SS 257. The SS 568 patch shown represents both ships.

Middle row, center: USS *Archerfish* (SS 311) has a unique namesake. The archerfish is named for its ability to shoot drops of water as far as 12 feet. It directs these watery bullets at insect prey whether in flight or at rest.

Middle row, right: USS *Crevalle* (SS 291) was named for a voracious fish, known for its fighting tactics and ability and nicknamed "bulldog of the sea." Hence, the patch features a torpedo-wielding dog riding a ferocious-looking fish with a jowly bulldog face.

Bottom row, left: The USS *Kentucky* (SSBN 737) patch was developed from a drawing submitted by a Kentucky resident. The horseshoe represents the state's rich racing heritage, and the Kentucky long rifle has historically been a symbol of freedom for the Bluegrass State.

patch featuring patriotic or historical symbols. A typical example was created for USS James K. Polk *(SSBN 645).* A sunburst and eagle in flight represent the "Spread Eagle" platform on which Polk ran for President in 1844.

With the Los Angeles *(SSN 688) class, designs based on features of the named cities naturally appeared; likewise, with the* Ohio *(SSBN 726) class, most designs reflect a tie to the namesake state. Many of these later patches include artwork or designs created by residents (often youths) of the namesake cities and states. In the mixed submarine force of today, patch designs reflect all of the above influences.*

Like the submarine patches, the exact origin of submarine battle flags has been lost through the years. Sometime early in World War II, submarines returning from a successful patrol began mounting a broom topside above the conning tower to indicate a "clean sweep" of the enemy. By 1944, submariners had begun attaching pennants to the brooms to indicate the number and type of

enemy ships they claimed to have sunk. Typically, a white flag with a red circle was used to represent Japanese merchant shipping sunk, and one with a rising sun was used to represent naval vessels sunk.

As the war continued, crews added the unofficial ship's patch, a colorful representation of the ship's name, other symbols for shore targets attacked, Allied pilots rescued, decorations and citations received until the flag elaborately reflected much of the boat's record. Among the more unique emblems is that found on the battle flag of USS Barb. Near the bottom center of this flag is the silhouette of a train labeled "Karafuto Exp." commemorating a train destroyed by a landing party of

Above: USS *Harder* (SS 257) was commissioned 2 December 1942 and was lost at sea in late August 1944 with all hands. Her fifth patrol was "the most brilliant of the war" as she sank five Japanese destroyers, driving off Admiral Ozawa's Mobile Fleet from its planned operating area, contributing significantly to a U.S. victory in the Battle of the Philippine Sea. *Harder* received the Presidential Unit Citation; her commanding officer, Commander Samuel D. Dealey, was awarded the Medal of Honor for this patrol.

Barb's sailors that was reportedly the only U.S. force to set foot on Japanese soil before the end of the war.

Another notable flag was that of USS Blackfin (SS 322). The battle flag features a "Varga" girl riding on a torpedo. Alberto Vargas, a noted painter of pinups during World War II, had given his painting to Blackfin. Members of the crew then used the pinup model as a central feature in the battle flag.

Whether born in the torpedo room or over a cup of coffee in the crew's mess, these flags represent and memorialize the exploits of the best submarine crews in the world. The stories are as varied as the designs of the flags. Each flag does not necessarily record all the

events of a submarine's war patrols but does include many specific events or situations. The flags would typically include all tonnage each ship claimed based upon the commanding officers' records. Postwar, the Joint Army-Navy Assessment Committee (JANAC) compiled the only official listing of Japanese sinkings (this did not include damaged ships), and only includes vessels of more than 499 tons. Therefore, the so-called official results may be less—in some cases considerably less—than what the submarine claimed. The flags, however, were never changed and thus a comparison today of battle flags to JANAC records is likely to show some disparity.

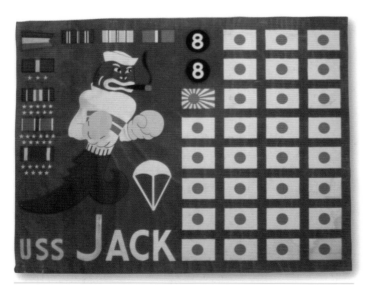

Top, left: USS *Pittsburgh* (SSN 720) is one of the few modern ships to sport a battle flag. She launched Tomahawk cruise missiles against targets in Iraq in the opening stages of Operation Desert Storm.

Top, right: The *Blackfin* girl was taken from a drawing by Alberto Vargas, who was famous for his "Varga Girl" pinup drawings. Vargas created the drawing specifically for *Blackfin*.

Bottom left: USS *Jack* completed nine successful war patrols. The flag shows her many awards.

Bottom, right: The striking and distinctive battle flag of USS *Tang* (SS 306) shows a black panther ripping through the center of the Japanese rising sun naval ensign. *Tang* was one of the most successful World War II submarines.

Top: Crew of USS *Jack* (SS 259) surround the ship's battle flag after returning from a war patrol. It is rather primitive compared to later versions.

Above: The USS *Ray* (SS 271) battle flag is characteristic of the development of battle flags later in World War II. In addition to a large array of sinkings, it reflects personal decorations awarded to members of the crew.

Above: USS *Flasher* sank 132,600 tons of enemy shipping, which was the highest total attributed to any American submarine in World War II. *Flasher* was awarded the Presidential Unit Citation for her third, fourth, and fifth war patrols. Her bridge, shears, and upper gun are now located at the National Submarine Memorial in Groton, Connecticut.

SUBMARINE
Museums &
Memorials
A Living Legacy

Sarah C. Page

For many years very little was publicized about the Submarine Force. The silence of the service was due not only to the quiet of the submerged vessels, but also to the tight lips of the crews who were forbidden to discuss the details of their work. Americans today, however, are becoming increasingly aware of the significance of the U.S. Submarine Force to our nation's security. In the twenty-first century, submarine museums and memorials afford us the opportunity to learn more about the invention of the submarine and its historic and present-day uses. They also serve to honor and remind us of the heroes who have helped keep our nation safe through the employment and improvement of submarines.

Submarine museums afford us the opportunity to explore the intriguing world of submarines, tracing the history of the submarine force from its inception to the present. Memorials honor those who have made the ultimate sacrifice in defense of our nation.

Museums with Permanent Submarine Exhibits

The common mission of submarine museums is to collect, preserve, interpret, and present the history of the U.S. Submarine Force. They keep the story of the Submarine Force alive in the hearts and minds of their visitors.

The World War II-era submarine USS Silversides *(SS 236), a national landmark and a museum, is seen at "full dress ship" in Muskegon, Michigan. A hardworking boat in World War II, she made fourteen war patrols and sank twenty-four ships.*

USS Marlin *(SST-2) is on display at Freedom Park in Omaha, Nebraska. She provided training services for naval ASW units from 1953 to 1973.*

Opposite: *The USS* Bowfin *Submarine Museum and Park is located adjacent to the Arizona Memorial visitor center in Pearl Harbor, Hawaii. It features the World War II submarine USS* Bowfin *(SS 287), a memorial honoring the fifty-two American submarines lost during World War II, and a museum with an impressive array of submarine-related artifacts.*

Artist Dan Price's rendition of the Submarine Force Library and Museum with the Historic Ship Nautilus *in the foreground. Located on the Thames River near the U.S. Submarine Base at Groton, Connecticut, the library is a world-renowned research facility and the museum hosts the largest collection of artifacts related to the history and operations of submarines in the United States.* Nautilus *is the first ship to have been "underway on nuclear power."*

UNITED STATES NAVY MUSEUM, WASHINGTON, D.C., displays artifacts related to the submarine service, from *Turtle* to the modern submarine. Extensive coverage of submarines may be found in three main permanent exhibitions that include photographs and personal artifacts from World War II submarines; an undersea exploration exhibit focusing on the scientific purposes of Navy submersibles including *Trieste*, a life-size model of *Alvin*, with diving equipment, and a simulated combat center where visitors learn about the fundamentals of submarine technology through interactive displays.

SUBMARINE FORCE LIBRARY AND MUSEUM, GROTON, CONNECTICUT, is home of the Historic Ship *Nautilus* and serves as the U.S. Navy's official submarine museum. It is the primary repository for artifacts, documents,

Visitors can tour the mostly unchanged interior of USS Clamagore (SS 343), *as well as other naval vessels, at Patriots Point Naval and Maritime Museum in Mount Pleasant, South Carolina.*

and photographs relating to U.S. Submarine Force history. The Submarine Force Museum maintains the world's finest collection of submarine memorabilia. The museum traces the development of the "silent service," from David Bushnell's *Turtle*, used in the Revolutionary War, to the modern *Los Angeles-*, *Ohio-*, and *Seawolf*-class submarines.

NAVAL UNDERSEA MUSEUM, KEYPORT, WASHINGTON, has one of the largest collections of naval undersea artifacts in the United States. With 20,000 square feet of exhibits, this museum combines naval history, undersea technology, and marine science to create an exciting and educational experience.

USS *BOWFIN* SUBMARINE MUSEUM AND PARK, PEARL HARBOR, HAWAII, allows visitors to go below decks on board the famous World War II submarine USS *Bowfin* (SS 287), a national historic landmark. The museum facilitates exploration of the history of submarines from their beginnings to the present day.

VALLEJO NAVAL AND HISTORICAL MUSEUM, VALLEJO, CALIFORNIA, features a functioning periscope from a World War II submarine, along with models, murals, photos, and other artifacts.

PATRIOTS POINT NAVAL AND MARITIME MUSEUM, MOUNT PLEASANT, SOUTH CAROLINA, includes USS *Clamagore* (SS 343), a World War II diesel-powered submarine, converted post-war to a Guppy III configuration. *Clamagore* and other naval vessels can be toured at Patriots Point.

USS Cod *(SS 224) is located on Lake Erie in downtown Cleveland, Ohio. Commissioned in June 1943, she made seven successful war patrols. The conning tower scoreboard includes a martini glass representing the rescue of the crew from the Dutch submarine O-19, which had grounded on Ladd Reef, deep in enemy waters, and the unforgettable thank-you party given by the crew of the O-19 once they were safely back in port.*

The deep submergence research vessel RV Trieste *is located at the Navy Museum in the historic Washington Navy Yard, Washington, D.C. She dove to a record-breaking depth of 35,800 feet in the Marianas Trench in 1960.* Trieste *also located the remains of the lost submarines USS* Thresher *and USS* Scorpion.

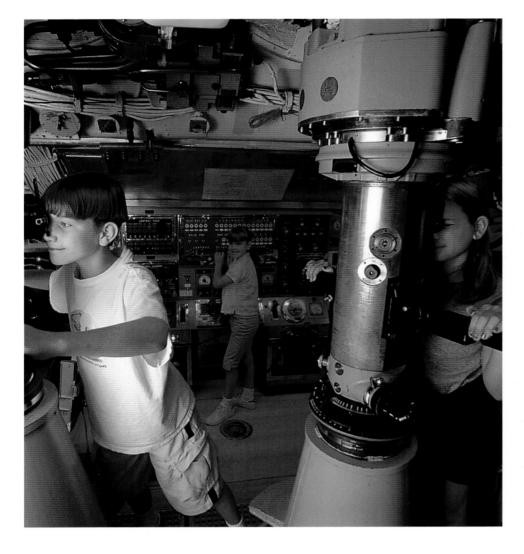

Above, left: *Children delight in trying out the working submarine periscopes at the Oregon Museum of Science and Industry, home of USS* Blueback.

Above, right: *With her bow planes neatly folded against her slender hull, USS* Becuna *(SS 319) nestles alongside the nineteenth-century cruiser* Olympia *at Philadelphia's Independence Seaport Museum.*

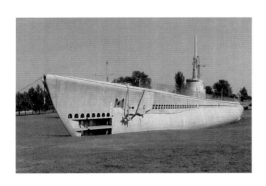

USS Batfish *(SS 310) was awarded nine battle stars and sank eight ships in World War II. Over a four-day period in February 1945, she sank three Japanese submarines. She was towed up the Arkansas River to Muskogee and placed in a dry berth as a memorial to Oklahoma submariners.*

Los Angeles Maritime Museum, San Pedro, California, is located at the site of the first operational submarine base on the West Coast. This museum features a small but very impressive display on submarine history.

Oregon Museum of Science and Industry, Portland, Oregon, is one of the nation's top ten science museums and one of Oregon's most popular tourist attractions. It features USS *Blueback* (SS 581), the only surviving diesel electric submarine built with the *Albacore* tear-drop-style hull.

Carnegie Science Center, Pittsburgh, Pennsylvania, is home to USS *Requin* (SS 481). Science-oriented exhibits demonstrate the engineering principles behind submarines, including how they move in water, the different metals used in their construction, and the workings of submarine engines.

East End Seaport Museum, Greenport, New York, features a life-size mock-up of the main compartment of *Holland*. A supporting exhibit explains why *Holland* was a success.

Independence Seaport Museum, Philadelphia, Pennsylvania, is home to the World War II submarine USS *Becuna* (SS 319). Very active during the war, the submarine was awarded four battle stars for her efforts.

Intrepid Sea-Air-Space Museum, New York, New York, features USS *Growler* (SSG 577), the only intact strategic missile submarine in the world that is open to the public. USS *Growler* offers museum visitors a firsthand look at life on board a submarine and enables a close-up inspection of the once "top-secret" missile command center. Launched in 1958 and on active duty for only six years, *Growler* remains in remarkably good shape.

NEW JERSEY NAVAL MUSEUM, HACKENSACK, NEW JERSEY, is home to USS *Ling* (SS 297), a *Balao*-class submarine. The museum contains many unique items, ranging from a SEAL delivery vehicle to personal photos and effects.

PATERSON MUSEUM, PATERSON, NEW JERSEY, features the effects and memorabilia of former Paterson schoolteacher John Philip Holland, who became known as the father of the modern submarine. On permanent display at the museum are the hulls of two of Holland's first three submersibles, as well as his bowler hat.

USS Drum *(SS 228), moored in Mobile, Alabama, is a National Historic Landmark. On her first war patrol from Pearl Harbor in April 1942, she sank the Japanese navy seaplane tender* Mizuho *and three merchant ships.* Drum *made thirteen war patrols and earned twelve battle stars in World War II.*

Memorials

USS *ALBACORE* (AGSS 569), IN PORTSMOUTH, NEW HAMPSHIRE, commissioned in 1953 at Portsmouth Naval Shipyard, served as an experimental submersible. She was noted for her innovative hull design and high submerged speed.

The USS Bowfin *Submarine Museum and Park in Pearl Harbor, Hawaii, honors the U.S. submarines and submariners lost during World War II.* Bowfin *was nicknamed the "Pearl Harbor Avenger," having been launched 7 December 1942, exactly one year after the attack on Pearl Harbor.*

Communications central: the radio room on board Lionfish *(SS 298). Visitors can board this National Historic Landmark, located in Fall River, Massachusetts.* Lionfish *was commanded during World War II by Edward Spruance, the son of Admiral Spruance.*

USS BATFISH (SS 310), on display in Muskogee, Oklahoma, sank three submarines. *Batfish* is a fine example of an early *Balao*-class submarine and compiled an aggressive record during World War II.

USS CAVALLA (SSK 244), in Galveston, Texas, received four battle stars for service in World War II, as well as the Presidential Unit Citation for sinking

the Japanese carrier *Shokaku* in the Battle of the Philippine Sea. *Cavalla* was reconfigured as an SSK in 1953.

USS Cobia *(SS 245), at the Wisconsin Maritime Museum at Manitowoc, is a memorial that keeps alive the heritage of the twenty-eight submarines built at Manitowoc during World War II.*

USS *Cobia* (SS 245), in Manitowoc, Wisconsin, is a World War II submarine similar to the twenty-eight submarines constructed at the shipyard in Manitowoc during the war. She is moored adjacent to the Wisconsin Maritime Museum.

USS *Cod* (SS 224), on display in Cleveland, Ohio, is credited with sinking ten enemy vessels totaling more than 27,000 tons of enemy shipping. All seven of her war patrols were considered successful and *Cod* was awarded seven battle stars.

USS *Croaker* (SSK 246), on display in Buffalo, New York, was awarded a Navy Unit Commendation for sinking a Japanese light cruiser during World War II.

USS *Drum* (SS 228), on display in Mobile, Alabama, sank fifteen vessels during World War II.

USS *Lionfish* (SS 298), in Fall River, Massachusetts, is a member of the fleet of historic ships located at Battleship Cove. A National Historic Landmark, *Lionfish* is berthed alongside USS *Massachusetts* (BB 59), destroyer USS *Joseph P. Kennedy, Jr.* (DD 850), and Russian missile corvette *Hiddensee*.

USS *Marlin* (SST 2), on display in Omaha, Nebraska, was dedicated at the opening of "Freedom Park," where she remains on display today.

USS *Pampanito* (SS 383), in San Francisco, California, was meticulously restored by the San Francisco Maritime National Park Association. The *Pampanito* Memorial is not only a memorial to the submariners of World War II but is also a museum of history, science, and technology.

USS *Silversides* (SS 236), on display in Muskegon, Michigan, was awarded the Presidential Unit Citation and sank twenty-four ships during World War II to rank third in sinkings by U.S. submarines.

Restored World War II submarine USS Pampanito *is open to the public for exploration every day (including holidays). She is located in San Francisco, California, at Fisherman's Wharf. (Photo: David Allen; courtesy of San Francisco Maritime National Park Association)*

USS *Torsk* (SS 423) moored in the inner harbor of Baltimore, Maryland, is available for tours. *Torsk* fired the last torpedoes and sank the last ship before the end of World War II.

DAVID H. MCCLINTOCK *DARTER/DACE* MEMORIAL, MARQUETTE, MICHIGAN, features a replica of USS *Darter's* (SS 227) conning tower, a three-foot scale model of *Darter*, a Mk 14 World War II torpedo, and a bronze plaque listing the crew members of *Darter* and USS *Dace* (SS 247). The memorial is part of the Marquette Maritime Museum.

SQUALUS MEMORIAL, PORTSMOUTH NAVAL SHIPYARD, KITTERY, MAINE, displays the bridge structure and conning tower fairwater of USS *Squalus* (SS 192), which foundered during sea trials in 1939. She was salvaged, and as USS *Sailfish* (SS 192) was awarded a Presidential Unit Citation for sinking a Japanese aircraft carrier.

SUBMARINE MEMORIAL PARK, SUBMARINE BASE, PEARL HARBOR, HAWAII, was dedicated 27 October 1960 to the crews of the fifty-two submarines lost during World War II. Between 1941 and 1945, the Submarine Force lost

Opposite, top: *The* Intrepid *Sea-Air-Space Museum, New York City, features USS* Growler *(SSG 577), the only intact strategic missile submarine open to the public anywhere in the world.* Growler *offers museum visitors a firsthand look at life on board a submarine and a close-up inspection of the once "top-secret" missile command center. Armed with Regulus nuclear-tipped cruise missiles, she helped usher in a new era of strategic defense.*

Opposite, bottom: *Retired crewmembers from USS* Darter *and USS* Dace *pose in front of the McClintock* Darter/Dace *Memorial, located in Marquette, Michigan.*

Left: *USS* Torsk *(SS 423) is a Tench-class fleet submarine located in Baltimore, Maryland. She made two war patrols and sank four ships in World War II. She was converted to a fleet snorkel in 1952 and has been restored to her 1960s configuration by a group of dedicated volunteers.*

Above: *The deep submergence vessel* Trieste II *(DSV 1) is located at the Naval Undersea Museum in Keyport, Washington.* Trieste II *is a bathyscaphe—able to sink to the ocean floor and then rise to the surface. Design depth is 20,000 feet.*

Bottom, left: *The Wall of Honor is part of the National Submarine Memorial-East, located in Groton, Connecticut. The names of submariners lost in World War II are engraved on this wall. (Photo: Tiffany Yost)*

Bottom, right: *The National Submarine Memorial-West, is located in Seal Beach, California. It honors the fifty-two submarines and crews lost during World War II. (Photo courtesy of James Burnett)*

over 3,500 officers and enlisted men. More than 16,000 men actually participated in war patrols. Their casualty rate of 22 percent was the highest of any branch of the U.S. Armed Forces.

NATIONAL SUBMARINE MEMORIAL-EAST, GROTON, CONNECTICUT, includes a Wall of Honor (on which is engraved the names of all submariners lost in World War II); a flagstaff and memorial plaque for each of the fifty-two submarines lost in the war; and the conning tower fairwater of USS *Flasher* (SS 249), the U.S. submarine credited with sinking the most tonnage during World War II.

NATIONAL SUBMARINE MEMORIAL-WEST, SEAL BEACH, CALIFORNIA, is a hallowed memorial to the fifty-two submarines lost during World War II and the submariners lost with them. Included are a Mk 16 torpedo and fifty-two stone monuments—each bearing a bronze plaque identifying the boat and listing the names of the crewmembers lost with it.

CEREMONIAL AREA, U.S. SUBMARINE BASE, SAN DIEGO, CALIFORNIA, is centered on the bridge structure and fairwater of USS *Roncador* (SS 301) and includes plaques in memory of the fifty-two submarines lost during World War II and fourteen other U.S. submarines lost before or after World War II.

CENTENNIAL OF THE SUBMARINE FORCE MEMORIAL, U.S. NAVAL ACADEMY— ANNAPOLIS, MARYLAND. Near Bancroft Hall is a striking sculpture, by Paul D. Wegner, of a submarine emerging from the sea attended by creatures of the deep. This memorial was dedicated in 2000 to celebrate the centennial of the U.S. Submarine Force.

JOHN HOLLAND'S GRAVE is located in the Holy Sepulchre Cemetery, Paterson, New Jersey. A new headstone was provided by the New Jersey Chapter of the Submarine Veterans of World War II with the help of people from all over the country.

Above: *USS* Albacore *(AGSS 569) is a national historic landmark at the center of Albacore Park in Portsmouth, New Hampshire. Albacore's mission was to be experimental: to be designed and redesigned, adapted and readapted. Albacore's innovative design features were a triumph. Submarine builders around the world copied them as best they could.*

Opposite, top: *Commissioned on 8 June 1945 USS* Ling *(SS 297) is now moored in the Hackensack River and is the official state Naval Museum of New Jersey. Never modified or converted,* Ling *is a good example of a World War II submarine.*

Opposite, center: *USS* Requin *(SS 481) is moored at the Carnegie Science Center in Pittsburgh, Pennsylvania. Commissioned in 1945,* Requin *was converted in 1946 to become the first United States radar picket submarine. New missions for the "migraine boats" included warning surface battle groups of incoming enemy aircraft, directing friendly air strikes in enemy-held areas, and providing mid-course guidance for submarine-launched Regulus missiles.* Requin *later returned to the role of attack submarine after a fleet snorkel conversion.*

Opposite, bottom: *USS* Croaker *(SS 246) is part of the historic fleet at the Naval and Military Park in Buffalo, New York.* Croaker *reached Pearl Harbor in the summer of 1944 and quickly made a name for herself. On her first war patrol, she sank a Japanese cruiser and three merchantmen. After the war,* Croaker *was one of the first submarines converted for an anti-submarine warfare role and was designated an SSK. The large passive sonar wrapped around her bow, able to detect snorkeling submarines at ranges in excess of 30 miles, is still a distinguishing feature.*

REFLECTING ON THE PAST: THE 2000 SUBMARINE FORCE CENTENNIAL

On 11 April 1900, the U.S. Submarine Force came into existence, when the U.S. Navy purchased inventor John Holland's submarine, Holland VI. The Navy commissioned the vessel as USS Holland on 12 October 1900. It was the first of a new type of warship that would devastate the Japanese navy and merchant marine in World War II, and play a prominent role in the outcome of the Cold War. The birth of the U.S. Submarine Force also marked the beginning of a series of technological innovations that have evolved into the formidable weapon that we know as the submarine of today.

Throughout the year 2000 the U.S. Submarine Force commemorated 100 years of submarine service and sacrifice to the country. As part of the Centennial year, the people of the Submarine Force, the Navy, and the nation celebrated with events and observances that highlighted both World War II and the Cold War and honored past and present founders, leaders, and heroes of the Submarine Force. Those who celebrated shared stories of service and sacrifice by American submariners who had demonstrated the effectiveness of power projection in combat, nuclear deterrence, and stealth; and whose deeds in defense of freedom still inspire us today and will continue to do so in the future.

For the U.S. Submarine Force, the Centennial year began as USS Topeka (SSN 754) rang in the year by straddling the International Date Line at the Equator, making the crew among the first to celebrate the new millennium. New Year's Day 2000 also brought another first as the Submarine Force participated in the Tournament of Roses Parade in Pasadena, California. Submarine Force sailors carried city and state flags representing the namesakes of today's submarines and flags emblazoned with gold and silver dolphins representing submariners throughout the century of service.

Activities throughout the rest of the Centennial year matched these early events with a variety of memorial services and dedications sponsored by both submarine veterans and active duty submariners. Centennial birthday balls were held all around the world as were scores of other activities and celebrations.

In March 2000, the U.S. Postal Service unveiled five new postage stamps honoring the Navy's Submarine Force in a ceremony at Dealey Center, U.S. Naval Submarine Base, New London, Connecticut. The five stamp designs depict different periods in submarine technology and were included in the first U.S. commemorative prestige booklet, containing text and photographs in addition to the stamps. This event was followed in April with the opening of a special exhibition, Fast Attacks and Boomers: Submarines in the Cold War, at the Smithsonian's National Museum of American History. This exhibit, together with the new Cold War exhibits at the Submarine Force Museum and Library in Groton, Connecticut, reveals some recently declassified Cold War submarine activities and explains how the U.S. Submarine Force contributed to ending the standoff that lasted for nearly half a century.

Other exhibits at submarine museums around the country also paid tribute to the 100-year history of the U.S. Submarine Force. New memorials were established, including the dedication of a pier at the Submarine Base Pearl Harbor in honor of Torpedoman's Mate Henry Breault—the first submariner to be awarded the Medal of Honor—and the placement of a Submarine Centennial Memorial Statue at the U.S. Naval Academy.

Taken individually or collectively, the events that celebrated the Submarine Centennial all recognized the enormous contributions of both American submariners and those involved with building and supporting our innovative submarines since the dawn of the twentieth century. In spirit and intent, the Centennial memorialized the contributions made by American submariners and gave the nation a glimpse at a living museum for the development and evolution of a Submarine Force second to none. It was a year to be remembered.

On 27 March 2000, submariners and supporters packed the theater at the Submarine Base in Groton, Connecticut, for the unveiling and first-day issue of five new postage stamps honoring the Navy's Submarine Force. Collectors received an additional bonus in the form of a "prestige booklet," which accompanied the stamps. A first in U.S. Postal history, the prestige booklet contained text and photographs detailing the long and distinguished record of the "Silent Service."

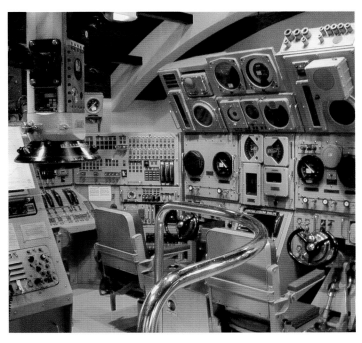

Top left, top right, and left: *The control stations on board a typical U.S. Navy nuclear-powered attack submarine of the Cold War era are displayed as part of the exhibition that opened to the public on 12 April 2000 at the Smithsonian's National Museum of American History. The exhibition, including videos and interactive displays allowing visitors to witness submarine operations and hear families discuss the demands placed on both the crew and their families, is scheduled to remain open through April 2003.*

Bottom, far left and left: *Admiral R. L. J. Long, USN (Ret), and the Submarine Memorial Statue at the U.S. Naval Academy. Admiral Long made the following remarks at the dedication ceremony: "This Submarine Memorial commemorates not one point in history, but one hundred years of innovation and dedication, both in war and peace. It is a monument to the inventors like Holland, to the early operators who saw the potential in the submarine like Nimitz, to the engineers who worked out the problems of production like L. Y. Spear, to the wartime leaders who sent their boats out like Lockwood, to the wartime skippers who brought about great things with diesel boats like Dealey, Fluckey, and Cutter. It also memorializes the technical skills and management acumen of Rickover and Levering Smith. The early nuclear legend-making trips of Nautilus, Triton, and the Skate-class boats are remembered here. The Cold War building program is a part of this memorial and was itself a monument to tenacity with 190 submarines built, tested, manned, and operated since Nautilus sent her "Underway on Nuclear Power" message. The end of the Cold War is also a part of the first century submarine story, and we can take justifiable pride in the large part played by this force in bringing about a peaceful end to that contest. The last decade of this first century is also represented here. There was no easy ride for submariners after the Berlin Wall came down."*

Exploration

AND THE Future

Science & Exploration

Captain James C. Hay, USN (Ret)

Page 328–329: *USS* Sennet *(SS 408) maneuvers in sea ice adjacent to the ice shelf of the Ross Sea near Antarctica, during Operation* High Jump *from 1946 to 1947. A World War II veteran still in wartime configuration,* Sennet *tested weapons and equipment under cold weather conditions.*

Above: *In addition to scientific expeditions, submarines experimented with many unusual operational capabilities to extend their warfighting capabilities. In this photograph, USS S-1 (SS 105) readies a seaplane for flight during tests at Hampton Roads. The aircraft when not in use was partially disassembled and stored in the large cylinder on deck. Successful development of this concept would greatly increase the reach of the submarine when on its scouting mission; however, the program was cancelled, since it was considered an idea ahead of its time.*

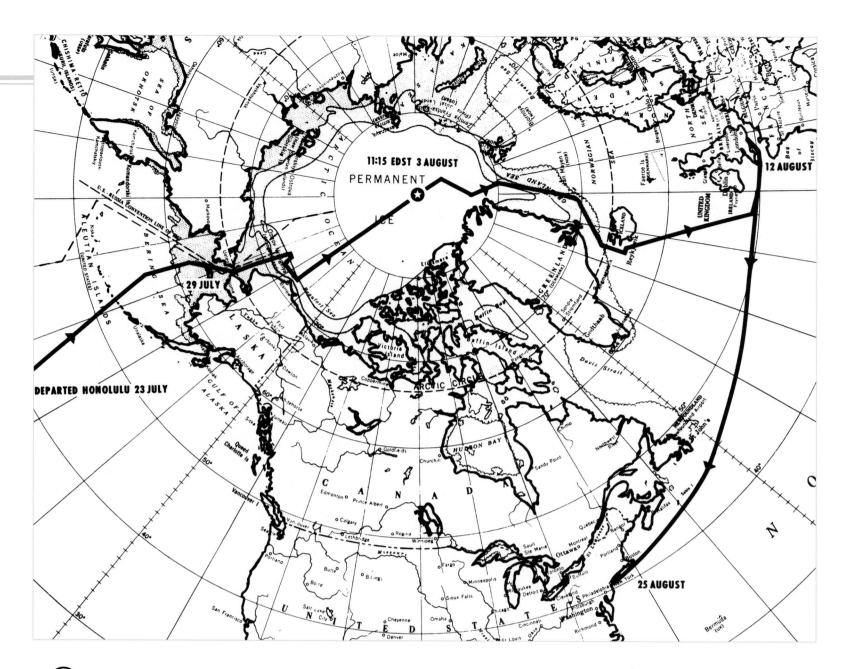

Over the years several submarine expeditions have been designed for the collection of scientific knowledge and the conduct of operations under conditions not normally encountered. These expeditions have gone to the farthest regions of the frozen north and south and to the very bottom of the sea.

Almost without exception, these expeditions were aimed primarily at the development of knowledge for the extension of military capability. The collection of pure scientific data was concurrently possible and civilian scientists from academia, government, and industry were on board for most of those trips.

While in these remote and forbidding places, submariners were able to test existing equipment under extreme conditions, evaluate the need to develop new hardware, and examine their procedures and doctrines in a new environment. The scientific efforts had a much wider utility with both meteorology and hydrography benefiting in the short to mid term and other marine sciences standing to advance from the collected data over the long term.

In 1930 the Arctic explorer Sir Hubert Wilkins, working through the firm of Simon Lake and Commander John Danenhower, leased for $1 the submarine USS *O-12* (SS 73) in order to cross the Arctic Ocean. *O-12* had been built by Lake in 1917 and was 175 feet long and displaced 566 tons submerged. After many materiel problems, he finally got to the edge of the ice and prepared to dive on 21 August 1931 only to find the stern

Nautilus's course across the top of the world marked the first passage of the Arctic Ocean by any vessel, surfaced or submerged. The voyage was truly an expedition into the unknown because both the thickness of the ice and the depth of the bottom could only be estimated while planning for the cruise.

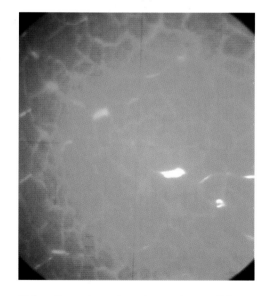

Taken through a submarine periscope, this photo shows the extremely uneven nature of the bottom of the ice shelf. Ridges can extend well below the nominal ice thickness and make submerged navigation particularly tricky in areas of relatively shallow ocean depths. Selection of the right place to attempt a surfacing through the ice naturally depends on the location and avoidance of such ridges.

DODGING ICE RIDGES

A submerged transit to the Arctic Ocean from the Pacific Ocean is always a challenging (and sometimes harrowing) feat. The Bering Straits, between Russia and Alaska, and the Chukchi Sea to the north are very shallow. For several hundred miles the water is only 125 to 180 feet deep. Since the submarine's keel to top of sail height is about 50 feet and since the ice ridges project down any number of feet from the surface, there is not much room for clearance. To avoid the deep ice ridges, the submarine cruises about 25 feet above sea bottom and uses a forward-looking iceberg detecting sonar to estimate the depth of the ice ridges ahead. With the submarine so close to the ice above and the bottom below, and considering that the submarine is about the length of a football field, any minor up or down angle could result in the rudder hitting the ice or the bottom. When the iceberg detector indicates a deep ice ridge ahead that will not clear the top of the sail by 25 feet, a course change is made to avoid it. This occurs frequently and for an extended period of time. In the winter, it can take several days to clear the ice-capped shallow waters; in the summer, the critical transit is much shorter. Occasionally there is no way to go, and one could literally get stuck between the rock and the hard place. A submariner is greatly relieved when his last shallow water watch is over, until he realizes that he may have it all to do over again on the way home.

—Captain Arne C. Johnson, USN (Ret)

NAVSHIPS 1111 (REV. 11-54)

SHIP'S POSITION

U. S. S. **NAUTILUS**

TO: COMMANDING OFFICER

AT (Time of day) 1915 U		DATE 3 August 1958
LATITUDE 90° 00.0'N	LONGITUDE Indefinite	DETERMINED AT —

BY (Indicate by check in box)
☒ N6A CELESTIAL   ☒ D. R.   ☒ MK19 LORAN   ☐ RADAR   ☐ VISUAL

SET —	DRIFT —	DISTANCE MADE GOOD SINCE (time) (miles) Honolulu 4844

DISTANCE TO North Pole	MILES Zero	ETA —

TRUE HDG. 180°	ERROR MK19 GYRO 3 E MK23 GYRO 0°	VARIATION 170° E

MAGNETIC COMPASS HEADING (Check one)
☐ STD   ☐ STEERING   ☒ REMOTE IND   ☐ OTHER   M 244 G 359 °

DEVIATION 126 E	1104 TABLE DEVIATION 3° W	DG: (Indicate by check in box) ☐ ON ☒ OFF

REMARKS

N6A DR
σ = 0
ν = 0

N6A
$n_x = 0$
$n_y = 0$
$n_z = 1$

RESPECTFULLY SUBMITTED (Navigator)

LT Shepherd M. Jenks, USN

CC:

planes had been too badly damaged to conduct any submerged operations. Wilkins's dream of submarine Arctic exploration was right; he just did not have a good enough boat to accomplish this feat.

A much different, and infinitely better equipped, U.S. naval group made a trip to Antarctica in 1946 with USS *Sennet* (SS 408) in company for further submarine ice operations in the Ross Sea. Once again, materiel problems—this time the failure of an upward beamed fathometer—caused cancellation of the under-ice work.

In 1958, however, the right type ship was available to make history with a significant transit under ice and attainment of a polar crossing. USS *Nautilus* (SSN 571), the world's first nuclear-powered ship and the first true submarine, passed under the North Pole at 90 degrees north latitude on 3 August. Military operations in the polar regions could now be envisioned, and the top of the world came to be looked at as an area of potential advantage in the Cold War.

The U.S. Navy continued its submarine under-ice operations for the next four decades, gaining both military experience and scientific knowledge. This phase of Arctic exploration culminated in a series of five planned scientific expeditions as a joint venture between the Navy and the National Science Foundation. On the last of the submarine under-ice expeditions (SCICEXs) an ice camp was established about 150 miles northwest of Point Barrow, Alaska.

The incorporation of nuclear power gave submarines a much needed step-change improvement in mobility. It meant not only the all-important increase in tactical mobility, which lifted the submerged submarine from almost stationary in relation to surface forces to being on a par with them, but also in strategic mobility. The submerged submarine could now go anywhere and remain undetected while doing its job. To properly examine and exploit that new-found capability, the Navy had to embark on a series of geographic cruises to examine the operational aspects of long distance, high-endurance submerged operations and the various physical phenomena associated with more advanced submarining.

Above: *In early March 1959, USS* Skate *(SSN 578) headed for the Arctic to pioneer operations during the period of extreme cold and maximum ice thickness. Skate steamed 3,900 miles under pack ice while surfacing through it ten times. On 17 March 1959, she surfaced at the North Pole to commit the ashes of the famed explorer Sir Hubert Wilkins to the Arctic waste.*

Opposite, top: *The navigator's report to the captain recorded USS* Nautilus's *(SSN 571) historic achievement in arriving at the geographic North Pole on 3 August 1958.*

Above: *Dr Waldo K. Lyons was the director of the Arctic Submarine Laboratory for four decades during the Cold War. He made immense contributions to Arctic submarine design and operations. He was a valued advisor and participated in most of the submarine under-ice expeditions.* (Undersea Warfare Magazine *Historic Photo Collection*)

Left: *Sophisticated ice operations continued through the Cold War. In May of 1986 three* Sturgeon-*class nuclear attack submarines worked together in the Arctic and surfaced simultaneously at the North Pole. Shown here are USS* Archerfish *(SSN 678), USS* Hawkbill *(SSN 666), and USS* Ray *(SSN 653).*

Commander William Anderson, commanding officer of USS Nautilus *(SSN 571), waves to admirers as* Nautilus *returns from its historic transpolar Arctic voyage.* Nautilus *proudly displays a flag specifically designed for the event from number two periscope.*

The first submerged circumnavigation by USS *Triton* (SSRN 586) in 1960 was such an expedition. It followed closely upon, and benefited greatly from, both the polar cruise by *Nautilus* and a subsequent two-month continuously submerged operation by USS *Seawolf* (SSN 575). The scientific goals of the world cruise were to examine bathymetry and submarine oceanography. The military purposes included high-speed

endurance testing of the power plant, sampling of worldwide submarine communications conditions, and the long-term performance of developmental submarine inertial navigation.

Other extended cruises made detailed surveys that were to become very useful to the Fleet Ballistic Missile (FBM) program. USS *Archerfish* (AGSS 311) spent long periods at sea making gravitational measurements throughout the oceans of the world. All submarines were tasked to collect bathymetric information wherever they operated and forward it for central processing and promulgation in constantly revised charts.

The military value of operations at greater depths by submarines has not yet been fully attained; however, as the United States learns

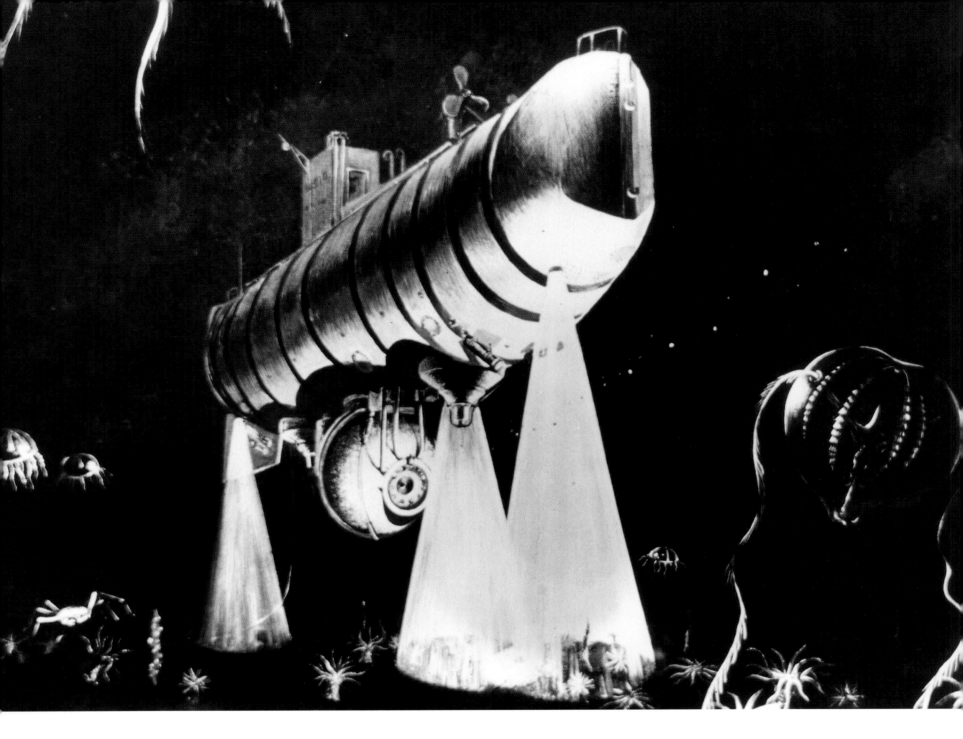

The historic dive of Trieste, *with Don Walsh and Jacques Picard, to the deepest spot on earth (37,800 feet down) in 1960 set another dimension to the rapidly expanding scope of U.S. submarine exploits.* Trieste *was essentially a manned, very strong sphere attached to a buoyancy shape filled with gasoline, which is less dense than sea water and allows it to be operated much like a high-altitude balloon. (U.S. Naval Historical Center)*

Opposite, top: *Deep submergence rescue vessels (DSRVs) can dive to a disabled submarine and connect with the survivors through a mating with one of the disabled submarine's hatches. The DSRVs were designed to be transported, launched, and recovered by an SSN or by a submarine rescue vessel. The crew of the DSRV can enter, while submerged, through the host submarine's hatch. The DSRV displaces 37 tons but can be air transported to any place on earth within a few hours.*

more about what can be done with hull forms and materials, we will be able to get deeper with our weapons-carrying, mission-capable submarines. As we learn more about the oceans' unique general properties and characteristics of specific locales, we will be able to develop more sophisticated tactics exploiting those properties and characteristics. Going deeper, with greater environmental knowledge, may well provide us with a step increase in capability.

The most dramatic exploration of the ocean depths was made in 1960 by Lieutenant Don Walsh and the Swiss scientist Jacques Picard in the bathyscaphe *Trieste*. They dove to the deepest spot on earth, at 37,800 feet in the Challenger Deep of the Marianas Trench in the western Pacific. Since that time great strides have been made in oceanography, expanding our knowledge of both the geography of the sea bottom and the vertical profile of seawater physics. In addition, the discovery of new features such as thermal vents in the sea floor has given added impetus to innovative research into military use of the sea. Deep submergence has been done, and science of the sea has advanced. It now remains to combine engineering and ocean technology to further the military effectiveness of the submarine.

Nuclear propulsion was successfully introduced into the deep submergence world with the Navy's research submersible *NR-1* that was launched in 1969. This vessel added both mobility and endurance to operations in

deeper waters. *NR-1* has performed admirably in high priority object recovery, such as the retrieval of the wreckage of the space shuttle *Challenger* off Cape Canaveral. It has also participated in the search for ancient ships in the Mediterranean Sea as part of undersea archeological expeditions.

USS *Dolphin* (AGSS 555) is an experimental submarine capable of deeper operations than the Navy's other submarines. She has operated extensively in both the Atlantic and the Pacific conducting physical surveys and furthering the Navy's body of oceanographic knowledge and submarine design. *Dolphin*, at 950 tons submerged and 165 feet length overall, was put into service in 1968. Although her hull is specially constructed to resist greater sea pressures, *Dolphin* more nearly resembles the operating mode of military mission submarines than does *NR-1*.

Deep submergence rescue vessels (DSRVs) constitute another branch of the Navy's deep submergence effort. Two DSRVs were built, *Mystic* and *Avalon*. They were designed specifically for the rescue of crew members from submarines disabled on the bottom. Each can carry up to twenty-four survivors in two of its three spheres.

The depths of the ocean have been called "inner space." We who inhabit the Earth's surface are nearly as fascinated by the mysteries of the sea bottom as we are by the remote galaxies of outer space. Inevitably, as improvements in technology permit, submariners and submarines will lead the further exploration of inner space.

USS Dolphin *(AGSS 555) is a deep diving non-nuclear submarine offering an excellent platform for research, and frequently is tasked to support various naval research facilities.* Dolphin *is not considered a combatant; however, she has been heavily involved in the development of ASW, advanced communications, sonar, and oceanography.*

THE Future

Vice Admiral Bernard M. Kauderer, USN (Ret)
Vice Admiral Roger F. Bacon, USN (Ret)
Commander Daniel K. Bacon, USN (Ret)

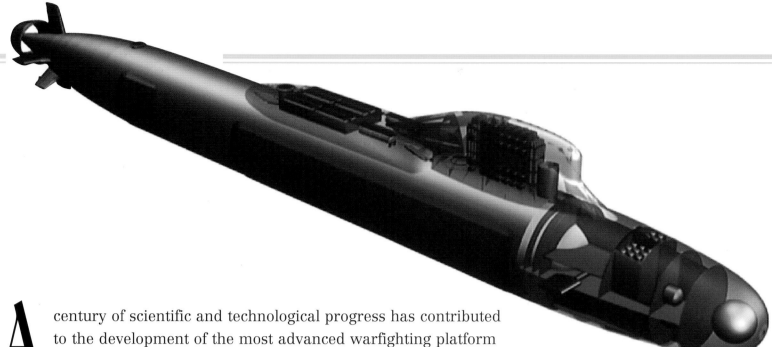

A century of scientific and technological progress has contributed to the development of the most advanced warfighting platform in the world—the modern nuclear-powered submarine. Submarines have become America's vehicle of choice for an increasing array of military missions. The enduring attributes of the submarine—stealth, endurance, fire power, and agility—will continue to make it a platform that can accomplish missions that no other platform is capable of performing. The submarine's unparalleled success is achieved through technology and innovation. The submarine lives through stealth, sees through sensors, controls through weapons, and extends mission capability through new off-board systems and communications capability.

The elemental and enduring characteristic of submarines is stealth—the ability to remain undetected by an enemy employing any means of detection. The hull itself is as hydrodynamically and hydro-acoustically pure as the ship design will permit. The shapes of the intersections of the sail and other appendages with the hull optimize flow without noise. To minimize the possibility that some errant noise might escape from the hull, and also to absorb active sonar pulses from either an attacking ship or a torpedo, the hull is coated with a material that dampens and traps acoustic energy.

The design of the mechanical components of the ship has received as much attention to technological detail as the design of the hull. The vast complexes of turbines, pumps, and valves that comprise the nuclear propulsion plant have been carefully designed and integrated to mini-

Above: *The near-term future of the U.S. Submarine Force is built upon USS* Virginia *(SSN 774) and variants that will provide payload and sensor flexibility. Shown here, considerations for the "Virginia-class Bundle One" include accommodations for a large unmanned undersea vehicle (UUV), composite sail, and large vertical aperture sonar arrays.*

Opposite: *USS* Asheville *(SSN 758) is underway with a battle group in the Pacific Ocean. For half a century, the Navy tried unsuccessfully to build a submarine fast enough to operate with the battle fleet. Finally, nuclear power provided the speed (and more) for the submarine to be integrated into the battle group. Today U.S. naval forces control the battle space from stratosphere to ocean floor.*

Above: *Shown is the left rear view of the Navy's Predator unmanned aerial vehicle (UAV) in-flight on a simulated Navy reconnaissance mission. Predator was controlled by USS* Chicago *(SSN 721) in an operational demonstration in June 1996.*

Left: *This conceptual hull is designed to maximize payload while minimizing hydrodynamic impact. The vehicle would contain three cylindrical pressure hulls, external weapons clips, two adjuvant vehicles, and conformal sonar arrays.*

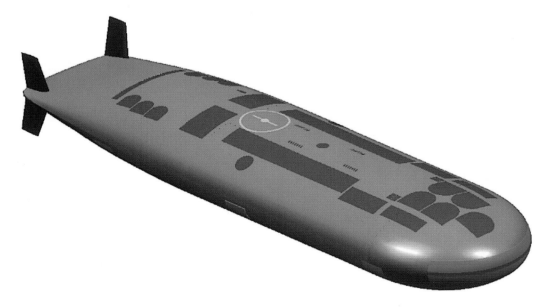

Right: *Unmanned undersea vehicles (UUVs), such as the Manta shown here, will be autonomous, re-usable, re-configurable, and multi-mission capable. These vehicles will be force-multipliers, extending the reach of the submarine with both sensors and weapons.*

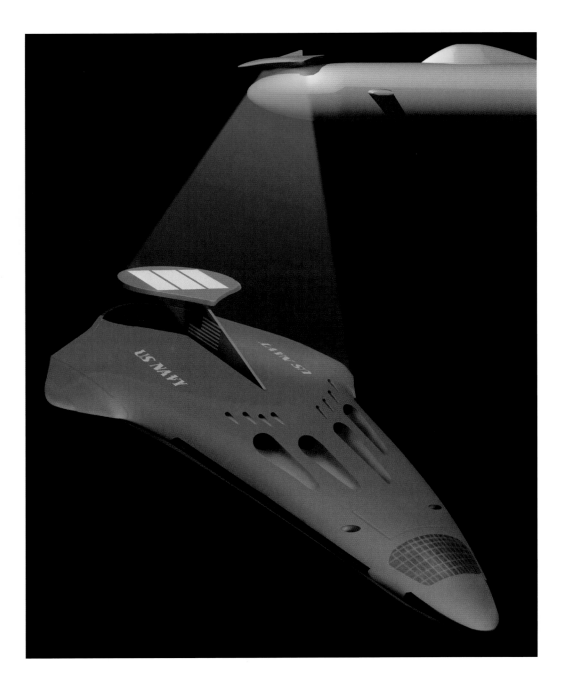

Above: *Unmanned undersea vehicles (UUVs) allow an SSN to safely gain access to denied areas with revolutionary sensors and weapons. These areas may be denied based on unacceptable risks to an SSN such as extremely shallow water, very poor acoustic conditions, or mined waters. UUVs provide unique capabilities and extend the "reach" of our platforms while reducing the risk to an SSN and its crew. The UUV depicted here is an element of the Long-term Mine Reconnaissance System (LMRS), which will greatly improve submarines' mine-hunting capabilities in the near future. Ultimately, a mission-reconfigurable UUV will also come into service, providing more capabilities and further reducing risk to future SSNs.*

Below: *The Advanced SEAL Delivery System (ASDS) was designed to reduce the risk to Navy Special Operations forces (SEALs) when requiring transit from submarine to shore. ASDS permits long-range Special Forces operations. It also enhances the effectiveness of the insertion teams by delivering them to their destination rested and better equipped, as well as the means of conducting shore surveillance prior to landing. The ASDS can be carried by six specifically modified* Los Angeles-*class SSNs, all* Virginia-*class SSNs, and also SSGNs (if SSGNs are made operational).*

Right: *Towed modules could provide additional weapons and sensors, as well as a possible habitat for special forces or a refueling station for unmanned underwater vehicles.*

mize the generation of noise that could radiate from the hull and be detected at long range. Conventional bearings have been replaced by magnetic bearings in which the machine shaft is levitated in a silent magnetic field. The main propeller, or propulsor, is a massive, finely balanced, precision finished, multiblade device designed to deliver the maximum horsepower with a minimum of radiated noise. The nuclear

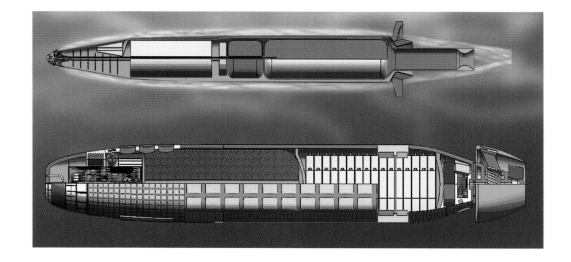

Advanced weapons, such as this rocket-propelled super-cavitating torpedo, will be able to break the underwater sound barrier, ensuring that it can catch up to high speed surface targets. Quiet submerged targets with acoustic sensors will never hear it coming.

Left: *A conceptual* Virginia-*class variant with external UUVs and modular hull plug.*

reactor core produces power for the lifetime of the ship, eliminating the need for refueling. Permanent magnet motors will drive the next generation all-electric ship, perhaps in pods external to the ship. Ultimately, electric energy will be produced from direct conversion of reactor heat, eliminating steam and mechanical systems and facilitating greater flexibility in ship arrangement. Directed energy weapons enabled by the transition to electric drive will create a fearsome new weapon—the Death Ray envisioned by President Reagan.

Deployed independently in the most forward areas where no other ship can survive, a submarine relies on a variety of sensors to establish and maintain an accurate "picture" of the surrounding environment. Gone is the traditional periscope. The view of the surface and the airspace above is now provided by a high-definition television camera augmented for night viewing by an infrared imaging system, combined with a variety of communications antennas in a photonics mast. The mast includes electronic surveillance system sensors for the detection and identification of signals across the entire radio frequency spectrum. The system also provides instant early warning of potential threats to the submarine such as ship or airborne radar and identifies and records signals for the intelligence collection mission.

Below the surface, a submarine is able to exploit sonar sensors to detect, track, and identify contacts. The acoustic advantage, the ability to detect a contact before being detected, derives from the capability of the system to process a whisper of a signal out of the background of ocean noise into a defined contact.

The basic submarine weapons arsenal includes a dual-purpose antiship or antisubmarine wire-guided torpedo, and several variations of a long-range land attack cruise missile. For special missions, the submarine may carry mobile mines that can maneuver to position themselves accurately (e.g., in the channel approaches to an enemy harbor) without placing the submarine at risk. A medium-range tactical ballistic missile,

The photonics mast is replacing the traditional periscope and provides operations with high-definition color, black-and-white, and infrared television images of the above-surface scene. The system's lack of optical hull penetrations provides increased flexibility in control room design and layout.

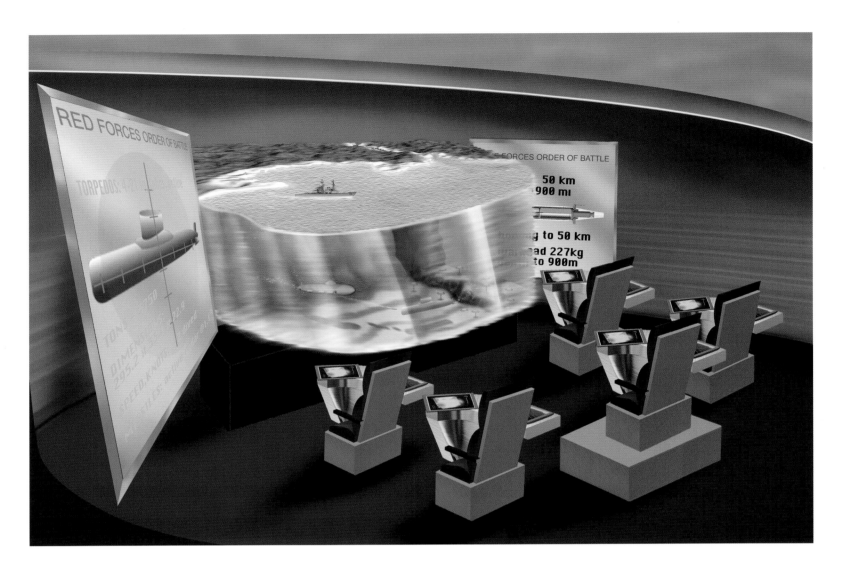

Above: *In future submarine combat systems, technology and connectivity combine to provide operators with detailed knowledge of their environment and the tactical scene.*

Above: *The SSGN is a transformational submarine, both physically and conceptually. Four Ohio-class ballistic missile submarines, also referred to as Trident submarines, will be decommissioned and inactivated by the Nuclear Posture Review. By capitalizing on the investment already made in these advanced submarines, new strike and special operations capabilities are possible.*

Right: *The next generation submarine is likely to be an electric drive, all-electric ship that provides architectural arrangement flexibility while preserving attributes necessary for today's enduring submarine missions. These submarines are likely to contain external weapons clips instead of the traditional torpedo room, modular UUV and payload handling systems, conformal sonar arrays, and an advanced signature controls system.*

launched from vertical tubes, will provide the battle force commander with a rapid response to mobile targets ashore. A rocket propelled, super-cavitating torpedo with a speed greater than 200 knots, is just over the horizon, as is a weapon to counter shallow draft, high-speed patrol craft.

Many exciting advances have been realized in a completely new field for submarines—the development and integration of adjuvant vehicles, the unmanned underwater vehicle (UUV) and the unmanned aerial vehicle (UAV), controlled by the submarine. Future armed, unmanned combat air vehicles (UCAV) will deliver ordnance on targets detected and tracked by UAVs, again, all under submarine control. If unmanned aerial vehicles can be made to operate effectively from submarines, it is conceivable that the capabilities of UAVs could evolve to approach those of manned air wings operating from aircraft carriers.

Submarine superiority depends upon a continuous infusion of technology to support both offensive and defensive capabilities. Chief among

the ideas that may come to fruition is that of platform and payload modularity. Payload modularity would be accomplished in a manner similar to the payload delivery capability of the Space Shuttle, with detachable payload modules that do not penetrate the submarine hull pressure boundary. In this concept, a submarine could be readily outfitted with payload modules that are designed to enhance the submarine's ability to execute a variety of missions, including Strike; Sea Control; Special Operations Force operations; and intelligence, reconnaissance, surveillance, and tracking (IRST). Such payload modules could be changed to outfit a particular submarine for a particular mission. Even today preliminary designs are on the drawing board for wasp-waist and drop-in hull forms to accommodate modular payloads. For example, a Strike Payload module is envisaged to evolve to accommodate over 300 land-attack missiles in the space required for eighteen of today's missiles and launchers. The U.S. Submarine Force will continue to be operationally exciting, technically challenging, and full of surprises. Submariners of extraordinary dedication, skill, and professionalism will make it so!

Commissioned in 1997, USS Seawolf *(SSN 21) was the first completely new design in approximately thirty years. The* Seawolf *class can carry up to 50 torpedoes/missiles, or 100 mines. Armed with Tomahawk cruise missiles,* Seawolf *can target about 75 percent of the earth's landmass for strike missions and can target surface ships at long range.* Virginia, *lead ship of the next new class of attack submarines, will be commissioned in 2004.* Virginia *breaks new ground as she has been designed specifically to fight in the world's littorals. She will operate in the shallower coastal regions to influence events ashore. Follow-on classes will draw on these predecessors.*

One option for increasing the submarine payload while keeping hull size down is shown here with a Towed Strike module capable of carrying hundreds of land-attack missiles.

343

Submarines Coming of Age

Captain Edward L. Beach, USN (Ret)

Years ago—more than I like to think about these days—I wrote something for The American Philosophical Society about the meaning of submarines. The ideas running around in my mind forty years ago were excited by the extraordinary capability we submariners suddenly found ourselves possessing. Those were great days for us because the just-developed nuclear power plant was an overwhelming success. No submariner of those days would ever forget the extraordinary operations of the first "nuke," the never-to-be-forgotten Nautilus. Our antisubmarine forces simply could not lay a hand on her. Then, along came the underwater-streamlined Skipjack, combining the Albacore research-hull form with the next generation reactor to establish wholly new parameters in speed and maneuverability. Finally, the nuclear submarine's enormous endurance and reliability were set positive by the voyage-around-the-world of my own ship, USS Triton (SSRN 586). This "subcircumnavigation" was in fact her shakedown cruise, converted at ten days' notice into a submerged around-the-world voyage at a sustained speed unattainable by surface ships.

Looking back at that fruitful time, today one can say that in an important sense nuclear power sent navies back a century and a half, to the days of sail, when ships stayed at sea for months, requiring only replenishment of provisions and water. The steam navy had become accustomed to frequent need to refuel, with the replenishment perquisites that went with it—and suddenly an enclosed recycling system of steam emanating from a virtually inexhaustible nuclear reactor freed us all not only from dependence on fuel but of the need, at the same time, for huge quantities of air. The nuclear ship has more than enough power to supply all its needs with ease, except food. If the United States was willing to build the ship big enough, it could do that, too.

The nuclear-powered aircraft carrier has proved in many ways to be the most useful naval ship since World War II, but the steady growth of the unmanned, computer-guided missile with huge destructive power creates the logical possibility that the carrier, too, may be reaching the end of her reign as the "queen of battles." The history of all warships says this must ultimately be so, but we cannot yet predict with certainty that they won't be needed. So, why should not these "most potent warships" be submerged, if they can there function better than two-dimensional predecessors confined to the surface membrane?

Radical changes have taken place, and change in combat is potentially the greatest change that has yet affected the world. We now have proof overwhelming that the glorious days of individual combat are over—

Above: A Tomahawk missile, launched from a submerged submarine 400 miles away, destroys its target during a test off the California coast.

be they on land, at sea, or in the air. Soon it will be possible for ships to be wiped out in the blink of an eye. Today we must think carefully how we steer, for we are in a time warp of combat capabilities.

It is said that military leaders, unless they plan aggression, prepare only for the last war, never for the next. Our concern today is that events move too fast. We can no longer expect to begin a naval building program at the start of a big war and see the new ships at sea before its end. Today, we must have the right fleet at the ready when the big war starts. Better yet, we should have it in hand, and so well practiced, that such a war does not start.

We may indeed already have seen this. World War III remained "cold" because of the unimaginable deterrent posited by our nuclear submarine armada. Would that it will always be so, and that ultimately even deterrence will no longer be necessary. For now, however, it is necessary. Yet the proudest boast of that submarine armada is that not once has one of its terrible weapons been fired in anger. Considering human frailty, here is the lesson for mankind: not a pleasant one, certainly not an easy one, but it has worked for half a century, arguably longer than any comparable peacetime period in the history of man.

If the nuclear submarine can give us a century of peace on top of the half-century it has already given, the world may be able to make real progress in some of its other pressing problems.

Above: Submarines and aircraft carriers have demonstrated their value as warships ever since World War II. Operating together, they provide a combination of air and sea power projection second to none, with perhaps infinite potential to affect the outcome of any armed conflict.

Left: Trident submarines converted to SSGNs could operate in otherwise denied areas to provide unique capabilities that would support other U.S. forces. These capabilities include cruise missiles that can be launched at rapid rates, Special Operations Forces (SOF) personnel, a swimmer lockout shelter, and an Advanced SEAL Delivery System (ASDS).

Suggested Reading

This short list of books is a representative sample of the submarine literature available from the bookstore, library, or internet. These titles comprise a subjective selection chosen by the editors. We hope that readers of this book who are interested in expanding their exposure to submarines find items of interest in this list.

NON-FICTION—EARLY YEARS

Alden, John D., *The Fleet Submarine in the U.S. Navy: A Design & Construction History* (1979)

Cable, Frank T., *The Birth and Development of the American Submarine* (1924)

Compton-Hall, Richard, *Submarine Boats: The Beginnings of Underwater Warfare* (1984)

Compton-Hall, Richard, *The Submarine Pioneers* (2000)

Ellsberg, Commander Edward, *On the Bottom* (1929)

Friedman, Norman and Christley, Jim, *U.S. Submarines Through 1945: An Illustrated Design History* (1995)

Lake, Simon, *The Submarine in War and Peace* (1918)

Lake, Simon, *Submarine: The Autobiography of Simon Lake as Told to Herbert Corey* (1938)

Maas, Peter, *The Terrible Hours: The Man Behind the Greatest Submarine Rescue in History* (2000)

Morris, Richard Knowles, *John P. Holland, 1841-1914: Inventor of the Modern Submarine* (1998)

Parsons, William Barclay, *Robert Fulton and the Submarine* (1922)

Weir, Gary E., *Building American Submarines, 1914-1940* (1991)

NON-FICTION—WORLD WAR II

Blair, Clay, *Silent Victory: The U.S. Submarine War Against Japan* (1975)

Calvert, James F., *Silent Running: My Years on a World War II Attack Submarine* (1997)

DeRose, James, F., *Unrestricted Warfare* (2000)

Fluckey, Eugene B., *Thunder Below! The USS Barb Revolutionizes Submarine Warfare in World War II* (1997)

Holmes, Harry, *The Last Patrol* (1994)

Hoyt, Edwin P., *Bowfin: The True Story of a Fabled Fleet Submarine in World War II* (1998)

Hoyt, Edwin P., *Submarines at War: The History of the American Silent Service* (1983)

LaVO, Carl, *Back from the Deep: The Strange Story of the Sister Subs Squalus and Sculpin* (1994)

Lockwood, Charles A. and Adamson, Hans C., *Hellcats of the Sea* (1955)

Lockwood, Charles A. and Adamson, Hans C., *Through Hell and Deep Water; the Stirring Story of the Navy's Deadly Submarine, the USS Harder, Under the Command of Sam Dealey, Destroyer Killer!* (1956)

O'Kane, Richard H., *Wahoo: The Patrols of America's Most Famous WWII Submarine* (1996)

O'Kane, Richard H., *Clear the Bridge!: The War Patrols of the USS Tang* (1997)

Padfield, Peter, *War Beneath the Sea: Submarine Conflict During World War II* (1998)

Roscoe, Theodore, *United States Submarine Operations in World War II* (1949)

Ruhe, William J., *War in the Boats: My World War II Submarine Battles* (1996)

Schratz, Paul R., *Submarine Commander: A Story of World War II and Korea* (1988)

Trumbull, Robert, *Silversides* (1945)

Wheeler, Keith, *War Under the Pacific* (1998)

NON-FICTION—1945 TO 2000

Anderson, William R. and Blair, Clay, *Nautilus 90 North* (1959)

Blair, Clay, *The Atomic Submarine and Admiral Rickover* (1954)

Beach, Edward L., *Around the World Submerged; the Voyage of the Triton* (1962)

Beach, Edward L., *Salt and Steel: Reflections of a Submariner* (1999)

Calvert, James E., *Surface at the Pole: The Extraordinary Voyages of the USS Skate* (1996)

Clancy, Tom, *SSN: A Strategic Guide to Submarine Warfare* (2000)

Clancy, Tom, *Submarine: A Guided Tour Inside A Nuclear Warship* (1993)

Duncan, Francis, *Rickover and the Nuclear Navy: The Discipline of Technology* (1990)

Friedman, Norman, *The Fifty-Year War: Conflict and Strategy in the Cold War* (2000)

Friedman, Norman and Christley, Jim, *U.S. Submarines Since 1945: An Illustrated Design History* (1994)

Kaufman, Steve and Kaufman, "Yogi," *Silent Chase, Submarines of the U.S. Navy* (1989)

Kaufman, "Yogi," *Sharks of Steel* (1993)

Lederer, Commander William J., *The Last Cruise* (1950)

Rockwell, Theodore, *The Rickover Effect: The Inside Story of How Admiral Hyman Rickover Built the Nuclear Navy* (1995)

Sapolsky, Harvey, *The Polaris System Development: Bureaucratic and Programmatic Success in Government* (1972)

Stumpf, David K., *Regulus, The Forgotten Weapon* (1996)

Weir, Gary E., *Forged in War; The Naval-Industrial Complex and American Submarine Construction, 1940–1961* (1998)

NON-FICTION—GENERAL

Compton-Hall, Richard, *Submarine Warfare: Monsters & Midgets* (1985)

Friedman, Norman, *Submarine Design and Development* (1984)

Kemp, Paul, *Submarine Action* (2000)

Kemp, Paul, *Underwater Warriors: Midget Submarine Operations in War* (1996)

Leary, William M., *Under Ice: Waldo Lyon & the Development of the Arctic Submarine* (1999)

Middleton, Drew, *Submarine, the Ultimate Naval Weapon: Its Past, Present & Future* (1976)

Preston, Antony, *Submarine Warfare: An Illustrated History* (1999)

Preston, Antony, *Submarines: The History & Evolution of Underwater Fighting Vessels* (1975)

Rindskopf, Mike and Morris, Richard, *Steel Boats, Iron Men: History of the U.S. Submarine Force* (1994)

Sontag, Sherry and Drew, Christopher, *Blind Man's Bluff: The Untold Story of American Submarine Espionage* (1999)

FICTION

Beach, Edward L., *Dust on the Sea* (1989)

Beach, Edward L., *Run Silent, Run Deep* (1986)

Clancy, Tom, *The Hunt for Red October (A Jack Ryan Thriller)* (1985)

Clancy, Tom, *SSN: Strategies of Submarine Warfare* (1996)

Smith, Ron, *Torpedoman* (1993)

Verne, Jules, *20,000 Leagues Under The Sea*

CHILDREN AND JUVENILE

Anderson, Joan, *Sally's Submarine* (1995)

Appleton, Victor, *Tom Swift and his Submarine Boat, or, Under the Ocean for Sunken Treasure* (1910)

Armentrout, Patricia, *Under the Sea* (1998)

Green, Michael, *Submarines* (1998)

Humble, Richard, *A World War Two Submarine* (1991)

Humble, Richard, *Submarines and Ships* (1997)

Kloeppel, James, *Danger Beneath the Waves: A History of the Confederate Submarine H.L. Hunley* (1992)

Lawhead, Steve, *Howard Had a Submarine* (1987)

McManners, Kelsey, *Underwater Attack: The First Submarines* (1978)

Osborne, Mary Pope, *Dolphins at Daybreak* (1999)

Roddy, Lee, *Secret of the Sunken Sub* (1991)

Swanson, June, *David Bushnell and His Turtle: the Story of America's First Submarine* (1991)

Woodman, Nancy, *Sea-Fari Deep* (1998)

Acknowledgments

The editors are greatly indebted to many people without whose assistance this book would not have been completed. First we must thank project editor Jim Muschett of Hugh Lauter Levin Associates and designer Lori S. Malkin for their patient explanation of the publisher's requirements; and add more thanks to Captain Dave Cooper of the Naval Submarine League for organizing our sources of information in the Washington, D.C., area. Also, we are grateful to Rear Admiral Jerry Holland and Ron Chambers of the U.S. Naval Institute for their advice and support, and we thank Dianne Moore of the Dolphin Scholarship Fund for her thorough description of that fine organization. The authors are introduced individually—to them collectively go our deep thanks for their patience and fine work.

As the book is primarily a "picture book," we need to recognize those who selected and provided the 700-plus images. We are most grateful to Jeanine McKenzie Allen and Eleanor Boyne for the zeal and good taste they displayed in choosing images from the several major sources in the Washington area. In addition, we thank the following organizations and individuals for their help in providing the pictures promptly and cheerfully: Naval Historical Foundation Photographic Service (Janea Milburn); U.S. Naval Institute Photo Service (Dawn Stitzel and Sarah Moreland); Defense Visual Information Center (Kathy Vinson); Navy Office of Information (Christopher Madden, Lieutenant David Blackwood, Lieutenant Richard Naystatt, Lieutenant Ron Steiner, Mrs. Henrietta Wright); Navy Office of Information East (Lieutenant Kathy Sandoz); Electric Boat Division, General Dynamics Corporation (Neil Ruenzel, Dave Tela, Kevin Flanagan); Historic Naval Ships Association (Channing Zucker); USS *Bowfin* Submarine Museum and Park (Captain Jerry Hofwolt); Chief of Naval Operations, Submarine Warfare Division N77, (Commander Chris Williams); *Undersea Warfare Magazine* (Lieutenant Commander Thomas Monroe, John Whipple); the Submarine Force Library and Museum (Wendy Gulley); Strategic Systems Project Office Public Affairs officer (Amanda Rogers); and the Atlantic and Pacific Submarine Force Public Affairs officers (Commander Robert Mehal and Lieutenant Commander Dave Werner). Further, we thank the many private individuals who offered and shared with us their treasured photographs, patches, battle flags, and other artifacts.

Not to be forgotten are the Sonalysts team members whose unflagging support sustained our efforts: Mark Patnode, whose graphics grace the Chronology; Jennifer Blaskovich, who designed and created the insignia graphics; Craig Kovacs, responsible for creation of graphics for the Future; Rena DeBartoli, photographic rework; Gerardo Orioli creation of chartlets; and Stephen Freitas, who designed and rendered the Memorial page of World War II losses. Also deserving recognition are Chip Yates, leader of a pack of avid researchers, and his henchmen, Jonas Sanchez, Robert Stack, Eric Toriello, and Cata Bingham; our local graphics and layout guru, Lisa Peringer; Nancy Moore, our charmingly tenacious technical editor; indefatigable typist, Donna Bonelli (supported by Eleanor Chapman and Mary LaForce). We thank Mike Hewitt for his research on submarine auxiliaries and finally the heavy-hitting review squad of Andy Toriello, Larry Clark, Dave Samuelson, Fred Litty, and Dave Boyd.

Editors and Authors

EDITOR-IN-CHIEF

COMMANDER DAVID RANDALL HINKLE, USN (Ret), a 1954 Naval Academy graduate, enlisted in the Navy at age 17 and earned silver dolphins in USS *Dogfish* (SS 350). Selected by Admiral Rickover in 1958, he served in four nuclear attack submarines, including command of USS *Pargo* (SSN 650) and three tours in SUBDEVGRU TWO. Called "Mr. Sonar" by his contemporaries, he received numerous awards for his contributions to submarine research and development. Commander Hinkle retired in 1973 and with his wife Muriel founded Sonalysts, Inc. The company boasts twenty-six former commanding officers as part of the one hundred plus submariners on its staff.

EDITOR

CAPTAIN HARRY H. CALDWELL, USN (Ret), became involved with submarines in 1939 when he was first employed by the Electric Boat Company. He attended U.S. Naval Academy (1940 to 1943) and served in submarines or submarine jobs for about twenty years. This included four war patrols, a trip to the Antarctic, and two submarine commands. Captain Caldwell is delighted to let a little light shine on his father's illustrious tour as the Navy's inaugural submarine skipper—and on the Submarine Force in general.

EDITOR

CAPTAIN ARNE C. JOHNSON, USN (Ret), is a 1953 Rensselaer Polytechnic Institute graduate. After duty in a destroyer escort, he entered the submarine service in 1956 serving on board six submarines. He had command of USS *Flasher* (SSN 613), USS *Mariano G. Vallejo* (SSBN 658), and Submarine Squadron TWO. Retiring in 1979, he joined Sonalysts, Inc. Captain Johnson became its Chief Operating Officer in 1994 and was named a corporate director upon his retirement in 1997. He is president of the Submarine Force Library and Museum Association.

LIEUTENANT COMMANDER DON C. LAFORCE, USN (Ret), was the project leader and coordinator for this book and also wrote the chapter *Submarine Family*. He served on submarines as an enlisted submariner and was commissioned through the Naval Enlisted Scientific and Education Program (NESEP) at the University of Idaho. Following graduation in 1972, he served on three fleet ballistic missile submarines. He retired from the Navy in 1983, and works as a multimedia producer developing program materials for the Submarine Force and other Defense Department activities.

COMMANDER JOHN D. ALDEN, USN (Ret), a World War II veteran, is considered an authority on the U.S. fleet submarine. The editors are grateful for his chapter on World War II boats, *America's Victorious Submarines in World War II*. A prolific writer, Commander Alden has authored numerous books and articles on naval history and technology, including *The Fleet Submarine in the U.S. Navy* and *The American Steel Navy*.

JEANINE MCKENZIE ALLEN, a graduate of Longwood College, taught for Norfolk, Virginia, and Brevard, Florida, schools. Her father, Lloyd Charles McKenzie, "plankowner" of USS *Triton* (SS 201) was lost in action with *Triton* and its crew in the spring of 1943. Her research of declassified records has led to helping families of other World War II servicemen killed or missing in action.

COMMANDER DANIEL K. BACON, USN (Ret), served on active duty in the U.S. Navy for twenty-one years, retiring on completion of his service as commanding officer, USS *Haddock* (SSN 621). Since 1980, he has been with Sonalysts, Inc., currently as executive vice president. His work has focused on the development and use of large-scale simulation systems to support command and control training of Joint Force and Navy commanders.

VICE ADMIRAL ROGER F. BACON, USN (Ret), served on active duty in the U.S. Navy for thirty-four years (1959 to 1993), including assignment as Assistant Chief of Naval Operations for Undersea Warfare (OP02). Vice Admiral Bacon also served as Commander, U.S. Submarine Force, Atlantic Fleet, Commander Submarine Group EIGHT/Commander Allied Submarines Mediterranean in Naples, Italy and as commanding officer of USS *Hunley* (AS 31), USS *Patrick Henry* (SSBN 599), and USS *Flasher* (SSN 613).

CAPTAIN E. L. BEACH, USN (Ret), a 1939 Naval Academy graduate, made eleven war patrols during World War II—the last one in command of USS *Piper* (SS 409). In subsequent years he commanded USS *Amberjack* (SS 522), served as naval aide to President Eisenhower, commanded USS *Triton* (SSRN 586) in which he circumnavigated the world submerged in 1960, and later commanded Submarine Squadron EIGHT. Paralleling Captain Beach's exceptional military career, he became a distinguished author having written eleven books and many professional articles. His first novel, *Run Silent, Run Deep*, was made into a movie in 1958.

JIM CHRISTLEY retired from the U.S. Navy in 1982 as a senior chief petty officer having served on seven submarines ranging from diesel to nuclear fast attacks to ballistic missile boats. A student of U.S. submarine technical history, he has written numerous articles and a book on the subject in addition to providing technical illustrations to several notable books on submarine design and history.

ADMIRAL WILLIAM J. CROWE, JR., USN (Ret), graduated from the Naval Academy in 1946, and holds a PhD in political science from Princeton University. His early naval career was in submarines, including command of USS *Trout* (SS 566). Gaining a reputation as a political-military specialist, he commanded the U.S. Naval Forces in the Persian Gulf; was Commander-in-Chief of Allied Forces, Southern Europe; and Commander-in-Chief of the U.S. Pacific Command. In 1985 he became the eleventh Chairman of the Joint Chiefs of Staff.

CAPTAIN JOHN M. DONLON, USN (Ret), a 1949 Naval Academy graduate, served in two destroyers, four diesel submarines and an SSN prior to ten years of submarine force commands: USS *Shark* (SSN 591), USS *Woodrow Wilson* (SSBN 624), Submarine Division FORTY-TWO, tender USS *L. Y. Spear* (AS 36), and Submarine Squadron SIX. He retired after thirty years of active duty and worked fourteen years for Electric Boat.

REAR ADMIRAL THOMAS W. EVANS, USN (Ret), a native of Jacksonville, Florida, is a 1959 graduate of Rice University. He served on board two destroyers and four submarines including command of USS *Batfish* (SSN 681). Selected for flag rank in 1984, Rear Admiral Evans directed key submarine and antisubmarine research and development programs in the Naval Sea Systems Command (NAVSEA). He became the Deputy Commander of NAVSEA in 1990.

WILLIAM P. "BUD" GRUNER, a 1935 graduate of the Naval Academy was serving as executive officer of USS *Pike* (SS 173) on the Asiatic station at the outbreak of World War II. After making seven war patrols as executive officer, Commander Gruner took command of USS *Skate* (SS 305) for three more patrols. *Skate* sank a cruiser and a destroyer among other ships and brought back five Japanese prisoners. In recent years he was technical advisor for production of the submarine game, "Silent Hunter."

WENDY S. GULLEY, a graduate of Lock Haven University, currently serves as the archivist at the Navy's Submarine Force Museum. Married to a U.S. Navy veteran whose family can claim three generations of men who served on submarines, she enjoys the opportunity her work affords her to spread the proud story of America's "Silent Service."

ROBERT A. HAMILTON, joined the staff at *The New London Day* in 1987, first as the science and technology reporter, then as city editor, and most recently as the military reporter. Mr. Hamilton teaches journalism at the University of Connecticut and has written articles for more than seventy-five magazines and newspapers.

CAPTAIN JAMES C. HAY, USN (Ret), served in seven submarines and commanded two of them, as the submarine force progressed from converted fleet boats to Poseidon fleet ballistic missile (FBM) submarines. He also was commanding officer of Submarine Base, New London, Connecticut, and followed that with a tour in Italy as Chief of Staff, Commander Submarine Group EIGHT. Jim has been Editor of *The Submarine Review* since 1990.

CAPTAIN HARRY JACKSON, USN (Ret), was deeply involved in design of submarines, beginning with the *Tang* class and through the 688 class and the Trident submarines. The deputy chief of NAVSEA recently referred to him as the grand master of submarine design. Captain Jackson has taught submarine design fundamentals to well over 750 naval students at Massachusetts Institute of Technology.

CAPTAIN F. T. (TERRY) JONES, USN (Ret), a 1966 Rensselaer Polytechnic Institute graduate, served in five submarines and was commanding officer of USS *Billfish* (SSN 676) and USS *Nevada* (SSBN 733) (Gold). During his years at sea, he operated in the Mediterranean Sea and the Atlantic, Indian, Pacific, and Arctic Oceans. Since his retirement from the Navy in 1992, he has continued his support of the submarine force by conducting naval research and development at Sonalysts, Inc.

VICE ADMIRAL BERNARD M. KAUDERER, USN (Ret), a 1953 Naval Academy graduate, commanded USS *Barb* (SSN 596), the submarine tender USS *Dixon* (AS 37), and, following selection to flag rank, Submarine Group FIVE. Vice Admiral Kauderer had the rare fortune to command both the Pacific and Atlantic Submarine Forces. He was president of the Naval Submarine League for five years and the originator and perennial chairman of its Submarine Technology Symposium.

CAPTAIN DONALD H. KERN, USN (Ret), is a graduate of the Massachusetts Institute of Technology. As the project manager for submarines in the Naval Ship Systems Command for six years, he strongly influenced the design, construction, overhaul, and conversion of diesel-electric and nuclear submarines.

CAPTAIN ARNOLD O. LOTRING, U.S. Navy, graduated from the College of The Holy Cross in 1978. Captain Lotring served in four submarines and subsequently commanded USS *Minneapolis-St. Paul* (SSN 708). Captain Lotring was assigned as Submarine Force Atlantic Prospective Commanding Officer instructor in 1997 and took command of the Naval Submarine School in 1999.

CAPTAIN DAVID C. MINTON III, USN (Ret), a 1956 graduate of the Naval Academy, served on board six submarines including command of USS *Guardfish* (SSN 612) and USS *George Washington* (SSBN 598). He also served as SUBRON THREE Deputy for Readiness and as the SUBPACREP for nuclear overhauls at the Bremerton Naval Shipyard.

SARAH CLARK PAGE graduated from Smith College in 1996 and joined the Sonalysts staff at the Naval War College. Her submarine roots include her father, Michael Gary Page, who worked at the Electric Boat Company, and was involved in the installation and testing of the first towed sonar array.

CAPTAIN MICHAEL G. RIEGEL, USN (Ret), a 1970 graduate of the University of Texas, spent his entire career in submarines, commanding the fast attack submarine USS *Archerfish* (SSN 678), the Trident fleet ballistic missile submarine USS *Kentucky* (SSBN 737), and the Naval Submarine Base, New London, Connecticut. He currently serves as executive director of the Submarine Force Library and Museum Association.

REAR ADMIRAL MAURICE H. RINDSKOPF, USN (Ret), a 1938 graduate of the Naval Academy, commissioned USS *Drum* (SS 228) just prior to the start of World War II and completed eleven war patrols in *Drum*, the last two as commanding officer. Post-war he commanded USS *Sea Cat* (SS 399), USS *Higbee* (DDR 806), Submarine School,. USS *Fulton* (AS 11), and Submarine Flotillas 2 and 8. He was Director of Naval Intelligence in 1966. He retired in 1972 as a Rear Admiral.

NEAL STEVENS took an early interest in submarines. As a youngster he devised his own submarine games. With the advent of personal computers, he began to develop submarine simulations. This led in 1997 to the popular Internet webjournal, *SubSim Review* (www.subsim.com).

ADMIRAL JAMES D. WATKINS, USN (Ret), was picked for the nuclear submarine program by Admiral Rickover, and worked for two years as an assistant in his office. Subsequently, Admiral Watkins commanded USS *Snook* (SSN 592), Cruiser-Destroyer Group ONE, the Sixth Fleet, and the U.S. Pacific Fleet before becoming the twenty-second Chief of Naval Operations in 1982. In 1989 Admiral Watkins was appointed Secretary of Energy in the Bush Cabinet.

COMMANDER RAYMOND V. WELCH, SR., USN (Ret), graduated from the U.S. Naval Academy in February 1941. He completed eight successful war patrols in USS *Nautilus* (SS 168), USS *Stingray* (SS 186), and USS *Seahorse* (SS 304). He commanded USS *Guitarro* (SS 363) and USS *Hank* (DD 702) after World War II.

VICE ADMIRAL JOE WILLIAMS, JR., USN (Ret), commanded USS *Bluegill* (SSK 242), USS *Robert E. Lee* (SSBN 601), USS *George Bancroft* (SSBN 643), the Norfolk Naval Shipyard, and the U.S. Atlantic Submarine Force. Before his retirement, Vice Admiral Williams had held all rates and ranks from seaman recruit through Vice Admiral and acquired a baccalaureate from the University of Maryland. Subsequently, he was Director of Nuclear Submarine Construction for General Dynamics.

CAPTAIN RAYMOND D. WOOLRICH, USN (Ret), a Naval Academy graduate, served in six submarines and commanded USS *Trepang* (SSN 674) during four extended deployments, including an Arctic Ocean patrol and North Pole surfacing. He was the commanding officer of Naval Facility, Brawdy, Wales, then served as Commander Undersea Surveillance, U.S. Pacific Fleet. He currently is vice-president of the Submarine Force Library and Museum Association.

CAPTAIN RICHARD T. WRIGHT, USN (Ret), graduated from the Naval Academy in 1953 and served twenty years in the submarine force—most of it in the strategic (*Polaris/Poseidon*) force. His assignments included command of USS *James Monroe* (SSBN 622), duty on the Joint Strategic Targeting Planning Staff, and senior SSBN staff positions in the Pentagon and on the fleet commander's staff in Norfolk. Also, he taught at the Naval War College in Newport, Rhode Island.

Index